e-food

Food and technology

Book 2

Leanne Compton   Carol Warren

OXFORD
UNIVERSITY PRESS

OXFORD

UNIVERSITY PRESS

253 Normanby Road, South Melbourne, Victoria 3205, Australia

Oxford University Press is a department of the University of Oxford.
It furthers the University's objective of excellence in research, scholarship,
and education by publishing worldwide in

Oxford New York

Auckland Bangkok Buenos Aires Cape Town Chennai
Dar es Salaam Delhi Hong Kong Istanbul Karachi Kolkata
Kuala Lumpur Madrid Melbourne Mexico City Mumbai Nairobi
São Paulo Shanghai Taipei Tokyo Toronto

OXFORD is a trade mark of Oxford University Press
in the UK and in certain other countries

© Leanne Compton, Carol Warren 2003

First published 2003
Reprinted 2004

National Library of Australia
Cataloguing-in-Publication data:

Compton, Leanne.
 e-food: food and technology.

 Includes index.
 For secondary students.

 ISBN 0 19 551602 8 (bk. 2).
 ISBN 0 19 551697 4 (teacher CD 2).

 1. Food—Juvenile literature. 2. Nutrition—Juvenile literature.
 3. Quick and easy cookery—Juvenile literature. I. Warren, Carol Joan.
 II. Title.

641.3

Typeset by Sylvia Witte
Printed through Bookpac Production Services, Singapore

OWLS

**OXFORD
DICTIONARY
WORD AND
LANGUAGE
SERVICE**

Do you have a query about words,
their origin, meaning, use, spelling,
pronunciation, or any other aspect
of international English? Then write to
OWLS at the Australian National
Dictionary Centre, Australian
National University, Canberra ACT
0200 (email ANDC@anu.edu.au).
All queries will be answered using
the full resources of *The Australian
National Dictionary* and *The Oxford
English Dictionary.*

The Australian National Dictionary
Centre and Oxford University Press
also produce OZWORDS, a
biannual newsletter which contains
interesting items about Australian
words and language. Subscription is
free – please contact the OZWORDS
subscription manager at Oxford
University Press, GPO Box 2784Y,
Melbourne, VIC 3001, or
ozwords@oup.com.au

CONTENTS

INTRODUCTION

e-Food Book 2 recognises that, after a core study of Home Economics at Year 7 and/or Year 8, students often undertake semester electives. The four sections in *e-Food Book 2* cover the types of electives offered in many schools, such as nutrition, meal planning, international foods and food technology. With this in mind, the four sections have been developed to incorporate a relevant and contemporary approach, acknowledging the fast-paced technological society for which we are preparing our students, yet maintaining a focus on the importance of healthy eating.

This book also aims to complement the focus on the Australian Guide to Healthy Eating in *e-Food Book 1*. Recognising that students study Home Economics for differing amounts of time, the topics and content from both books may be used together. For example, when studying snacks and junk food in *e-Food Book 2*, the information found in the chapters on fat, salt and sugar in *e-Food Book 1* will provide useful background information.

As with *e-Food Book 1*, a fresh, fun and interactive approach to food has been taken, which reflects the impact of technology and the electronic age. More than ever, it is important to prepare our students with a wide range of knowledge and skills. The development of knowledge and skills in the purchase, preparation and cooking of food is important for students to become educated consumers. Recipes, which form a major component of the book, have been developed to reflect our multicultural, busy lifestyle, while promoting the aim that food should be easy to prepare, fresh and nutritionally good for us.

The broad range of activities and visual appeal throughout *e-Food Book 2* has been designed to incorporate the thinking-oriented curriculum and provide plenty of choice for teachers to engage students with a range of abilities and learning styles. *e-Food Book 2* has a strong focus on student enquiry, and the broad range of questions, investigations, puzzles, newspaper articles and case studies encourages students to take responsibility for their own learning, providing them with experiences to feel empowered about making their own life choices. The inclusion of assessment tasks, addressing outcomes from the Technology and Health and Physical Education Key Learning Areas, is also a feature of *e-Food Book 2*.

The *e-Food Book 2 CD-ROM* for teachers will facilitate the use of *e-Food Book 2*. It has been designed to save preparation and marking time by offering activity worksheets, shopping lists, answers to activities, assessment tasks and assessment criteria sheets.

We hope that you will find this book to be a fun, interactive and educational resource that will help to meet the needs of our young people in a technologically diverse and challenging world.

THE TECHNOLOGY DESIGN PROCESS

The Technology Design Process involves the four phases of investigating, designing, producing and evaluating.

When you research or gather information, you are investigating. This can be done by searching on the Internet, reading books or listening to your teacher or other people.

Designing involves considering your options and making decisions about how you will go about your tasks, which resources you will use and how you will utilise your creative ideas to meet the requirements of the task (design brief).

Producing is when you undertake the task or make a product. This could be in the form of practical work, when you complete some of the recipes in this book or when you complete a project or assignment.

Evaluating is when you look back and reflect on the decisions made, the outcomes and how you might do things differently next time.

All phases involve making decisions, managing situations or solving problems. There is not necessarily a particular sequence to the phases of the Technology Design Process; however the four phases often flow sequentially, and it is more likely that they overlap and repeat continually. This is seen in the diagram below, which shows a continuous, flowing yet random connection between the four phases.

e-fact

A design brief is a defined situation, usually in the form of a statement, that outlines guidelines for a task.

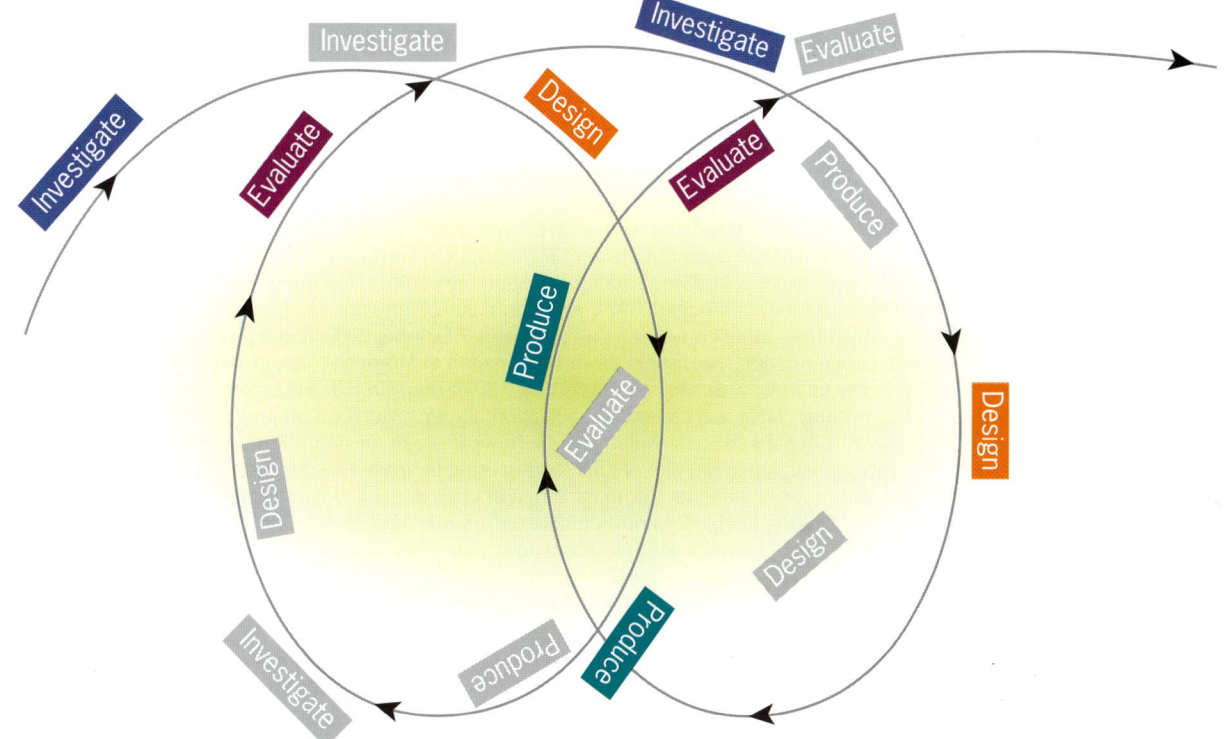

ACKNOWLEDGMENTS

The author and publisher wish to thank the following writers, artists and copyright holders whose material has been reproduced in this book:

Patrick McDonald, 'Fussy eaters make life tough for our chefs' and 'Few have true food allergy', *Advertiser*, 2 February 2002; 'Children's junk food slammed', *Agra Food News*, 22 June 2000; Steve Dow, 'Good food but there's a snag', *Age*, 22 July 2001; Stephen Cauchi, 'Diabetes in children reaching epidemic levels, experts warn', *Age*, 6 April 2002; Melissa Marino, 'GM ruling sparks fears', *Age*, 5 Jan 2003; Jane Rocca, 'Getting hyper about a bar of chocolate', *Age*, 13 August 2001; Minette Marrin, 'The seeds of suspicion', *Age*, 22 May 2000; Daniel Dasey, 'The end of the line for the checkout chicks?', *Age*, 21 July 2002; David Wroe, 'Most vitamin pills a waste of money, study finds', *Age*, 6 July 2002; 'Japanese woman finds finger tip in rice ball', *Age*, 2 June 2002; Steve Dow, 'Soy a key to healthy heart', *Sunday Age*, 4 May 2000; 'Taste for change', *Australian*, 24 November 1998; Vivienne Reiner, 'Coffee purists' short blacklash', *Weekend Australian*, 27–8 May 2000; 'Nation goes out more for breakfast', *Mercury*, 5 November 2002; 'Food in Australia', *Australian Tourist Commission Fact Sheet*, 2002; 'Pre-prepared meals' and 'Home meal replacements—where to now?', ACNielsen; 'Kilojoule, fat and salt content of some popular fast-food meals', Australian Consumers Association; 'Kilojoule, fat and salt content of some popular fast-food fries/chips', Australian Consumers Association; 'Glowing chook—food from the X-files?' and 'Food styling', www.choice.com.au; Allan Borushek, Sodium content of common takeaway foods', www.dietclub.com.au. Reproduced by permission; Bianca Nogrady, 'Send in the sensors', www.dietclub.com.au, copyright Family Health Network Pty Ltd.; 'Draft dietary guidelines for Australians' and 'Draft dietary guidelines for children and adolescents', National Health and Medical Research Council; Margaret Fraser, 'Witch's fingers', *Canadian Living's Family Cookbook*, 1995; 'Cafe Zest breakfast menu', Cafe Zest, Port Melbourne; 'The Australian guide to healthy eating', Commonwealth of Australia; 'Go for 2 & 5', Department of Health, Western Australia; '7-a-day', Coles Supermarkets; Anna Floate, 'Lowan repositions itself in the cereal market', Consolidated Foods Australia Ltd; 'Electronic nose—sniffing out commercial applications', *Food Facts* Winter 2001; Huyi Jin Elizabeth Kim, 'Stressed-out teens need to learn how to "chill"', Knight Ridder Newspapers; 'GI symbol', University of Sydney, in collaboration with Diabetes Australia and the Juvenile Diabetes Foundation; Holly Hayes, 'Is the internet refridgerator cool enough to purchase?'; 'Chinese market gardens', *Heritage* NSW, Vol.6 No.3; Sarah Stock, 'Would you like meat with that pie?', *Herald Sun*, 16 April 2002; David Wilson, 'Dob in dodgy souvlaki', *Herald Sun*, 1 September 2002; Peta Hellard, 'Family meals a thing of the past', *Herald Sun*, 27 April 2001; Simon Plant, 'Good oil from neighbours', *Herald Sun*, 7 March 2000; Ian Royall, 'Tuck in at Tucker Road', *Herald Sun*; Robyn Riley, 'Aussie fat epidemic' and 'Percentage of people who are overweight, or obese, in several major countries', *Herald Sun*, 26 November 2000; 'New food rules "to save lives"', *Herald Sun*, 19 December 2002; Flip Shelton, 'Seven secrets to good cooking', *Herald Sun*, 7 March 2000; Sasha Baskett, 'The weight of a lifetime', *Herald Sun*, 19 December 2002; 'Lazy lifestyles', *Herald Sun*, 24 June 2001; Evonne Barry, 'Alcohol gives students learning curves', *Herald Sun*, 10 July 2002; Catherine Lambert, 'A nation of tele-tubbies', *Herald Sun*, 24 June 2001; Tanya Taylor, 'Health watch', *Herald Sun*, 10 May 2000; Bronwen Gora, 'Fat's back in fashion', *Herald Sun*, 10 May 2000; Karen Collier, 'Deadly snack attack', *Herald Sun*, 23 February 2002; 'You are what you eat', *Herald Sun*, 23 February 2002; 'Broccoli a cancer buster', *Herald Sun*, 26 May 2000; Michele Curtis, 'Dot com and get it!', *Herald Sun*, 18 June 2002; Tanya Taylor, 'Pills fad in young diets', *Herald Sun*, 14 July 2000; 'Meet macca's number 1 fan', *Herald Sun*, 25 August 2000; 'Brains nut out answer', *MXNews*, 15 November 2001; 'Sticky date pudding', *MXNews*, 27 May 2002; Chloe Adams, 'New McMenu', *MXNews*, 5 September 2001; 'Homing in on cooking', *MXNews*, 28 February 2002; 'Name is food for thought', *MXNews*, 19 April 2002; 'Time not on cooks' side', *MXNews*, 8 January 2002; 'Unhealthy appetites—value comes at a cost', *MXNews*, 7 October 2002; 'Italy's pizza resistance', *MXNews*, 20 September 2002; Lubna Khader, 'The distinct flavor of Ramadan in Morocco', *Star*, 14 January 2003; John Merriman, 'Star oyster on its way', *Sunday Mail*, 3 February 2002; Brad Crouch, 'Focus on fussy eaters', *Sunday Mail*, 3 February 2002; '4 vitality', Meat and Livestock Association; 'Experts want ban on junk food advertising', and 'Tuckshop smartcard a healthy success', National Nine News; 'Taste of Australia', Red Ochre Grill restaurant, www.redochregrill.com.au; 'American diet of junk food causing increased health concerns', Sparks Companies Inc.; 'Thai Terrace menu', www.thaiterrace.com.au; 'Africa in crisis appeal', Oxfam Community Aid Abroad, www.caa.org.au; Joel Dullroy, 'Recipe for nutrition disaster', *Courier Mail*, 13 July 2000; 'Comparison of the fibre content for different types of bread', www.tiptop.com.au.

Nuts aBout Nutrition

Pepato

Pecorino

ALWAYS FRESH

Spanish

EXTRA LIGHT

OLIVE OIL

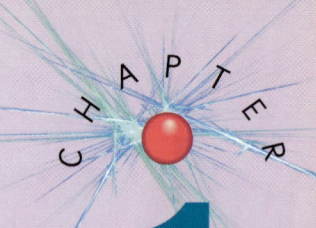

CHAPTER 1

FOOD STUFF: DISCOVER NUTRIENTS

Carbohydrates

Carbohydrates are made up of the elements carbon (C), hydrogen (H) and oxygen (O). This is useful to know, as the term *carbohydrates* is often abbreviated to CHO. Carbohydrates contribute energy to the diet, with 1 gram of carbohydrate providing 16 kilojoules. Plants produce carbohydrates during the process of photosynthesis.

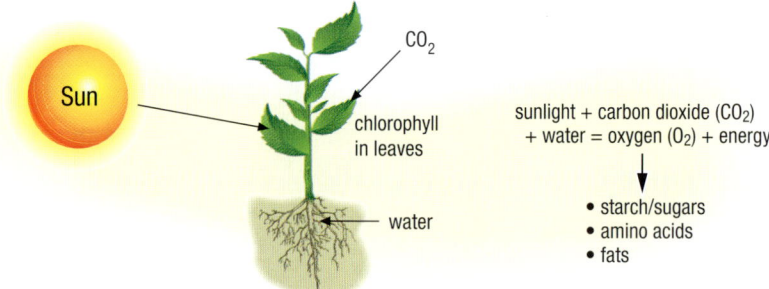

sunlight + carbon dioxide (CO_2) + water = oxygen (O_2) + energy

- starch/sugars
- amino acids
- fats

Carbohydrate is often wrongly termed a food. It is actually a component of food—or, more correctly, a nutrient. Carbohydrate-rich sources of food include cereals, starchy vegetables, sugars, fruits and milk products. In Australia, it is recommended that carbohydrates from a variety of food sources provide about 55 per cent of our daily kilojoule intake. On average, we tend not to consume enough carbohydrates and should increase our daily intake by about 50 grams, which is equivalent to the amount of carbohydrate found in four slices of bread, two bananas or two serves of breakfast cereal. Features of carbohydrates are shown in the following table.

Foods that contain starch may also provide fibre (see 'Fibre' on page 10).

Type of carbohydrate	Source	Solubility	Taste
Starch	Cereal grains, root vegetables, legumes	Does not readily dissolve in water	Not sweet to taste
Sugars	Added sugars and naturally occurring sugars found in foods: • fructose in honey and fruit • galactose in fruit • glucose in honey and fruit • lactose in milk • maltose in malt • sucrose in sugar	Readily dissolves in water	Sweet to taste

e-fact

Sucrose, maltose and lactose are broken down into fructose, glucose and galactose when they enter the small intestine.

@-faCt

Starch may consist of up to 10 000 sugars connected together. Once consumed, starch is digested to glucose. This occurs at different rates according to the type of starch and if fibre is present.

Glucose is absorbed into the bloodstream. Under the influence of insulin, the body tissues use the glucose as energy and the rest is stored in the liver and muscles as glycogen.

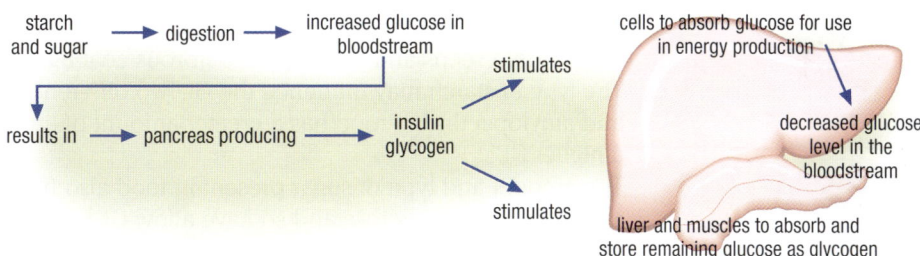

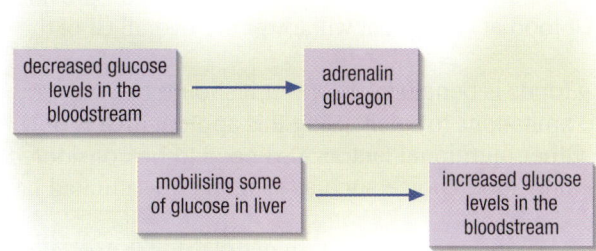

If the blood glucose levels fall, hunger will occur. Adrenalin and glucagon mobilise some of the glucose in the liver and restore the levels of blood glucose. After twelve hours, all glycogen stores are used. If the hunger pains are ignored, the body will begin breaking down lean muscle protein to form glucose. This only occurs in the liver and is known as gluconeogenesis. Fat cannot be converted to blood glucose. Muscle glycogen cannot be broken down to supply glucose to the blood. Glycogen in muscles is exclusively used for activity.

Scientists now consider classifying carbohydrates as 'simple' or 'complex' as redundant and unnecessary, as these terms do not reflect the nature and function of carbohydrates. It was once thought that the body quickly digested simple sugars, and complex carbohydrates were digested more gradually. However, the latest way of thinking about carbohydrate foods is referred to as the Glycemic Index (GI).

Focus on Glycemic Index of Foods

The GI is an approach to rating carbohydrates in food. The rating is between 0 and 100 and is based on the carbohydrates' effects on blood glucose in the body.

- High-GI foods are those that score 70 or more. These foods contain carbohydrates that are digested and absorbed quickly, resulting in a rapid increase in blood glucose levels.
- Foods with a low GI score 55 or less. These foods contain carbohydrates that are digested and absorbed more slowly and so have less of an impact on blood glucose levels.
- Foods with a medium GI score between 55 and 70.

The links between GI and health have been studied and findings suggest that including low-GI foods in your overall diet may be beneficial to your health. Consuming low-GI foods could be especially beneficial for:

- people who have diabetes or are at risk of developing this disease
- people who want to manage their weight
- people who have elevated blood cholesterol levels, poor insulin response or are at risk of heart disease

There are many factors that can influence the GI of a food.

- Processing methods, such as milling, grinding and extruding, may make foods quicker to digest and have been linked with a higher GI. For example, wholemeal

@-DEFINE

Adrenalin is a hormone that stimulates the conversion of glycogen in the liver to glucose to restore sugar levels in the blood.

Glucagon is a hormone produced in the pancreas that causes glucose to move from the liver to the blood.

bread has ground grains and a higher GI than multigrain bread in which the grains are not crushed or ground.

· The presence of soluble fibre or fat in foods can lengthen the digestion process and so lower their GI.

· The physical form of food can slow down its digestion and therefore lower the GI; for example, seeds and beans have a fibrous coating.

· The type of starch may influence the GI. Two different types of starch are amylose and amylopectin. If a food has a greater amount of amylopectin starch, it will have a higher GI.

· The amount and type of sugar present in food also has an impact. Apples and pears are high in fructose and so have a low GI. Foods that contain sucrose and glucose have a higher GI.

It is recommended that you try to include one low-GI food at each meal. This does not mean that you should only include low-GI foods in your diet. There is scope for high-GI and moderate-GI foods in a healthy diet, as many of these foods can provide other nutrients. Having one low-GI food at each meal will lower the overall GI of the meal.

The use of GI when choosing foods is beneficial; however, it should be remembered that there are some limitations to solely using this approach. GI is only one nutritional aspect of a food. Other nutritional factors also need to be considered when deciding if the food is a healthy food choice, such as its total and saturated fat, fibre, sodium and sugar content.

Researchers at the University of Sydney, in collaboration with Diabetes Australia and the Juvenile Diabetes Foundation, have created a symbol to indicate that a food has been tested for GI.

The GI symbol began appearing on food labels in Australia in 2002. The GI rating is located near the nutritional information panel on the food label. There is also a brief statement explaining the GI concept.

Other approved GI testing facilities can test foods and use the new GI logo. However, foods must also satisfy other nutritional guidelines, including the following:

· low in saturated fat
· moderate sodium content
· at least 10 grams of carbohydrate per serve
· source of fibre (if relevant)

Only proper testing will ascertain the GI of a food. There are several factors in food that can influence GI and often the GI of a food is not what we would expect.

· Wholemeal and white bread have a similar GI. However, wholemeal bread is more nutritious, due to its fibre and phytochemical content.

· Well-cooked pasta tends to have a higher GI than al dente pasta. Some great low-GI food ideas are:

· Include fresh fruits with milk and breakfast cereals, as this will assist in lowering the overall GI of breakfast.

· Select grainy, dense breads with whole seeds.

· Include legumes, barley or macaroni in soups and casseroles.

· Consume breakfast foods based on wheat bran, oats and barley.

· Incorporate pasta, noodles, sweet potato, legumes or rice (basmati or Doongara) in your main meal as an alternative to potato.

Toasted muesli contains a higher fat content, but has a lower GI than untoasted muesli. The fat can delay the emptying of the food from the stomach; this explains why some foods that are high in fat have a low GI. However, to decrease excess fat intake, low-GI foods that are low in fat should be consumed in preference to low-GI foods that are high in fat.

The GI of particular fruits and vegetables may change due to the variety, season and degree of ripeness.

QUESTIONS

1 What does GI stand for?

2 Outline the three main ratings of GI foods.

3 Describe the findings linking GI and health.

4 Identify the factors that may influence the GI of food.

5 Why should you consume at least one low-GI food at each meal?

6 Is there room for high-GI and medium-GI foods in one's diet?

7 Do you think the GI symbol is a useful tool for food selection?

8 Should GI be the sole criterion for food selection? Why or why not?

9 Who created the GI logo?

10 Provide examples of how low-GI foods can be incorporated into meal planning.

Carbohydrate loading

The term *carbohydrate loading* is commonly used in regard to athletes when they increase the amount of glycogen in muscles. It usually begins about a week prior to endurance events.

· **Phase 1:** The athletes should exhaust the glycogen in their muscles by exercising hard and eating little carbohydrate foods for several days. The small intake of carbohydrate foods can result in dizziness and headaches for the athletes.

· **Phase 2:** The athletes will begin to eat lots of carbohydrate foods to replenish their stores. Their exercise is kept to a minimum.

Carbohydrate loading will produce greater stores of glycogen in the muscles for the athletes. However, it has been suggested that a high-carbohydrate, low-fat diet can also achieve the desired effect for the athletes.

▶ Let's remember

1 Why is carbohydrate often abbreviated to CHO?

2 How many kilojoules are found in 1 gram of carbohydrate?

3 **a** What is photosynthesis?

    b Describe the process of photosynthesis. Diagrams may be useful.

4 What percentage of the average daily kilojoule intake should come from carbohydrates?

5 Outline the main differences between sugars and starches.

6 Describe how starch is absorbed into the bloodstream.

7 Describe the role that insulin plays in the digestion of carbohydrates.

8 **a** What causes hunger?

    b What may cause lean muscle protein to break down?

9 What is the current way of classifying carbohydrate foods?

10 Describe the process of carbohydrate loading.

▶ Let's investigate

1 Investigate the main food sources of carbohydrate for the following countries or regions.

a Australia	**d** Italy	**g** Samoa
b China	**e** India	**h** Russia
c United Kingdom	**f** USA	**i** Middle East

j	Mozambique	**o**	Spain	**t**	Egypt
k	Norway	**p**	Germany	**u**	Ghana
l	Brazil	**q**	Thailand	**v**	South Africa
m	Canada	**r**	Malaysia		
n	Mexico	**s**	Japan		

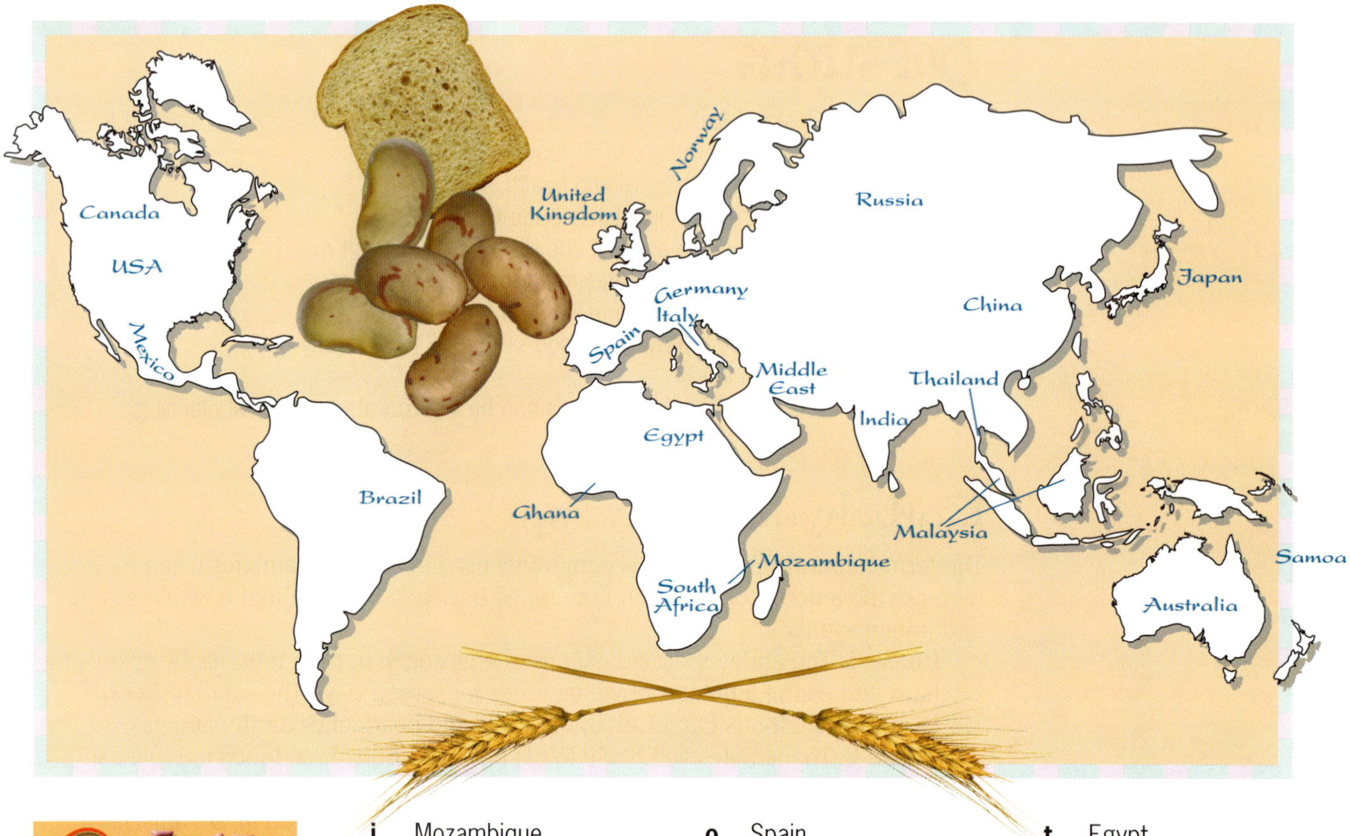

e-FACT

A potato plant can reproduce itself from its own tubers. When the eyes of the potato develop shoots, the potato can be used as seed to grow more potatoes.

e-FACT

If you store potatoes with onions, the onions will impart a natural gas that increases the deterioration of the potatoes.

2 Investigate the types of carbohydrate found in the following foods: apple juice, sweet potato, parsnip, white bread, wholemeal bread, skim milk, pasta, watermelon, peaches, dried apricots, baked potato, lentils, mixed-grain bread, sweet corn, sultanas, grapes, oranges, rolled oats, jelly beans, brown rice, pumpkin, honey, basmati white rice, cantaloupe, baked beans, bananas, dates, cornflakes, sugar, Nutri-Grain breakfast cereal. Indicate whether these foods have a high, medium or low GI. The following website may be useful: www.calvin.biochem.usyd.edu.au/GIDB/search.htm.

3 Design a poster or pamphlet to illustrate the key characteristics of the following types of sugars: glucose, fructose, sucrose, lactose and maltose.

4 Investigate the terms: *monosaccharide*, *disaccharide* and *polysaccharide*.

5 Investigate the various types of rice. Design a poster, datashow presentation or webpage to present your information.

6 Investigate the various types of potatoes. Design a poster, datashow presentation or webpage to present your information.

e-Carbohydrate

www.irishfood.com/history/potatoes.html

1 List the various names given to the potato.

2 Which country is the world's biggest producer of potatoes?

3 Outline the history of the potato.

4 Describe the various types of potatoes and their uses in food preparation.

5 Outline the history of the Irish potato famine. Present your information as a datashow presentation.

www.dfst.csiro.au/spuds.htm

1   Why do potatoes turn green?
2   Are green potatoes safe to eat?
3   Outline the criteria that you should use when purchasing potatoes.
4   Describe how you should store potatoes.

▶ Puzzled

CarboMaths

How many kilojoules are found in the following amounts of carbohydrates?

1   10 grams
2   34 grams
3   1 kilogram
4   $\frac{1}{2}$ gram
5   59 grams

Word puzzle

How many words can you create from the term *photosynthesis*? You can only use each letter once.

Fill in the gap

Complete the following sentences by using the words from the box.

| liver | glucose | glucose | glucose | hunger | adrenalin | restoring | glucagon | decreases |

_____ will result if the level of _____ in the blood _____. Two

hormones, _____ and _____ will activate some of the _____ found in

the _____. This will result in _____ the level of _____ in the blood.

CarboFind

Find each of the words from the box in the puzzle.

```
L D F K V Q C E L L U L O S E
S A D R K A G C E I A W N H G
E S I Y U V D L I E V I K L J
L C G G D C J R U M T E Y D E
C D E R B D T G E C E C R S A
S I S E N E G O E N O C U L G
U N T N P P B P S G A S Y R L
M L I E E B W T E E D L E L E
P H O T O S Y N T H E S I S G
Z V N E S O T L A M C P I N U
I I N S U L I N B J Z R Q S M
V E G E T A B L E S X Y A H E
P O T A T O E S O R C U S T S
E T A R D Y H O B R A C M X S
E S O T C A L A G M P C P A F
```

adrenalin	insulin
carbohydrate	legumes
cellulose	liver
digestion	maltose
energy	muscles
fructose	pectin
galactose	photosynthesis
gluconeogenesis	potato
glucose	starch
glycemic	sucrose
glycogen	vegetables

WEBExTRas

www.westernpotatoes.com.au
Western Potatoes is a statutory marketing organisation for potatoes. This site has a range of information about potatoes, including their nutritional content, varieties and recipes.

www.potatoesforschools.org.uk/winhome.htm
This is the British Potato Council website. The information is very student-friendly.

www.woolworths.com.au/dietinfo/rsa26.asp
The Woolworths site has information about potatoes, including 'Potatoes for All Seasons', 'Types of Potatoes', 'Potato Variety Planner' and 'How to Make the Best Mashed Potato'.

www.woolworths.com.au/dietinfo/rsa19.asp
The Woolworths site has information about 'The Humble Spud', including facts about nutritional value, varieties of potatoes and correct storage of potatoes.

www.potatohelp.com
This is the United States Potato Board website. It provides information on a range of topics, including nutrition, varieties, storage and potato history.

www.sunrice.com.au
The Sunrice website provides a wealth of information about rice, rice products and recipes that have rice as a major ingredient.

FARRINGDON COMMUNITY SPORTS COLLEGE

8

Concentrating on carbohydrates

Across

3 Abbreviation for carbohydrates

7 Hunger results when the levels of this substance drop

8 Recommended percentage of the kilojoule intake that should come from carbohydrates (two words)

9 One gram of carbohydrate is equivalent to _____ kilojoules

10 Where glycogen may be stored

Down

1 Plants produce carbohydrates through this process

2 Type of sugar found in milk

3 The process of increasing the amount of glycogen in one's muscles is _____ loading

4 Converts blood glucose to glycogen

5 Converts glycogen in the liver to blood glucose

6 The type of carbohydrate that is not sweet-tasting

7 The _____ Index is an approach to rating the carbohydrate found in foods

LET'S PRODUCE

Ingredients
¾ cup water
30 grams caster sugar
1 cinnamon stick
2 pears, peeled, quartered and cored

Risotto
2½ cups milk
20 grams butter
½ cup Arborio rice
50 grams dark chocolate, chopped
30 grams caster sugar (extra)

Ingredients
1 egg, lightly beaten
½ cup cream
5 tablespoons golden syrup
2 slices raisin bread
10 grams butter
icing sugar

Ingredients
250 grams new baby potatoes, cut into halves
2 teaspoons olive oil
1 zucchini, cut into halves and sliced
½ red onion, sliced
100 grams cherry tomatoes, cut into halves
½ bunch asparagus, cut into halves
2 tablespoons fresh basil
200 grams chicken breast

Dressing
2 tablespoons plain yoghurt
1½ tablespoons sweet chilli sauce
1 clove garlic, crushed
1 tablespoon lemon or lime juice

Poached pears with risotto (serves 2)

Method
1 Combine water, sugar and cinnamon stick in saucepan and bring to the boil.
2 Add pears and simmer, uncovered, for ten minutes, or until pears are tender.
3 In the meantime, bring milk to the boil and simmer.
4 Heat butter in a frypan and add rice, stirring for three minutes. Gradually add ½ cup of simmering milk at a time, stirring until all the liquid is absorbed and all the milk is added to the rice. This should take about thirty minutes.
5 Add chocolate and extra sugar and stir for five minutes, until mixture is well combined.
6 Spoon risotto into serving bowls and place pears on top.

Raisin bread and butter pudding (serves 2)

Method
1 Preheat oven to 200°C and grease ramekins.
2 Combine egg, cream and 4 tablespoons of golden syrup with a fork.
3 Cut the raisin bread to fit the ramekin and butter both sides.
4 Pour the egg mixture into two ramekins and place a slice of raisin bread, syrup side up, gently on top. Drizzle with remaining golden syrup.
5 Place on baking tray and cook for twenty minutes.
6 Dust with icing sugar before serving.

Warm chicken and potato salad (serves 2)

Method
1 Preheat oven to 200°C.
2 Toss potatoes in olive oil and cook in baking dish for thirty minutes, turning occasionally.
3 Add zucchini, onion, tomatoes and asparagus to the baking dish and cook for an additional fifteen minutes, or until vegetables are tender.
4 Toss basil leaves through the vegetables, cover and keep warm.
5 In the meantime, grill chicken until cooked. Cut into large chunks.
6 Combine all dressing ingredients.
7 Place vegetables on serving plates, top with chicken and drizzle with dressing.

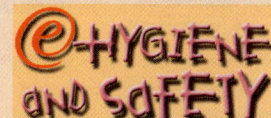
HYGIENE AND SAFETY

Ensure that the chicken is cooked thoroughly to kill any bacteria that may be present.

Fibre

Fibre is an essential part of a healthy diet. It is not one substance, but a combination of a variety of components. Fibre is present in both processed and unprocessed foods. It is found in foods of plant origin only, such as grains, breads, cereals, vegetables, fruit, legumes, seeds and nuts. It has the same chemical structure as starch, yet it is quite different.

Unprocessed foods

Processed foods

Fibre is found in parts of food not digested in the stomach and small intestine. However, fibre is digested in the large intestine by bacteria during fermentation. Bacteria multiply by the millions and, once they die, they contribute significantly to the faeces. Fibre plays an important role in preventing constipation, some cancers and heart disease.

There are a number of different types of fibre. The three major types are:
· soluble fibre
· insoluble fibre
· resistant starch

Although resistant starch is not really a fibre, it is now being accepted as a member of the 'fibre family' due to its comparable effects on the body.

Each type of fibre will have its own action within the body.

Soluble fibre binds and holds the end products of cholesterol metabolism and takes them out in the faeces. This means that these end products cannot re-enter the bloodstream and, therefore, the cholesterol level in the blood is lowered.

Soluble fibre

Soluble fibre can remove cholesterol from the body and slow the rate of digestion.

Soluble fibre includes:
· gums in oats and legumes, and is also added to some foods
· pectin, which is found in fruits and citrus peels

- some polysaccharide substances in legumes, such as lentils and soybeans, and oats
- vegetables
- rice

These fibres are completely digested by bacteria, which manufacture helpful acids.

Insoluble fibre

Insoluble fibre helps to keep us 'regular', by providing bulk in our diet and ensuring that we go to the toilet regularly. Foods that provide insoluble fibre in the diet include wheat-based products, such as wholegrain and wholemeal breads, cereals and pasta.

Resistant starch

For many years, it was thought that all dietary starch was digested entirely in the small intestine. However, we have realised recently that this is not necessarily the case.

Resistant starch is a type of carbohydrate that 'resists' digestion in the small intestine and so appears in the large intestine undigested. Bacteria in the large intestine break it down, resulting in the formation of beneficial fatty acids that encourage the manufacture of healthy cells that may play a vital role in the prevention of some bowel diseases.

Resistant starch also has a slight laxative effect and promotes the growth of healthy bacteria. It also may help prevent constipation. It is present in most carbohydrate-rich foods, but is high in firm bananas, cold cooked potatoes, legumes, such as roasted chickpeas and baked beans, boiled long-grain white rice, pasta and certain types of corn. Hi-Maize is a new variety of corn that is high in resistant starch and is being used to improve the fibre of breakfast cereals, bread and hamburger buns. Hi-Maize is undetectable, as it does not alter the flavour, colour or texture of the foods.

It is recommended that adults consume at least 30 grams of fibre daily, as well as drink plenty of liquids to assist with the action of fibre. There is no recommended daily intake of fibre for children or adolescents. However, as a guide, it is suggested that they should consume the amount of fibre in grams that is equivalent to their age in years plus five; for example, a fifteen-year-old should consume 15 + 5 = 20 grams of fibre. A healthy diet in early childhood, with a high amount of fibrous foods, contributes to a much healthier adult life in regard to digestive problems.

Soluble fibre

Insoluble fibre

Resistant starch

▶ Let's remember

1   Define fibre.
2   Identify a variety of foods where is fibre found.
3   What diseases does fibre play a role in preventing?
4   Identify the main types of fibre.
5   Outline the characteristics of each type of fibre.
6   What is Hi-Maize?
7   Why is Hi-Maize undetectable in foods?
8   How much fibre is recommended for an adult?
9   What other nutrient assists the action of fibre?
10 **a**   What is the suggestion for the amount of fibre that adolescents and children should consume?
   b   How much fibre should you consume?

▶ Let's investigate

1   Investigate which dietary related diseases might be prevented by consuming a diet high in fibre. Identify which type of fibre is linked to each disease. Design a poster, pamphlet or datashow presentation to present your findings.
2   Investigate a range of breakfast cereals by examining their nutritional label. How much fibre is found in each brand of breakfast cereal? What types of fibre are found in each breakfast cereal? Present your findings as a graph or a table. Evaluate each type of breakfast cereal in terms of its fibre content ☺ ☻ ☹. Which brands would you consider healthy? Write up your findings and present as a word-processed document.
3   Investigate a range of foods that are labelled as being 'high in fibre'. How much fibre is found in each food? Are all types of fibre present?
4   Design a day's diet that you would consume and that contains all of the three different types of fibre.
5   Design a poster or pamphlet that illustrates the different characteristics of the three types of fibre. Include information about the functions and food sources of each type of fibre.
6   Investigate a range of recipes. Find one that you can adapt to make it high in a range of fibre types, identifying the fibre-rich ingredients. Design your recipe. Produce and evaluate your recipe ☺ ☻ ☹.

▶ ℮-Fibre
www.hi-maize.com.au

1   What is the working definition that includes all non-starch polysaccharides (NSP) and lignin from plants and resistant starch?
2   How much resistant starch is recommended?
3   According to the website, what is the relationship between the consumption of resistant starch and colon cancer?
4   Outline the health benefits of resistant starch in the small and large bowel.
5   What is produced when resistant starch ferments in the bowel? What are the health benefits of this substance?
6   Why is Hi-Maize suitable for those who cannot consume fibrous foods?

 **Puzzled**

Fibre match

Match the following characteristics with the correct type of fibre.

Soluble fibre	Insoluble fibre	Resistant starch

Characteristics

1 Breaks down in the large intestine.
2 Keeps us regular.
3 Is found in pectin, gums, fruits and legumes.
4 Resists digestion in the small intestine.
5 Binds and holds the end products of cholesterol.
6 Is found in cold cooked potatoes, pasta and firm bananas.
7 Provides bulk in the diet.
8 Results in the formation of helpful fatty acids.
9 Promotes the growth of healthy bacteria.
10 Is found in wholegrain breads and cereals.

 ## Fibre advice

Work out the code to complete a sentence about fibre.

A	B	C	D	E	F	G	H	I	J	K	L	M	N	O	P	Q	R	S	T	U	V	W	X	Y	Z
													7				5	12	18						

```
 _  _  S  T  R  _  _  _  _  N  S  _  N  _  _  _  _  T  _  _  _  N  S  _  _  _
19 16 12 18  5 19 13 22 19  7 12    7 26 26 20   18 11   10 11  7 12 16  6 26

 _  _  R  _  _  _  _  R  _  _  N  _  T  _  _  _  R  _  _  _  _  T
 6 11  5 26    8 22  1  5 26   22  7    18 24 26 22  5   20 22 26 18
```

Corn fritters

(serves 2)

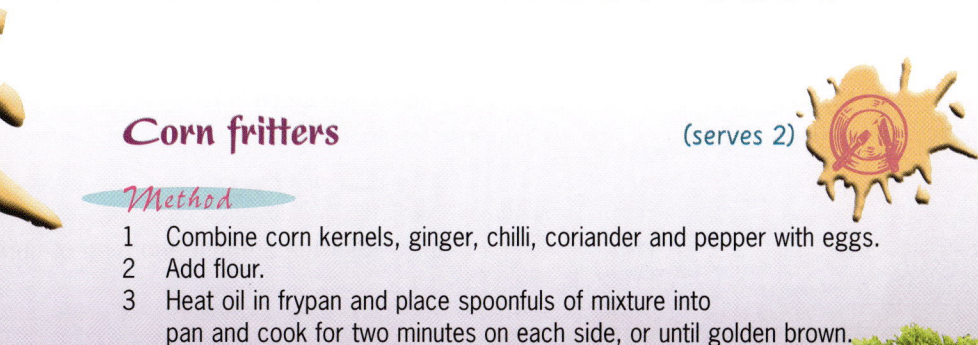

Method

1 Combine corn kernels, ginger, chilli, coriander and pepper with eggs.
2 Add flour.
3 Heat oil in frypan and place spoonfuls of mixture into pan and cook for two minutes on each side, or until golden brown.
4 Drain on absorbent paper and serve with lettuce and sweet chilli sauce.

Ingredients

1 cob corn
5-centimetre piece ginger, finely grated
1 red chilli, finely chopped
3 shakes black pepper
2 tablespoons fresh coriander, chopped
2 eggs, lightly beaten
1/3 cup flour, sifted
1 tablespoon oil
sweet chilli sauce
50 grams mixed lettuce

QUESTIONS

1 Investigate the sources of fibre in this recipe.
2 What type or types of fibre are present?
3 Outline two additional ways to further increase the fibre content of this meal.

Ingredients

1 tablespoon olive oil
$\frac{1}{2}$ brown onion, finely diced
$\frac{1}{2}$ leek, finely sliced
1 carrot, finely diced
1 clove garlic, crushed
$\frac{1}{2}$ cup red lentils, rinsed
500 millilitres vegetable stock
1 tablespoon fresh parsley, finely chopped
1 tablespoon fresh coriander, finely chopped
3 shakes black pepper
2 tablespoons natural yoghurt
2 small ovals pita bread

Thick lentil soup

(serves 2)

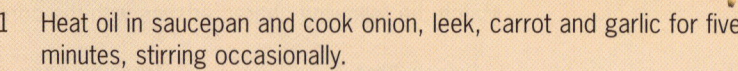

Method

1. Heat oil in saucepan and cook onion, leek, carrot and garlic for five minutes, stirring occasionally.
2. Add lentils and stir for another minute.
3. Add stock and bring mixture to the boil. Simmer, uncovered for twenty to twenty-five minutes, or until ingredients are tender.
4. Stir in parsley, coriander and pepper.
5. Place in serving bowls and top with yoghurt. Serve with warmed pita bread.

QUESTION

Investigate the types and sources of fibre in this recipe.

Ingredients

300 grams rhubarb stalks, washed and cut into 3-centimetre lengths
1 tablespoon apple juice
100 grams frozen raspberries, thawed
1 tablespoon sugar

Topping

1 teaspoon butter
$2\frac{1}{2}$ tablespoons self-raising flour
$2\frac{1}{2}$ tablespoons self-raising wholemeal flour
$\frac{1}{4}$ teaspoon cinnamon
3 teaspoons almond meal
3 teaspoons brown sugar
1 tablespoon rolled oats
40 millilitres apple juice
extra apple juice for glazing
ice cream

Rhubarb and raspberry dessert

(serves 2)

Method

1. Preheat oven to 200°C.
2. Place rhubarb and apple juice in saucepan and cook for five minutes, covered, until tender. Set aside to cool.
3. Add raspberries and sugar and spoon into greased baking dish.
4. To make topping, rub butter into sifted flours and cinnamon. Add almond meal, sugar and oats.
5. Add apple juice to make a dough. Extra juice may be required.
6. Lightly knead on floured boards and roll out to 1-centimetre thick. Cut into 3-centimetre diameter rounds.
7. Place rounds of dough around the edge of the rhubarb mixture, slightly overlapping them and leaving the centre exposed.
8. Brush with remaining apple juice and cook for twenty minutes, or until golden.
9. Serve with ice cream.

QUESTION

Investigate the amount and type of fibre found in rhubarb.

Protein

Protein is required throughout our life to produce, maintain and renew our body cells. Protein is also required to make antibodies, enzymes and haemoglobin.

Protein is made from chains of amino acids. About twenty amino acids are found in food, but the number of combinations in which the amino acids can be arranged is unlimited. Eight of these amino acids cannot be made by the body and so are called essential amino acids. The essential amino acids are:

- isoleucine
- leucine
- lysine
- methionine
- phenylalanine
- threonine
- tryptophan
- valine

There is a ninth essential amino acid for children, which is called histidine. The non-essential amino acids can be made by the body from the essential amino acids or from each other.

Animal sources of protein, such as meat, eggs and dairy products, contain all the essential amino acids and are called complete proteins. Plant sources of protein, such as grains, legumes and nuts, have at least one of the essential amino acids missing or in limited amounts. These are called incomplete proteins. Soybean is the exception to the rule.

For example, protein from wheat lacks lysine and dried beans lack methionine. However, a mixture of two plant proteins can complete one another; for instance, a dish of grains served with dried beans can provide the correct balance of all essential amino acids.

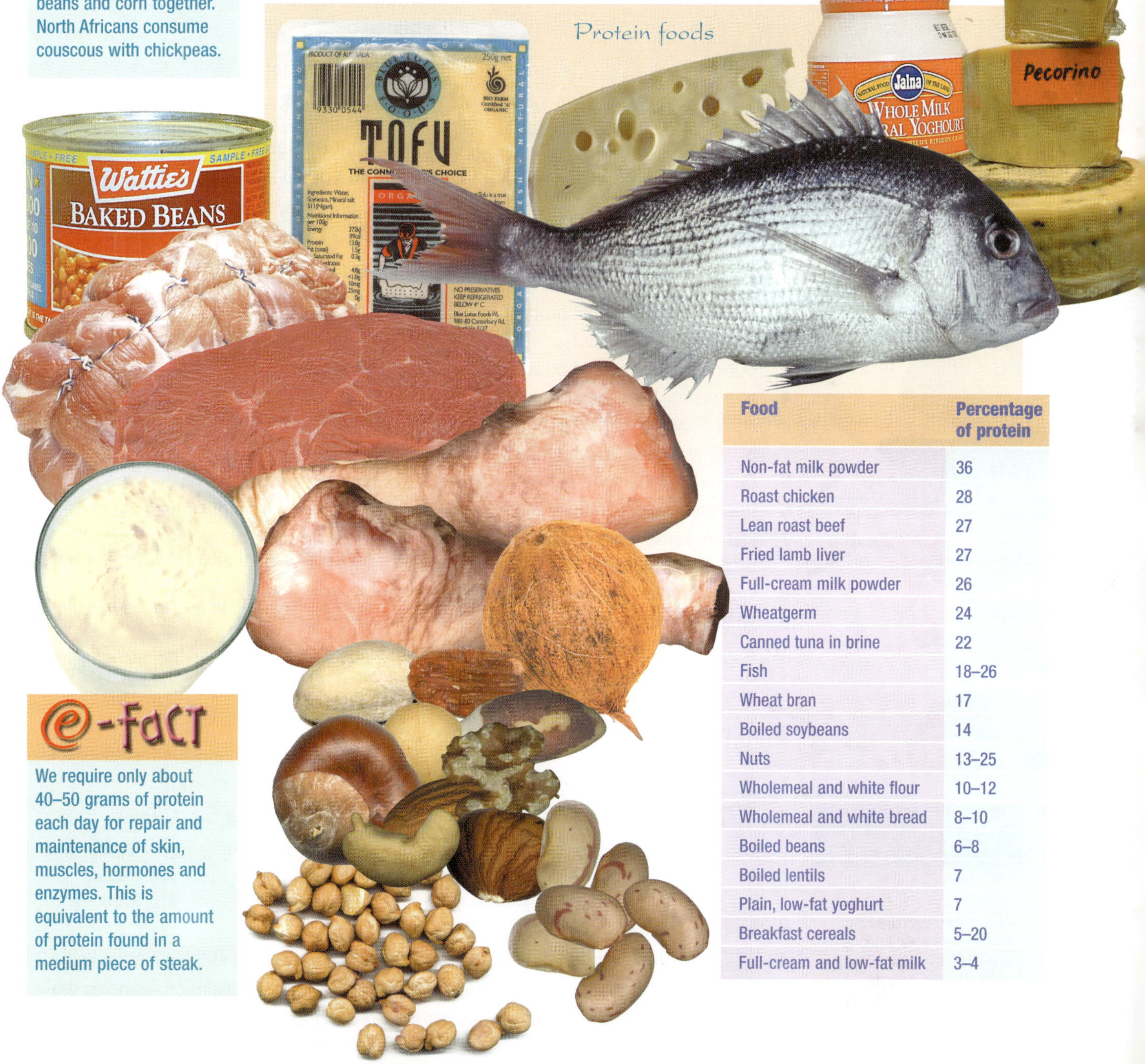

Protein foods

Food	Percentage of protein
Non-fat milk powder	36
Roast chicken	28
Lean roast beef	27
Fried lamb liver	27
Full-cream milk powder	26
Wheatgerm	24
Canned tuna in brine	22
Fish	18–26
Wheat bran	17
Boiled soybeans	14
Nuts	13–25
Wholemeal and white flour	10–12
Wholemeal and white bread	8–10
Boiled beans	6–8
Boiled lentils	7
Plain, low-fat yoghurt	7
Breakfast cereals	5–20
Full-cream and low-fat milk	3–4

4 vitality.

For a really satisfying meal, red meat is the ideal choice. **RED MEAT.**
Eat lean red meat 3-4 times a week and you'll feel better for it. Feel good.
www.redmeat-foodgood.com.au

Although we refer to foods as being high in protein, these foods are not made entirely of protein, as shown in the table on page 15.

Protein's main function is for growth, repair and maintenance of body cells, but excess amounts may be converted into kilojoules and can be used as energy. Protein is used as a source of energy if there is insufficient carbohydrate and fat consumed. This is why protein is referred to as a secondary source of energy. Excess protein that is not utilised is stored as body fat. Those who experience growth, such as children, adolescents and pregnant and lactating women, require more protein in relation to their body weight than adults. Adults require 1 gram of protein per kilogram of body weight.

QUESTION

Consider what messages this advertisement is conveying to you. Discuss your thoughts with a classmate. Share your thoughts with the class.

▶ Let's remember

1 What is the function of protein?
2 What are amino acids?
3 Outline the differences between essential and non-essential amino acids.
4 **a** Identify the essential amino acids for:
     i   adults   **ii**   children
   b Why is there a difference between the two groups?
5 Outline the difference between complete and incomplete proteins.
6 How can you obtain all of the essential amino acids solely from plant foods?
7 Identify some foods (both animal and plant) that are high in protein. Are they made solely from protein?
8 Why is protein also referred to as a secondary source of energy?
9 What happens to excess protein that is not required for energy?
10 **a** How much protein should adults consume?
   b Which groups require more protein in relation to their body weight than adults? Why?

▶ Let's investigate

1 Investigate Meat Standards Australia.
2 Investigate what meats are consumed in other countries or regions, such as:

a	USA	**d**	Middle East	**g**	New Zealand	**j**	Ghana
b	Sweden	**e**	Japan	**h**	Russia	**k**	Mexico
c	Italy	**f**	Korea	**i**	Germany	**l**	India

3 Investigate how eggs should be stored.
4 Investigate the various varieties of hen eggs that are available in the supermarket. Evaluate the protein content of each variety ☺ ☺ ☹. What conclusions can you draw about protein content of the various varieties of hen eggs?

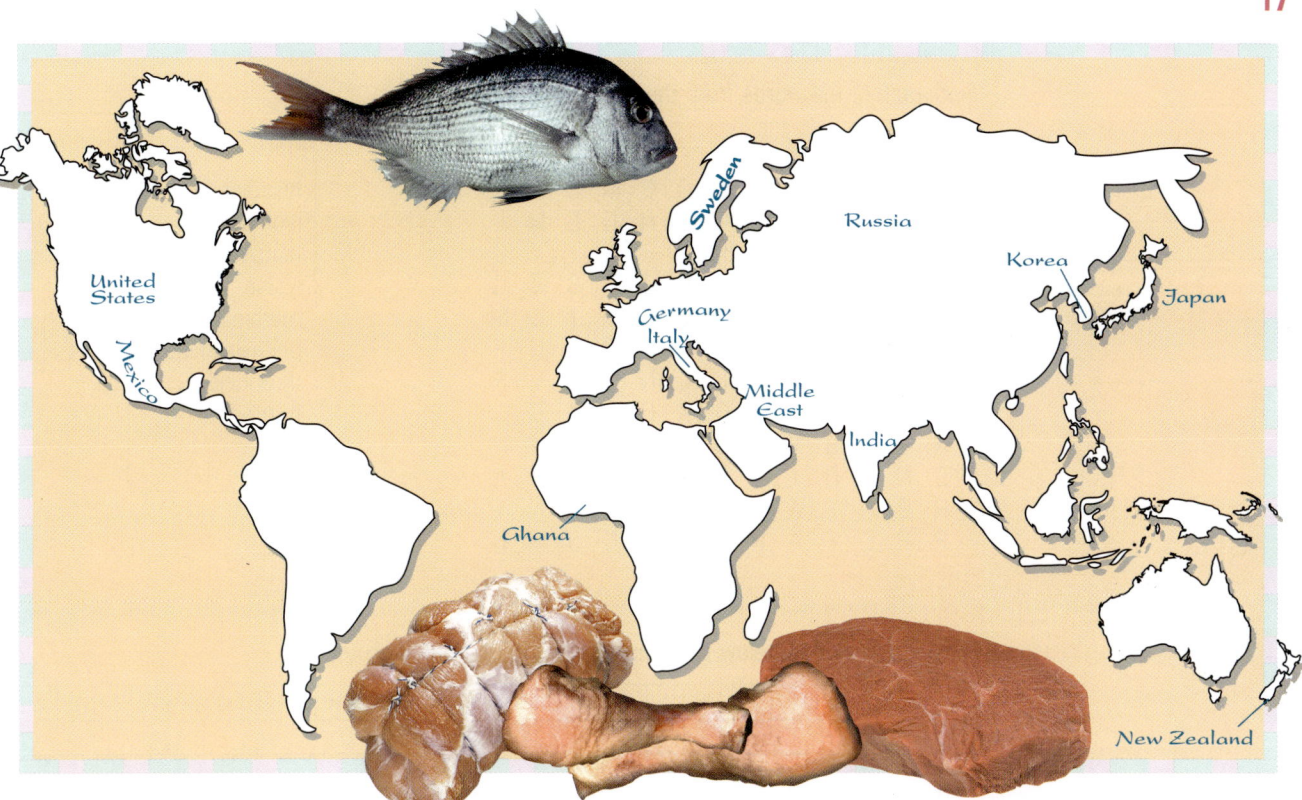

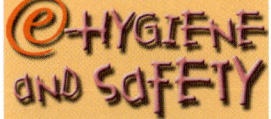

e-HYGIENE and SAFETY

Meat should be thawed in the refrigerator. Meat that has been thawed in this way can be safely refrozen.

5 Investigate how vegans could obtain protein in their diet. Design a menu that would ensure the consumption of all the essential amino acids.

6 Investigate the growth cycles that occur throughout the lifespan, i.e. pregnancy and lactation, infancy, childhood, adolescence, adulthood and late adulthood. Investigate what the Recommended Dietary Intake of protein is at each stage and provide reasons why protein is required at each stage. Present your information as a written report, datashow presentation, webpage or poster.

▶ **e-Protein**

www.redmeat-feelgood.com.au

Visit the Feel Good Campaign website and design a poster to promote red meat as part of a healthy diet.

▶ **Puzzled**

Protein puzzle

Unscramble the tiles below to complete a sentence about the function of protein.

L L S .	B O D	E O F	T H E	M A I N	R A N
E P A I	I S	D M A	C T I O	N O F	Y C E
T E I N	G R O W	T H R	N A N C	F U N	F O R
I N T E	P R O				

Essential amino acids

Find each of the words from the box in the puzzle.

```
E K Q A K L X F B H O I A
N X O C N X E Q C M C A X
I S O L E U C I N E E M L
N A H P O T P Y R T I Y Z
A D E P T F M B J H S V G
L H H M V H C Q O I T D M
A G L S A C R E N O L N F
L V E M L G L E N N W V R
Y S U G G J Q K O I Z G G
N Y C B V H D O L N L K H
E N I D I T S I H E I A A
H P N F W F P P U R Z N V
P P E F A K P T H E S M E
```

histidine
isoleucine
leucine
lysine
methionine
phenylalanine
threonine
tryptophan
valine

Protein code

Work out the code below to complete a sentence about protein.

A	B	C	D	E	F	G	H	I	J	K	L	M	N	O	P	Q	R	S	T	U	V	W	X	Y	Z
9												17		14		11									

P R _ _ _ _ _   _ _   M A _ _   _ R _ M   _ _ A _ _ _
14 11 13 3 2 16 23   16 19   17 9 5 2   24 11 13 17   4 20 9 16 23 19

_ _   A M _ _ _   A _ _ _ _
13 24   9 17 16 23 13   9 4 16 5 19

LET'S PRODUCE

Ingredients
½ brown onion, chopped
2 cloves garlic, crushed
40 millilitres beef stock
125 grams beef mince
½ × 435 gram can crushed tomatoes, undrained
150 grams red kidney beans, drained and rinsed
1 tablespoon tomato paste
1 teaspoon chilli powder
½ teaspoon sugar
3 shakes black pepper
4 20-centimetre diameter Mexican tortillas
2 tablespoons sour cream
1 spring onion, chopped
30 grams lettuce, shredded

Tortilla wraps

(serves 2)

Method

1   Place onion, garlic and stock in saucepan. Bring to boil and simmer, covered, for ten minutes.
2   Stir in mince with a wooden spoon and cook for five minutes.
3   Add tomatoes, kidney beans, tomato paste, chilli powder and sugar and bring to the boil. Simmer for twenty-five minutes, until mixture becomes thick. Season with black pepper.
4   Spoon mixture onto tortillas and top with sour cream, spring onion and lettuce. Roll up.

Variation

Use vegetable stock instead of beef stock and replace the beef mince with an additional 125 grams of red kidney beans.

QUESTION

Investigate the sources and types of protein in this recipe.

Lamb cutlets and pilaf

(serves 2)

Ingredients
4 lamb cutlets
1 teaspoon ground cumin
$\frac{1}{2}$ teaspoon oil
5 teaspoons vegetable oil
$\frac{1}{4}$ cup slivered almonds
1 brown onion, finely chopped
1 clove garlic, crushed
1 teaspoon fresh ginger, grated
pinch cardamom seeds
$\frac{1}{2}$ teaspoon cinnamon
3 whole cloves
pinch chilli powder
$\frac{3}{4}$ cup basmati rice, rinsed
1 cup chicken stock
$\frac{1}{4}$ cup coconut milk
$\frac{1}{4}$ cup currants
2 tablespoons fresh coriander, chopped

Method

1 Rub cumin and oil into cutlets and set aside.
2 Cook almonds in 2 teaspoons of oil in frypan for five minutes. Remove and drain on absorbent paper.
3 Add 3 teaspoons of oil and cook onion and garlic for five minutes. Add ginger, cardamom seeds, cinnamon, cloves and chilli powder and cook for another minute.
4 Add rice and stir to ensure that it is coated with oil. Add stock and coconut milk and bring to the boil. Reduce heat and simmer for fifteen minutes, or until all liquid had been absorbed. Stir currants and coriander through rice.
5 Grill cutlets and serve accompanied with rice and top with toasted almonds.

QUESTION

Investigate the sources and types of protein in this recipe.

Mini egg and bacon pies

(serves 2)

Method

1 Preheat oven to 180°C.
2 Make pastry by rubbing in butter to sifted flour and mustard powder.
3 Combine egg yolk and water and add to flour mixture.
4 Lightly knead on floured board and divide mixture into two.
5 Roll out each portion into a 15-centimetre circle half a centimetre thick.
6 Carefully press into greased muffin pans. Leave for fifteen minutes to rest.
7 In the meantime, cook bacon in frypan and drain on absorbent paper.
8 Combine parsley, chives and cheeses in bowl and add cooled bacon. Place half the mixture on base of the pastry cases.
9 Combine eggs and black pepper and place into each pastry case. Sprinkle with remaining bacon mixture.
10 Brush pastry edges with extra egg to glaze and cook for twenty minutes, or until cooked.
11 Cool slightly before removing from muffin trays.
12 Serve with lettuce and tomato.

Ingredients
2 rashers bacon, chopped
2 teaspoons fresh parsley, chopped
2 teaspoons fresh chives, chopped
10 grams parmesan cheese, grated
10 grams cheddar cheese, grated
2 eggs, lightly beaten
3 shakes black pepper
50 grams lettuce, washed
1 tomato, quartered

Pastry
60 grams butter, chopped
100 grams flour
$\frac{3}{4}$ teaspoon mustard powder
2 teaspoons egg yolk
2 teaspoons water, chilled

QUESTION

Investigate the sources and types of protein in this recipe.

Fats

Fats are made up of the same elements as carbohydrates—carbon, hydrogen and oxygen—but in different proportions. They are found in both animal and plant foods. Fats are a concentrated source of energy, with 1 gram supplying 37 kilojoules.

Other functions of fats include:

- making food more appetising
- carrying the fat-soluble vitamins—vitamins A, D, E and K
- providing essential fatty acids

Percentage of fat found in foods

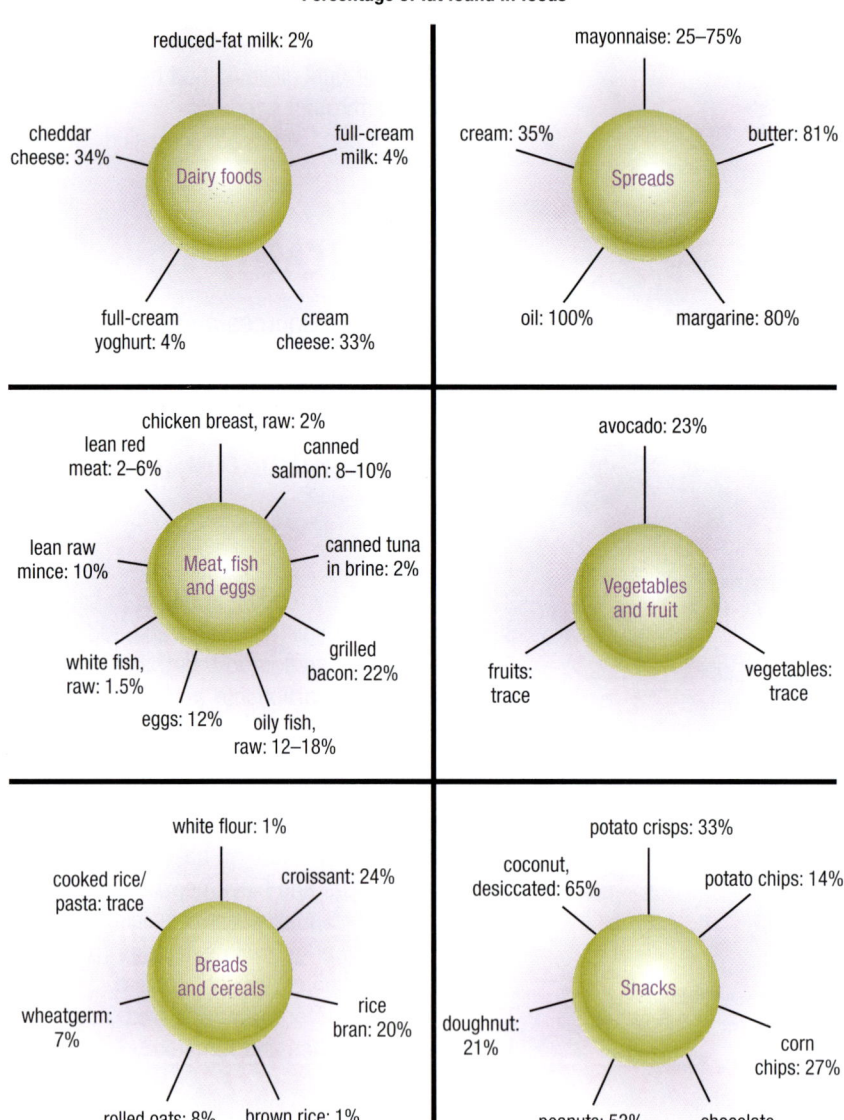

reduced-fat milk: 2%
cheddar cheese: 34%
full-cream milk: 4%
Dairy foods
full-cream yoghurt: 4%
cream cheese: 33%

mayonnaise: 25–75%
cream: 35%
butter: 81%
Spreads
oil: 100%
margarine: 80%

chicken breast, raw: 2%
lean red meat: 2–6%
canned salmon: 8–10%
lean raw mince: 10%
Meat, fish and eggs
canned tuna in brine: 2%
white fish, raw: 1.5%
grilled bacon: 22%
eggs: 12%
oily fish, raw: 12–18%

avocado: 23%
Vegetables and fruit
fruits: trace
vegetables: trace

white flour: 1%
cooked rice/ pasta: trace
croissant: 24%
Breads and cereals
wheatgerm: 7%
rice bran: 20%
rolled oats: 8%
brown rice: 1%

potato crisps: 33%
coconut, desiccated: 65%
potato chips: 14%
Snacks
doughnut: 21%
corn chips: 27%
peanuts: 53%
chocolate cake: 18%

Fat = fatty acids + glycerol

There are some fatty acids, known as non-essential fatty acids, that can be made by the body. Essential fatty acids are those that must be provided by food, as the body cannot make them.

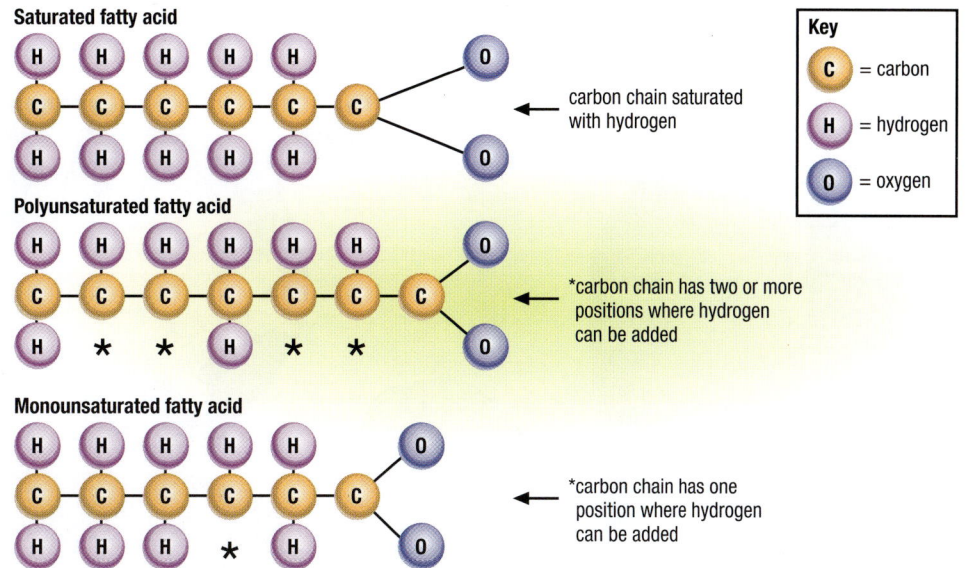

Saturated fatty acid

carbon chain saturated with hydrogen

Polyunsaturated fatty acid

*carbon chain has two or more positions where hydrogen can be added

Monounsaturated fatty acid

*carbon chain has one position where hydrogen can be added

Key

C = carbon

H = hydrogen

O = oxygen

Would you believe that coconut cream or milk may contain 11–36 per cent fat, most of which is saturated fat? Currently, there is no standard that defines coconut cream or milk, so manufacturers can call their product whatever they want.

Trans-fats are usually created by the hydrogenation of vegetable oils into margarines and can be found in baked goods, such as biscuits and pastries. Recent research has shown than these fats can have an undesirable effect on blood cholesterol.

It is recommended that we reduce our fat consumption to 30 per cent or less of all kilojoules consumed, with a greater proportion of monounsaturated and polyunsaturated fats rather than saturated fats.

e-DEFINE

Triglyceride = glycerol + three fatty acids.

Classifying fats

Fats are classified according to the amount of hydrogen that they contain. The two main groups of fats are:

- saturated fats, which contain the maximum amount of hydrogen
- unsaturated fats, which do not contain the maximum amount of hydrogen

Most foods contain a mixture of each type of fat, but are classified according to the fat of which they contain the greatest percentage.

Saturated fats

- Saturated fats are found in both animal and plant foods, such as fatty meat, dairy products, palm and coconut products, and commercially baked products.
- Saturated fats tend to increase low-density lipoproteins (LDL), which can elevate cholesterol levels and therefore increase your chance of heart disease.
- It is best to consume a smaller amount of food that is high in saturated fats or to choose lean or low-fat alternatives.

Unsaturated fats

- Unsaturated fats can be classified as either monounsaturated or polyunsaturated.
- Polyunsaturated and monounsaturated fats are often called 'good' fats because they can assist to decrease cholesterol.
- Unsaturated fats are found in sunflower, olive and canola oils and margarines, as well as in many nuts, seeds and soy foods.

Fat-soluble vitamins and fatty acids occur in small quantities in foods such as fish, lean meat, eggs, oats, seeds, nuts, vegetables and fruit. However, most of us would be surprised to know how much fat we really consume. We are usually aware of fat in butter, cream, margarine, oils and meats, but we often are oblivious to the fat that is hidden in biscuits, pastries, cheese, chocolate, fried and takeaway foods, cakes and potato chips and crisps.

We need fat in our diet, but in our well-nourished and under-exercised society, we tend to consume too much and too much of the wrong type of fat. A diet high in saturated fats can also be high in cholesterol and triglycerides in the blood, which can lead to dietary related diseases, such as coronary heart disease, high blood pressure, diabetes and gallstones. We will explore these diseases in more detail in chapter 2.

'Good' fats

'Bad' fats

▶ **Let's remember**

1 Define the term *lipid*.
2 Of what elements does fat consist?
3 How much energy is contained in 1 gram of fat?
4 Identify the various functions of fat.
5 What does fat comprise?
6 Distinguish between essential and non-essential fatty acids.
7 **a** How are fats classified?
    b What are the two main types of fats?
8 What are the health concerns with consuming a diet high in saturated fat?
9 Which types of fat are recommended?
10 Why may we be unaware of the total amount of fat that we consume?

e-fact

Light olive oil is not lighter in kilojoules, but rather lighter in taste and viscosity.

▶ Let's investigate

1 Investigate current labelling laws concerning fat content in food. Present your information as a pamphlet.
2 Investigate trans-fatty acids. Design a brochure to present your information.
3 Undertake a K-W-L. Write down:
   a two things that you **k**new about fats before reading this section
   b two things that you **w**ant to know about fats (find out the answers to these)
   c two things that you have **l**earnt about fats

▶ *e*-Fat

www.goldncanola.com.au

1 What is omega-3?
2 Outline what research has shown in regard to omega-3.
3 Which foods provide omega-3?
4 What role did the Greenland Eskimos play in the discovery of the importance of omega-3?

www.dietclub.com.au/createameal/?menu = 2
www.dietclub.com.au/createameal/?menu = 1

These two websites provide you with information about the amount of fat in common takeaway foods found at McDonald's and Pizza Hut. Undertake a PMI, outlining five 'Pluses', five 'Minuses' and five 'Interesting points' associated with these websites. Select a meal and graph the nutrients found in this meal. Write a 200-word summary about the nutritional value of this meal.

▶ Puzzled

The good oil

Answer the following and work out the fat-soluble vitamins by selecting the letters in each box.

1 One of the elements that make up fat
2 The general term for fats and oils
3 Fat is made up of fatty acids and
4 1 gram of fat supplies 37

Vitamins __, __, __ and __ are fat-soluble.

Fat chance

Work out the code below to complete a sentence about fat.

A	B	C	D	E	F	G	H	I	J	K	L	M	N	O	P	Q	R	S	T	U	V	W	X	Y	Z
A		D												B					G						

_ A T C O _ _ _ _ T _ O _ C A _ _ O _
I A G D B P Q V Q G Q B I D A T E B P

_ _ _ _ _ O _ _ _ _ A _ _ O _ _ _ _
S N U T B M W P A P U B L N M W P

Fat fun

Across

3 Type of fatty acid that can only be supplied by food
5 A diet high in saturated fat is often high in this substance
8 It is recommended that infants do not consume _____-fat products
9 One of the elements that fat consists of
10 These fats contain the maximum amount of hydrogen
11 Term used to describe glycerol plus three fatty acids
13 Type of fat created by the hydrogenation of vegetable oil into margarine
14 Term used to describe fats and oils

Down

1 Vitamins A, D, E and K are known as the fat-_____ vitamins
2 Mono and poly are examples of this type of fat
4 This type of fat is considered 'good' for your health
6 Percentage of energy intake that should come from fat
7 Abbreviation for low-density lipoprotein
12 Number of kilojoules supplied by one gram of fat (two words)

LET'S PRODUCE

Ingredients

1 tablespoon olive oil
1 red capsicum, chopped
½ zucchini, chopped
½ red onion, sliced
1 clove garlic, crushed
100 grams cherry tomatoes, cut into halves
1 sheet frozen puff pastry
½ egg, lightly beaten
2 tablespoons vegetable pesto
¼ cup parmesan cheese, grated
1 tablespoon fresh basil leaves, chopped

Ingredients

2 carrots, peeled and cut into 1-centimetre batons
2 potatoes, peeled and cut into 1-centimetre batons
1 tablespoon olive oil
2 fillets fish
1 lemon
3 shakes black pepper
2 spring onions, chopped finely
10 grams butter
⅓ cup light sour cream
2 teaspoons capers
2 teaspoons fresh dill, chopped

Vegetable tarts

(serves 2)

Method

1 Preheat oven to 220°C.
2 Combine oil with capsicum, zucchini, onion and garlic in a large baking dish and cook for thirty minutes, or until vegetables are slightly tender.
3 Add tomatoes and cook for another ten minutes.
4 Remove vegetables and let cool.
5 Turn oven down to 200°C.
6 Cut pastry sheet into quarters and place two quarters on greased oven tray, and brush edges with egg.
7 Cut remaining two quarters into 2-centimetre-wide strips and attractively arrange around the edges of each square.
8 Spread pesto over pastry squares and sprinkle with parmesan cheese.
9 Top each pastry square with cooled vegetable mixture and brush edges of pastry with remaining egg.
10 Cook for twenty minutes, or until pastry is lightly brown.
11 Garnish with basil leaves.

Fish and vegetable chips

(serves 2)

Method

1 Preheat oven to 230°C and line shallow roasting pan with baking paper.
2 Toss carrots and potatoes in oil and place in a single layer on roasting pan. Bake for fifteen minutes, turning once.
3 In the meantime, cut two 60-centimetre lengths of foil and fold each piece in half lengthways. Place each fillet of fish in the opening of the foil.
4 Cut lemon in half and juice one half. Cut the other half into thin slices and place slices in with fish, together with spring onion, black pepper and butter. Enclose fish in foil and place on baking tray and place in oven with vegetables.
5 Cook fish for eight minutes, or until tender and vegetables are tender and golden.
6 Mix sour cream, capers, dill and lemon juice.
7 Place fish on serving plates and serve with vegetable chips and sour cream mixture.

HYGIENE AND SAFETY

Remove the fish from the foil parcels carefully, as the entrapped steam can be dangerous.

QUESTIONS

1 What types of fats are found in fish?
2 Why are the vegetable chips healthier than the chips you may buy from a takeaway shop?

Ingredients

½ teaspoon olive oil
250 millilitres chicken stock
20 grams fresh breadcrumbs
40 grams walnut halves,
  finely ground
3 teaspoons sweet paprika
2 chicken thigh fillets, skin
  removed
½ teaspoon olive oil (extra)
75 grams spinach
black pepper
10 grams walnut halves
  (extra), roughly chopped

Chicken with walnuts　　　　(serves 2)

Method

1　Preheat oven to 200°C and grease baking dish with olive oil.
2　Bring stock to boil in saucepan. Remove from heat before adding breadcrumbs and walnuts.
3　Return to medium heat, stirring constantly for twenty-five minutes, or until sauce thickens slightly. Let cool for ten minutes.
4　Sprinkle chicken with paprika and place in baking dish and cook for fifteen minutes. Turn over and cook for a further three minutes, or until juices run clear.
5　Heat extra olive oil in frypan and cook spinach leaves for two minutes, or until just wilted. Add pepper.
6　Serve chicken on bed of spinach and topped with walnut sauce. Garnish with extra walnuts.

QUESTIONS

1　Why was the skin removed from the chicken?
2　Investigate the sources of oil in the various ingredients and explain whether these fats are beneficial to one's health.

Minerals

Minerals play a very important role in the body. They are classified as either major or trace. Major elements are required in large amounts and include calcium, iron, sodium, magnesium, phosphorus, potassium, chlorine and sulphur. Trace elements are required in small amounts and include zinc, copper, selenium and iodine, to name a few.

Calcium

Calcium has various functions in the body, including:
· forming a hard structure of bones and teeth
· assisting in muscle contractions and nerve functioning
· assisting in blood clotting and enzyme activity
Calcium is also being researched to discover its role in the prevention of high blood pressure, premenstrual tension and kidney stones.
Good sources of calcium include:
· all dairy products, such as milk, cheese and yoghurt
· canned fish with edible bones, such as salmon and sardines
· nuts, such as almonds, hazelnuts and Brazil nuts
Foods such as broccoli also contain calcium, but it is not as easily absorbed as from other sources.
Factors that inhibit the absorption of calcium include smoking, caffeine, alcohol and salt. A high protein intake also interferes with the absorption of calcium.

e-fact

The lifecycle of the red blood cell is 120 days. The iron is reused when red blood cells die. Men usually lose only small amounts of iron from the body, whereas women lose much more due to the loss of menstrual blood.

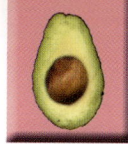

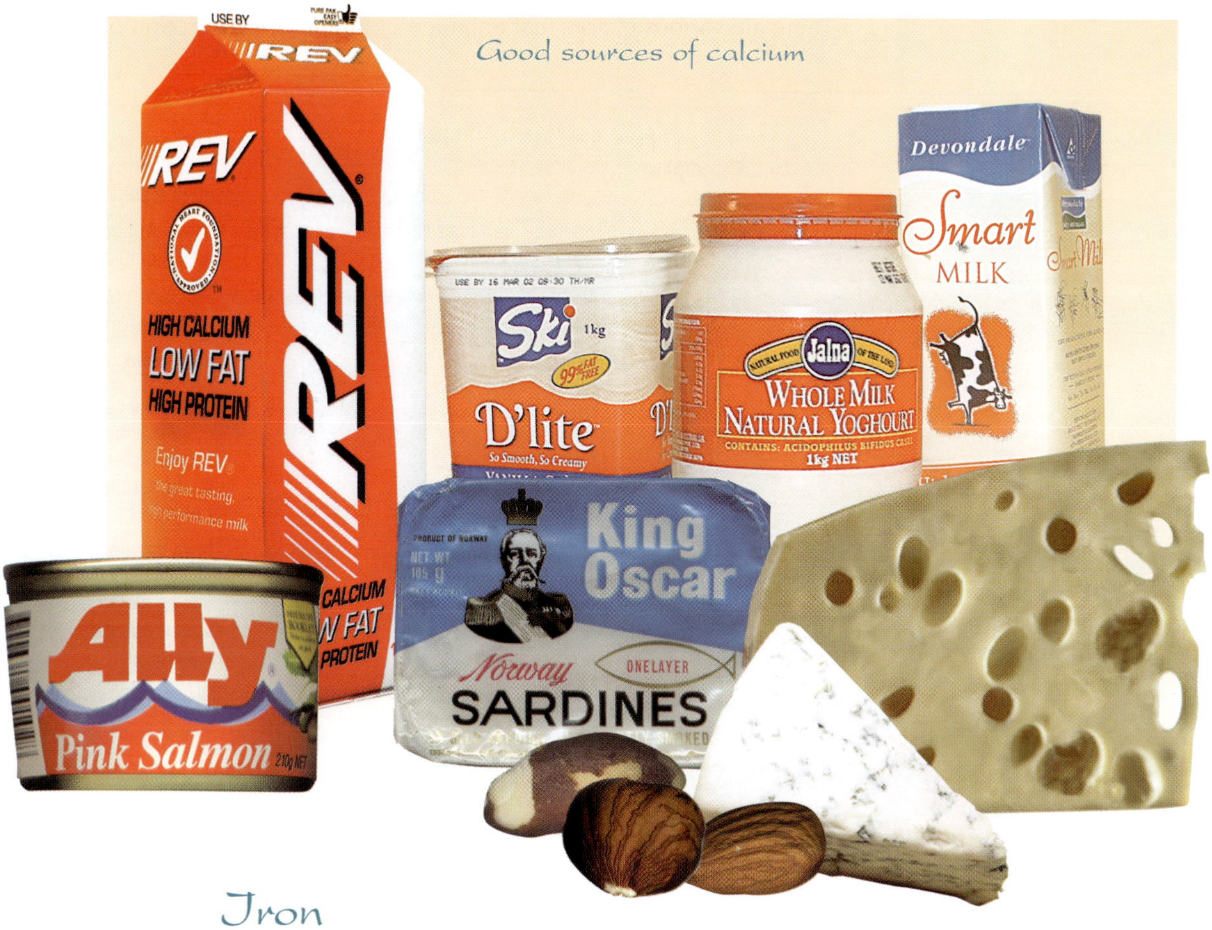

Good sources of calcium

Iron

The body uses iron to form haemoglobin, one of the essential components of red blood cells. The role of haemoglobin is to carry oxygen around the body. Iron is also a necessary component of myoglobin, which is another name for the protein found in muscles. Myoglobin is responsible for providing oxygen to the muscles during strenuous physical activity.

Iron also plays a role in the body's chemical reaction that produces energy.

Infancy, adolescence and pregnancy are critical stages in the lifespan when iron intake should be increased due to rapid periods of growth. Iron is required to assist in increasing the number of red blood cells and provide blood for new body tissue.

There are two main types of iron found in food.

e-fact

The Recommended Dietary Intake for iron nearly doubles during the last trimester (three months) of pregnancy, to supply the growing foetus and placenta with new red blood cells.

Types of iron	Comments	Food sources
Haem iron	• Is well absorbed by the body • About 10–30 per cent in healthy people	Animal foods, such as: • liver • meat • seafood • poultry
Non-haem iron	• Is not well absorbed by the body • About 2–10 per cent in healthy people	Plant foods, such as: • legumes • wholemeal breads • wholegrain cereals • green leafy vegetables • nuts • seeds Eggs

e-fact

A healthy person will absorb about 10 per cent of iron from food intake if their sources are a variety of plant and animal foods.

There are various factors that enhance or inhibit the absorption of iron.

Enhancers	Examples	Food sources
These substances assist in increasing the absorption of iron	Vitamin C	Fruits and vegetables, such as berries, citrus fruits, capsicum and broccoli
	Vitamin A and beta-carotene—especially iron found in rice, wheat and corn	Yellow, orange and green fruits and vegetables
	Animal meats—can slightly increase the absorption of non-haem iron	Beef, chicken, fish

Inhibitors	Examples	Food sources
These substances decrease the absorption of iron	Phytates	Wholemeal cereals, bran and legumes. Vitamin C (and to some extent meat) can counteract the inhibiting effect of phytates
	Polyphenols	These compounds are found in tea, coffee and certain grains such as barley, and vegetables such as onion and herbs such as parsley
	Calcium—decreases the absorption of both haem and non-haem iron	Dairy products

Phytates are compounds found in the outer layers of cereal grains. They can trap minerals, such as iron, calcium and zinc, and make these unavailable to the body.

Good sources of haem iron

Good sources of non-haem iron

Sodium

Sodium plays a role in:
· controlling of the transmission of nerve impulses
· maintaining water balance within the body
· transportation of amino acids and glucose in the bloodstream

It is found naturally in most foods and the best way to obtain sodium is from fresh, unprocessed foods, such as vegetables. Unfortunately, processed foods such as meats and takeaway foods tend to be too high in sodium. This is where Australians tend to consume too much sodium. Such foods include soy sauce, packet soups, potato crisps, cornflakes, salami, ham and cheeses.

Naturally occurring sodium | Added sodium

▶ Let's remember

1 Outline the two classifications of minerals.
2 Complete the following table.

Mineral	Functions	Good food sources
Calcium		
Iron		
Sodium		

3   What current research is occurring in regard to calcium?

4   Identify factors that inhibit the absorption of calcium.

5   Outline the difference between haem and non-haem iron.

6   Why should infants, adolescents and pregnant women increase their iron intake?

7   What happens to the iron when the red blood cells die?

8   Identify factors that enhance the absorption of iron.

9   Identify factors that inhibit the absorption of iron.

10 Where would most Australians obtain their sodium?

Let's investigate

1   Investigate one of the following major nutrients: phosphorus, magnesium, potassium, chlorine, sulphur. Include information about its functions and food sources. Present your information as a poster or datashow presentation.

2   Investigate the food sources and functions of three of the following trace minerals: zinc, copper, iodine, fluorine, manganese, chromium, selenium, molybdenum, cobalt. Present your information as a poster or datashow presentation. Include pictures of foods that contain the minerals being investigated.

3   Design a menu that includes ingredients that enhance the absorption of iron. Identify these ingredients. Be sure to include foods that you would consume.

4   Investigate the range of foods in your pantry or refrigerator by reading the labels. Make a list of ten foods that contain salt.

5   Investigate the Recommended Dietary Intake for calcium, sodium and iron over the lifespan. Graph your results and discuss reasons for trends and patterns apparent in each of the three graphs. Think about the growth and development that is occurring throughout the lifespan.

6   Investigate which minerals are associated with the following chemical symbols: NA, K, Ca, Fe, Zn, P, Mg, I, Se, Cu.

@ -Minerals

www.foodsciencebureau.com.au/nutrit/calcium.htm

1   Why is calcium regarded as an essential part of one's diet?

2   Why should we consume calcium every day?

3   How much calcium is required?

4   What happens if you consume too little calcium?

5   What happens if you consume too much calcium?

6   Design a diet that is high in calcium. Include foods for breakfast, lunch, dinner and snacks.

www.foodsciencebureau.com.au/nutrit/salt.htm

1   Why is salt an important part of our diet?

2   What minerals make up salt?

3   Outline the dietary related diseases that are associated with salt.

4   How can you monitor your salt intake?

5   In what ways is salt used in food preparation?

WEBExTras

www.woolworths.com. au/dietinfo/rsa17.asp
The Woolworths site provides information about lean meat and iron, including the importance of iron and the different types of iron.

www.woolworths.com. au/dietinfo/rsa22.asp
The Woolworths site provides an overview of milk, outlining the numerous varieties of milk.

WEBExTras

www.woolworths.com. au/dietinfo/ras13.asp
The Woolworths site presents a summary of the various types of vitamins and minerals.

www.foodwatch.com. au/iron.html
Catherine Saxelby provides a summary about the importance of iron in one's diet on the Foodwatch website.

 **Puzzled**

Scrambled minerals

Unscramble the following minerals.

1	cclamui	**4**	nori	**7**	manemugis	**10**	phlurus
2	doneii	**5**	pocpre	**8**	amssutiop	**11**	cinz
3	dosmiu	**6**	meelsinu	**9**	norilech	**12**	ernioulf

 ## Mineral find

Find each of the words from the box in the puzzle.

```
C E R C N I Z P R M
H N U O C O H H P U
L I H P L U S O S I
O R P P Q K T S E S
R O L E L A I P L E
I U U R S R O H E N
N L S S O V V O N G
E F I N H O I R I A
M U I C L A C U U M
M S O D I U M S M Z
```

calcium	phosphorus
chlorine	potassium
copper	selenium
fluorine	sodium
iron	sulphur
magnesium	zinc

Ingredients

3 teaspoons olive oil

1 teaspoon cumin

200 grams butternut pumpkin, peeled and cut into 1.5-centimetre wedges

$1\frac{1}{2}$ teaspoons curry powder

4 lamb cutlets

$\frac{1}{2}$ cup condensed tomato soup

$\frac{1}{3}$ cup coconut milk

1 tablespoon water

$\frac{1}{3}$ cup frozen peas

1 tablespoon fresh coriander, chopped

Curried lamb with pumpkin   (serves 2)

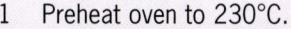 ### Method

1 Preheat oven to 230°C.
2 Line baking tray with foil.
3 Combine 1 teaspoon oil and cumin, then brush over pumpkin.
4 Place pumpkin on tray and cook for twenty minutes, or until tender and golden.
5 Heat remaining oil in frypan, add curry powder and cook for thirty seconds. Add lamb and cook for two minutes on each side.
6 Add tomato soup, coconut milk and water, then bring to boil. Simmer, uncovered for ten minutes, stirring occasionally.
7 Add peas and cook for a further two minutes, until sauce thickens.
8 Place two cutlets on each serving plate, top with sauce and place pumpkin wedges to the side. Garnish with coriander.

QUESTIONS

1 Investigate the type of iron that is present in this recipe.
2 Identify other ingredients that enhance or inhibit the absorption of iron in this recipe.
3 Design your own version of this recipe to include other ingredients to assist with the absorption of iron.

Cheese pull-apart

(serves 1)

Ingredients

750 grams easy-bake bread mix

3 teaspoons dried yeast

$\frac{1}{2}$ teaspoon salt

6 teaspoons olive oil

450 millilitres water, lukewarm

1 teaspoon olive oil (extra)

120 grams tasty cheddar cheese, grated

100 grams parmesan cheese, grated

Method

1 Preheat oven to 220°C. Line tray with baking paper.
2 Combine bread mix, yeast and salt and make a well in the centre.
3 Mix oil and water together and add to dry ingredients.
4 Turn onto floured board and knead for two minutes, until smooth and elastic.
5 Grease bowl with extra oil and add dough, turning to coat it in oil.
6 Cover and leave in warm place to rise.
7 Punch down dough and roll out to a 30 x 40-centimetre rectangle.
8 Sprinkle with cheeses and press into dough.
9 Starting from the long side, roll up the dough. Trim to neaten the edges and cut into eight even slices.
10 Arrange the slices touching one another in two rows on the tray.
11 Leave in warm place to rise again and then place in oven for twenty-five minutes, or until cooked.
12 Serve warm or at room temperature.

QUESTIONS

1 Identify the minerals found in this recipe.
2 Investigate what other ingredients could be added to this recipe. Design and produce your own pull-apart. Evaluate your pull-apart using a Y-chart as shown.

```
        Y    Tastes
             like
 Smells     Looks
 like       like
```

Vegetable rolls

(serves 2)

Ingredients

1 onion, chopped

$\frac{1}{2}$ clove garlic, crushed

$\frac{3}{4}$ cup cabbage, shredded

1 carrot, grated

$\frac{1}{2}$ cup corn kernels

2 medium potatoes, cooked and mashed

$\frac{1}{4}$ cup cheddar cheese, grated

2 teaspoons fresh parsley, chopped

4 cabbage leaves

Pumpkin sauce

$\frac{3}{4}$ cup water

$\frac{1}{2}$ onion, chopped (extra)

125 grams pumpkin, chopped

125 grams ricotta cheese

2 teaspoons fresh parsley chopped (extra)

Method

1 Preheat oven to 190°C.
2 Sauté onion and garlic in frypan.
3 Add shredded cabbage, carrot and corn and cook for a further two minutes.
4 Remove from heat and stir through potatoes, cheese and parsley.
5 Place cabbage leaves in boiling water for thirty seconds and turn under cold water.
6 Divide cooked vegetable mixture into four and place on each cabbage leaf. Roll up tightly and place in ovenproof dish.
7 Bring water, extra onion and pumpkin to boil in saucepan and simmer until pumpkin is tender. Process until smooth.
8 Fold in ricotta cheese and pour over cabbage parcels.
9 Sprinkle with extra parsley and cook for thirty minutes.

QUESTION

What minerals are found in this recipe?

Vitamins

There are two types of vitamins: fat-soluble and water-soluble.

Fat-soluble vitamins	Functions	Food sources
Vitamin A—occurs as retinol and beta-carotene	• Essential for eyesight, as it prevents night blindness • Normal growth during childhood • Healthy skin and mucous membranes	Carrots, broccoli, spinach, egg yolk, butter, cheese, sardines, herring and milk
Cholecalciferol (vitamin D)	• Works in conjunction with calcium and phosphorus for the development of strong bones and teeth	Sunlight, oily fish such as sardines, margarine and butter
Tocopherols (vitamin E)	• Maintenance of healthy cell membranes	Wheatgerm, nuts, wholegrain cereals, vegetable oils, fish
Phylloquinone (vitamin K)	• Assists in the clotting of blood	Green leafy vegetables, broccoli, eggs, cheese; also made by the bacteria in the intestines

Water-soluble vitamins	Functions	Food sources
Ascorbic acid (vitamin C)	• Healthy gums, teeth and bones • Assists in healing of wounds and resistance to infection • Collagen formation • Assists in the absorption of non-haem iron	Citrus fruits such as oranges and lemons, berries, mango, capsicum, broccoli, cabbage
B group vitamins		
Thiamin (vitamin B_1)	• Release of energy from carbohydrates • Correct functioning of heart and nervous system • Normal appetite and digestion	Vegemite, yeast, legumes, green leafy vegetables
Riboflavin (vitamin B_2)	• Healthy skin and eyes • Metabolism of carbohydrate, protein and fat	Milk, liver, Vegemite, nuts, green vegetables, liver
Niacin (vitamin B_3)	• Metabolism of carbohydrate, protein and fat • Essential for growth	Vegemite, yeast, legumes, peanuts, liver
Folate (folic acid)	• Essential for normal cell multiplication • Assists in the prevention of spina bifida and encephalitis • Helps in the usage of protein • Necessary for the production of red blood cells	Yeast, meat, green leafy vegetables, oranges

e-fact

A fat-soluble vitamin means that it needs fat to be absorbed and that it can be stored in the body's fat tissue.

e-fact

Another name for fat tissue is adipose tissue.

e-fact

The liver of the polar bear is so high in vitamin A that some of the early explorers who consumed its liver died from an overdose of vitamin A.

e-DEFINE

Vitamin A can be found preformed in foods, or as beta-carotene, which is then converted to vitamin A in the wall of the small intestines and liver. Other carotenoids can also be converted to vitamin A.

e-fact

The correct name of vitamin A is retinol.

e-fact

In the 1930s, when chickens were denied tidbits of alfalfa and decaying fish meal, they bled profusely and developed fatal diseases.

e-fact

Low-fat dairy products do not contain vitamin A and this is one reason why it is recommended that infants should not consume such products unless under medical supervision. It is not a real problem for adults, as they are likely to consume vitamin A from other sources.

Let's remember

1 Identify the two types of vitamins.
2 Outline the main differences between the two groups of vitamins.
3 Outline the difference between retinol and beta-carotene.
4 Explain why most Australians obtain enough vitamin D, while people in countries like Norway do not.
5 Using the table above, identify the vitamins found in green leafy vegetables.
6 What do thiamin, riboflavin and niacin have in common?
7 Why are pregnant women encouraged to consume foods that are high in folate prior to and during pregnancy?
8 Explain why it is recommended that infants do not consume low-fat products.
9 Why is thiamin often incorrectly spelt?
10 Why is your urine often bright yellow after you take a multivitamin?

e-Fact

If you consume a multi-vitamin and then burp, ribo-flavin, one of the B group vitamins, is responsible for the aftertaste in your mouth. It is also responsible for the bright yellow urine! Only a maximum of 25 milligrams will be absorbed, so the excess is excreted in the urine.

Let's investigate

1 Investigate the validity of the statement 'Eating carrots helps you to see in the dark'.
2 Investigate the functions and food sources of the following vitamins: pyridoxine (vitamin B$_6$), cyanocobalamin (vitamin B$_{12}$), biotin, pantothenic acid.
3 Investigate the role of folate in the prevention of neural tube effects. Present your findings as a pamphlet.
4 Investigate one of the following vitamin-deficiency diseases that are more prevalent in low-income countries : pellagra, scurvy, xerophthalmia, beriberi. Include information about signs and symptoms and dietary considerations. Present your information as a written or oral report.

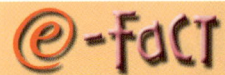

e-Fact

Folate comes from the Latin word *folia*, which means leaf. Folate is found in green leafy vegetables.

@-Vitamins

www.foodwatch.com.au/vitamins

1 Define the term *vitamin*.
2 How many vitamins are there?
3 Outline the different groups of vitamins and the differences between the two groups.
4 Why do we need vitamins?
5 Outline the advantages of consuming vitamins in food rather than as supplements.
6 Summarise the problems with overdosing on vitamins.
7 Construct a concept map to illustrate the functions and food sources of the various vitamins.
8 Graph the Recommended Dietary Intakes for all the vitamins for both men and women and summarise the trends and patterns in your graphs.

▶ **Puzzled**

VitaMatch

Match the following terms.

1 Ascorbic acid   a Vitamin B_1
2 Niacin   b Vitamin E
3 Cyanocobalamin   c Vitamin B_2
4 Phylloquinone   d Vitamin B_6
5 Thiamin   e Vitamin C
6 Tocopherols   f Vitamin B_{12}
7 Pyridoxine   g Vitamin D
8 Riboflavin   h Vitamin K
9 Cholecalciferol   i Vitamin B_3

 Split the vitamins

Match two boxes to create the names of six vitamins.

RIBO	NIA	QUINONE
CIN	PHEROLS	PHYLLO
MIN	CHOLE	TOCO
CALCIFEROL	THIA	FLAVIN

 Vitals of vitamins

Unscramble the tiles to create a sentence about classifying vitamins.

S O L U	T W O	E F A	D W A	T H E	T Y P E
B L E .	A M I N	L U B L	S O F	V I T	E A N
T S O	S	A R	T E R		

LET'S PRODUCE

Ingredients

1¼ cups self-raising flour

½ teaspoon baking powder

½ cup mashed pumpkin

½ egg, lightly beaten

1 tablespoon milk

60 grams shaved ham

2 slices cheese

1 tomato, sliced

mayonnaise

Pumpkin damper rolls   (serves 2)

Method

1   Preheat oven to 200°C.
2   Sift flour and baking powder. Make a well in the centre.
3   Mix pumpkin, egg and milk together and add to the dry ingredients. Add extra milk if desired to create a soft, sticky dough.
4   Turn dough onto floured surfaces and knead until smooth.
5   Divide in half and shape into round portions, then cut a cross on the surface of each.
6   Bake on a greased oven tray for about twenty minutes, or until each roll sounds hollow when tapped.
7   Let each roll stand on tray for five minutes before transferring to a wire rack to cool.
8   Cut each roll in half and fill with ham, cheese, tomato and mayonnaise.

QUESTION

Investigate the various vitamins found in this recipe. Classify them and list their functions.

Ingredients

¾ cup fresh basil leaves, finely chopped

½ white onion, finely chopped

1 clove garlic, crushed

1 heaped tablespoon flour

180 millilitres milk

¾ teaspoon olive oil

225 grams chicken mince

3 shakes black pepper

60 grams instant cannelloni

15 grams shredded mozzarella

50 grams spinach

Chicken cannelloni with spinach   (serves 2)

Method

1   Preheat oven to 230°C.
2   Combine basil leaves, onion, garlic, flour, 2 tablespoons of milk and oil.
3   Add 1 tablespoon of basil mixture to mince and pepper.
4   Fill the cannelloni tubes and place in a single layer in greased baking tray.
5   Heat remaining milk with rest of basil mixture in saucepan, stirring constantly for two minutes, or until mixture thickens. Pour over cannelloni and sprinkle with cheese.
6   Bake for fifteen to twenty minutes, or until tender.
7   Rinse spinach and cook in microwave for one minute.
8   Place on serving plates and top with cannelloni tubes.

QUESTIONS

1   What vitamins are found in the various ingredients in this recipe?
2   What factors may inhibit the availability of these vitamins?
3   What factors should be taken into consideration to ensure that the maximum amount of vitamins is available?

Ingredients

4 Roma tomatoes, halved lengthways
2 teaspoons brown sugar
pinch dried chilli
3 shakes black pepper
8 stalks asparagus
50 grams baby spinach, washed
50 grams bocconcini cheese, quartered
crusty bread

Dressing

2 teaspoons balsamic vinegar
2 teaspoons lemon juice
$\frac{1}{2}$ teaspoon Dijon mustard
1 teaspoon honey
1 teaspoon olive oil
black pepper

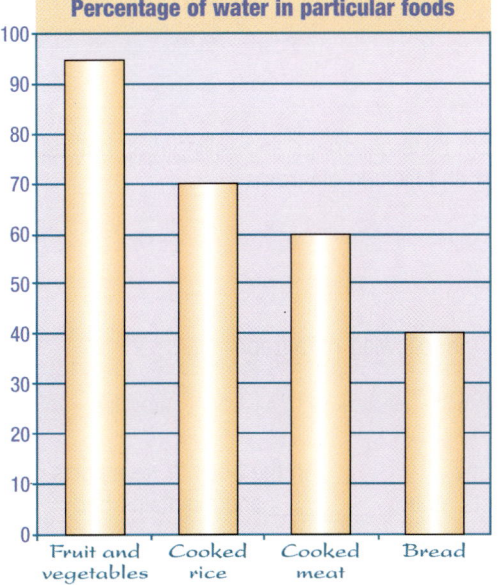

Tomato and asparagus salad   (serves 2)

Method

1 Preheat oven to 200°C.
2 Place tomato halves cut side up on a baking tray with non-stick baking paper. Sprinkle tomato with sugar, chilli and pepper and bake for twenty-five minutes, or until slightly wrinkled.
3 In the meantime, cook asparagus in boiling water until tender, about two minutes. Drain and refresh under cold running water.
4 Make dressing by placing dressing ingredients in a small bowl and whisking with a fork until combined.
5 To serve, place spinach leaves in serving bowls, top with roasted tomatoes, asparagus and bocconcini and drizzle with dressing. Serve with crusty bread.

QUESTION

Draw the following table and complete it using the recipe above.

Vitamin	Food sources	Functions

Water

Water is very important for good health. It is required:
·   for the regulation of body temperature through perspiration
·   as an important component of blood to carry other nutrients around the body
·   for the removal of wastes from the body

Percentage of water in particular foods

(Bar chart showing: Fruit and vegetables ≈ 95, Cooked rice ≈ 70, Cooked meat ≈ 60, Bread ≈ 40)

Focus on dehydration

Our body contains 70 per cent water. The body's water content can fluctuate to some extent, but lack of water leads to dehydration. We lose an average of 2.5 litres of water each day and this does not include obvious perspiring. We tend to drink when we are thirsty; by this time, we are already dehydrated. We should ensure that we constantly drink water throughout the day. Our blood volume decreases when we are dehydrated and the output of the heart is reduced, resulting in less blood flow to the skin. Perspiration decreases and there is no way to disperse heat from the body, so the body temperature increases. In severe cases, such as in marathon runners who do not drink regularly, the kidneys fail to function as the blood becomes thicker and waste products accumulate in the body. The rising body temperature causes the heart output to decrease and cardiac shock can cause death. A loss of over 5 per cent of the body's water content can lead to fatigue, mental confusion and lethargy. Water loss of 15–20 per cent is fatal.

Caffeine and alcohol both have a diuretic effect on the body.

We obtain water from beverages and foods.

Most people would consume about a litre of water each day from food and about 1.5 litres from beverages. They would also obtain another 300 millilitres of water from the metabolism of food. The precise amount of water required depends on the individual's:

· body surface area
· amount of physical activity
· amount of sodium consumed in the diet

On average, an individual should consume 1.5 to 2.5 litres of water each day.

▶ Let's remember

1 Why is water in the diet important?
2 How much water do we lose each day?
3 What does thirst indicate?
4 Why is there less blood flow to the skin when one is dehydrated?
5 Explain why one's body temperature increases when dehydrated.
6 Why do the kidneys fail when one becomes extremely dehydrated?
7 Outline the signs and symptoms of dehydration.
8 Identify the various ways in which water is gained in the body.
9 Identify factors that determine the amount of water that should be consumed.
10 What effect does consuming caffeine and alcohol have on the body?

Leaner people have a greater percentage of water than those with higher levels of body fat.

▶ Let's investigate

1 Investigate the various ways in which water is lost from the body. Present your information as a poster, with diagrams.
2 Survey the class to find out how often people drink water. Investigate how this water is obtained; for example, bottled water, drink bottle, from bubble taps at school. Investigate how active each class member is and evaluate his or her water consumption ☺ ☺ ☹. Investigate reasons why he or she does or does not regularly consume water. Can you draw any conclusions or make any recommendations?
3 Investigate the range of bottled water on the market. Investigate the various ways in which manufacturers encourage us to consume more bottled water.

WEBExTRaS

www.bottledwater.org.au
The Australasian Bottled Water Institute Incorporated is the peak industry council and certifying organisation for water bottlers.

▶ @ -water

www.neverfail.com.au

Investigate the process of obtaining water from mineral springs and selling it as bottled water. Present your information as a flow chart and include diagrams.

▶ Puzzled

Water fill

Unscramble the words in the box to complete the following paragraph.

tenisutnr	ameeettprru	tiocufnns	taniburcl	reppistarnoi	ropcutsd	ssnetliae

Water is _____ for life. It carries out many _____ in the body. It transports _____, removes waste _____, acts as a _____ and maintains body _____ via _____.

WEBExTRaS

www.foodwatch.com.au/water.html
The Foodwatch website outlines the importance of consuming water regularly in the diet.

CHAPTER 2

SCIENCE FICTION: DISCOVER FOOD MYTHS

There are many issues to do with food of which you should be aware. Too often, the information is incorrectly interpreted. In this chapter, we will dispel some food myths.

Carob

Carob is often used as a substitute for chocolate. It comes from the beans of the carob, or locust bean, tree. Because it has a bitter taste, manufacturers often add sugar and fat, particularly saturated fat, to make the product more appetising. If you read the labels of carob products, often the main ingredient is glucose syrup; therefore, in this context, carob is not that healthy. Other carob products have up to 45 per cent fat. Now, that is a lot of fat!

Soy Crisps

Soy crisps are not a healthy substitute to potato crisps. Although their fat content tends to be more unsaturated, soy crisps are likely to have a kilojoule and fat content similar to regular crisps. Soy crisps also may have one and a half times as much salt as regular crisps.

Healthy Life provides the highest quality products available. Our product range is available for your convenience at over 80 retail outlets throughout Australia, and our Quality Guarantee is the assurance of consistency that you can always expect.

For further information on this, or any other Healthy Life products, please call us on (02) 9905 8144.

You can also visit at www.healthylife.et.au.

Healthy Life is fully Australian Operated & Owned.

Healthy Life Pty Ltd
8/98 Old Pittwater Road
Brookvale, NSW 2093
Australia

Nutrition Information Servings Per Package: 3 Serving Size:	
	100g
	Average Qty Per 100gm
Energy	2225kj
Protein	15g
Fat, total	32g
- saturated	31.1g
Carbohydrate	
- total	46g
- sugars	41g

Ingredients
Vegetable Oil, Milk Solids, Buttermilk powder, carob powder, skim milk powder, emulsifiers (322, 492), flavour.

QUALITY GUARANTEED

9 314137 080417

Best Before:
Product Origin:
Storage:
Dry, cool conditions a...

Batch No: 021006
09 SEP

Controlled scientific trials in Australia have shown no link between the consumption of milk and mucus. Milk does leave a soft filmy coating in the throat or mouth, but it is merely the milk's natural, creamy texture.

Uncle Tobys Muesli Bars are quality products from Goodman Fielder Ltd

NUTRITION INFORMATION

SERVINGS PER PACKAGE: 8
SERVING SIZE: 31.3g (1 BAR)

	PER 31.3g SERVE	PER 100g
ENERGY	610kJ	1900kJ
PROTEIN	2.6g	8.3g
FAT	6.9g	22.0g
CARBOHYDRATE		
– TOTAL	19.5g	62.3g
– SUGARS	5.5g	17.5g
DIETARY FIBRE	2.2g	6.7g
SODIUM	100mg	320mg
POTASSIUM	100mg	320mg

INGREDIENTS

UNCLE TOBYS OATS, DESICCATED COCONUT, ROLLED WHEAT, SUNOLA VEGETABLE OIL, RAW SUGAR, GOLDEN SYRUP, PUFFED CEREAL (RICE, OATS, CORN), GLUCOSE SYRUP, MINERAL SALT (SODIUM BICARBONATE), SALT, NATURAL EMULSIFIER (LECITHIN), FLAVOUR. MAY CONTAIN TRACES OF PEANUTS AND OTHER NUTS.

CONSUMER QUALITY GUARANTEE

Uncle Tobys guarantee the quality of this product. If you are not completely satisfied with this product, we'll replace it. If you have any questions or comments, write or telephone at our expense to: **Australia** Consumer Relations, Reply Paid 63943, Barkly Street Wahgunyah, VIC 3687. Free Call 1800 025 768. **New Zealand** Consumer Relations, 124 Wiri Station Road, Manukau City, Auckland. Toll Free 0800 730 123. If writing, please PRINT your name, address, **phone number,** and include the product's "Best Before" date and place of purchase.

Sport and Health Bars

Sport and health bars tend to contribute a vast amount of kilojoules to one's diet. If you read the ingredients list on sport and health bars, you will find that they contain a variety of sugars as the main ingredients. Some bars may provide added vitamins. However, it is more beneficial if you consume fresh fruits and vegetables for these additional vitamins. Muesli and other breakfast bars, in particular, are often low in fat but are very high in sugar. There is some debate about whether they should remain in the breakfast cereal section of the supermarket or be positioned with confectionery items.

Fruit Bars

Fruit bars are essentially fruit pastes. Some such bars actually do not contain any of the fruit stated on their label whatsoever, only the fruit flavour. Some bars have extra sugar, but do not provide the same amount of fibre as in a piece of fruit. Because of this, fruit bars may contribute to dental caries. Read the ingredients list carefully on fruit bars and select those that include only dried fruit, seeds and nuts and contribute no added sugar or fat. Or better still, eat fresh or dried fruits instead of fruit bars.

Popcorn

Popcorn is a healthy snack if you pop it yourself. The best way is to place it in a brown paper bag in the microwave, as it requires no oil. Packaged popcorn tends to provide a lot of fat—about 29 per cent, compared with the 3 per cent found in straight corn. Therefore, packaged popcorn cannot be regarded as a healthy snack.

Red Meat

Often, people wrongly think that red meat plays no part in a healthy diet. Red meat that is lean and trimmed of fat is nutritious; it is a valuable source of iron, zinc, the B group vitamins and protein.

Bread

Bread is an essential part of one's diet. It is an essential source of carbohydrates, fibre, vitamins and minerals. It is often what is eaten with the bread that contributes energy-dense kilojoules and makes it not that nutritious; for example, butter or jam. Toasting does not reduce the kilojoules in the bread. There are many low-carbohydrate diets, such as the Zone, that encourage people to consume high amounts of protein at the expense of carbohydrates. Much of the initial weight loss is water. The body will begin to break down fats for energy. Ketones—the fatty by-product—accumulate in the bloodstream. Ketones can spill over into the urine, and the body is then said to be in a state of 'ketosis'. Fat will begin to disappear from the body. Unfortunately, this condition is also associated with tiredness, dehydration, constipation and nausea. Not healthy at all!

Although dried fruits are regarded as a healthy snack, be aware that they contain a more concentrated amount of sugars than fresh fruit because they have been dried.

SCIENCE FICTION

41

► Fat's back in fashion

Read the newspaper article and then answer the questions that follow it.

By Bronwen Gora

FAT is the food of the moment. It sounds like anathema to anyone who has ever tried to watch their weight.

But advocates of the latest trends believe we should adopt diets similar to those of cavemen—lots of protein and a lot less carbohydrates.

Low-carb diets are all the rage. Jennifer Aniston and Sharon Stone sing their praises.

Stone recently ate cream straight off the spoon in front of one interviewer, proclaiming: 'Cream has fewer carbohydrates than milk, so if you're on a low-carbohydrate diet, you drink cream.'

Diet junkies are following suit. Each morning, computer programmer Ron Glasgow, 39, eats a three-egg omelette and 340 g of bacon.

During the rest of the day, he eats all the pork rind, sausage and steak he wants. No carbs in sight. After 11 months on this diet, he has gone from 191 kg to 149 kg.

Nutritionists say his diet will raise cholesterol levels and possibly cause kidney problems and a calcium deficiency.

'I'm aware of that, but for me right now it seems to be working,' he says.

Many people seem determined to follow this controversial dietary path, which has been given added weight by a radical new theory.

Researchers are saying meat and fat should comprise 60 per cent of our diet, and fruit and vegetables the rest.

And they advise cutting carbohydrates such as wholemeal bread, rice and pasta.

When this theory was announced in Sydney at the 10th World Conference on Food Science and Technology by evolutionary biologist Loren Cordain and researcher Boyd Eaton, it set the diet world spinning.

The pair studied more than 200 hunter-gatherer groups and found two-thirds of their food was meat, with more than half of it fat.

The pair supported their claims that this is the way we should eat by pointing to the scrawny skeletons of ancient races of grain-eaters and to the fact humans lack the essential amino acid taurine. While herbivores manufacture their own, we get taurine from meat.

But the theory has angered nutritionists. The president of Sports Dietitians Australia, Dr Helen O'Connor, says the low-carb diet is a fad which has caught on because results are almost immediate. Weight does drop off, at least in the beginning.

'That's the initial hook,' Dr O'Connor says. 'But some of the weight loss is muscle and water, and people don't know this, so it's very tempting.'

Dr Susanna Holt, from Sydney University's human nutrition unit, says too many laymen have painted a misleading picture of carbohydrates.

The truth is some carbs are far better, and less likely to add weight, than others, she says.

Dr Holt says we should stick to the carbohydrates that are the least processed.

These release energy slowly into the bloodstream, are used more efficiently by the body and leave us feeling fuller for longer.

They include sweet potatoes, yams, beans, chickpeas, porridge and wholegrain bread.

The carbohydrates causing all the trouble, the ones that pack on kilos, are more refined.

These foods are burned rapidly and send blood sugar levels soaring before plunging a short-time later, leaving us tired, hungry and craving for more.

'Even wholemeal bread is not healthy because all the fibre is processed, it just gives the bread a brown color,' Dr Holt says.

Another concern of nutritionists is the fact low-carb devotees do not realise they are starving their brains as well as their bodies.

'Your mood, alertness, concentration and ability to think are affected,' Dr Holt says.

But nutritionists are facing an uphill battle because anyone following such a diet could lose a kilogram a week—mostly water.

If they stick to it they lose fat, but in the unhealthiest way possible.

'High-protein, high-meat, high-fat diets cause weight loss by causing ketosis,' says Sydney University senior lecturer Jenny O'Dea.

'This is a metabolic imbalance where you lose lots of weight, but it's mainly water and muscle.

'Ketosis also causes weakness, dizziness, nausea, headaches and bad breath.'

Whatever diet gurus say, science shows carbohydrates provide essential vitamins and minerals. And the real fight lies not with food.

'People seem to think it's our diet, but the predominant problem is lack of exercise,' Dr Holt says. 'We don't move enough.'

Emotions, feelings, hunches
How do I feel?

Caution, judging and assessing the negatives
What are the problems?

Information
What information do we have or need?

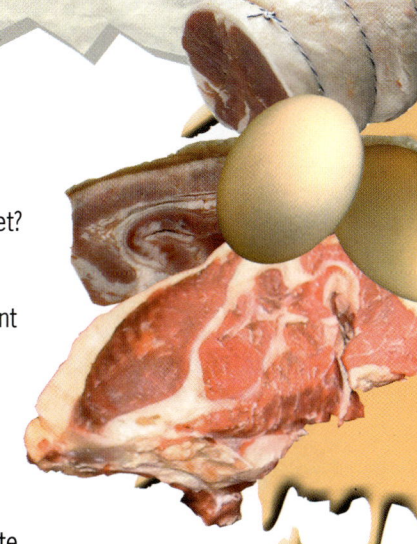

QUESTIONS

1 Why are nutritionists concerned about this type of diet?
2 What is the radical new theory regarding the consumption of meat and fat?
3 Why has the fad caught on, according to the president of Sports Dietitians Australia?
4 Outline what Dr Susanna Holt, from Sydney University's human nutrition unit, says.
5 Which carbohydrates are better for you?
6 Why is this diet unhealthy?
7 Write a comment using the following de Bono hats:
   a red   **b** black   **c** white

▶ Potato—a carbohydrate-rich food

excellent source of carbohydrates

good source of
niacin, vitamin B$_6$,
thiamin and folate

no cholesterol

low in kilojoules

fat-free

good source of
minerals, such
as iodine

source of protein

good source of dietary fibre

QUESTION

Why should you include high-carbohydrate foods in your diet?

Case Study

Low-Fat Products

Compare the following two yoghurt products.
   Both are Swiss Vanilla flavoured; however, one is low-fat. Read the nutrition information panel of each product and answer the questions on the following page.

LOW FAT VANILLA FLAVOURED YOGURT

NUTRITION INFORMATION
SERVINGS PER PACKAGE: 5 SERVING SIZE: 200g

	AVERAGE QUANTITY PER SERVING 200g	AV. QTY. PER 100g
ENERGY	954 kJ, 228 Cal	477 kJ, 114 Cal
PROTEIN	10.8 g	5.4 g
FAT: TOTAL	2.0 g	1.0 g
SATURATED	1.5 g	0.7 g
CARBOHYDRATE:	40.9 g	20.4 g
SUGARS	38.6 g	19.3 g
SODIUM	177 mg	88 mg
CALCIUM	345 mg (43% RDI*)	172 mg
POTASSIUM	497 mg	249 mg

* RECOMMENDED DIETARY INTAKE.

VANILLA FLAVOURED YOGURT

NUTRITION INFORMATION
SERVINGS PER PACKAGE: 5 SERVING SIZE: 200g

	AVERAGE QUANTITY PER SERVING 200g	AV. QTY. PER 100g
ENERGY	1056 kJ, 253 Cal	528 kJ, 126 Cal
PROTEIN	8.2 g	4.1 g
FAT: TOTAL	7.9 g	4.0 g
SATURATED	5.7 g	2.9 g
CARBOHYDRATE:	36.7 g	18.3 g
SUGARS	34.5 g	17.2 g
SODIUM	141 mg	71 mg
CALCIUM	257 mg (32% RDI*)	128 mg
POTASSIUM	368 mg	184 mg

* RECOMMENDED DIETARY INTAKE.

QUESTIONS

1 Identify the kilojoule amount for 100 grams for both products.
2 How much is the difference between the two products? Which product has the greater amount of kilojoules? Are you surprised? Why or why not?
3 Identify the total fat amount for 100 grams for both products.
4 How much is the difference between the two products? Which product has the greater amount of total fat? Are you surprised? Why or why not?
5 Identify the saturated fat amount for 100 grams for both products.
6 How much is the difference between the two products? Which product has the greater amount of saturated fat? Are you surprised? Why or why not?
7 Identify the carbohydrate amount for 100 grams for both products.
8 How much is the difference between the two products? Which product has the greater amount of carbohydrate? Are you surprised? Why or why not?
9 Identify the sugar amount for 100 grams for both products.
10 How much is the difference between the two products? Which product has the greater amount of sugar? Are you surprised? Why or why not?
11 Identify the sodium amount for 100 grams for both products.
12 How much is the difference between the two products? Which product has the greater amount of sodium? Are you surprised? Why or why not?
13 Using the information collected above, what comments can you make about the nutritional differences between low-fat and full-cream Nestlé Swiss Vanilla yoghurt?
14 Which product is healthier? Explain your response.
15 Compare other low-fat and full-cream products. Are your findings similar to those found here?

Case Study LEAN CUISINE

QUESTIONS

1 What does '97% Fat Free' imply to you?
2 Look at the ingredients list and comment on the fat content of this meal.
3 Investigate the fat content of other Lean Cuisine meals by visiting www.leancuisine.com.au.
4 Write a comment using the following de Bono hats:
a red
b white
c black

Nutrition Information Servings per package – 1 Serving size – 380g	Ave Quantity Per Serving	Ave Quantity Per 100g
ENERGY – KILOJOULES	1580kJ	415kJ
– (CALORIES)	(378 Cal)	(99 Cal)
PROTEIN	7.6g	2.0g
FAT – TOTAL (2% of meal)	5.7g	1.5g
– Saturated fat (75% of TOTAL FAT)	Less than 1g	Less than 1g
– Trans Fat (Less than 1% of total fat)		
– Polyunsaturated fat (7% of TOTAL FAT)	0.4g	0.1g
– Monounsaturated fat (18% of TOTAL FAT)	1.5g	0.4g
CHOLESTEROL	15mg	4mg
CARBOHYDRATE	61g	16g
– SUGARS	4.6g	1.2g
SODIUM	705mg	185mg

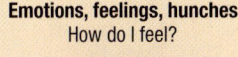

Emotions, feelings, hunches
How do I feel?

Information
What information do we have or need?

Caution, judging and assessing the negatives
What are the problems?

▶ Fussy eaters make life tough for our chefs

Read the newspaper article and then answer the questions that follow it.

By Patrick McDonald, Social Issues Writer

EXTENSIVE menus are no longer enough for fussy South Australian diners, who want dishes modified to suit their tastes—and their waists.

Restaurateurs say an increasing number of customers are demanding that cream, cheese, oil, garlic or other ingredients be left out of meals or replaced with alternatives.

Many claim to be allergic to certain things, while others are on diets which require eliminating certain food groups.

'It's getting quite impossible,' said leading chef Cheong Liew, of the Hilton Adelaide's Grange restaurant.

'We try to accommodate as much as we can but, especially with my kind of food, the whole dish is a design.'

Removing ingredients from Mr Liew's creations upsets the delicate balance and flavour.

'If anybody comes in and tries to say they are allergic to onions, I would not try to sell them any of my dishes. I'd rather cook them something very, very simple.'

About one in four customers now asked for changes to dishes, said David West, owner of To Relish at Hyde Park.

'I've had a guy on New Year's Eve who was allergic to four types of cheeses and he can't have any of those, otherwise he needs to be rushed to hospital,' Mr West said.

'I've had a young lady in who was allergic to peppers, lettuce, rocket, tomato, cream—that was a bizarre one.

'I've had vegans who don't eat tofu as well, all sorts of things.'

Mr West said his four chefs were good at meeting requests.

'It's just a bit sad that people don't ring to warn us—it's hard when you've got a full restaurant to start modifying menus,' he said.

Salvatore Pepe, of Cibo Ristorante Pasticceria in North Adelaide, said the type of requests had changed. Ten years ago, customers wanted to add extra ingredients—now they wanted things left out. 'There is a lot of demanding,' he said.

'Now they start to say 'no cream' or 'no garlic'. They are more allergic or they don't like certain ingredients.'

Not all establishments were aware of ingredients in the food they sold, said Carolyn Cattrall of Nailsworth.

She had to avoid dairy products and eggs because her baby daughter Harriet, who was being breastfed, was allergic.

'Sometimes people look at you as if you are just being fussy, when it was actually for a real need,' Mrs Cattrall, 30, said.

At one coffee shop, despite being busy, a waitress happily rang the person who had baked a semolina cake to check the ingredients.

However, during a set menu function at a North Adelaide hotel, staff could not say what ingredients were used.

QUESTIONS

1 What demands are customers making in regard to ingredients in dishes on menus?
2 What reasons do customers provide for changes to ingredients?
3 Why do the customer demands upset chefs?
4 To what types of foods do customers say that they are allergic?
5 How have these requests changed from requests made ten years ago?

▶ Few have true food allergy

Read the newspaper article and then answer the questions that follow it.

By Patrick McDonald, Social Issues Writer

FEW people are really allergic to specific foods, says Tania Ferraretto, spokeswoman for the Dietitians Association of Australia.

Genuine allergies cause people to produce antibodies against a certain substance.

'If you get an immediate reaction (such as vomiting or swelling) it is an allergy and you need to be careful,' Ms Ferraretto says.

The Australian Food and Grocery Council says about 2 per cent of people have true food allergies.

Other people have intolerances to chemicals in a range of foods, which can build up and cause a gradual reaction.

However, Ms Ferraretto encourages people on diets to ask for dishes in restaurants to be modified.

'Most chefs are pretty good about modifying things, if you want something grilled instead of fried or you want the sauce left off, or the cream left out of the sauce,' she says.

Many people are eating out more often. 'If it's a regular part of your lifestyle, you need to be thinking about things you can do while you are out to still be healthy.'

The management of the Fellini Cafe at North Adelaide noticed so much demand for modified meals that it introduced special Shape-Up dishes to the menu. 'People are more health-conscious. They don't want too much salt or cheese,' says co-owner Teresa Bruno.

The Shape-Up menu was devised in conjunction with a friend who ran a fitness company.

'We just came up with a few ideas with the chef—no butter, no oil,' Mrs Bruno says.

The Shape-Up menu had proved popular with sporting identities 'and girls trying to watch their weight a bit'.

QUESTIONS

1 What do genuine food allergies cause? What reaction is evident?
2 According to the Australian Food and Grocery Council, what percentage of people have genuine food allergies?
3 What occurs if you have a food intolerance?
4 Why did the management of Fellini Cafe introduce special Shape-Up meals?
5 What groups of people consume the Shape-Up meals?

 Viva

Juice bars are one of the trendiest food places at the moment. They are emerging in various parts of Melbourne. One such chain is Viva Juice, the brainchild of Simon McNamara and Anna McArdle. Viva markets its juices as low-fat and nutritionally sound products. It also sells smoothies, wraps, muffins and soups.

Viva smoothies are promoted as a 99 per cent fat-free 'Meal In a Cup'. Viva states that high-quality ingredients, such as A-grade fruits, are used to make 100 per cent juice and yoghurt. Viva guarantees that it uses products that are low in sugar, and sorbet that is dairy-free.

Viva includes a free 'booster', which is a blend of additional vitamins, minerals, amino acids and herbs, in each of its smoothies, to provide supplementary nutritional value. According to Viva, the smoothie ingredients are selected specifically to keep the goodness in and the fat and kilojoules out. Extra fruit is included to achieve the desired thickness.

Viva smoothies are marketed as an amazing health experience, with everything that one needs to lead an active and healthy life.

Booster	Ingredients	Promoted benefits
Energy	Guarana	For an additional energy boost
Total health	Minerals such as folate and calcium and vitamins such as vitamins A, B, D and E	To boost one's total health
Immunity	Vitamin C and Echinacea	To improve the immune system
Slimmer	Citrin formula	To assist you succeed in the fight against flab
Protein	A complete vegetarian protein	To invigorate your working muscles
Brain power	Ginkgo Biloba	To enhance short-term and memory concentration

QUESTIONS

1 How does Viva market its juices?
2 Why are Viva and other juice bars popular with consumers?
3 What are boosters and why do consumers request boosters in their juices?
4 Using your nutritional knowledge, consider whether the promoted benefit of each booster is accurate. Discuss your thoughts with a classmate. Write down a summary of the discussion and share your comments with the rest of the class.
5 Are fruit juices healthy? Explain your response.

 ## Let's remember

1 Why is a carob bar no better for you than a chocolate bar?
2 Why do some people wrongly consider soy crisps to be a healthy alternative to potato crisps?
3 Are health bars healthy? Explain your answer.
4 Why should you consume fruit instead of fruit bars?

5 How would you be able to select a nutrient-dense health bar?

6 Is popcorn a healthy snack? Explain your answer.

7 Why is red meat good for you?

8 Explain why bread should be a regular part of your diet.

9 Why was bread wrongly considered to be fattening?

10 Are low-carbohydrate foods recommended for good health? Explain your answer.

▶ Let's investigate

1 Investigate Kellogg's Disney Muesli bar. Evaluate how healthy this product is ☺ ☺ ☹.

2 Investigate the value of vitamin pills in the diet. Ensure that you obtain a range of views. Summarise your findings in a 500-word report, which could be presented as a newspaper article, pamphlet, poster, datashow presentation or webpage.

3 Investigate the accuracy of the following statements.

   a Honey and brown sugar are better for you than white sugar.

   b White bread is fattening.

   c Brown eggs are more nutritious than white eggs.

   d Vegetable oils do not contain cholesterol.

   e Consuming grapefruit dissolves fat.

   f Butter contains more kilojoules than margarine.

▶ *e*-Food myths

www.goodmedicine.ninemsn.com.au/goodmedicine/Factsheets/db/fitness/eathealthy/1156.asp

Summarise the food safety myths.

▶ Puzzled

Fact find

Provide answers to the following statements.

1 Carob comes from this plant.

2 Fruit bars increase the risk of this dietary related disease.

3 Red meat contributes these nutrients.

4 Bread contributes these nutrients.

5 This is a healthy alternative to fruit bars.

6 Breakfast bars tend to be high in this ingredient.

7 This is wrongly believed to be a healthy substitute for potato chips.

8 Fruits bars are generally made from this.

9 This is a healthy alternative to breakfast bars.

10 This is the amount of fat contained in packaged popcorn.

 Upper crust

Work out the code to complete the following sentence.

A	B	C	D	E	F	G	H	I	J	K	L	M	N	O	P	Q	R	S	T	U	V	W	X	Y	Z
		19					15							7				9							

_ O _   C _ _   O H _ _ _ _ _ T _   _ _ _ _ T   _ _ _
8 7 23   19 25 21 12 7 15 2 17 21 25 9 20   17 24 20 9 3   25 21 20

_ O T   H _ _ _   T H _
16 7 9   15 20 25 8   9 15 2

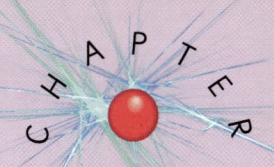

BaD TaSTE: DISCOVER DIETaRY RELaTED DISEaSES

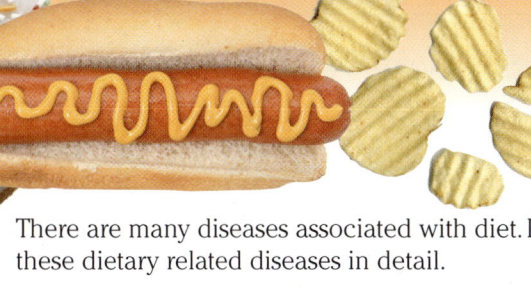

There are many diseases associated with diet. In this chapter, we will explore some of these dietary related diseases in detail.

Obesity

Obesity is increasing at a staggering rate in both high-income and low-income countries. Obesity can contribute to the development of heart disease and diabetes. The World Health Organisation believes that the rise in obesity rates is mainly due to the increase in sedentary lifestyles and high-fat, energy-dense diets. Although excess amounts of energy from both sugar and fat may contribute to obesity, the exact role of sugar as a cause of obesity is not really clear.

After sugar is eaten, the levels of glucose in the blood rapidly increase. This results in the body producing more insulin. An increase in insulin may hinder the body's ability to use fats as an energy source.

Research suggests that the body uses carbohydrates and proteins as the preferred source of energy, so these two nutrients are used up before fat; the body prefers to store fat. Very high amounts of carbohydrates can be converted to fat, and this high intake of carbohydrates can prevent the body from burning some of the stored fat. Carbohydrates are only converted to fat when an excessive quantity—more than 500 grams—of carbohydrate is consumed. This is equivalent to the carbohydrate found in thirty-two slices of bread! Under normal circumstances, carbohydrates do not increase stores of body fat, as previously thought. However, there is some evidence that diets containing carbohydrate foods with a high GI factor may increase body fatness. This is probably linked to the overall diet being high in energy input.

In many low-income countries, starches contribute a large proportion of the energy in the diet. Unfortunately, in many high-income countries, starches are crowded out by foods high in fat, and simple sugars, such as sucrose and protein. Nutritionists prefer people to replenish the body's glucose levels from starches or from sugars found in fruits and milk, rather than sucrose. Fruits and milk also provide additional nutrients. Carbohydrates only contribute 16 kilojoules per gram and should not be labelled as fattening. However, sucrose can be easily consumed in excess amounts and exceed the body's requirements.

Adults can use the Body Mass Index (BMI) to calculate if they have too much body fat.

$$BMI = \frac{\text{weight in kilograms}}{\text{height in metres}^2}$$

Obesity is defined as being 20 per cent or more overweight.

Did you know that about 14 kilograms of excess weight means about 40 kilometres of extra blood vessels through which the blood must be pumped?

Classification of BMI in adults

Men are more likely to be overweight and obese than women at every age, despite the fact that more women are on diets!

BMI	Classification	Risk of ill health
18.5–24.9	Normal range	Average
25.0–29.9	Overweight	Increased
>30	Obese	Greatly increased

The takeaway test

The National Nutrition Survey indicated that 67 per cent of all Australians had low levels of exercise.

Item	Weight (grams)	Energy (kilojoules)	Sodium*	Fat (grams)
Red Rooster Skin-free sub meal: two chicken breast strips, Mediterranean glaze with Kraft Free mayonnaise, lettuce, on nine-inch roll	320	1830	46	3
McDonald's Grilled chicken burger without sauce	206	1340	35	8
Pizza Haven Vegetarians' choice original crust 3 slices large	189	1680	25	13
Pizza Hut Super supreme grand pan 3 slices regular	187	2260	54	20
McDonald's Happy meal: cheeseburger, small fries	208	2420	33	28
Battered fish and chips	240	2520	36	36
KFC Chicken fillet burger combo: chicken fillet burger, regular chips	276	2600	38	37
McDonald's Grilled chicken McValue meal: grilled chicken burger, medium fries	349	3290	50	37
McDonald's Fillet-o-fish McValue meal: fillet of fish, medium fries	274	3160	41	38
Meat pie and chips	285	2780	56	39
McDonald's Big Mac McValue meal: Big Mac, medium fries	348	3820	43	47
Burger King Whopper value meal: whopper burger, medium fries	376	4130	53	55

French fries/chips	Weight (grams)	Energy (kilojoules)	Sodium*	Fat (grams)
Red Rooster Regular chips	140	1450	15	15
Burger King Medium chips	116	1560	15	18
Hungry Jack's Medium fries	114	1570	11	18
KFC Regular chips	117	1380	6	20
McDonald's Medium fries	128	1700	10	22

*Sodium per cent of upper daily limit per serve
Source: Australian Consumers Association

The weight of a lifetime

Read the newspaper article and then answer the questions that follow it.

By Sasha Baskett, Health Reporter

AUSTRALIA has a big problem with its smallest citizens.

More than one quarter of the nation's children are now overweight or obese.

And it is not just a problem for the younger set. Those who start life overweight will usually have a hard time taking it off later on.

Even if they can shed the excess in later life, children who are overweight or obese are at greater risk of health problems, restrictions on their enjoyment of sport, and schoolyard taunts.

Sedentary lifestyles and sugary high-fat diets have both been blamed for the nation's obesity epidemic.

Doctors and consumer advocates are now calling for restrictions on the marketing of fast food and sweets.

The Australian Consumers Association's senior health policy officer, Nicola Ballenden, wants voluntary restrictions on advertising to children.

'Aggressive marketing of fast food and confectionery to children can influence their dietary choices early in life, putting them at greater risk of becoming overweight and obese,' she said.

'Children can be extremely vulnerable to advertising messages. Promoting fast food and confectionery can also make it more difficult for parents to provide their children with fresh and healthy food.'

The association wants manufacturers and retailers to volunteer to stop advertising their products on television during the peak children's viewing times from 4 pm–7 pm.

Fast food should also not be included in publications, movies or websites aimed at children.

'This would ensure that children are protected from the aggressive marketing of food products that have little nutritional value,' Ms Ballenden said.

But the Australian Food and Grocery Council argues that food advertising is not to blame.

Chief executive Mitchell H. Hooke said the link between advertising and obesity was 'superficial and unsubstantiated'.

He said the Australian Consumers Association had not been able to convince the Australian Broadcasting Authority of the merit of its case.

'The real issue in childhood, and indeed adult, obesity is the missing link between energy intake and energy output—decreased levels of physical activity,' he said.

He said independent scientific studies showed the intake of kilojoules for Australian children had fallen in the past 10 years.

'There is no such thing, in nutritional terms, as bad food—only bad diets or bad food habits,' he said.

The nation's food authority wants children to be taught the dangers of junk and fatty foods at school.

The Australia New Zealand Food Authority's managing director, Ian Lindenmayer, said food companies also needed to take some responsibility for the obesity epidemic.

He wants food education, including the reading of food labels, to be taught in schools. 'I believe it would be highly desirable for the education system to also now take up with much greater vigour the enhancement of skills in an area which is literally an everyday part of every child's life—eating,' Mr Lindenmayer said.

'The alarming figures on childhood obesity and its links with diabetes and a range of other diseases represent a very persuasive case for this,' he said.

Mr Lindenmayer said food manufacturers could increase their market share by promoting healthy and inviting products.

Dr Julie Thompson, chair of the Australian Division of General Practice, said there was a demonstrated link between obesity in children and health problems such as heart disease later in life.

She supports the call for restrictions on advertising to children.

'Unless we act now to reduce the high rates of obesity among children we will create a generation of Australians at high risk of heart attacks, strokes, and premature death,' she said.

Parents who are concerned about their child's weight should see their doctor, she said. GPs can give advice on healthy weight ranges, diet and exercise to help parents improve their child's health.

She said children should not be on a kilojoule-controlled diet unless there were exceptional circumstances.

Children should be encouraged to eat a wide variety of fresh food.

'Foods that are high in fat, sugar and salt, with little nutritional value, should be eaten only occasionally and not form a regular part of children's diets,' she said.

QUESTIONS

1 Identify the big problem with small citizens in Australia.
2 Why is being overweight in childhood a health concern?
3 What two causes of childhood obesity are identified in the article?
4 How would restrictions on the marketing of fast foods and sweets help to address the problem of childhood obesity?
5 Why is it suggested that such foods not be advertised between 4 pm and 7 pm?
6 In what other ways is it suggested that children be protected from the aggressive marketing campaigns of manufacturers?
7 What does the Australian Food and Grocery Council argue is the real issue concerning childhood (and adult) obesity?
8 What evidence is there to support the Australian Food and Grocery Council's claims?
9 In your own words, explain what is meant by the statement 'There is no such thing, in nutritional terms, as bad food—only bad diets or bad food habits'.
10 How would food education assist with childhood obesity?
11 What does the article suggest that manufacturers do to benefit themselves as well as assist in decreasing childhood obesity?
12 Outline what advice general practitioners could provide in regard to childhood obesity.
13 Should overweight children be placed on kilojoule-controlled diets?
14 What advice would you give to an overweight child to assist him or her?

▶ Lazy lifestyles

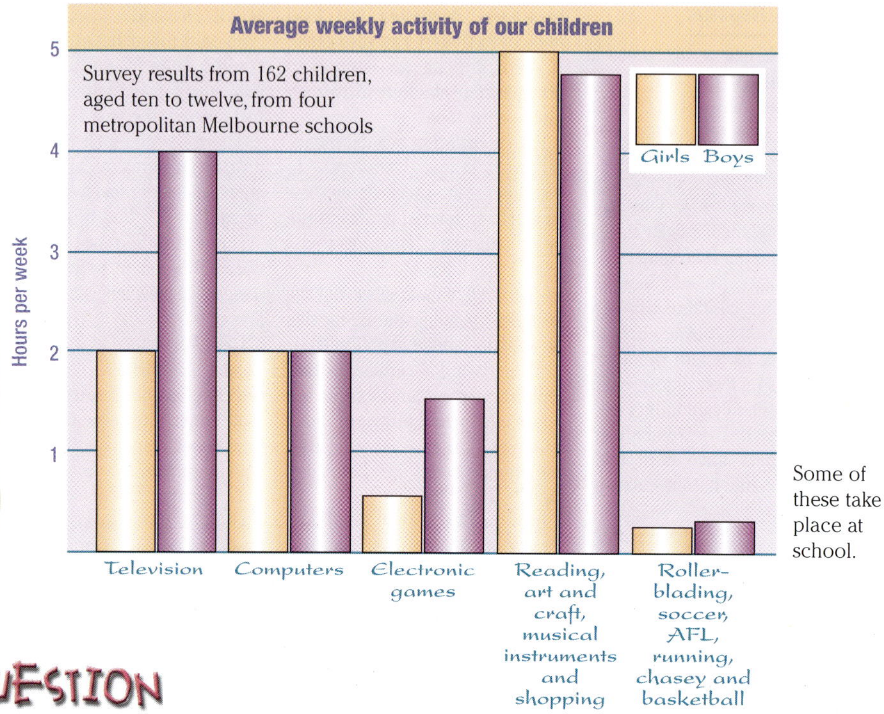

Average weekly activity of our children

Survey results from 162 children, aged ten to twelve, from four metropolitan Melbourne schools

Hours per week

Girls Boys

Television Computers Electronic games Reading, art and craft, musical instruments and shopping Roller-blading, soccer, AFL, running, chasey and basketball

Some of these take place at school.

QUESTION

Select each of the de Bono hats and make an appropriate comment. Share your comments with a classmate.

Emotions, feelings, hunches	Caution, judging and assessing the negatives	Creativity	Optimistic, judging and assessing the positives	Information	Organising thinking
How do I feel?	What are the problems?	What new ideas can I propose?	Why is this worth doing?	What information do we have or need?	What have we achieved?

▶ Alcohol gives students learning curves

Read the newspaper article and then answer the questions that follow it.

By Evonne Barry, Health Reporter

UNIVERSITY study is usually served with a big helping of socialising—and alcohol is a typical side dish.

The health risks, and potential benefits, associated with drinking are well documented. But what of the damage to students' waistlines?

When Sophie left her family home in Ballarat to study four years ago, she revelled in the party scene.

Living on-campus at Melbourne University, she found herself drinking alcohol three or four nights every week.

'It's part of the uni lifestyle,' said Sophie, 21.

'It's not like I was having one or two drinks. You drink excessively. There's always alcohol at the parties and events you go to and there's pressure to drink.'

But while Sophie's circle of friends was growing, so too was her dress size.

Now a law student at La Trobe, she estimates she has put on 10 kg since leaving secondary school.

According to Karen Inge, the VIS dietitian overseeing Sophie's progress in Health-Watch's Great Winter Work-out, alcohol was largely responsible for this gain.

'Alcohol is very high in kilojoules, and they are empty kilojoules because they have no nutritional value,' she said. 'Alcohol has more kilojoules than sugar and protein. And that's just pure alcohol.'

Add the creamy and fizzy drinks you mix with it—as well as the greasy foods you develop a taste for—and your kilojoule intake can rocket.

'Sophie attributes a lot of her weight gain, which accelerated at uni, to going out and drinking,' Ms Inge said.

'When you drink alcohol, you feel the need to eat high-fat foods with it.

'Eating slows down the absorption of alcohol.'

Hunger is also the result of the liver working overtime to free itself of alcohol, which is poisonous in large amounts.

Ms Inge says excessive drinking can also lead to learning difficulties.

QuEstions

1 Explain the impact that alcohol consumption has on weight.
2 What other factors would increase one's kilojoule intake?
3 Why do you usually feel hungry when you drink alcohol?

▶ **Let's remember**

1 What causes obesity and why is its rate increasing?
2 Outline the health problems associated with obesity.
3 What types of foods contribute to obesity?
4 Explain why carbohydrate and sugars are not thought to greatly contribute to obesity.
5 What does BMI stand for and how it is calculated?

Did you know that 1 gram of alcohol contributes 29 kilojoules?

Coronary Heart Disease

Would you believe that heart and blood vessel disease is the leading cause of death in Australia, and someone dies every ten minutes from this disease? There are many risk factors associated with this disease, such as age, sex and genetics, that we cannot change. We should also undertake regular physical activity most days of the week, to reduce the risk of developing heart disease. However, coronary heart disease is also associated with a diet in high saturated fats and cholesterol. We can change this!

The different fats—monounsaturated, polyunsaturated and saturated—have different effects on the level of cholesterol in the blood.

Saturated fats	Increase low-density lipoprotein cholesterol (i.e. bad cholesterol) and total cholesterol levels in the blood. This can clog arteries when present in high amounts.
Polyunsaturated fats	Tend to lower low-density lipoprotein and total cholesterol levels in the blood.
Monounsaturated fats	Increase the level of high-density lipoprotein cholesterol (i.e. the good cholesterol). This cholesterol 'soaks' up the fats in the blood and prevents their build-up in the artery walls.

We should replace much of the saturated fats in our diet with polyunsaturated and monounsaturated fats to reduce the blood cholesterol levels. However, it should be noted that all fats provide the same amount of kilojoules.

Research has shown that those who regularly eat nuts tend to have lower cholesterol levels and experience fewer heart attacks.

Focus on cholesterol

Cholesterol is an important part of cell membranes and some hormones. It is an essential substance for good health, but we do not need to consume it as our body can make its own supplies. Problems arise with cholesterol when people consume too much and excess builds up, along with other substances, in the arteries. Clogged arteries hinder blood flow and enable blood clots to settle. A build-up of cholesterol occurs usually when the diet is high in unsaturated fats. To decrease blood cholesterol, one must decrease saturated fats in the diet. Oats, legumes and some fruits and vegetables, all high in soluble fibre, tend to increase the amount of cholesterol that is excreted in the faeces.

Cholesterol in the blood is attached to a protein molecule called a lipoprotein. High-density lipoproteins (HDL) are beneficial to health, as they remove cholesterol from the artery wall and return it to the liver. In this way, HDL can protect against heart disease. Low-density lipoproteins (LDL) are not considered to be beneficial to one's health, as they deposit cholesterol in the cell, resulting in a build-up of cholesterol. Saturated fats increase the levels of LDL in the blood.

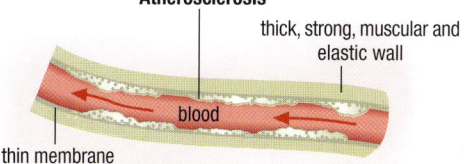

Atherosclerosis

thick, strong, muscular and elastic wall

blood

thin membrane

A nation of tele-tubbies

Read the newspaper article and then answer the questions that follow it..

e-Fact

Cholesterol that already exists in foods such as prawns and eggs is known as *preformed cholesterol*. Research has indicated that preformed cholesterol is not detrimental to one's health. These foods do not contribute a large amount of saturated fat to the diet. However, if you deep-fry the prawns or fry the eggs with bacon, they do become high in saturated fat.

e-Fact

Did you know that cholesterol is a waxy substance that looks similar to the wax that accumulates in your ears?

e-Fact

Cholesterol is required by the body to make vitamin D.

By Catherine Lambert

MELBOURNE school-children are at risk of heart disease because of their slovenly lifestyles.

Television, electronic games and computers are keeping children so entertained they only have time for 10 minutes of vigorous activity each day.

Researchers at Deakin University's Department of Health Sciences are the first in Australia to monitor children's daily movements for a month.

Project co-ordinator Jackie Arbuckle said Australian children were following the US trend where 60 per cent of children had at least one coronary risk factor by the time they were nine years old.

'It's just too easy for kids and parents to sit inside because there's so much to do there,' Ms Arbuckle said.

'They are over-stimulated and under-challenged and it's essential they become more physically active.'

The study involved 162 children from four schools. Children in prep and grades five and six wore a matchbox-sized motion detector on their wrists from when they got out of bed until they went to sleep.

The prep children were found to be vigorously active for 30 minutes a day, which was acceptable. But the older children had an average of only 10 minutes vigorous activity a day.

Television proved a drawcard with boys watching the box for an average of four hours a day and girls watching for an average of two and a half hours a day. The study was carried out over the summer and was part of wider research into the activity levels of 1000 children, which would be released in January.

'We were extremely surprised by the findings,' Ms Arbuckle said. 'They should be having at least 30 minutes of exercise a day, where they are sweating and their temperature is raised, especially in summer.'

The executive director of the Victorian division of the Heart Foundation, Robyn Charlwood, said the study had major health implications for today's generation of children and future generations of adults.

'In terms of cardiovascular disease, being physically inactive is up there with smoking, high blood pressure and cholesterol,' Ms Charlwood said.

'It's not enough for us, as parents, to assume kids run around a lot. We should be encouraging them to be more physically active in their play.'

Ms Arbuckle said parents mistakenly believed children were exercising during physical education classes at school.

A State Government report in 1993 recommended at least three hours of physical education classes a week, but Ms Arbuckle said few schools involved in the study met that government guideline.

'Many schools don't have the resources or physical education specialists and a lot of schools are only offering one and a half hours a week,' she said.

But according to Ian Maddison, manager of the education department's health, physical and sport education unit, 75 per cent of primary schools met the government's guidelines last year.

QUESTIONS

1 Explain why Australian children are at risk of heart disease.
2 Identify the United States trend in regard to childhood health.
3 Why is it easy for children and parents to lead sedentary lifestyles?
4 Outline the study undertaken by researchers at Deakin University's Department of Health Sciences.
5 Outline the findings of this study.
6 What are the major health implications associated with these findings?
7 What should parents do to address this problem?

Let's remember

1 What factors contribute to coronary heart disease?
2 Explain whether cholesterol is good or bad.
3 What is preformed cholesterol?
4 How does cholesterol contribute to coronary heart disease?
5 Explain the terms *LDL* and *HDL* and outline the differences between the two.

Hypertension and Stroke

Hypertension is the term used to describe high blood pressure. It can be the result of a high-salt diet. Other factors that contribute to this dietary related disease include:

· being overweight
· a sedentary lifestyle
· high fat intake

Hypertension results when the heart is forced to pump blood around the body under too much pressure. A high-salt diet can lead to the build-up of sodium in the smooth muscle cells of the small blood vessels. This results in the blood vessels pumping more vigorously, resulting in increased blood pressure. The circulatory system is put under a great deal of strain when the blood pressure is increased, and the inner lining of the arteries will become damaged. Fatty tissues can build up in the damaged area, leading to heart disease and stroke.

A stroke causes damage to the brain, because the blood supply is interrupted. A stroke can result if a blood vessel breaks and blood leaks into the surrounding brain tissue. Hypertension can cause the blood vessels to become damaged and lead to them rupturing; this can also be caused by a build-up of fatty deposits.

Although we need salt in our diet, Australians tend to consume too much salt due to their high consumption of processed foods, such as salted crisps and biscuits, pickled vegetables, cured meats and takeaway foods.

Signs of stroke

Most strokes are caused by a clot lodging in a blood vessel in the brain

Tissue death in area deprived of blood

Symptoms to look for

Dizziness, confusion

Headache

Visual disturbance

Trouble speaking

Difficulty swallowing

Weakness or paralysis on one side of the body

▶ Let's remember

1 Define the term *hypertension*.
2 Explain how hypertension occurs.
3 What is a stroke?
4 How does a stroke occur?
5 What factors contribute to hypertension and stroke?

Osteoporosis

Another name for osteoporosis is brittle bones. This means that the bones become thinner, and more porous. Osteoporosis is linked to a lack of calcium. It is important to build up bone density by consuming calcium-rich foods, such as dairy products, during childhood and adolescence.

The majority of calcium consumed is used for bone and teeth development.

Amount of calcium in foods

white bread
1 slice
15 mg

carton of regular milk
285 mg

tub of low-fat fruit yogurt
420 mg

200 g

tub of cottage cheese
80 mg

100 g

cheddar cheese
275 mg

35 g

15 almonds
80 mg

broccoli
1 cup/100 g
30 mg

cooked soybeans
150 g
115 mg

canned salmon
230 mg

cooked spinach
170 mg

1 cup/340 g

Of the body's calcium, 99 per cent is stored in the bones and teeth. One per cent of calcium is found in body fluids, as calcium plays a role in blood clotting and healthy functioning of nerves and muscles.

Swimming is not a weight-bearing exercise, although it is a healthy activity.

e-faCT

It is thought that, in Australia, about 60 per cent of women and 30 per cent of men over the age of sixty years experience fractures associated with osteoporosis.

e-faCT

The trend for extreme thinness in women can intensify osteoporosis. This is because these women eat too little or exercise too much and their body fat level becomes so low that they stop menstruating. Because of this, they do not build up bone density mass for later in life. They also suffer the withdrawal of calcium, which usually does not occur until menopause.

After about thirty years of age, you will lose 1 per cent of your bone density, even though you may consume calcium in your diet. Weight-bearing exercise, such as walking and cycling, assists in the prevention of osteoporosis. This is because this exercise places stress on the bones and stimulates the bones to remodel and therefore improve their strength.

Women are susceptible to osteoporosis because of their hormones. During menopause, there is a decrease in oestrogen which results in an increase in calcium loss from the bones, resulting in a decrease in bone density mass.

Girls who begin to menstruate later, especially ballet dancers and athletes, are more prone to osteoporosis. This is because the delayed onset of menstruation means that oestrogen levels are lower and therefore calcium loss from bones is greater.

Caffeine, salt, smoking and alcohol may all interfere with the absorption of calcium.

Menopause:

↓ oestrogen

leads to

↑ calcium loss from bones

= ↑ chances of osteoporosis

▶ **Weightlessness reduces astronauts' bone density**

Read the newspaper article and then answer the question that follows it.

By Tanya Taylor

SPACE travel should come with a health warning, scientists have claimed.

They have concluded that astronauts' bone density could be reduced after just a month of weightlessness.

The French researchers called for more research into gravity after their study of 15 cosmonauts from the Russian Mir station showed bone loss continued throughout space missions.

'Bone loss was especially striking in four cosmonauts,' the scientists reported in *The Lancet*.

They examined cosmonauts who had spent one, two and six months in space, and measured the bone mineral density in the radius, a bone in the forearm, and the tibia in the lower leg.

The loss was significant in the tibia, which is a weight-bearing bone, but was barely changed in the radius.

'Our results indicate the need to investigate not only different bones, but also different areas of the same bone since not all sites of the skeleton are similarly affected by space conditions,' the scientists reported.

Without gravity bones do not bear any weight. As a result, calcium, which makes strong bones, is drained into the bloodstream.

QUESTION

Read the article and undertake a PMI—list two 'Pluses', two 'Minuses' and two 'Interesting Points' about the article. Share your thoughts with a classmate.

▶ Let's remember

1 What does osteoporosis mean and what causes it?
2 Why is it important to build up one's bone density mass prior to thirty years of age?
3 Why is weight-bearing exercise important?
4 Which groups of people are more susceptible to osteoporosis? Why?
5 Identify factors that interfere with the absorption of calcium.

Anaemia

Fatigue means lacking energy.

Anaemia results in a lowered level of haemoglobin, which is the pigment in red blood cells. Haemoglobin carries the oxygen around in the bloodstream. Anaemia is due to a lack of iron in the diet. Symptoms of anaemia include irritability, faintness and fatigue.

Lack of iron is a common nutrient deficiency in many high-income countries. Symptoms of iron deficiency include:

· weakness
· tiredness
· decreased ability to maintain a constant body temperature
· decreased ability to perform physical activity

Type 1 diabetes is when the pancreas produces little or no insulin. It is also known as insulin-dependent or juvenile-onset diabetes.

Prolonged iron deficiency can lead to anaemia, which means that there are decreased levels of haemoglobin in the blood and therefore less oxygen is reaching the body tissues. This means that the body is not able to operate normally.

Adolescent girls and women are more prone to anemia, as they often wrongly believe that red meat is fattening. Iron-rich foods are essential for women to meet the high needs of blood losses from menstruation and the demands of pregnancy and lactation. Other groups at risk of anaemia include athletes and vegetarians.

▶ Let's remember

1 Define the term *haemoglobin* and outline its role in the body.
2 Outline the cause, signs and symptoms of anaemia.
3 Why does the body not operate normally when one suffers from anaemia?
4 Why are women more prone to anaemia?
5 Which other groups are also susceptible to anaemia? Provide reasons for your answer.

Diabetes Mellitus

Insulin resistance occurs when a person produces enough insulin, but the insulin cannot carry out its normal role of removing the glucose from the blood and into the body cells.

Diabetes occurs when the body cannot make proper use of the glucose in the blood. There are two types of diabetes. Diabetes mellitus (Type 2 diabetes) occurs in 90 per cent of all diabetes cases and is dietary related. Insulin is manufactured, but the body resists its action and the glucose cannot enter its cells.

The resistance to the action of insulin occurs because of the increasing levels of fat in and around the cells, most often seen in overweight or obese people. When the insulin cannot get the glucose into the cells, the body will respond by producing more insulin. If this continues to happen over a long period of time, diabetes mellitus may develop. In many cases, being overweight or obese results in high insulin levels and insulin resistance.

Many people wrongly believe that consuming excess amounts of sugar causes diabetes. This is because diabetes itself results in a high level of blood sugar. However, consuming too much sugar does not cause diabetes. People with diabetes used to be told to avoid all sugars, as sugar was thought to cause blood sugar levels to increase more than other factors in food. However, we now know that this is not always the case. Sugar does not cause blood glucose levels to rise very high at a rapid rate. The

effect of food on blood glucose levels depends on many factors, including the composition of food and how it is processed. Foods with a low Glycaemic Index (GI) tend to cause a lower, more steady rise in blood glucose levels and so are more beneficial to those people with diabetes. Low-GI foods consumed as part of a meal can decrease the overall GI of the meal, and therefore slow the increase of glucose in the bloodstream after the consumption of the meal.

Consuming a diet high in fibre and low in fat, and based mainly on plant foods, is recommended for those with diabetes. It is also recommended that a healthy weight is maintained and regular physical activity is undertaken.

▶ Diabetes in children reaching epidemic levels, experts warn

Read the newspaper article and then answer the questions that follow it.

Obesity and diet are driving an illness tipped to rise twentyfold in a decade.

Stephen Cauchi reports.

Sally Hoss, 15, has a disease that a decade ago mostly affected overweight men in their 60s, or children who were born without insulin.

Thanks to modern food and a less physically active society, thousands of obese Australian children and teenagers, some as young as 10, have diabetes.

Ten years ago, children with type-two diabetes—brought on by obesity—were virtually unheard of. Now diabetes is set to reach epidemic levels.

Endocrinologists predict a twentyfold rise in the disease over the next decade, among teenagers. Unless the disease is diagnosed and treated, diabetic children may suffer from heart attacks/blindness and kidney disease in their late 20s.

'We're now seeing it (diabetes) in 25-year-olds, 18-year-olds and 10-year-olds. You never would have seen that,' said Professor Paul Zimmet, head of the International Diabetes Institute, in Caulfield. 'Twenty years ago the textbooks would say you see it in people 60 years and over.'

Professor Martin Silink, head of the Institute of Endocrinology at Sydney's Royal Alexandra Hospital, said his clinic, was handling 30 cases. They included a boy, 14, who weighed 135 kilograms; a girl, 14, over 100 kilograms and two boys, 12 and 15, who weighed 80 kilograms.

'Until the last four or five years, we never used to deal with childhood diabetes in adolescents,' he said. 'It's almost like a new disease.'

Sally Hoss was only 11, a grade five pupil in 1997, when she was diagnosed with diabetes. She is taking medication daily, and will do so for years to come.

'At first it was really upsetting for me because I had been diagnosed with a disease. I never thought I would,' she said.

'For about two or three years after I was diagnosed I used to cry myself to sleep thinking so many things could happen to me and all the things I have to do.'

Sally came from a high-risk group. Not only was she over-weight, but she was Lebanese. Her mother and uncle have diabetes, too. Luckily, regular testing diagnosed the disease early.

Although all overweight children are susceptible, some ethnic groups, including Aborigines and others not used to Western food, are especially vulnerable.

Sally has consulted a dietician, plays sport at school, and tries to be active at home.

Type-two diabetes affects both overweight and obese children. Sally, medium height and 60 kilograms, is not grossly fat.

'Sometimes I feel good, some-times I feel bad about the way I look,' she said. 'There are people much bigger than me.'

Professor Silink said some obese girls, even those not yet diabetic, faced distressing side-effects. 'Basically, their ovaries are being stimulated by the high insulin level to produce male hormones. These girls become hirsute,' he said.

'In the last 10 days, literally, I've been referred two girls, both of them of Arabic descent, both obese, and both had beards. By beards, I mean they're shaving.'

The girls, aged 13, weigh more than 90 kilograms.

There are one million diabetics in Australia. Type-one diabetes occurs when the pancreas fails to produce insulin, needed to break down glucose in the blood. Such diabetics usually inject insulin from childhood.

Type-two diabetes occurs when the blood's glucose levels are too high, because of diet and lack of exercise, and overwhelm the insulin the body produces.

Obesity drives it, but it also depends on the amount of genetic susceptibility to diabetes,' Professor Zimmet said.

He said that 'at a guess' 5000 children under 18 in Australia had type-two diabetes, dwarfed by the 100 000 who had insulin-dependent type-one diabetes.

However, numbers of the former, virtually non-existent five years ago, were rocketing.

The mean age of onset of type-two diabetes was 60 two decades ago but is now 40. 'In 10 years' time, there will be more children and adolescents with type-two diabetes than there are with type-one,' Professor Zimmet said.

Both he and Professor Silink blamed childhood obesity on a diet of fatty foods and lack of exercise. Since 1985, the numbers of obese and overweight children in Australia had doubled, part of a world-wide trend.

Child type-two diabetics often don't take medication properly, eat well or exercise because there are no immediate side-effects to their illness.

Sally Hoss is an assumed name.

QUESTIONS

1 What factors are attributed to the increase in diabetes in children?
2 What health problems are associated with undiagnosed diabetes?
3 Sally Hoss has diabetes. What indicated that she came from a high-risk group?
4 Explain why some obese girls become hairy.
5 Explain the difference between Type 1 diabetes and Type 2 diabetes. Include the number of children less than 18 years who have each disease.
6 What was the mean age of onset of Type 2 diabetes twenty years ago compared to today?

► Let's remember

1 What is diabetes mellitus?
2 Explain the term *insulin resistance* and how it occurs.
3 Why were people with diabetes wrongly told not to consume sugar in their diet?
4 What factors influence the level of blood glucose?
5 Outline dietary considerations for those with diabetes.

Constipation, Haemorrhoids, Diverticulitis and Bowel Cancer

Did you know that constipation is the most common dietary related disease in childhood? It is a condition of hard and/or infrequent bowel motions. It is very common in high-income countries.

Constipation is caused by a lack of insoluble fibre in the diet, mainly due to the consumption of a high percentage of refined foods. There is no Recommended Dietary Intake of fibre for children, but it is suggested that children should consume the amount of fibre in grams that is equivalent to their age in years plus five (see chapter 1). It is recommended that adults consume at least 30 grams of fibre daily. It is also recommended that more water be consumed, as fibre absorbs water and so produces soft, bulky faeces that are easy to pass.

Haemorrhoids can also result from a lack of fibre. Haemorrhoids are varicose veins in the anus. The constant pressure of straining to pass faeces causes the veins to become swollen. Symptoms include bright red blood in the faeces and agonising bowel movements. Haemorrhoids are not dangerous, just painful.

Constipation can also lead to diverticulitis, which is when small, sac-like swellings occur in the wall of the large intestine. Inflammation of these swellings results in pain, nausea and sometimes bleeding. Eating fibre regularly throughout the lifespan assists in the prevention of diverticula.

There is also convincing evidence that cancer of the lower part of the large intestines—the colon and rectum—can be prevented with physical activity and a diet that is high in plant foods. Dietary fibre was found to be the likely nutrient to decrease the risk of bowel cancer.

All these diseases are linked to a lack of dietary fibre, which is found in fruits, vegetables, legumes and starchy foods that have not been highly processed, such as rice, oats and potatoes.

e-DEFINE

Cirrhosis of the liver occurs when healthy liver tissue is replaced by scar tissue. This is often caused by the consumption of a large amount of alcohol over many years.

e-FACT

Scientific research shows that sugar contributes to dental caries. The sugar becomes acidic due to the action of bacteria in the mouth. This acid attacks the tooth enamel. The stickiness of the food and how often we consume sugary foods affects the chances of dental caries.

e-DEFINE

Gallstones occur more commonly in overweight people, but are known to occur in thin people who consume a high-fat diet. They consist of cholesterol, bile pigments and mineral salts. Gallstones form when the liver makes bile that is extremely saturated with cholesterol.

▶ Deadly snack attack

Read the newspaper article and then answer the questions that follow it.

By Karen Collier, Consumer Reporter

CHILDREN are eating foods stacked with shockingly high levels of fat, salt, sugar and caffeine.

The trend is raising the risk of child obesity, tooth decay, diabetes and heart disease.

Leading dietitian Karen Inge urged parents to carefully check labels, because many were unaware of just what was in the food they buy.

A team of dietitians randomly checked products popular with children for a *Herald Sun* food study. The team found:

SOFT drinks contain up to 10 teaspoons of sugar in each can.

SWEETENED breakfast cereals are fortified with vitamins and minerals—and up to three teaspoons of added sugar per serve.

COLA drinks have as much caffeine as half a cup of strong coffee.

A SINGLE snack bar can be crammed with up to four teaspoons of sugar.

SEASONED instant noodles and savoury biscuits can be saltier than potato chips.

A SINGLE fried dim sim has more salt than very young children need for an entire day.

A BUCKET of hot chips contains about three teaspoons of fat.

TWO slices of luncheon meat are fattier than a slice of pizza.

DAIRY desserts tend to have less calcium, more sugar, and up to six times the fat of fruit yoghurt.

FRUIT drinks are often pumped with artificial colours and have as little as 25 per cent real juice.

FAST food hamburgers are up to four times as fatty as healthier homemade versions.

'In many cases foods that target children are full of taste but offer low nutritional value from vitamins and minerals,' Ms Inge said.

'They are OK as treats but should not be handed out every day.

'Children who get hooked on heavily sweetened, salted or fatty foods early find it harder to change as they get older.'

The warning comes as record numbers of Australian children pile on weight. About one in four youngsters are too chubby, studies show.

Research also shows one in three children under 12 are not eating enough fruit, and more than one in five do not eat enough vegetables.

Parental advice

LEAD by example. Parents are a greater influence than advertising.

FEED children about two fruits and five vegetables a day.

SELECT breakfast cereals that are a good source of fibre.

FILL sandwiches with cooked meat leftovers or lean ham instead of fatty luncheon meats.

ENCOURAGE them to drink water and plain milk instead of soft drinks.

IDEAL snacks include fruit, wholemeal bread spread with jam, yoghurt, cheese sticks, raisin and fruit breads, low-fat rice snacks, crispbreads and snack bars with real fruit, fibre and grains.

FATTY yoghurt powder flavouring is a common fruit bar coating.

QUESTIONS

1 Describe the nutritional value of foods that children consume.
2 To what dietary related diseases are these foods contributing?
3 What does dietician Karen Inge encourage parents to do to overcome this problem?
4 Complete the following table.

True constipation is associated more with the consistency of the faeces rather than the regularity.

Some studies have suggested that a third of older people in high-income countries suffer from diverticular disease.

Food	Description of nutrients
Soft drinks	
Sweetened breakfast cereals	
Cola drinks	
Single snack bar	
Seasoned instant noodles and savoury biscuits	
Single fried dim sim	
Bucket of hot chips	
Two slices of luncheon meat	
Dairy desserts	
Fruit drinks	
Yoghurt fruit bars	
Fast-food hamburgers	

5 Can children consume the foods in the table?
6 Which foods do children tend to miss out on?
7 Refer to the section entitled 'Parental advice'. Using this information, create a pamphlet or poster that outlines some of the advice provided.

▶ You are what you eat

Study the table and then answer the questions that follow it.

What's in your food

	Serve size	Total sugars (g)	Total sugars approx. tsp	Total fat (g)	Total fat approx. tsp	Saturated fat (g)	Sodium (mg)	Salt approx. tsp	Caffeine (mg)
Breakfast cereal									
Kellogg's Honey Smacks	30 g	15.3	3.0	0.2	0.0	Neg.	5	Neg.	—
Kellogg's Humungo Froot Loops	30 g	12.2	2.5	0.8	Neg.	Neg.	156	$\frac{1}{13}$	—
Snack Bar									
LCMs chocolate-coated coco pop bar	40 g	19.7	4.0	7.3	1.5	N/A	84	Neg.	—
Pop-Tarts double chocolate	50 g	15.5	3.0	4.8	1.0	N/A	228	$\frac{1}{9}$	—
Savouries									
Arnott's cheddar shapes	35 g	0.2	0.0	9.4	2.0	N/A	448	$\frac{1}{4}$	—
Chips/Crisps									
Samboy extra salt and vinegar	20 g	0.3	0.0	6.8	1.5	N/A	248	$\frac{1}{8}$	
Smith's Cheetos cheese and bacon balls	20 g	0.0	0.0	7.1	1.5	3.4	217	$\frac{1}{9}$	
Mini chocolate									
Kenman Harry Potter chocolate frog	25 g	13.5	2.5	7.7	1.5	4.9	<5	Neg.	—
Picnic	25 g	12.6	2.5	7.9	1.5	4.0	N/A	N/A	—
Cake slice									
White Wings chocolate fudge cake bar	56 g	21.8	4.5	11.1	2.0	N/A	145	$\frac{1}{14}$	
Dairy snack									
Nestlé Milky Bar white chocolate	100 g	17.8	3.5	14.9	3.0	N/A	40	Neg.	—
Yogo Mix and Choc Chips	100 g	17.6	3.5	7.9	1.5	4.9	177	$\frac{1}{11}$	
Ice cream									
Cadbury Freddo rainbow railside	84 mL	23.4	4.5	6.1	1.0	4.3	50	Neg.	
Streets Paddle Pop choc rock	82 mL	14.0	3.0	13.7	3.0	N/A	49	Neg.	
Other food									
Maggi beef two-minute noodles	85 g	2.8	0.5	14.8	3.0	N/A	1820	1	
Supreme pizza slice	85 g	0.8	0.0	7.6	1.5	2.9	633	$\frac{1}{3}$	—
Hot dog with bun	85 g	1.9	0.5	13.0	2.5	4.2	900	$\frac{1}{2}$	—
Strassburg (2 slices)	50 g	0.3	0.0	9.6	2.0	3.4	435	$\frac{1}{4}$	—
Fried dim sim	50 g	3.0	0.5	4.3	1.0	1.8	535	$\frac{1}{4}$	—
Tomato sauce (1 tbsp)	22g	5.1	1.0	0.0	0.0	0.0	200	$\frac{1}{10}$	—
McDonald's Big Mac	217 g	11.5	2.5	20.8	4.0	9.5	840	$\frac{1}{2}$	—
KFC nuggets six-pack	108 g	0.5	0.0	16.6	3.0	6.9	660	$\frac{1}{3}$	—
Soft drink									
Fanta can	375 mL	48.7	10.0	0.0	0.0	0.0	56	Neg.	—
Coke can	375 mL	40.7	8.0	0.0	0.0	0.0	45	Neg.	49
Pepsi can	375 mL	40.7	8.0	0.0	0.0	0.0	45	Neg.	40
Energy drink									
Red Bull can	250 mL	30.0	6.0	0.0	0.0	0.0	N/A	N/A	80
Chocolate (extra caffeine)									
Viking bar	60 g	34.1	7.0	11.0	2.0	8.2	140	$\frac{1}{14}$	58

Daily energy and nutrient needs for children

Age	Energy (kJ)	Sodium (mg)	Total fat (g)	Total sugars (g)
4–7	6400–8300	460–1730	49–63	60–78
8–11	7700–9800	600–2300	59–75	72–92
12–18	8100–13 500	920–2300	62–103	76–127

Key

5 g fat	1 teaspoon fat
5 g sugar	1 teaspoon sugar
2000 mg sodium	1 teaspoon salt
Neg.	Negligible
N/A	Not available

QUESTIONS

1 In pairs, select a group of foods from the table and graph the information. Display your graph in the classroom.
2 Which foods, if any, in the group that you have chosen do you consider to be 'healthy'? Justify your response.
3 What dietary related diseases may result if these foods are consumed regularly?
4 Identify some healthier foods that could replace the foods you consider to be 'unhealthy'.

▶ **Let's remember**

1 What is constipation and how prevalent is this disease?
2 What dietary considerations are recommended to decrease the chances of constipation?
3 What are haemorrhoids and what causes them?
4 What is diverticulitis and what causes it?
5 What dietary recommendations are suggested to decrease the chances of bowel cancer?

▶ **Let's investigate**

1 Investigate the current research being undertaken in regard to cancer and diet. Outline the relationship between different types of cancers and diet.
2 Investigate factors that increase the absorption of iron in the diet and factors that inhibit the absorption of iron in the diet.
3 Investigate which dietary related diseases are more common during childhood, and which are more common in late adulthood. Are there any diseases that are more common in females than in males? Design a concept map to summarise your findings.
4 Investigate the costs of dietary related diseases.
5 Investigate a disease that is more common in low-income countries, such as rickets, osteomalacia or kwashiorkor. Include information about signs and symptoms, dietary considerations and who is most affected by this disease.
6 Investigate which dietary related diseases are more common in high-income and low-income countries. Are there diseases that are prevalent in both types of countries? Complete a Venn diagram, as shown below, to present your information.

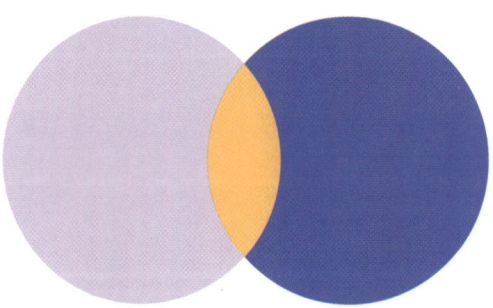

Dietary related diseases

low-income countries   high-income countries

7 Investigate the term *diseases of affluence*. What does it mean?
8 Investigate kidney stones. Design a pamphlet to display your findings.
9 Investigate the term *lactose intolerance*, outlining its causes and symptoms.

10 Investigate coeliac disease, outlining its causes and symptoms. Design a pamphlet to present your information.

11 Discuss the health implications that are associated with companies offering 'mega meal deals' and offering the consumer super-sized takeaway foods at a small increase in price from the regular size.

@-Dietary related diseases

www.heartfoundation.com.au/school/index_fr.html

Click on 'Nutrition and Cardiovascular Disease'

1 What does RDI stand for?
2 Identify the factors that influence the food habits of Australians.
3 Outline the major dietary problems associated with Australians.
4 What does CVD mean and to which disease does it refer?
5 Outline the risk factors associated with CVD.
6 What statistics did the National Survey by the Heart Foundation present in regard to blood pressure?
7 Which groups are more susceptible to high blood pressure?
8 What is the cost to the community in regard to high blood pressure?
9 Why is exercise a public health priority?
10 Outline the benefits of exercise.
11 Identify the risk factors for heart disease. Categorise them as either modifiable or non-modifiable.
12 Discuss the modifiable risk factors for heart disease in detail.

▶ Puzzled

Dietary discover

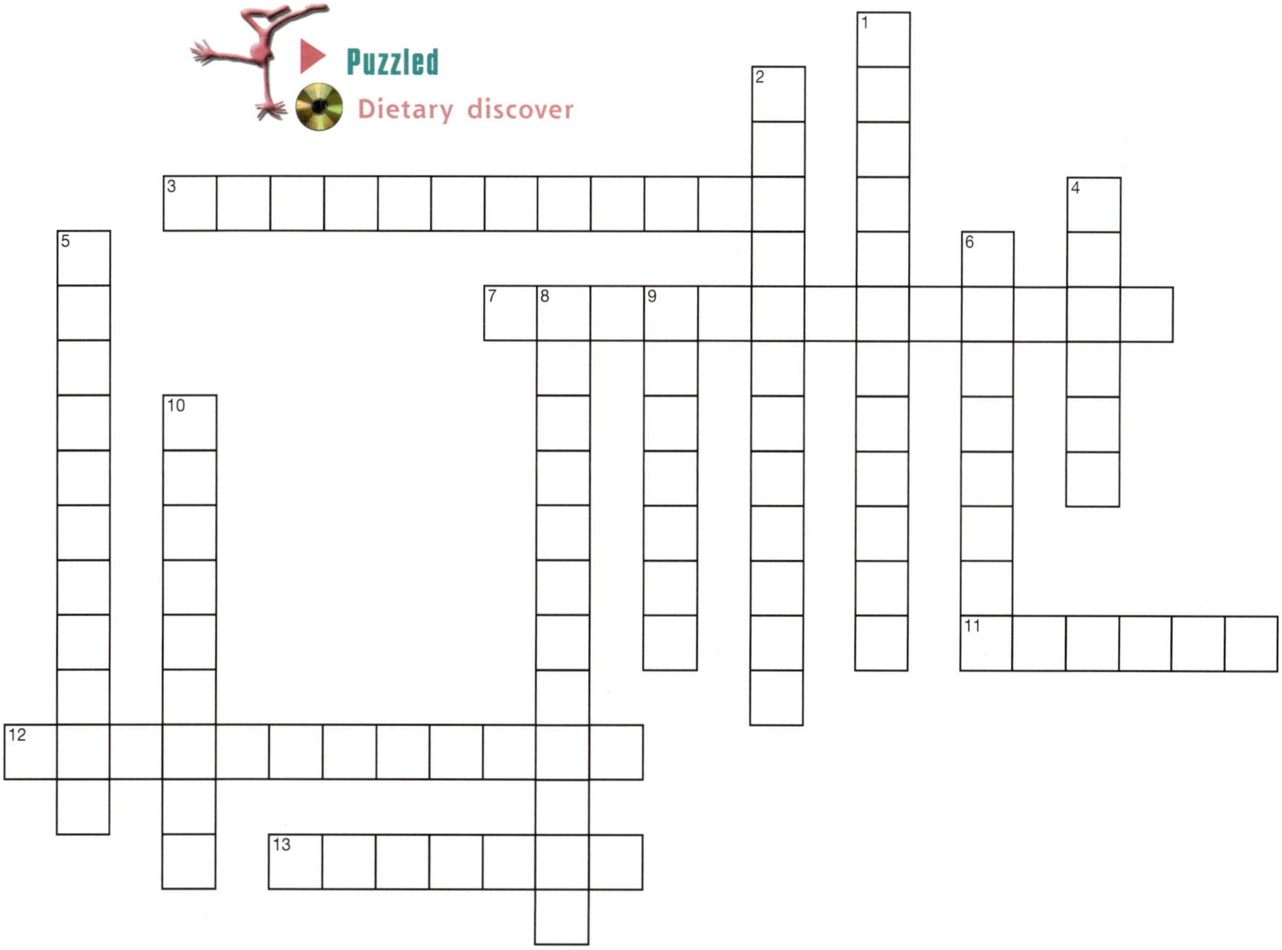

Across

3 Another name for high blood pressure

7 The major cause of death in Australians is _____ _____ disease.

11 Lack of vitamin C may result in this disease

12 This dietary related disease is common among children because they do not consume an adequate amount of fibre

13 Lack of iron may result in this disease

Down

1 Too much vitamin C may cause these (two words)

2 Sweet, sticky foods can result in these (two words)

4 This disease may be a long-term effect of a high-salt diet

5 Lack of water results in this

6 Type of diabetes caused by being overweight

8 Weight-bearing exercise and calcium assist in the prevention of this disease

9 This dietary related disease results when one's energy input is much greater than one's energy output

10 One of the major causes of this disease is the consumption of a large amount of alcohol over a long period of time

Dietary decisions

Match the following diseases with nutrients that are linked to them. More than one nutrient may be linked to a disease, and nutrients can be linked to several diseases. Decide whether it is a deficiency or excess of the nutrient that is linked to the disease.

1	osteoporosis	**7**	hypertension
2	anaemia	**8**	stroke
3	diabetes mellitus	**9**	constipation
4	coronary heart disease	**10**	haemorrhoids
5	kidney stones	**11**	dental caries
6	cirrhosis of the liver	**12**	obesity

calcium   fibre   water   sugar   fat   salt   iron   vitamin C   alcohol*

* not a nutrient

LET'S PRODUCE

Grilled chicken and rice   (serves 2)

Ingredients

2 chicken fillets (200 grams)
2 teaspoons vegetable oil
1 cinnamon stick
2 cloves
$\frac{1}{2}$ teaspoon cumin
pinch cardamom seeds
$\frac{1}{2}$ onion
2 cloves garlic, crushed
$\frac{1}{2}$ cup basmati rice, rinsed
1 cup vegetable stock
3 shakes black pepper
30 grams spinach leaves, washed and chopped
1 cup frozen peas, thawed
$\frac{1}{3}$ cup natural yoghurt
$\frac{1}{4}$ tablespoon fresh coriander, chopped

Method

1 Grill chicken until cooked. Transfer to a plate, cover and keep warm.

2 Heat oil in saucepan and cook cinnamon, cloves, cumin and cardamom for one minute. Add onion and garlic and cook for a further five minutes.

3 Stir in rice, then add stock and black pepper. Bring to boil and reduce heat to low. Cover and cook for twenty minutes.

4 Remove from heat and stir through spinach and peas with a fork. Replace lid and set aside for ten minutes.

5 In the meantime, mix yoghurt and coriander together and thinly slice chicken.

6 Place rice mixture on serving plate and top with chicken and yoghurt mixture.

QUESTIONS

1   Which nutrients are found in this recipe?
2   Investigate which dietary related diseases are related to the nutrients identified in question 1.

Ingredients

1 tablespoon olive oil
$\frac{1}{2}$ brown onion, cut into wedges
$\frac{1}{4}$ cup yellow split peas, rinsed
1 clove garlic, crushed
1 teaspoon fresh ginger, grated
$\frac{3}{4}$ teaspoon ground cumin
1 cup stock
250 grams tomatoes, chopped
200 grams sweet potato, peeled and chopped
1 carrot, peeled and chopped
1 cup couscous, cooked
2 tablespoons fresh coriander, chopped

Vegetables with couscous   (serves 2)

Method

1   Heat oil in frypan and cook onion for five minutes.
2   Add split peas, garlic, ginger and cumin and cook for a further two minutes.
3   Add stock and simmer for twenty minutes.
4   Add tomatoes, sweet potato and carrot and simmer for another ten minutes.
5   Stir coriander through and serve with couscous.

QUESTIONS

1   Which nutrients are found in this recipe?
2   Investigate which dietary related diseases are related to the nutrients identified in question 1.

Chinese omelettes   (serves 2)

Method

1   Beat eggs with sesame oil and add prawns, ham, bean sprouts, spring onion and pepper.
2   Heat peanut oil in frypan and add $\frac{1}{4}$ cup of egg mixture. Cook until base of omelette sets and becomes golden brown.
3   Flip omelette over and cook for another two minutes, or until golden brown. Remove and place on plate and keep warm.
4   Cook remaining egg mixture.
5   To make sauce, combine stock, soy sauce and sesame oil in frypan and bring to boil.
6   Combine water and cornflour together and add to frypan, stirring constantly. Reduce heat and boil for another minute, until mixture thickens.
7   Pour over omelettes and garnish with spring onion.

Ingredients

3 eggs
$\frac{1}{2}$ teaspoon sesame oil
125 grams prawns
125 grams ham, cut into strips
$\frac{1}{2}$ cup bean sprouts, rinsed and trimmed
1 spring onion
3 shakes black pepper
1 tablespoon peanut oil

Sauce

$\frac{1}{3}$ cup chicken stock
2 teaspoons soy sauce
1 teaspoon sesame oil
1 tablespoon water
2 teaspoons cornflour
1 spring onion, finely chopped

Variations

Include any of the following ingredients in the omelettes: red capsicum, corn kernels, water chestnuts, bamboo shoots.

QUESTION

What could you serve with this recipe to ensure a balance of all nutrients?

Tuscan tomato soup

(serves 2)

Ingredients

1 teaspoon olive oil
1 rasher bacon, finely diced
½ onion, finely diced
½ stalk celery, finely diced
½ carrot, finely diced
¼ cup corn
½ zucchini, finely diced
125 millilitres tomato pasta sauce
325 millilitres vegetable stock
1 bay leaf
3 shakes black pepper
1 tablespoon pasta
1 tablespoon parsley
crusty bread
parmesan cheese,
 coarsely grated

Method

1 Heat oil in saucepan and gently fry bacon, onion and celery for five minutes.
2 Add carrot, corn and zucchini and cook for another minute.
3 Add pasta sauce, stock, bay leaf and black pepper and bring to boil. Simmer with lid on for thirty minutes.
4 Add pasta and boil for another ten minutes, with lid off.
5 Sprinkle with parsley and serve with crusty bread and parmesan cheese.

QUESTIONS

1 Identify the nutrients contained in this recipe.
2 Why do soups tend to retain most of the vitamins found in their ingredients?
3 Investigate the dietary related diseases that lycopene, the antioxidant found in tomatoes, is considered to prevent.
4 Investigate what other ingredients you could add this to recipe to increase its nutritional value.
5 Design, produce and evaluate your new soup recipe ☺ ☺ ☹.

Thai lamb salad

(serves 2)

Ingredients

250 grams lamb (for example, backstraps)
2 teaspoons peanut oil
½ Spanish onion, thinly sliced
4 radishes, thinly sliced
½ stalk celery, thinly sliced
50 grams bean sprouts
2 teaspoons coriander, chopped
1 tablespoon basil, chopped
1 small red chilli, thinly sliced
1 clove garlic, crushed
1 teaspoon ginger, grated

Method

1 Heat oil and cook lamb on high for three minutes, turning once.
2 Reduce heat and cook for a further three minutes.
3 Remove from pan and rest for five minutes. Cut into 1-centimetre strips. Cover with foil to keep warm.
4 Mix onion, radish, celery, sprouts, coriander, basil, chilli, garlic and ginger together.
5 Combine dressing ingredients in small bowl.
6 Place salad ingredients on two plates, top with warm lamb and drizzle with dressing.

Dressing

1 teaspoon fish sauce
2 teaspoons lemon grass, thinly sliced
2 teaspoons soy sauce
½ teaspoon sesame oil
1 tablespoon lime juice
½ teaspoon brown sugar

WHaT'S HOT?: DISCOVER NUTRITIONAL ISSUES

Plant Sterols

Sterols are a group of substances that are part of the composition of cell walls in plants and animals. Cholesterol is a familiar sterol that is found in the cells of mammals. Plants manufacture sterols called phytosterols; they look similar to cholesterol, but the human body cannot make them.

Nuts	Almonds, pecans, cashews
Seeds	Sunflower, sesame
Grains	Rice bran, wheat germ
Legumes	Soybeans, peanuts

Plant sterols are the natural components of all vegetable oils and are found in a variety of foods, such as those shown in the table.

As early as the 1950s, plant sterols were shown to lower blood cholesterol levels. The manufacture of effective cholesterol-lowering drugs overtook the use of these sterols. However, there has been a recent renewal of interest in plant sterols. Plant sterols from soy, sunflower and canola oils have been added to margarines and have been shown to reduce blood cholesterol levels.

As plant sterols pass through the human digestive system, they hinder the absorption of cholesterol. Cholesterol that is produced within the body is also inhibited. Instead of entering the bloodstream, the majority of the cholesterol, together with the plant sterols, will pass directly through the body. Therefore, the overall levels of cholesterol in the blood are reduced and plant sterols may assist with reducing the risk of heart disease.

Studies have shown that the consumption of 2–3 grams of plant sterols per day may reduce the total cholesterol by about 10 per cent and the 'bad' low-density lipoprotein (LDL) cholesterol by 10–15 per cent.

Although very few unfavourable effects have been seen with the short-term consumption of plant sterols, the long-term safety studies have yet to be completed.

There have been concerns raised about the consumption of foods enriched with plant sterols reducing the levels of a variety of fat-soluble compounds, such as carotenoids and vitamin E. Food Standards Australia New Zealand has proposed that infants, children and pregnant or lactating women avoid foods that have been enriched with plant sterols. It should be noted that plant sterols can be obtained naturally by consuming a variety of plant foods.

How plant sterols reduce cholesterol uptake

Without plant sterols

Cholesterol enters the gut from food and bile

About half of the cholesterol is absorbed from the gut into the bloodstream

About half of the cholesterol passes out of the body

With plant sterols

Less cholesterol is absorbed from the gut into the bloodstream

More cholesterol passes out of the body

▶ Let's remember

1 What are sterols?
2 Identify a sterol found in animals.
3 Identify a sterol found in plants.
4 List five foods that contain plant sterols.
5 Where are plant sterols found?
6 Describe how plant sterols inhibit the absorption of cholesterol.
7 What is a plant-sterol-enriched food? Identify one type of food that is plant-sterol-enriched.
8 To what can the consumption of two to three grams of plant sterols per day lead?
9 What are the concerns with consuming plant sterols?
10 Which groups of people should not consume foods that have been enriched with plant sterols? Explain why these people should not consume such foods.

▶ Let's investigate

1 Think of reasons why products other than margarine that contain plant sterols were withdrawn from sale. Discuss your thoughts with a classmate. Share your discussion with the class.
2 Investigate plant sterols. Design and produce a pamphlet to inform consumers about plant sterols. Ensure that you include current information about this topic.

▶ @·Plant sterols

www.florapro-activ.com.au

1 Where are plant sterols found?
2 Compare plant sterols with cholesterol, listing similarities and differences.
3 Using diagrams, explain how plant sterols can lower blood cholesterol levels.
4 What are the benefits of adding plant sterols to margarine?

▶ Puzzled

Missing words

Complete the following sentences with the words from the box below. Some words may be used more than once.

cholesterol	hinder	digestive	naturally	decrease	phytosterols

Plants manufacture _____. Plant sterols _____ the absorption of _____ that passes through the _____ system and _____ that is manufactured within the body. Plant sterols have been shown to _____ blood _____ levels and may _____ the risk of heart disease. They can be obtained _____ by consuming a variety of plant foods. Plant sterols may _____ the levels of carotenoids and vitamin E.

 Scrambled sterols

Unscramble the following terms to discover different types of food. Copy the letters in the numbered cells to cells with the same number in the grid below, to complete a sentence about plant sterols.

MIRNARGAE — □□□□□□□□□ 8 3 28 30

LANCAO LOI — □□□□□□ □□□ 12 16 10 21 2

LASODMN — □□□□□□□ 15 22 4 23 11

REOLNFUSW SESDE — □□□□□□□□□ □□□□□ 20 9 17 27 19 6 18 26

GELUSME — □□□□□□□ 24 25 7 31

TUAPSNE — □□□□□□□ 1 29 13 14 5

□□□□□ □□□□□□ □□□ □□□□□
1 2 3 4 5   6 5 7 8 9 10 11   12 13 14   15 16 17 18 19

[B]□□□□ □[H]□□□□□□□ □□[V]□□
20 21 22 23   12   16 24 25 26 5 27 28 21 2   2 29   30 24 31

Organic Foods

An organic food is described as a food that has been grown without artificial fertilisers, pesticides or herbicides. Organic animal meats may be treated with vaccines, but cannot be fed any growth-regulating hormones, drugs, steroids or antibiotics. No organic food should be exposed to irradiation or to the use of genetic engineering.

A farm is only certified as 'organic' after it has operated in accordance with the organic principles listed above for at least three years. Organic farming also takes into consideration the conservation of water, soil and energy, as well as the use of renewable resources and natural cycles in farming. Organic farmers tend to go to great efforts to reduce damage to the environment by endeavouring to achieve a natural balance between the soil and its natural inhabitants, food crops and animal life. For example, organic farmers will use:

- physical weed control, through hand-weeding or expensive weeding equipment, instead of pesticides and herbicides
- animal and green manure to maintain natural soil fertility
  Organic foods tend to be more expensive than other foods for various reasons.
- Organic farming is more labour-intensive and cost-intensive than non-organic farming.
- The crop yields are usually lower in organic food production.
- Organic foods adhere to strict production and processing standards and so are separated from other foods, such as genetically modified and conventional foods, at all stages of the food chain.

Many people select foods on the basis of price. However, what is paid for cheap foods does not represent the full costs. The ecological damage should be considered as well. If more people purchase organic foods, the price of such foods should decrease.

Organic farming has become more popular because the excessive use of agricultural and horticultural chemicals and conventional farming systems has caused tremendous environmental damage, including:

- decline in soil fertility
- salinity problems
- blue-green algae in waterways

Studies on the texture, taste and nutritional properties of organic foods have not shown any considerable differentiation between these foods and non-organic foods. There may be minor benefits with such foods as carrots, apples and tomatoes, but overall the major gain with consuming organically grown foods is linked to environmental issues.

Compared to non-organic farming, organic farming:
· is more beneficial to the environment
· is more sustainable
· produces foods with generally lower pesticide residues

Organic foods that meet the national standard in Australia carry a 'certified organic' label from one of seven Quarantine and Inspection Service accredited certifying groups.

Let's remember

1 Define the term *organic foods*.
2 How is organic meat defined?
3 What is irradiation?
4 When can a farm be certified as being organic?
5 Provide two examples of how organic farmers endeavour to reduce the risk to the environment.
6 Why do organic foods tend to be more expensive than conventionally grown foods?
7 Outline some environmental concerns that have resulted from conventional farming techniques.
8 Are there any differences in regard to the taste, texture and nutritional value of organic foods when compared to those grown with conventional standards? Explain your answer.
9 Can organic foods be described as 'pesticide-free'? Explain your response.
10 Draw the symbol that represents that a food is certified as being organic.

Let's investigate

1 Think about the advantages and disadvantages of consuming organic foods. Discuss your thoughts with a classmate. Share your discussions with the rest of the class. Compile your findings in a table. Write a paragraph explaining why you would or would not consume organic foods. Provide reasons for your response.
2 Investigate one of the following environmental concerns.
   a salinity problems
   b blue-green algae
   You may present your findings as a written report, poster, pamphlet or webpage.

e-Organic

www.tasteoflife.com.au

1 Why did Kraft Foods create Taste of Life?
2 According to this website, what do the terms *organic* and *biodynamic* mean?
3 What does BFA Certification stand for and what does it mean to the consumer?
4 Draw the BFA Certification symbol.
5 How long does the organic certification of an ingredient take and why?
6 Identify products that are available under the Taste of Life brand.

www.heinz.com.au

1 Where are Heinz Wattie's Australasia's certified organic production facilities located?
2 What does the BIO-GRO trademark mean?
3 When and where did Heinz Wattie's Australasia begin its organic program?
4 To whom does Heinz Wattie's Australasia market its organic products?
5 Why are organic yields generally below conventional yields?
6 How have organic growers successfully replaced conventional agrichemical control?
7 Why have organic growers benefited from plant-breeding work?
8 How have organic growers ensured that soil fertility remains in balance?
9 Explain how Heinz Wattie's Australasia helps growers improve yield and quality.
10 What is so special about Kowhai Farm?

▶ Puzzled

All organic!

Find the ten words associated with organic foods from the box in the puzzle.

```
P N T U C U T V P H U S C E I
I E S N Z I O P G Q C X E L Q
G N S Z E W N L E I I R R B X
G J M T O M E A T B E B T A H
A A F V I M N O G N Q M I N C
X V M I Q C I O E R M J F I N
W T C Y T B I W R X O I I A D
S N E A I D A D K I M H E T X
L J B T W B D T E R V W D S T
M B N K L N K V M S D N Y U E
U A Q E Y T I N I L A S E S S
E C O L O G I C A L O U F L C
M T G P E C D P P X O X E U L
N O I T A I D A R R I A Q H M
I U U K V T V V A B N D A K P
```

antibiotics	organic
certified	pesticides
ecological	renewable
environment	salinity
irradiation	sustainable

Guarana

Guarana is a plant extract that is high in caffeine. It comes from the crushed seeds of a climbing Brazilian vine. Guarana has been used as a stimulant for thousands of years in South America.

Today, guarana is an ingredient in trendy carbonated 'energy' soft drinks and confectionery bars throughout the world.

The main active ingredient in this herb is caffeine, which is responsible for the increase in alertness and vitality that people may experience after consuming guarana. However, guarana's high caffeine content makes it unsuitable for consumption by a range of people, including children, pregnant and lactating women, diabetics and those who are caffeine-intolerant.

At the moment, the food industry seems to be infatuated with guarana and caffeine found in energy drinks and various chocolate bars. Nutritionists are recommending that we steer clear of food products that contain guarana, as our bodies do not need caffeine. It is an additive substance that is quite harmful to certain groups of people.

Nutritionists are also very concerned that guarana bars should not be displayed with confectionery, as they are not suitable for children.

Information about the high caffeine content is often not easy to find on packaging of products that contain guarana.

Case study

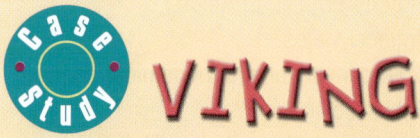

Cadbury's Viking is marketed as 'chocolate with horns', implying that it will provide an energy boost due to its guarana content. The Viking bar contains 58 milligrams of caffeine and recommends a 'dose' of up to three bars per day. If you followed this advice, you would be consuming 174 milligrams of caffeine. This is not healthy, as it is the equivalent of two cups of strong coffee and about six teaspoons of saturated fat!

The Viking bar's label states that consumption of the product is not recommended for specific groups of people and contains advice that the product should be consumed under medical or dietetic supervision. Unfortunately, this information is concealed under the same flap as the recommended daily dose.

QUESTIONS

1   How is the Viking bar marketed? To whom would this type of marketing appeal?
2   Is the Viking bar healthy? Explain your answer.
3   Is it a sensible idea to provide information about who should not consume this type of bar in an inconspicuous place on the packaging?
4   Would children under fifteen years of age heed the warning on a chocolate bar? Explain your answer.
5   Would people consuming this chocolate bar expect to require medical advice before consuming one? Explain your answer.

Getting hyper about a bar of chocolate

Read the newspaper article and then answer the question that follows it.

By Jane Rocca

When is a chocolate bar no longer an ordinary chocolate bar? When it comes with horns.

Confectionery companies such as Cadbury are following in the steps of energy drinks and topping up their chocolate bars with guarana in an effort to lure the 18 to 24-year-old market.

Given the bad publicity some energy drinks have endured over the past few months, it may be surprising that Cadbury has launched a chocolate bar called Viking that promises guarana-spiked energy. The chocolate bar comes with a warning that the product could be harmful to pregnant women, children and diabetics.

According to Cadbury's corporate public affairs manager, Karma O'Meara, the confectionery company was ready for the bad publicity.

'Naturally we expected that this would create noise and possibly a little controversy,' says O'Meara. 'We have this with many new products and would expect nothing less. Ultimately the consumer will decide if this product succeeds.'

Cadbury's Viking is the first chocolate bar containing guarana. Cadbury's technical director Dr Phillip Downing worked on the development of Viking over eight months before its launch in June this year. 'People aged between 18 and 24 feel a strong association with guarana because of its presence in energy drinks,' he says. 'We wanted to go in this direction because we felt we were breaking new ground.'

Lydia Buchtmann, program manager of public affairs for the Australia New Zealand Food Authority, says there are concerns about guarana in chocolate because it contains caffeine. She says ANZFA's expert group on caffeine found it did not pose a health risk, but could cause sleeplessness and anxiety in caffeine-sensitive people, even at low levels.

'The new requirement to label foods containing guarana as containing caffeine was made because of concerns that, while people are aware that caffeine is found in tea, coffee and chocolate, they may not be aware that it is also in guarana,' says Buchtmann.

Viking has about 58 milligrams of caffeine, equivalent to about a cup of instant coffee.

Cadbury was not under legal obligation to put a warning message on the Viking bar, but felt it their duty to cover themselves.

Leanne Mundy is an accredited dietitian based in Hobart who is concerned about caffeine in chocolate bars, and that they are being sold alongside ordinary bars in supermarkets and milk bars. She is particularly concerned about bars such as Viking being sold in school canteens. Mundy says the voluntary

warning label is placed under the flap of the wrapper making it difficult to notice.

'These products are typically marketed at young people, which is my main concern and then placed among other chocolates that don't contain caffeine,' says Mundy.

'Anxiety, tension, headaches and insomnia are some side effects of caffeine (on adults), but the problem is we don't know if children experience these as well. Pregnant women who consume a guarana product may affect the growing child's sleeping pattern. It could be dangerous.'

Downing says the chocolate bar is not a threat to consumers. He says consumers are more likely to drink more than one energy drink a day, but says it is unlikely they would eat more than one bar per day.

Mundy says more needs to be done to educate the public about guarana. 'We need to educate parents to be aware of this as well as educate the average consumer,' she says. 'But I think the fact that school canteens are requesting information on caffeine-enhanced products and wanting to know more about them is a start. They are playing a role in helping get the message out that chocolate is not necessarily what it used to be.'

Select each of the de Bono hats and make an appropriate comment. Share your comments with a classmate.

Emotions, feelings, hunches	Caution, judging and assessing the negatives	Creativity	Optimistic, judging and assessing the positives	Information	Organising thinking
How do I feel?	What are the problems?	What new ideas can I propose?	Why is this worth doing?	What information do we have or need?	What have we achieved?

▶ Let's remember

1 What is guarana and where does it come from?
2 What ingredient is guarana high in?
3 What had guarana traditionally been used for?
4 How is guarana used in today's food industry?
5 What are the physical effects that may be associated with consuming guarana?
6 Which groups should not consume products containing guarana?
7 Why do nutritionists recommend that we do not consume food containing guarana?
8 What is the concern regarding products containing guarana being sold near other confectionery products?
9 Have you ever consumed a product containing guarana? If yes, what types of products did you consume and why?
10 What is your opinion of the addition of guarana to food products? Explain your response.

▶ Let's investigate

1 Investigate the effects that caffeine has on the body. Present your findings in the form of a poster or pamphlet.
2 Investigate the range of products available in the supermarket that contain guarana. Compile a list. Evaluate how well the recommendations as to who should not consume this product are displayed ☺ ☺ ☹. Select one product and design a label that clearly displays this recommendation.

▶  @-Guarana

www.nutritionaustralia.org/Food_Facts/FAQ/caffeine_and_energy_drinks.asp

Write a 300-word magazine article about high-caffeine drinks. Include information about the potential effects on health from the amount of caffeine in these drinks, the difference between high-caffeine and sports drinks and the use of high-caffeine drinks to aid athletic performance.

▶ Puzzled

Scrambled

Unscramble the following words that relate to guarana.

1 reenyg   **2** lizbra   **3** eeinffac   **4** vitedadi   **5** latnmistu

 Stimulated?

Work out the following code to complete a sentence about guarana.

A	B	C	D	E	F	G	H	I	J	K	L	M	N	O	P	Q	R	S	T	U	V	W	X	Y	Z
25						18		4																	

G _ A _ A _ A _ _ I _ _ A _ _ _ I _ _ _ _ A _ _ _ A _
18 6 25 8 25 20 25   4 23   25   23 1 4 10 6 22 25 20 1   25 23

_ I _ _ I _ _ _ I G _ _ _ I _ _ _ A _ _ _ I _
4 1   4 23   11 4 18 11   4 20   19 25 21 21 14 4 20 14

WEBExTRAS

www.burkesbackyard.com.au/facts/2001/recipes/guaranabar_28.html
In this section of the Burke's Backyard website, Rosemary Stanton explodes various myths about chocolate bars containing guarana and provides factual information about this ingredient.

www.guarana.com.au
This website is about The Guarana Company Pty Ltd and provides information about the herbal supplement guarana.

Antioxidants

Antioxidants include vitamins A, C and E, and beta-carotene. They are found in such foods as fruit, vegetables and wholegrain products. In particular, such foods as carrots, tomatoes, red capsicum, oranges, green leafy vegetables, soybeans, tea and red wine are frequently mentioned for their antioxidant properties.

Oxygen is essential to life. However, oxygen may contribute to human ageing and illness because, when it is metabolised, cells form natural by-products called 'free radicals'. Free radicals pass through the cell, disturbing the arrangement of other molecules and causing damage to the cell. This damage is thought to contribute to ageing and a variety of health problems, such as coronary heart disease and cancers.

Research has shown that antioxidants can counteract the harmful effects of free radicals.

e-FaCT

Free radicals are chemicals without paired electrons. Therefore, they steal electrons from other molecules and cause damage.

e-DEFINE

Rancid is when fats become oxidised and develop an 'off' flavour and odour.

e-DEFINE

Angina usually occurs when the arteries are blocked and there is insufficient blood reaching the heart. There is pain in the chest or radiating to the neck, shoulder or arms.

e-FaCT

Research suggests that antioxidant supplements do not work as effectively as those naturally occurring in foods.

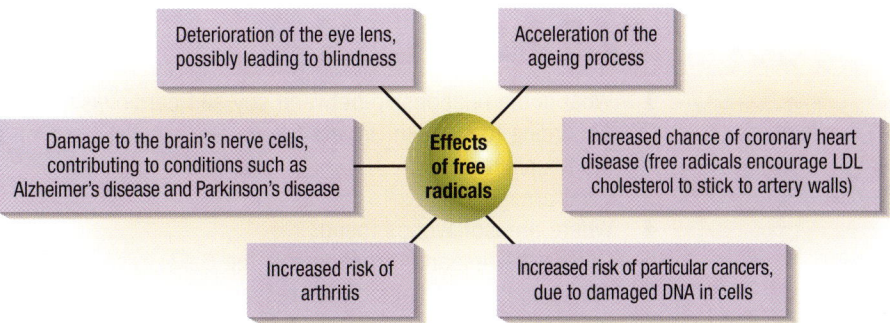

Antioxidants protect key cell components from damage by neutralising the free radicals. Antioxidants that occur naturally in the body or are consumed through the diet may prevent a large amount of the damage.

In food, antioxidants prevent oxygen from making the food become rancid or from affecting discolouration or flavour loss. In the body, antioxidants appear to work by hindering the 'bad' low-density lipoprotein (LDL) cholesterol from being oxidised and manufacturing cells that develop fatty streaks in the walls of blood vessels. Ultimately, these cells will cause coronary heart disease, resulting in atherosclerosis and arterial narrowing and an elevated risk of angina, heart attack and stroke.

Our understanding of how free radicals work is quite limited at this stage, so it is not recommended that we consume large doses of antioxidants. However, scientists are researching the effects of increasing antioxidant levels through the diet and dietary supplements in individuals, in an effort to gain a comprehensive understanding of free-radical activity.

Research has revealed that the antioxidants beta-carotene and vitamin E are found in the interior of the LDL unit. It is acknowledged that providing considerable amounts of vitamin E can delay oxidation *in vitro*. However, further research into the role of antioxidants in hindering heart disease needs to occur. Currently, data suggests that people with a history of cardiovascular disease may benefit most from greater consumption of fruits and vegetables.

We should consume a variety of foods in moderation for a healthy lifestyle. Consuming a well-balanced diet while regularly partaking in physical activity and maintaining a healthy weight is the best approach for a healthy life.

Soy a key to healthy heart

Read the newspaper article and then answer the questions that follow it.

By Steve Dow

The decade of soy 'therapy' to prevent heart disease is dawning, with Australian scientists poised to unlock the secret of why it appears to work so well. Soy as a component of Asian diets has long been associated with a reduced risk of cardiovascular illness. More recently, the United States Food and Drug Administration has approved the labelling of soy products as significant for cholesterol lowering.

A week ago, Monash University's cardiovascular research group presented to a

Melbourne scientific meeting the results of the largest controlled trial performed to date of soy on the cardiovascular system. The study, of 220 men and post-menopausal women, confirms that soy lowers fatty lipids, including cholesterol. The study also discovered that soy may even help lower blood pressure slightly.

The question not immediately answered was: why does soy have such effects? Monash and Melbourne's Baker Medical Research Institute are about to join forces to begin a new clinical trial concentrating on a

mysterious component that may be responsible: isoflavones.

The scientists suspect isoflavones are the active ingredient. They are a sub-group of agents known as phytoestrogens: plant-based compounds that mimic the female hormone oestrogen, which is thought to provide a protective effect against heart disease. Isoflavones are found in soy as well as other foods such as the plant red clover. Armed with this theory, the Baker Institute has carried out two studies on 50 menopausal women using isoflavones extracted from red clover and from soy, or a placebo.

Menopause is often associated with the stiffening of arteries and subsequent rising blood pressure.

The Baker researchers, led by Professor Paul Nestel, found the women who took isoflavones had significantly improved elasticity of the arteries; equivalent to that experienced by women on hormone replacement therapy. Separate research at the Baker by doctors Chin Dusting and Krishna Sudhir, using a synthetic form of isoflavones, has shown improved artery flow and prevention of early arterial atherosclerosis, the disorder causing heart attacks.

QUESTIONS

1 What is the relationship between soy and cardiovascular disease?
2 According to Monash University's cardiovascular research group, what has their recent study confirmed?
3 What are isoflavones?
4 Where are isoflavones found?
5 Outline the research procedure of the Baker researchers, led by Professor Paul Nestel.
6 What were the findings of this research, in regard to the intake of isoflavones by menopausal women?
7 What were the findings of the doctors who used a synthetic form of isoflavones?

▶ Let's remember

1 List some antioxidants.
2 Identify foods that are known for their antioxidant properties.
3 What are free radicals?
4 Describe how free radicals may contribute to ageing and illness.
5 What is the relationship between antioxidants and free radicals?
6 What does research say about the role of antioxidants and ageing?
7 Describe the role of antioxidants in food.
8 Describe the role of antioxidants in the human body.
9 Identify diseases that antioxidants may assist in preventing.
10 Why is further research in antioxidants desirable?

▶ Let's investigate

Sources of vitamin C

Food	Milligrams per 100 grams of food
Capsicum	231
Blackcurrants	209
Broccoli, cooked	92
Brussels sprouts, cooked	83
Strawberries	58
Cabbage	56
Orange juice	49
Mango	41

1 Investigate vitamin C.
  a Find out another name for vitamin C.
  b Graph the data presented in the table labelled 'Sources of vitamin C'. Give your graph an appropriate title and remember to label the axes.
  c Which food contains the most amount of vitamin C per 100 grams of food?
  d Investigate what the Recommended Dietary Intake of vitamin C is for your age group.
  e Design a meal that would provide the Recommended Dietary Intake of vitamin C for you. Include foods that you would consume.

Sources of vitamin E

Food	Milligrams per 100 grams of food
Sunflower oil	48.7
Polyunsaturated margarine	25.0
Hazelnuts	21.0
Almonds	20.0
Wheatgerm	11.0
Tuna, canned	6.3
Peanuts	5.6
Olive oil	5.1

2 Investigate vitamin E.
  a Find out another name for vitamin E.
  b Investigate the functions of vitamin E.
  c Investigate the Recommended Dietary Intake of vitamin E for all members of your family.
  d Design a meal that would provide adequate vitamin E for your family. Include foods that you would all consume.

@-Nutritional issues

www.foodwatch.com.au/antiox.html

1 Why is a daily diet high in antioxidants considered to be 'good insurance'?
2 Where are antioxidants found?
3 What are the three best known antioxidants?
4 Explain the benefits of consuming antioxidants.
5 Why are free radicals detrimental to one's health?
6 What are oxidants?
7 Select three antioxidants and summarise their key features.

▶ Puzzled

Word puzzle

How many words can you make from the term *antioxidant*? Each letter can be used only once.

Reordering antioxidants

Unscramble the following names of foods that are thought to have antioxidant properties.

1 ate   2 rotcar   3 yosnabe   4 der niwe   5 tamoot

Scrambled!

Unscramble each of the words to form the names of seven foods that are high in antioxidants. Take the letters that appear in ◯ boxes and unscramble them for the final word.

OTTAOM ☐☐☐☐☐☐

ATE ☐☐◯

RAONGE ☐☐☐☐◯☐

NESOBAY ☐☐☐☐☐◯◯

ROTCAR ☐☐☐☐◯◯

DER WENI ☐☐◯ ☐☐☐☐

DRE PACMUSCI ☐☐☐ ☐☐☐☐☐◯☐☐

☐☐☐☐☐X☐☐☐☐☐

LET'S PRODUCE

Ingredients
2 tablespoons hot water
1 teaspoon caster sugar
1 teaspoon fish sauce
½ lime, juiced
1 small red chilli, finely chopped
1 clove garlic, crushed
8 rice paper sheets
150 grams red cabbage, finely shredded
1 carrot, peeled and shredded
60 grams bean sprouts
1 cup fresh coriander, chopped
1 cup fresh mint, chopped

Rice paper rolls (serves 2)

Method

1 To make dipping sauce, stir sugar into water until it dissolves. Add fish sauce, lime juice, chilli and garlic. Set aside.
2 Fill a bowl with 5 centimetres of warm water and dip one sheet of rice paper into water for fifteen seconds. Drain.
3 Top with a quarter of cabbage, carrot, bean sprouts, coriander and mint and fold in sides and roll up to enclose filling.
4 Repeat with remaining rice paper sheets. Serve with dipping sauce.

Ingredients

75 grams brown rice
200 grams chicken thigh fillets, skin removed and thinly sliced
100 grams firm tofu, drained on absorbent paper and chopped
$2\frac{1}{2}$ tablespoons soy sauce
3 teaspoons olive oil
1 carrot, peeled and cut into 2-centimetre batons
6 sheets nori

Chicken and tofu in nori   (serves 2)

Method

1   Cook rice until tender. Keep warm.
2   In the meantime, marinate chicken and tofu in soy sauce.
3   Heat 1 teaspoon of oil in frypan and stir-fry a third of the chicken mixture for three minutes. Transfer to bowl and repeat with remaining oil and chicken mixture.
4   Add carrot mixture and stir-fry for three minutes, or until tender.
5   Add chicken mixture and cooked rice to frypan and heat through.
6   Divide the chicken mixture into six equal quantities and place down the centre of each nori sheet.
7   Roll each sheet up firmly and cut each in half diagonally.

Ingredients

$\frac{1}{4}$ capsicum, brushed with 1 teaspoon oil
2 cups self-raising flour
270-gram can corn kernels, drained
40 grams cheddar cheese, grated
$\frac{1}{4}$ cup fresh chives, chopped
1 cup soy milk
1 egg, lightly beaten
80 grams butter, melted
1 tablespoon polenta

Corn and soy muffins   (makes 12)

Method

1   Preheat oven to 200°C. Grease muffin tray.
2   Grill capsicum until skin blackens and blisters, then place in plastic bag to cool. When cool, peel skin from capsicum and chop into small pieces.
3   Sift flour and mix in capsicum, corn, cheese and chives.
4   Whisk milk, egg and butter together and add to flour mixture.
5   Stir until just combined and place into muffin tray.
6   Sprinkle with polenta and cook for twenty minutes, or until golden brown. Allow to cool before turning onto cake cooler.

Ingredients

$1\frac{1}{2}$ tablespoons olive oil
325 grams Spanish onions, sliced thinly
150 grams carrots, peeled and grated
250 grams sweet potato, peeled and grated
3 spring onions, sliced
2 tablespoons fresh coriander, chopped
1 teaspoon cumin
$\frac{1}{3}$ cup cornflour
$1\frac{1}{2}$ eggs, lightly beaten
1 tablespoon olive oil (extra)
$\frac{1}{4}$ cup organic plain yoghurt
100 grams feta cheese, crumbled

Vegetable fritters with caramelised onions   (serves 2)

Method

1   Preheat oven to 180°C and grease oven tray.
2   Heat olive oil in frypan and add onions, stirring occasionally over a low heat for twenty minutes, or until onions become soft and caramelised.
3   In the meantime, combine carrot, sweet potato, spring onions, coriander, cumin, cornflour and egg.

4   Divide mixture into four patties and cook in extra oil until golden brown.
5   Place on tray and cook for ten minutes, or until cooked through.
6   Place two fritters on each plate and top with yoghurt, onions and feta cheese.

QUESTION

Investigate the range of health benefits associated with the ingredients of this recipe.

Vegetarian curry   (serves 2)

Method

1   Preheat oven to 200°C.
2   Put brown rice in boiling water and cook until tender.
3   Place tofu on oiled tray and sprinkle with salt. Bake for twenty minutes. Set aside.
4   Heat oil in frypan and add onion, garlic and ginger. Stir-fry for seven minutes.
5   Add tomato, tomato paste, turmeric, coriander, chilli and sultanas and bring to boil. Simmer for fifteen minutes. Cool slightly.
6   Process mixture in food processor until smooth.
7   Return to pan and add soy milk, carrot and potato. Cover and cook for a further ten minutes, or until vegetables are tender.
8   Add peas and tofu.
9   Serve on bed of rice and garnish with fresh coriander.

Ingredients

1 cup brown rice
150 grams firm tofu, cut into half-centimetre slices
1 tablespoon oil
3 shakes salt
1 onion, finely sliced
1 clove garlic, crushed
$\frac{1}{4}$ teaspoon fresh ginger, grated
1 tomato, chopped
1 tablespoon tomato paste
$\frac{1}{2}$ teaspoon turmeric
$\frac{3}{4}$ teaspoon ground coriander
$\frac{1}{4}$ teaspoon chilli powder
2 tablespoons sultanas
$\frac{1}{3}$ cup soy milk
1 carrot, sliced
1 potato, peeled and chopped
$\frac{1}{2}$ cup frozen peas, thawed
1 tablespoon fresh coriander, chopped

QUESTION

Outline the benefits of consuming soy products.

Pad Thai   (serves 2)

Method

1   Cover noodles in hot water in an ovenproof bowl, let stand for about thirty seconds and then separate the noodles gently. Drain.
2   Heat 1 teaspoon of oil in frypan and cook the egg. Remove from pan and roll up. Cut into thin strips.
3   Heat another teaspoon of oil in frypan and cook onion, garlic and spring onions for about five minutes, or until transparent.
4   Mix sweet chilli sauce, soy sauce, fish sauce, tomato sauce and sugar together and add to frypan. Add noodles, peanuts, tofu, sprouts, coriander and egg. Stir until heated through.

Ingredients

250 grams fresh rice noodles
2 teaspoons olive oil
1 egg, lightly beaten
$\frac{1}{2}$ onion, sliced thinly
1 clove garlic, crushed
2 spring onions, sliced thinly
2 tablespoons sweet chilli sauce
2 teaspoons soy sauce
$1\frac{1}{2}$ tablespoons fish sauce
2 teaspoons tomato sauce
$1\frac{1}{2}$ tablespoons sugar
2 tablespoons chopped peanuts, roasted
100 grams tofu, cubed
1 cup bean sprouts
2 teaspoons fresh coriander, chopped

FOOD FOR THOUGHT: DISCOVER IMPACT OF TECHNOLOGY

Genetically Modified Foods

The science of biotechnology includes genetic modification. It has seen improvements in conventional methods of making products such as cheese, beer, bread and vitamins. However, the use of genetic modification in commercial food crops is new in Australia, although it has been widely used in the USA for many years.

Genetic modification involves acquiring genes from the cells of a plant, animal or microbe and introducing them into another cell to provide a desired characteristic. Food products that are derived in this way are known as genetically modified foods.

Farmers have used cross-breeding techniques for many centuries to modify and improve the quality, yield and taste characteristics of plants and animals. Genetic modification is a new technique of distinguishing and transferring particular characteristics.

There is a wide range of diverse opinions in the community about genetically modified foods. The state and federal governments are working together to consider how to best meet the information needs of consumers in regard to genetically modified foods. This includes labelling considerations, so that consumers can make informed decisions.

The arguments for genetically modified foods include the following.
· It is claimed that genetically modified foods will be more nutritious, taste better and keep longer.
· Genetically modified crops, such as maize and tomatoes, will be more efficient for farmers to grow and will result in decreased use of pesticides. This will make it better for the environment.

Researchers are aiming to develop foods that offer many consumer benefits, such as:
· increased vitamin and protein contents
· removal of allergy-causing properties
· inclusion of properties that prevent chronic diseases, such as cancers and heart disease
· inclusion of fewer chemicals in agricultural production

The Australian Commonwealth Scientific and Industrial Research Organisation (CSIRO) believes that Australia needs to assess carefully the potential risks as well as the benefits available from gene technology. It believes that there is a window of opportunity for Australia to benefit economically and to remain competitive in the international food arena.

However, some people are concerned about the effects of genetically modified foods on human health and the impact of genetically modified crops on the environment. The arguments against genetically modified foods include the following.
· We do not have any specific data that genetically modified foods are harmless.
· The practice of genetic modification is vague and the science too recent to guarantee that we will not come across problems in the future.

Did you know that gene technology is used to create vaccines against hepatitis and safer insulin for diabetics?

Genetic modification

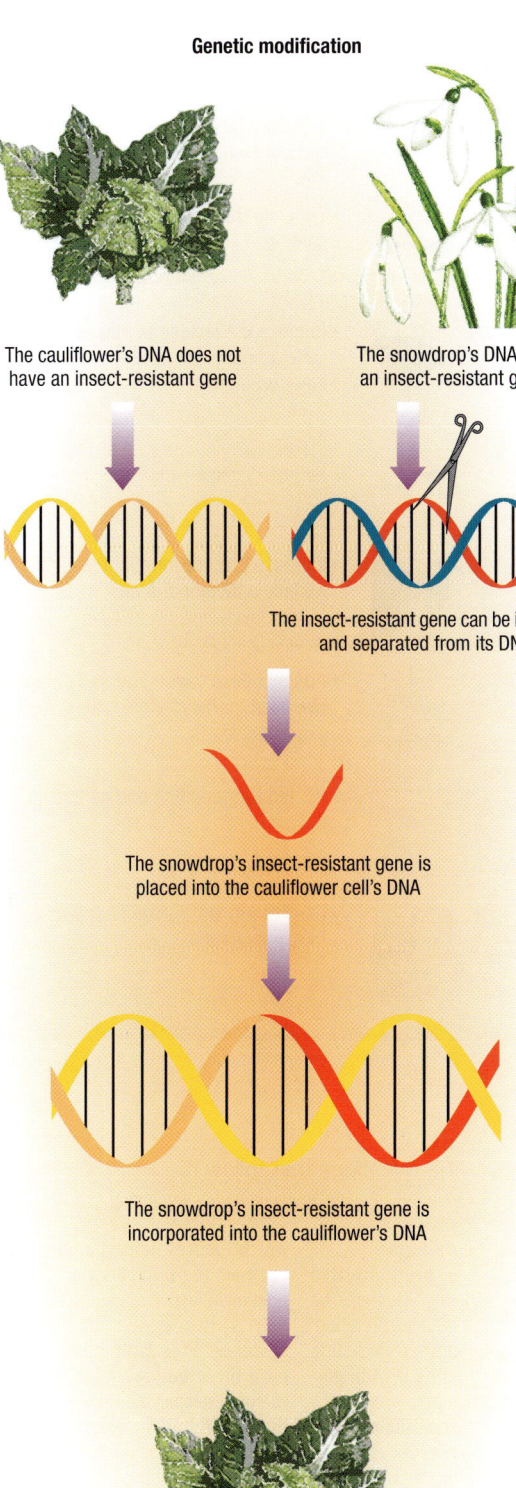

The cauliflower's DNA does not have an insect-resistant gene

The snowdrop's DNA has an insect-resistant gene

The insect-resistant gene can be identified and separated from its DNA

The snowdrop's insect-resistant gene is placed into the cauliflower cell's DNA

The snowdrop's insect-resistant gene is incorporated into the cauliflower's DNA

This cauliflower is now resistant to insects

· We already have established plant and animal breeding techniques that can improve our food, so we do not need genetically modified foods.

The table below lists reasons why some foods or food sources could be genetically modified.

Food sources	Reason for genetic modification
Soybean	• Increase resistance to herbicides, so that farmers can spray weeds without damaging the crop
Legumes, such as chickpeas	• Increase nutritional value • Improve yields, so that the plants have natural protection from fungal and bacterial disease
Oil seeds, such as canola and sunflower	• Improve health, so that mono-unsaturated (omega-3) fatty acids are increased in margarines and oil, which will contribute to improved cardiovascular/heart health
Sugar	• Increase the amount of sucrose produced in each plant • Enhance resistance to disease
Wine grapes	• Increase colour, flavour and sweetness • Increase productivity by enhancing resistance to pests and disease and making the plant more effective at absorbing nutrients from the soil
Barley	• Increase productivity by enhancing resistance to pests and disease • Improve brewing efficiency
Wheat	• Improve health by increasing the amount of fibre • Enhance the exportability of wheat by designing varieties of wheat to suit different market demands
Apples and pears	• Decrease the use of pesticides by increasing the natural resistance to insect pests
Grapes and citrus fruits	• Produce seedless varieties to meet consumer demands
Potatoes	• Produce non-browning varieties to meet consumer demands • Decrease the use of pesticides by increasing the natural resistance to insect pests
Poultry	• Increase poultry health by enabling infectious bursal disease to be detected

Continued on next page ➡

A vitamin A-enriched rice, called Golden Rice, has been developed to increase the nutritional value of rice.

Bacillus thuringiensis (Bt) is a bacterium found in the soil. When it is consumed by some insects, Bt manufactures a protein that disrupts the digestive system of the insect. Bt has been genetically added to cotton to naturally resist pests. This cotton is referred to as Bt cotton.

Labelling laws that were introduced in September 2001 should assist Australians to identify products that contain genetically modified foods. To date, there are no genetically modified vegetables or fruit on sale in Australia, but imported products, such as tomato paste, may have been made from genetically modified tomatoes. In Australia today, bread and cheese may be prepared with genetically modified enzymes. An assortment of processed food products containing soy may be made from imported genetically modified soybeans.

Food additives, including flavouring agents and sweeteners, may have also been created using genetically modified organisms. The oil produced by Bt cotton, grown in Australia, may also be used in cooking.

Food sources	Reason for genetic modification
Pigs	• Increase pig health by increasing the pig's natural immunity to infection and so decrease the use of antibiotics
Salmon	• Enhance the growth rate and size of salmon
Dairy cattle	• Remove the lactose in milk, so that lactose-intolerant people can consume dairy products
Fish	• Increase growth as well as increase natural disease resistance
Livestock	• Increase disease immunity and so replace antibiotic therapy
Cheese	• Adapt cheese flavours to suit differing overseas markets and so improve exportability
Yeast	• Hasten fermentation and enhance flavour
Preserving foods	• Use natural anti-bacterial agents as food preservatives

Broccoli a cancer buster

Read the newspaper article and then answer the questions that follow it.

SUPER broccoli loaded with natural compounds to help prevent cancer could be on dinner tables within a few years.

British researchers at the John Innes Centre, a government-funded plant research unit, produced the super broccoli by cross-breeding the normal plant with a wild Sicilian species in the same family.

The new plant, which is not genetically modified, contains up to 100 times more sulphor-aphane—a compound that helps lower the risk of cancer—than normal broccoli.

'It's much more potent than normal broccoli,' said Prof. Richard Mithen, head of the research team that produced the plant.

'Our best lines have 100 times more sulphoraphane than a normal broccoli.'

The activity of the compounds is well known and has for years been the focus of research, particularly in the United States. But Prof. Mithen said the super-broccoli was one of the first plants in which scientists had intensified their effects.

'No gene has been inserted through genetic modification,' he said. 'This is classical breeding. But we speeded that breeding program up by using DNA finger-printing technology.'

Normally the breeding program would have taken about 10–15 years, but thanks to DNA technology Prof. Mithen has done it in four. The institute owns the patent on the breeding method.

The super broccoli looks and tastes like normal broccoli but is packed with sulphoraphane, which induces natural protective enzymes to rid the body of carci-nogens before they can do harm.

'It switches on our body's defences,' Prof. Mithen said. 'We have these natural defences but in some people they work better than in others. If we eat broccoli it switches them on and makes them more effective.'

Breeding work on the super broccoli is nearly finished and the researchers hope to begin testing it on humans next year. It could be available within a few years.

QUESTIONS

1 Define the term *super broccoli*.
2 How would super broccoli be produced?
3 Why has the breeding program for the development of super broccoli been so fast?
4 Outline the similarities and differences between broccoli and super broccoli by completing a Venn diagram.
5 What are the advantages of consuming super broccoli?

The federal government, through various agencies, regulates the use of gene technology. These agencies include:

- Food Standards Australia New Zealand
- Australian Competition and Consumer Commission
- Australian Quarantine and Inspection Service
- Interim Office of the Gene Technology Regulator
- Genetic Manipulation Advisory Committee
- Therapeutic Goods Administration
- National Registration Authority
- National Occupational Health and Safety Commission

▶ The seeds of suspicion

Read the newspaper article and then answer the question that follows it.

'Tinkering' with nature freed us from famine and disease. The greatest risk lies in not tinkering.

By Minette Marrin

IT IS both sad and shocking that Prince Charles has used his considerable influence, in a lecture on sustainable development last week, to cast grave doubt upon science. He suggested science is somehow at odds with nature; that 'scientific rationalists' are at odds with proper feeling and a sense of wonder at the world; in his call for a sense of the sacred, he even suggested that a purely secular approach is more or less bound to be environmentally irresponsible—in other words, the godless are unlikely to be green, and so are 'scientific rationalists'.

He spoke of balance, but in effect he has set up a series of false dichotomies. It is bad enough that this kind of thinking represents a serious misunderstanding of what science truly is; worse still, it will support the Luddite tendencies of the world's highly professional environmental pressure groups, in their irrational and unscrupulous determination to prevent scien-

tific developments that could do wonderful things—that already have done wonderful things—to feed the hungry, enrich the poor and protect the environment.

That is precisely the opposite of what they say they want to achieve, of course, but they are opposed to reason and to scientific investigation; Prince Charles' lecture will only encourage them. They will also have been very encouraged by the news story of the day after Prince Charles' speech, that, as one headline put it, 'Rogue GM seeds taint UK crops'.

The British Ministry of Agriculture had to admit that large quantities of genetically modified oilseed rape had been sown by mistake, last year and this, in British farmland; unknowing farmers had been sold, by mistake, Canadian seed of which about 1 per cent was genetically modified. Of course, this added to the deep opposition to anything to do with biotechnology, and a general New Age feeling that we must stick to what is 'natural' and 'organic'.

It's a wholly understandable feeling, and very powerful. It is sometimes right, too. But it is

usually wrong—feelings are of no use in judging empirical evidence, or indeed without it.

The public was disgusted by Jenner's experiments in the 18th century with cowpox, and his invention of vaccination seemed horribly unnatural. There were cartoons at the time of humans with lots of little cow's udders growing from their arms. Had public sentiment prevailed, smallpox would probably be still with us.

Tinkering with nature, flying in the face of common sense, as science seems to do, can be very scary. But the truth is that tinkering with nature and flying in the face of common sense—to put it in those emotive and misleading terms—are what has made the West rich, powerful and in a position to be compassionate to less-developed countries. Tinkering with nature has freed the West from back-breaking peasant labor, famine, malnutrition and disease—all those evils from which mankind has begged the gods for deliverance. But deliverance came from science; scientists have been the great heroes and heroines of the modern era.

The truth is that traditional or organic farming, however desirable it might be in some ways, cannot feed the world. What's more, genetic modification is, in fact, very much the same as evolution, but simply speeded up. Its risks are largely misunderstood and usually wildly exaggerated. Its benefits could be dazzling.

Many minds in the European Union are no longer open. In the United States, by contrast—home of extreme consumer caution and massive class-action lawsuits—a House Committee on Science sub-committee has recently issued a report on the risks and benefits of GM plants, named Seeds of Opportunity. It concluded that there is no significant difference between GM plants and similar plants created using traditional cross-breeding.

Biotechnology can reduce farmers' reliance on chemicals. The report dealt with many of the common fears about biotechnology—including the scares about the monarch butterfly, antibiotic resistance, allergens, cross-breeding with nearby plants and so on—and

concluded that GM plants and foods pose no greater risks than those developed through traditional methods.

It also found that there is no evidence that transferring genes from unrelated organisms to plants—stories of fish genes in tomatoes and so on—poses unique risks. (Incidentally, humans share 50 per cent of their genes with bananas.)

In fact, according to this report, biotech procedures allow for much more careful control and monitoring of risk than classical breeding techniques. According to Nick Smith, the chairman of the committee, 'in the case of agricultural biotechnology, the scientific community is as united as I have ever seen it on any major issue'.

This won't be enough for anti-science, anti-any-unknown-risk zealots, but isn't it enough for the rational man or woman? One of the most exciting things about biotechnology is that it is actually very green. GM plants can produce higher yields, in less favorable climates, with less ploughing, less fertiliser and less insecticide, or less toxic insecticide. That means less pollution, less soil erosion, less soil exhaustion, fewer chemicals in the food chain and less back-breaking work for humans and animals.

It means using less or no new land, leaving more land uncultivated and wild; organic farming would certainly mean cultivating more land than now. It means that more wild life could survive; scares about butterflies have proved insubstantial.

Of course there are all kinds of problems. The worst is the problem of trust. Hardly anyone really trusts big business or governments any more; perhaps we should have an international Citizens' Advice Bureau of disinterested, world-class scientists.

But biotechnology for farming is an opportunity not to be missed. As Darwin said: 'It is not the strongest of the species that survive, nor the most intelligent, but the one most responsive to change.'

QUESTION

Undertake a PMI of the article—list three 'Pluses', three 'Minuses' and three 'Interesting Points' related to the article.

 ### GM ruling sparks fears

Read the newspaper article and then answer the questions that follow it.

By Melissa Marino

Conservationists and farmers say new rules for growing genetically modified canola in Australia are inadequate and will lead to contamination of organic produce.

The guidelines call for a five-metre buffer zone between GM and non-GM canola crops. But opponents say that is not enough to prevent contamination.

They are also concerned non-GM farmers will have to pay the costs of segregating crops, resulting in higher prices for non-GM foods.

The rules were released by the Gene Technology Grains Committee just before Christmas.

Chairman Bob Watters has accused dissenters of running a fear campaign. He said the guidelines would give farmers the choice to take up new technology and grow GM crops while protecting non-GM interests.

The Canola Industry Stewardship Protocols provide the basis for industry self-regulation of commercial GM canola crops.

Commonwealth Gene Technology Regulator Sue Meek had been waiting for the guidelines before deciding whether to approve two applications for the commercial release of GM canola.

Two multinational companies, Monsanto and Bayer, have applications before Dr Meek to supply herbicide-resistant GM canola seeds to Australian farmers. If approved, crops could be growing by April.

Scott Kinnear, a spokesman for Biological Farmers of Australia, which certifies organic crops, said the protocols were supposed to ensure GM and other crops could co-exist. But, he said, the five-metre buffer zone required by the guidelines was ludicrous.

Mr Kinnear said organic crops must have no detectable GM residue to be classified GM-free, but the guidelines were based on keeping contamination below 1 per cent. He said 16-kilometre buffer zones would be more realistic, as well as strict penalties for breaching the regulations.

Mr Watters said he was confident the five-metre buffer would limit contamination of non-GM crops to a commercially acceptable standard.

But Greenpeace GM campaigner John Hepburn said canola plants could be contaminated from a distance of 2.6 kilometres. This translated to the contamination of more than half a million seeds in one season.

'Our point is that contamination will increase exponentially over time,' he said. 'You might be able to keep contamination low in the first year and maybe in the second year, but come year three, four or five it will be everywhere.'

Mr Hepburn said non-GM farmers would face rising costs to keep their canola GM-free.

'What has happened in other countries, and what we're fearing will happen here, is that it will be the normal growers that foot the bill for the introduction of GM crops,' he said.

Mr Hepburn said serious environmental, health and economic implications were possible if GM crops were allowed to be grown commercially in Australia.

But David Vaux, a head scientist at Melbourne's Walter and Eliza Hall Institute of Medical Research, said GM crops were being vilified and trials should be allowed.

'There is a fear of technology and a fear of anything . . . that comes from people wearing white coats and I can't work out what the reason is behind it,' he said.

'You can never prove that something is going to be bad in 100 years unless you do trials for 100 years. You've got to use common sense.'

QUESTIONS

1 Outline the concerns of conservationists and farmers regarding the new rules for growing genetically modified canola in Australia.
2 List all the people who are identified in the article, and their organisations. Outline their points of view, and indicate whether they are for or against growing GM canola in Australia. A table may be a useful way to present your information.
3 Explain what David Vaux, a head scientist at Melbourne's Walter and Eliza Hall Institute of Medical Research, meant when he stated 'You can never prove that something is going to be bad in 100 years unless you do trials for 100 years. You've got to use common sense.'
4 Would you support or oppose the introduction of GM canola in Australia? Justify your answer.

▶ Let's remember

1 How are genetically modified foods created?
2 Outline the arguments for genetically modified foods in terms of human health issues.
3 Outline the arguments for genetically modified foods in terms of environmental issues.
4 What are the concerns with the production and use of genetically modified foods?
5 Does Australia produce genetically modified crops?
6 What have farmers been using cross-breeding techniques to achieve?
7 Complete a table, as shown below, by identifying five foods that could be genetically modified and providing reasons for this.

Food	Reasons for genetic modification

8 Why were new labelling laws introduced in Australia?
9 What genetically modified foods may be consumed by Australians?
10 Who regulates the use of gene technology in Australia?

▶ Let's investigate

1 Organise a class debate on the topic: 'That the introduction of genetically modified foods will result in more harm than good'. Alternatively, you could write your own individual response to this topic and develop an A4 pamphlet outlining the key arguments for your point of view.
2 Investigate the current labelling laws for genetically modified food. What information is provided to consumers? Are these laws comprehensive enough?
3 Investigate wax-tipped bananas by visiting the website www.eco-banana.com.au. Include information about the advantages of these bananas and how they are produced and marketed.
4 Investigate the steps that are necessary in the approval process for genetically modified food.
5 Identify five foods that have faults that could be genetically modified to improve consumer demand for the products; for example, eliminate the browning of potatoes. Consider whether these faults should be removed with genetic manipulation to improve the appeal of the food. Investigate what other methods could be used to eliminate the identified faults. Discuss your thoughts with a classmate. Share your discussion with the rest of the class. Write up a summary of the discussion.

🅔·Genetically modified foods

www.foodsciencebureau.com.au/food/genetech.htm

WEBExTRAS

www.betterhealthchann el.com.au
The Better Health Channel provides quality assured information from the Victorian government on a range of topics. Undertake a search for 'genetically modified foods' or 'organic foods' to find out more specific information on these topics.

1   What do consumers want in regard to gene technology?
2   Describe how long humans have been improving foods.
3   Define biotechnology.
4   Define gene technology.
5   What are the disadvantages associated with traditional breeding methods and cross-breeding?
6   How can gene technology overcome these disadvantages? Discuss two reasons.
7   Identify the various areas in which gene technology is utilised. Provide examples of each.
8   What are the potential advantages of using gene technology?
9   How can consumers benefit from gene technology?
10 Provide some examples of food products that could be created using gene technology.
11 Why does Australia have strict regulatory controls concerning gene technology?
12 Who is responsible for setting Australia's food standards?
13 What is Standard A18?
14 Identify the two categories of food made from gene technology, and discuss the labelling requirement for each.
15 What action is the federal government undertaking in regard to allaying fears associated with gene technology?

www.foodstandards.com.au

Click on 'GM Foods'.

1   Define the term *genetically modified foods*.
2   What reasons are provided for the development of genetically modified foods?
3   Identify the genetically modified foods sold in Australia.
4   What guarantee do consumers have that genetically modified foods are safe now and that they will be safe in the future?
5   How can consumers tell if they are buying a genetically modified food? Discuss whether all genetically modified foods can be identified.
6   What is the role of Food Standards Australia New Zealand in regard to genetically modified foods?

Additional information can be found on this website by selecting 'Media Releases and Publications', then 'Fact Sheets' and then 'Fact Sheets 2000'. Scroll down the index to find relevant articles on genetically modified foods.

▶ Puzzled

Genetic mix and match

Complete the following sentences by using the words in the box. Write your sentences in your workbook.

harmless	genes	nutritional	biotechnology	environment

Genetic modification belongs to the science of _____. Genetic modification involves obtaining the _____ from the cells of a living organism and introducing them into the cell of another organism. One of the reasons for genetically modified foods is that it will be better for the _____. One of the reasons against genetically modified foods is that we do not really know if it will be _____. One of the reasons given to genetically modify legumes is to increase their _____ value.

WEBExtras

www.foodsciencebureau.com.au

The Australian Food and Grocery Council's Food Science Bureau is an initiative of the consumer food, drink and grocery products industry. It aims to provide balanced and impartial facts about food science. Click on the 'Food Technology' tab to discover further information about gene technology, including irradiation and functional foods.

Twenty-one foods

The box contains the names of twenty-one foods and food sources that some people argue would be advantageous to genetically modify. Find them in the puzzle.

S	Z	L	M	S	Q	Y	C	W	S	D	P	T	C	N
N	U	C	E	J	E	H	E	E	H	P	R	I	N	A
O	K	N	L	P	E	O	M	L	O	E	T	U	D	E
M	W	X	F	E	C	U	T	R	R	R	A	C	A	B
L	X	V	S	L	G	A	K	A	U	A	D	T	I	Y
A	C	E	A	E	O	P	N	S	T	R	B	C	R	O
S	G	J	L	H	Y	W	F	O	A	O	K	A	Y	S
J	S	U	G	A	R	R	E	M	L	O	P	P	C	P
O	S	R	P	O	U	L	T	R	Y	A	D	P	A	T
C	T	I	D	I	H	S	I	F	S	F	A	L	T	Y
A	O	K	T	D	Y	I	A	W	H	E	S	E	T	E
S	A	E	P	K	C	I	H	C	W	R	E	S	L	A
R	C	Y	B	Y	E	L	N	Y	A	K	O	D	E	S
H	S	E	P	A	R	G	P	E	R	Y	R	A	S	T
T	C	N	X	F	P	K	P	L	I	M	L	L	L	C

apples	pork
barley	potatoes
canola	poultry
cheese	salmon
chickpeas	soybean
citrus fruit	sugar
dairy cattle	sunflower
fish	seeds
grapes	wheat
legumes	yeast
pears	

Irradiation

Food irradiation is the process of preventing food spoilage by exposing the food to ionising energy or radiation to extend the shelf-life of the food. The dose of radiation does not make the food radioactive.

Irradiation is not a new process, but it was only recently that the health ministers in Australia and New Zealand lifted the ban on food irradiation. Food Standards Australia New Zealand will look at each application individually for the use of irradiation as a food preservation method.

Below is a table outlining the advantages and disadvantages of food irradiation.

e-fact

Irradiation is also referred to as cold pasteurisation.

Advantages	Disadvantages
Irradiation reduces the likelihood of food poisoning, as it makes food safer by controlling bacteria and moulds.	Irradiation will not necessarily kill the micro-organisms that can make people ill; the toxins that these micro-organisms produce may be left intact.
There is less wastage, as food is kept fresh for longer.	Vitamins such as vitamin C and thiamin are destroyed.
Irradiation may be a better alternative to chemical fumigation to control pests found in herbs and spices.	Irradiation may undermine the efforts to improve food hygiene standards and so give people a false sense of security.

In small amounts, irradiation extends the shelf-life of foods by:

- destroying or inactivating insects, bacteria, yeast and moulds
- hindering the ripening of fruit, such as strawberries
- restricting unwelcome budding of vegetables, such as potatoes

At higher doses, irradiation helps to decrease quantities of dangerous bacteria present in such foods as chicken and dry herbs and spices.

Irradiation causes only minor alterations to the nutritional value of food, comparable to the effects of cooking. Usually, the individual components of irradiated food are not distinctive and cannot be identified from those in other foods. Research indicates that nutrients such as protein, carbohydrates and fat are not affected during irradiation. In most cases, tests can identify irradiated foods. However, identifying an irradiated ingredient, when it is a minor component of a larger food product, may not necessarily be possible.

e-fact

Irradiation is used to destroy bacteria and parasites that cause illness in humans, such as E. coli, campylobacter and salmonella.

There are plans to ensure that irradiated food is labelled. At this stage, the international symbol for irradiation is optional.

▶ Let's remember

1 What is irradiation?
2 Outline the purpose of irradiation.
3 List the advantages of irradiation.
4 List the disadvantages of irradiation.
5 Is food in Australia irradiated? Explain your answer.
6 Should the international symbol for irradiation be optional? Explain your answer.
7 How do low doses of irradiation affect food?
8 What effects do higher doses of irradiation have on food?
9 Can you identify irradiated food? Explain why labelling irradiated food is important.
10 Draw the international symbol for irradiation.

▶ Let's investigate

Investigate which companies have lodged applications to use irradiation with their products. Provide a summary report of the types of foods that these companies wish to irradiate.

▶ *e*-Irradiation

www.foodsciencebureau.com.au/food/irradiation.htm

1 Why do health experts encourage the use of irradiation?
2 What are the advantages of irradiation?
3 Identify the agencies that have endorsed the use of irradiation.
4 Identify some foods that are not suitable to be subjected to irradiation.
5 Describe the process of irradiation.
6 Outline Standard A17.
7 Can tests identify foods that have been subjected to irradiation?
8 Is irradiated food labelled?
9 Explain what the following statement means: 'Irradiation complements—but doesn't replace—proper food handling practices'.
10 Can irradiation improve the appearance, flavour and aroma of spoiled foods?

▶ Puzzled

Irradiation puzzle

Work out the code to complete a sentence about irradiation.

A	B	C	D	E	F	G	H	I	J	K	L	M	N	O	P	Q	R	S	T	U	V	W	X	Y	Z
D								V				F													

I _ _ A _ I A _ I _ N   I _   _ N _ _ N _ A _
V J J D X V D T V L F   V Y   E F L M F   D Y

_ _ _ _   A _ _ _ _ _ _   I _ A _ I _ N
B L S X   H D Y T I Q J   V Y D T V L F

WEBEXTRAS

www.foodstandards.gov.au

Click on 'Media Releases and Publications' at the top of the page. Then click on 'Fact Sheets' and then 'Fact Sheets 2000'. Scroll down the index to find relevant articles on irradiation.

Irradiation tiles

Unscramble the tiles to reveal a message about the process of irradiation.

T E N D	E S S	I F E .	I S	N T I N	O N T
B Y E	R E V E	I A T I	S H E	L F L	T O
P R O C	X P O S	O D S	R A D	F O O D	O F P
G F O	I T S	T H E	F O O D	T H E	P O I L
T I O N	A G E	O E X	I N G	A D I A	I R R

Other Technological Developments

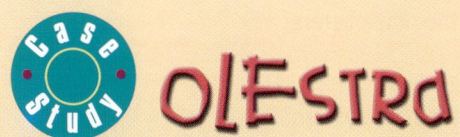

Olestra is a fat substitute that has the taste and texture of fat, but does not contain 'real' fat or its kilojoules. Olestra passes through the digestive tract without being absorbed. Olestra is not used in products in Australia, but is marketed as Olean in potato crisps and biscuits in the USA. The US Food and Drug Administration mandates that all foods containing olestra have an information statement outlining for consumers the possible side-effects of olestra, including the hampering of the absorption of fat-soluble vitamins.

Advantages	Disadvantages
People may reduce their fat intake if they consume foods containing olestra rather than fatty foods; this will assist with reducing their fat intake and reduce their blood cholesterol levels and weight.	Some consumers of olestra have experienced diarrhoea, bloating and abdominal cramps.
Reduced-fat diets can be made more appealing and simpler to adhere to.	The absorption of fat-soluble nutrients, such as vitamins A, D, E and K, from foods that contain olestra is reduced.
Olestra can withstand heat and be used for deep-frying; this is not the case with other fat substitutes.	Those who consume olestra deny their body of antioxidants that may assist in protection against cancer and other diseases; olestra prevents the absorption of the antioxidants.

There is also concern that consumers of olestra may eat more when they select low-fat foods. Others may elect to consume fat-free snacks instead of breads, fruits and vegetables and omit essential nutrients from their diet.

QUESTIONS

1   What is olestra?
2   How does olestra work?
3   Where is olestra available?
4   List the advantages of olestra.
5   Outline the concerns with consuming olestra.
6   Argue why you believe that olestra should or should not be allowed to be used in Australia. Present your case in an A4 handout. A desktop publishing package could be used.

▶ Star oyster on its way

Read the newspaper article and then answer the questions that follow it.

By John Merriman

SCIENTISTS are developing a new 'stud oyster' that will be used to produce a super breed of shellfish.

The SA Oyster Research Council, Oyster Growers Association and Tasmanian Oyster Research Council formed Australian Seafood Industries to develop the superior oyster.

Using selective breeding, researchers are picking the premium oysters from each crop. A superior male oyster is used to fertilise just one female, which produces hundreds of offspring.

The best of the offspring are then chosen for mating and the process is repeated in single pair-families. The first of the new and improved oysters are expected on South Australian tables by September.

The breeding program began in 1996–97 and has entered its fourth generation.

In 1999–2000 financial year SA produced 2500 tonnes of oysters worth about $9.5 million. About 5 per cent were exported overseas, but this is expected to jump to 30 per cent within five years.

The oysters are being bred at commercial hatcheries at Bicheno on Tasmania's eastern coast.

After spawning, they are grown for 12–15 weeks before being transferred to two farms in SA and three in Tasmania.

QUESTIONS

1 How are Australian Seafood Industries planning to develop a new 'stud oyster'? A diagram may be useful to help explain the process.
2 When can consumers expect to consume the new oysters?
3 When did the breeding program begin?
4 Why has the process taken so long?
5 What will be the advantages of producing the new oysters?

ONLINE SHOPPING

Case study

We've been wary, but Victorians are getting an appetite for online food.

By Michele Curtis

THERE are 4.2 million internet subscribers in Australia.

And though most of us surf with confidence, we are behind the rest of the developed world when it comes to putting our money where our mouse is. The Australian Bureau of Statistics has reported continued widespread reluctance to give our credit-card details online.

And if an internet search is anything to go by, Melburnians are more reluctant to switch to the internet for food than shoppers in Sydney or Brisbane. NSW has three times as many food-based home-delivery sites as Victoria, including at least one offering online pizza ordering.

There are three big online food retailers in Victoria, one of which is greengrocer.com.au, established five years ago in Sydney by greengrocer Barry McDonald.

Melbourne got its taste of greengrocer.com.au, part-owned by Woolworths, 18 months later.

Sydney has embraced food e-commerce faster than Melbourne. This could be because of the Harbour City's bigger inner-city population but inferior produce markets, greengrocer.com.au Melbourne manager Allison Stewart says.

'The business is still growing. We are adding new products. There are more than 4000 items to choose from, and 50 per cent of our customers reorder each week,' Stewart says.

The introduction of a delivery fee last year has coincided with unexpected growth in the business.

'The customers' basket size increased dramatically. They felt to get better value, it was best to order more,' Stewart says.

'The average spend per customer used to be about $50 and it's now risen to $120 in Melbourne.'

Jackie Steedman, from eatfresh.com.au, feels that customer service is her company's key to staying in the business so long, when so many others have failed.

'We still have customers from day one. We are constantly in touch with customers, by phone and e-mail, to ensure we're meeting their needs,' Steedman says.

'Our business has been operating in Melbourne since 1998 and just over one month in Sydney.'

QUESTIONS

1 How many Australians subscribe to the Internet?
2 Why are Australians, and in particular Victorians, not confidently using the Internet to shop?
3 Identify three online retailers in Victoria.
4 What has the introduction of a delivery fee for online shopping resulted in?
5 Why do people shop online?
6 Outline the advantages and disadvantages of shopping online.

The end of the line for the checkout chicks?

Read the article, select three of the de Bono hats and write a comment relating to the article for each of the three selected hats.

By Daniel Dasey

New technology being considered by one of the nation's top retailers could spell the death of the 'checkout chick'.

Grocery giant Woolworths is investigating cost-saving technology that would see human cash-register operators replaced with sophisticated scan-and-pay stations in its stores.

The self-checkout system would require customers to scan and bag their shopping before feeding payment into a slot or moving to a special pay station.

A Woolworths spokeswoman last week confirmed the chain's interest in the self-checkout concept.

But in a one-line statement she denied strong industry rumours that self-scanners would be tested in a Big W store in Melbourne this year.

'Big W is looking at the system but has no plans for a trial at this stage,' the spokeswoman said.

A single self-checkout station sells for about $80 000, the equivalent of about two years' wages for a human checkout operator.

Grocery industry magazine *Retail World* reports on the new technology in its current edition.

Editor-in-chief Barry Flanagan said Woolworths had briefly tested a self-checkout system in Tasmania in the 1990s, but it was abandoned because of concern about stock loss.

That system relied on customers carrying barcode scanners and scanning each item before placing it in a trolley.

Mr Flanagan said the new system being examined by Woolworths had built-in theft prevention measures.

To use the checkout a customer advances with a trolley or basket and then scans each item on a laser reader before bagging it on an adjacent weighing table.

The weight of each item is recorded by the register and at the end of scanning, items on the weight table must tally with the weight of items scanned.

In a supermarket situation shoppers would bag and obtain bar codes for items such as fruit and vegetables before going to the checkout.

Finally, shoppers obtain a total and pay at the register or advance to a pay station to settle their account. To prevent theft, cameras and a staff member may watch shoppers.

Mr Flanagan said the system was used widely in the US where it is installed in 1300 Kmart stores as well as grocery shops. But he was unsure whether Australians would warm to the technology.

Emotions, feelings, hunches
How do I feel?

Caution, judging and assessing the negatives
What are the problems?

Creativity
What new ideas can I propose?

Optimistic, judging and assessing the positives
Why is this worth doing?

Information
What information do we have or need?

Organising thinking
What have we achieved?

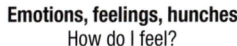

Is Internet Refrigerator cool enough to purchase?

Read the newspaper article and then answer the questions that follow it.

By Holly Hayes

If you think all a refrigerator is good for is keeping the OJ cold and serving as a metallic canvas for the family photo collection, you haven't met the newest icebox on the market.

The Internet Refrigerator, manufactured by LG Electronics, is being touted as the world's first 'multimedia' refrigerator, a 'gateway to the home'. On the flat monitor built into the right-hand door, you can use the touch-screen display to surf the Web, send and receive e-mail and watch television. Over its four hi-fi speakers, you can listen to FM radio or MP3 music files you've downloaded off the Net. Naturally, a remote can be used to control all this from your comfy kitchen table.

We presume the 26-cubic-foot appliance also keeps food cold. At a suggested retail price of $7900, we should hope so.

Oh, but it also keeps track of the food you have stored inside and will alert you when something's about to spoil or when it's time to change the water filter.

'Until now, the kitchen and home computer were kept in separate rooms in most households,' says Simon Kang, president of LG Electronics, a 44-year-old Korean company that entered the US market about three years ago.

He says the Internet Refrigerator is not meant to take the place of the home PC, but rather to 'bring multimedia technology and Internet connectivity into the kitchen—the center of home and family activity'.

The company says it has invested more than $12 million over three years to develop the Internet Refrigerator.

A research team of 55 sub-mitted a total of 75 patents both within and outside Korea.

In addition to letting you shop eBay and watch the latest episode of 'The Simpsons', the appliance is rigged to leave video messages for family members, keep track of appointments and shoot and e-mail digital pictures.

What's next? LG is about to un-veil its Internet Microwave, with an embedded modem and LCD panel that can be networked to the fridge. Users will be able to bookmark food-related sites, download recipes and auto-matically set cooking directions. And the Internet Turbo Drum Washer, available soon, will be able to download wash-cycle programs from the Internet for different kinds of fabrics, creating a customized wash for each load.

But will it be able to find that missing sock?

QUESTIONS

1 Outline the features of the Internet Refrigerator. You can visit www.lgappliances.com/demo.html to read about the features of the Internet Refrigerator in more detail. Click on the icons at the top of the page to view the various features.
2 Sketch the Internet Refrigerator and label its key features.
3 Comment on any other additional features that you would like the Internet Refrigerator to have. Add these to your sketch.
4 Discuss the advantages and disadvantages of having an Internet Refrigerator.
5 Would you purchase an Internet Refrigerator? Why or why not?
6 Who do you think would be the first type of consumers of the Internet Refrigerator? Create a profile for these consumers.
7 Outline the features of an Internet Microwave.
8 Can you think of other kitchen appliances that could be made into a multimedia item? Discuss.

Nuts about Nutrition: Assessment Task 1

This assessment task addresses the outcomes HPIP0601 and TEMA0602 from the Health and Physical Education and Technology Key Learning Areas.

▶ ## Part 1   Dietary supplements

Read the following newspaper articles and answer the questions.

Pills fad in young diets

By Tanya Taylor, Health Reporter

PARENTS are spending more than $11.5 million each year on herbal and dietary supplements for children as young as two.

Unable to make children stick to healthy diets, they are spending big dollars for quick-fix pills.

Mums and dads are also turning to century-old herbal remedies to boost their children's memory, attention spans and immune systems.

A spokesman for the Royal Australian College of General Practitioners, David Dammery, said the figure was astonishing.

'Combine working mums and dads, prepared foods (and) buying food on the run and you get to the point of, 'Better give the kids something to make up for it',' Dr Dammery said.

Child-health experts echoed this concern, saying many parents had given up trying to make their kids eat healthily.

Tweddle Child and Family Health Service education co-ordinator Rosey Cummings said parents became anxious when their children did not eat properly.

'Parents are extremely vulnerable because they just want to do what is best for their children,' she said.

'It is easy for them to just go into the supermarket and buy (the products) off the shelf without much in the way of advice and information.

'I would just hope that parents are not overdosing children on them, because we don't know what the long-term effects of these things are.'

The figure comes from research conducted by natural pharmaceutical company Black-mores.

Product manager Michele Fitzgibbon said it represented the sum spent on products for children aged two to 12.

She said the research showed multivitamins and vitamin C were the most commonly bought products.

'What mothers are saying is that sometimes it is hard to get children to eat a balanced diet,' she said.

'They are looking for nutritional supplements.'

A Newspoll study last year found 62 per cent of parents believed it was a good idea to give their children supplements.

But the chair of the Australian Medical Association's council of general practice, Mukesh Haikerwal, said dietary supplements were usually unnecessary.

He warned that some products, especially herbal remedies, could carry risks. 'There's a very common misconception that just because it's natural, it's safe, when that is patently not true,' Dr Haikerwal said.

The Therapeutic Goods Administration has urged practitioners to report any adverse reactions.

Last year it received 199 reports of suspected reactions to herbal and vitamin products, five of which involved children under 13 years.

Two involved the herb echinacea, two multivitamins, and the fifth a supplement bought online.

Family stays healthy

ALTHOUGH he thinks his daughters are healthy, Nick Livaditis believes some things are lacking in modern diets.

The Greensborough father said that while his girls ate well, he wanted to be certain they got all their vitamins and minerals. Mr Livaditis and his wife Anna have given their three daughters dietary supplements for years.

The girls, Jennifer, 11, Sophie, 9, and Ellie, 4, take multivitamins every day as a general pick-me-up and to make up for anything missing in their diet. They also take liquid echinacea at the first sign of coughs and colds to boost their immune systems.

'It's pretty much a part of their daily routine,' he said. 'We take them to the doctor too.'

Most common supplements

Multi-vitamins
Vitamin C
Echinacea
Cod liver oil
Calcium
Indian ginseng

Diet tips

Prepare meals using fresh ingredients.

If a child likes a particular meal, don't be afraid to serve it several times a week.

Do not offer sugary/fatty foods as a reward for eating healthy foods.

Be flexible. If a child prefers to eat fruits than vegetables, let them.

QUESTIONS

1   How much money do parents spend on herbal and dietary supplements for their children?
2   Why are parents spending so much money on dietary supplements?
3   What is so alarming about the information presented?

4 Identify some of the common dietary supplements purchased.

5 Why does the Australian Medical Association's council of general practice say that these dietary supplements are not necessary?

6 Why does Nick Livaditis encourage his daughters to consume dietary supplements?

7 Outline some dietary tips to encourage healthy eating, that do not include the consumption of dietary supplements.

Most vitamin pills a waste of money, study finds

David Wroe, Health Reporter

Most vitamin pills sold are a waste of money and do not protect against heart disease, cancer or a range of other illnesses, according to one of the biggest ever studies of food supplements.

Scientists from Britain's Oxford University found daily doses of vitamin C, vitamin E and beta carotene made no difference to the rate of heart disease, cancer, cataracts, bone fractures, asthma and mental decline.

These three vitamins are the most commonly-sold.

Rory Collins, co-author of the study, which followed 20 000 people over five years, said: 'Vitamin pills are a waste of time. They are safe, but they are useless.' The findings were published yesterday in *The Lancet* medical journal.

Co-author Jane Armitage said the findings showed vitamin pills

were also 'a waste of money'. 'People would be far better off spending the money on fresh fruit and vegetables,' Dr Armitage said. The three vitamins are all anti-oxidants. They are believed to mop up free radicals—harmful, unstable molecules that cause cholesterol to build up on the lining of artery walls, increasing the risk of heart disease and strokes. David Hare, senior cardiologist at the Austin and Repatriation Medical Centre, said the study showed the pill form of these vitamins did not work. 'This study has really killed off the idea that anti-oxidant vitamins reduce heart and blood vessel disease,' Professor Hare said.

Mark Wahlqvist, president of the International Union of Nutritional Sciences, said vitamin pills were no substitute for healthy eating because food included other important micronutrients such as trace elements and minerals.

'This study shows how simplistic people are about food and how they expect it can be replicated by way of pills,' he said.

He stressed the research was not a complete study of all the vitamin pills available. The study

did not consider the effectiveness of the B group vitamins, or vitamins D and K.

Val Johanson, executive director of the Complementary Healthcare Council of Australia, which represents the food supplement industry, said US research from Harvard University found last month nearly all adult Americans had inadequate diets and should be taking multivitamin supplements.

'The Harvard study shows … vitamins have a critical role to play in preventing the chronic diseases that plague Western society,' she said.

VITAMINS the conventional wisdom

VITAMIN A For healthy lungs, reproductive system, skin and linings of the digestive system, good vision and fighting infection. Found in fish, egg yolks and liver, carrots, sweet potatoes, mangoes.

FOLIC ACID (B GROUP) For healthy blood. Found in fortified breakfast cereals and bread, liver, black-eyed beans, brussels spouts, peanuts, spinach, broccoli, chickpeas.

VITAMIN B$_{12}$ For healthy blood, nervous system and growth. Found in liver, red meat, game, fish, eggs, fortified breakfast cereals, fortified yeast extract, brewers yeast.

VITAMIN B$_6$ To repair muscles and balance sex hormones. Found in wheatgerm, wheatbran, liver, cod, turkey, beef, bananas, brussels sprouts, cabbage, mangoes, avocados and potatoes.

VITAMIN C To heal wounds, fight free radicals and reduce the severity of colds. Found in berries, citrus fruit and juices, papaya, guava, peppers, dark green vegetables.

VITAMIN D For strong bones, teeth and muscles. Found In fresh tuna, sardines, salmon, cheddar cheese, eggs, margarine.

VITAMIN E For heart, circulation, skin and nervous system. Found in wheatgerm oil, sunflower oil, sunflower seeds, hazelnut, almonds, pinenuts, sweet potatoes, spinach muesli.

VITAMIN K For bloodclotting and strengthening teeth and bones. Found in broccoli, brussels sprouts, green cabbage, yoghurt, alfalfa sprouts, egg yolk, kelp.

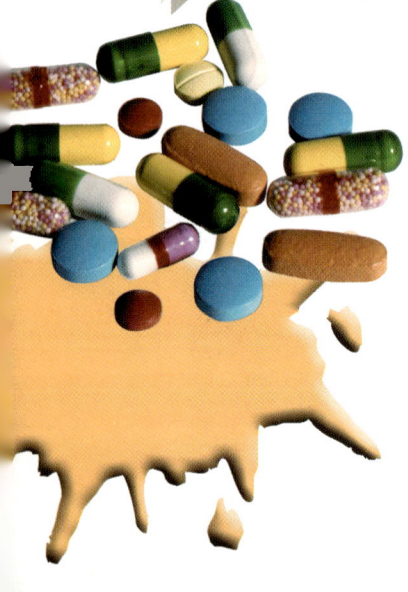

QUESTIONS

1 Outline the findings of the Oxford University study in regard to the consumption of vitamin pills.

2 Describe the study undertaken by Oxford University, including the number of people involved and the duration of the study. Make an assessment about the validity of this study.

3 What recommendations did Jane Armitage, co-author of the study, make?

4 The three vitamins studied—vitamin A, vitamin E and beta-carotene—were referred to as *antioxidants*. What does this term mean?

5 What recommendations does Mark Wahlqvist make? Why does he make these recommendations?

6 Outline the dietary supplements that were not part of this study.

7 What comments does Val Johanson, executive director of the Complementary Healthcare Council of Australia, make? Why has she made these comments?

8 Make a list of the various vitamins and outline their functions and food sources.

9 Write a 250-word report summarising your thoughts on dietary supplements.

▶ Part 2   Practical activity

Investigate which foods contain vitamin C, vitamin E and beta-carotene. Design a recipe that would include these nutrients, is quick to prepare and uses a range of complex equipment. Investigate ways in which food preparation processes can be employed to retain the vitamins in the recipe. Produce and evaluate your recipe using a Y chart as shown.

Tastes
like

Smells   Looks
like   like

Nuts about Nutrition: Assessment Task 2

This assessment task addresses the outcomes HPIP0601 and TEMA0602 from the Health and Physical Education and Technology Key Learning Areas.

▶ Dietary related diseases

Taste for change	What an Australian consumes each year							
Meat and poultry	1938–39	1968–69	1997–98	**Dairy**		1938–39	1968–69	1997–98
Beef and veal	63.6 kg	40.0 kg	38.4 kg	Milk		106.4 L	128.2 L	103.7 L
Lamb	6.8 kg	20.5 kg	10.9 kg	Cheese		2.0 kg	3.5 kg	10.9 kg
Mutton	27.2 kg	18.8 kg	5.9 kg	Butter		14.9 kg	9.8 kg	2.9 kg
Pork	3.9 kg	6.7 kg	17.8 kg	Margarine		2.2 kg	4.9 kg	6.7 kg
Chicken	N/A	8.3 kg	30.7 kg					

Beverages	1938–39	1948–49	1958–59	1968–69	1978–79	1988–89	1997–98
Tea	3.1 kg	2.3 kg	0.8 kg				
Coffee	0.3 kg	1.2 kg	2.3 kg				
Beer	53.2 L	76.8 L	99.7 L	113.5 L	133.2 L	113.1 L	95.0 L

1   Select five foods and graph the consumption rates for each over the time periods shown in the table.

2   Using the five selected foods, discuss possible reasons for their changing food consumption patterns over the years.

3   Referring to the information provided in chapter 2, outline possible dietary related diseases that could increase and possible dietary related diseases that could decrease. Provide reasons for your response.

4   For one of the dietary related diseases that you mentioned in question 3, complete a 'fishbone' as shown below. Include additional headings if required.

Fishbone

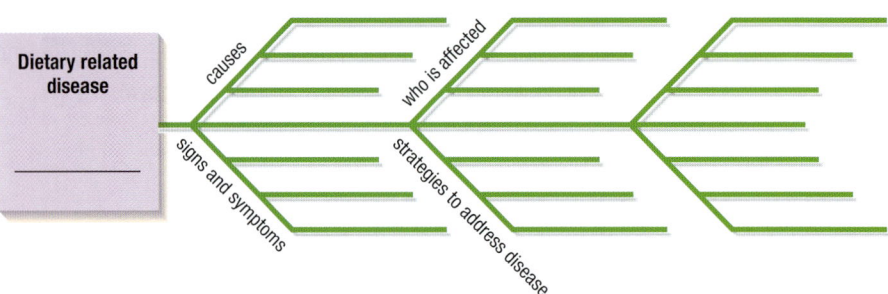

5   Design a campaign that could be employed to decrease the prevalence of the dietary related disease that you chose for question 4. Include reasons why you think this campaign would be successful.

6   Design a meal that would address some of the issues raised in question 3 by adapting a recipe. Include both the original and the redesigned recipe. Write a summary providing reasons for your alterations to the original recipe.

AROUND THE WORLD

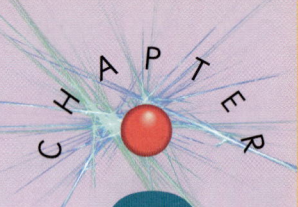

advance australia fare: Discover australian cuisine

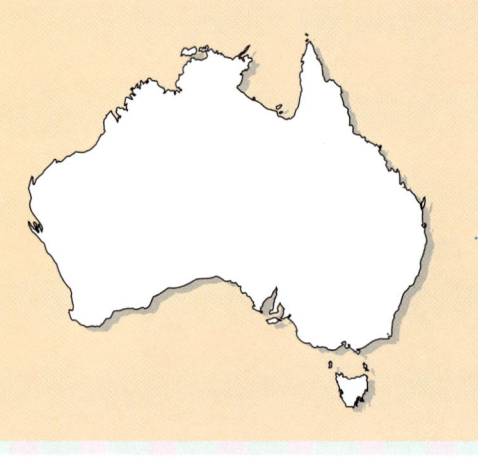

The Pacific region consists of Australia, New Zealand and the Pacific island nations. Australia, the largest island in the world, is one of seven continents and constitutes most of the Pacific region, both in size and population. The culture, history and food of each country within the region are influenced by both the indigenous people and those people who have migrated from other countries around the world.

History of Australia

For over 40 000 years, Australia's cuisine was derived from its indigenous foods, with the indigenous people leading a nomadic lifestyle as hunters and gatherers, moving from place to place and finding food as they went.

For more than two hundred years, influences from countries and cultures around the world have broadened the cuisine of Australia. Our contemporary Australian cuisine reflects this diversity of influence and embraces a wide range of new foods, tastes and products.

With European settlement came change. Some of these changes are still evident today. For example, some people still follow the British tradition of a hot Christmas meal with plum pudding and brandy custard for dessert.

e-fact

When the British settled in Australia over 200 years ago, they brought food customs and recipes with them. Some dishes still evident in Australia today are shepherd's or cottage pie, roast beef with Yorkshire pudding, Cornish pasties and apple pie.

During the gold rushes of the mid-1800s, many people came to Australia and the gold fields in Bathurst, Bendigo and Ballarat, intent on making their fortune. Most of these people came from Britain and China. After the gold rushes, many Chinese people settled in Australia and became market gardeners.

▶ **Chinese market gardens**

Read the newspaper article and then answer the questions that follow it.

Three market gardens in La Perouse, among the oldest in the State, have been listed on the State Heritage Register for their significant heritage values, particularly to Sydney's Chinese community.

Working farms with links to the life of 19th century Sydney, they are the last surviving examples of the market gardens which were originally fairly widespread in the Randwick area. For over 150 years the land has been used for market gardens, firstly by European settlers and then by Chinese.

The gardens were nominated as part of a Heritage Office program established in 1997 to encourage ethnic communities to nominate sites of heritage value in NSW. This will mean that the State Heritage Register can provide a more accurate picture of Australia's diverse heritage.

Market gardens played an important role in supplying the food needs of the growing settlements of NSW. By the end of the 19th century, these labour intensive farms had become almost synonymous with the Chinese and were part of the everyday life of many towns and cities.

The earliest farms in the La Perouse area were recorded in 1830. At first the gardens were tended by Europeans and supplied vegetables to some of the wealthiest homes in Randwick. But this changed after the gold rushes.

Karl Zhao, Chinese Heritage Officer at the NSW Heritage Office, explains:

'Chinese immigrants came to prospect for gold but soon realised not everyone could get rich from the gold fields and so started growing vegetables. At the end of the 1850s gold rushes, many Chinese came to the Sydney metropolitan area and became involved in market gardening.'

Many of the gardens in the La Perouse area survived well into the 20th century. Older residents still recall the market gardeners who worked on the farms and lived in corrugated iron huts.

The La Perouse gardens have special significance for the Chinese community.

'For many people, especially those from the Yiu Ming district of Guangdong, market gardens were their starting point in Australia. They worked hard and saved and then opened restaurants, grocery shops, their own businesses,' says Karl Zhao.

'This particular garden is important because it is so old. Many generations, many owners, many gardeners have connections with the La Perouse market gardens.'

The gardens have been managed by members of the Chinese community for over 90 years, passing from one generation to another without a break. The still working gardens have maintained features of a traditional market garden and even today, most of the work is done by manual labour with simple tools. Nowhere else so close to the modern, busy centre of Sydney is land still worked this way.

Gordan Ha's family have been involved with the La Perouse market gardens for over 40 years.

'My father came from overseas and worked on this farm with his cousin. He worked and studied English at the same time,' said Mr Ha.

The market gardens continue to be a part of Sydney life. In fact, with the increasing number of Asian immigrants over the last 20 years, long forgotten Chinese vegetables have been reintroduced to the Australian diet. 'When my Dad started on the farm 40 years ago, they grew mostly Australian vegetables such as celery,' says Gordan Ha. 'Now with the demand for new vegetables, we are growing Chinese vegetables like Bok Choy, Cho Sum and Chinese broccoli.'

e-Fact

ANZAC is an abbreviation for Australian and New Zealand Army Corps. During the First World War, the Anzac biscuit was developed as a long-lasting, nutritional biscuit to send to the Australian soldiers fighting in the war. Based on a Scottish recipe, these biscuits, originally known as soldier's biscuits, were renamed Anzac biscuits after the landing at Gallipoli.

QUESTIONS

1   Why have the market gardens at La Perouse been heritage listed?
2   How did the Chinese people come to manage the gardens?
3   Why do the market gardens at La Perouse have special significance for the Chinese community?
4   What impact have these gardens had on Australian cuisine?
5   How is most of the work in the gardens carried out?

After the Second World War, the government policy was to increase population with a subsidised scheme of migration. It was during this time that many people migrated to Australia from Britain, Italy and Greece. This migration brought with it an influence of the culture, customs and food patterns of these countries. The introduction of spaghetti bolognaise and souvlaki, for example, can be attributed to influences from Italy and Greece.

During the 1970s, migration from Asian countries such as Vietnam and Cambodia increased and this also had a significant impact on the foods and cuisines eaten in Australia. Today in Australia, we have migrants from all parts of the world, including the Middle East, Africa and China, to name a few. Globalisation has made us even more aware of the customs and food patterns of other countries and we are increasingly seeing the result of this in our food stores and markets. As you will read in chapter 7, we have seen an increase in the influence of Thai cuisine, with ingredients such as curry pastes, vermicelli and lemon grass becoming readily available in Australia.

QUESTIONS

1   Can you think of any more foods from other countries that have been introduced recently into Australian cuisine?
2   Choose five meals that you have eaten over the past week.
   a   Which, if any, of these dishes would you associate with other cuisines?
   b   List all of the ingredients included in each meal.
   c   Identify the cuisines with which we would most associate those ingredients. How many cuisines are represented?
   d   Write a summary of approximately 100 words or construct a concept map to illustrate the impact of other cuisines on your eating patterns.

Australian food today

Walk through the supermarket, the butcher's, the greengrocer's or the local produce markets and you will gain a sense of the types of foods that consumers in your part of Australia have available to them today. Alternatively, visit www.colesonline.com.au and do a 'virtual' shop. Look at the range of fresh meats, dairy products, fruits, vegetables, frozen products and home meal replacements (see page 178) available.

Next time you go to your local shopping centre, look at the types of restaurants, takeaway and fast-food establishments around. Consider how you would describe Australian cuisine in your town or city.

▶ Food in Australia

Read the fact sheet and then answer the questions that follow it.

It's no secret these days, but over the past decade Australia has become a culinary destination par excellence. Australians themselves have known it for years, and now the rest of the world is discovering the tastes of Australia.

'Australians have one of the most extraordinary assortments of basic ingredients of high quality anywhere in the world, and at exceptionally modest prices,' according to Barbara Kafka, one of America's most influential food writers.

'I've never had such tastes, such subtleties, such delights, such form, such colour,' wrote celebrity chef Robert Carrier when he visited Australia to judge the Gourmet Traveller Restaurant of the Year.

Glance in the window of one of the gourmet food stores scattered throughout Australia's capital cities and you'll be surprised. There's a huge variety available in every state—some examples are chevre from Queensland, prosciutto from Western Australia, brie and cold-pressed olive oil from South Australia, balsamic vinegars and snails from Victoria, milk-fed lamb from New South Wales, smoked salmon from Tasmania, mud crabs from the Northern Territory. It is only fitting that what Australia eats now comes from a collage of culinary influences that uses a splash of olive oil with one hand while tossing in a handful of chopped chillies with the other.

There are many reasons for Australia's culinary success, including a diversity of micro-climates that allows it to produce mangoes as well as strawberries, custard apples, citrus fruits and coffee beans. Its lush coastal pastures are well suited to farm-house cheeses, its native forests produce honeys of exceptional fragrance and flavour and its vast coastline yields succulent oysters, crayfish and tuna of tremendous delicacy.

Australian chefs have been quick to make the most of this natural bounty, experimenting with ingredients and drawing their inspiration from the cultural cross-currents of modern Australia. Over the past 30 years, Australia has become one of the most ethnically diverse nations on earth, and when the present generation of chefs took over the restaurant kitchens, their cultural heritage seasoned their food. So successful have they become that Australia is now exporting its chefs to the wider world. Recently, two Australian chefs were awarded Michelin stars—the ultimate accolade of the food world—at the London restaurants where they are carving out exalted reputations.

QUESTIONS

1 Read the 'Food in Australia' fact sheet, published on the official website for the Australian Tourism Commission. Do you think this accurately reflects our Australian cuisine?

2 Design and produce a tourism brochure for visitors to Australia. Include information about cuisine, lifestyle, sights to see, weather and a category of your own choice.

Focus on traditional Aboriginal foods

Early European settlers in Australia struggled to develop a healthy existence, as many of the foods, crops and animals brought with them from England either did not survive the journey or did not suit the conditions and climate of the new land. Had they been more aware of traditional Australian foods as discovered by the Aboriginal people over thousands of years, they may not have struggled so much in these early days. Today, Australians are more aware of traditional Aboriginal foods, also referred to by some people as bush foods.

Some traditional Aboriginal plant foods are listed in the table below.

Kakadu plum

Food	Description	Food	Description
Kakadu plum	A small green plum with a sharp taste, high in vitamin C	Bunya nut	The nut from the native Bunya pine tree
Riberry	A variety of lilly-pilly with a clove taste	Kurrajong flour	Flour produced from the seeds of the Kurrajong tree
Quandong	The most well-known outback fruit, also known as a wild desert peach	Warrigal green	A groundcover plant, like spinach
Bush tomato	The berries from a desert shrub related to the tomato family	Wattle seed	Dry roasted seeds from different varieties of Acacia trees

bunya nut

wattle seed

bush tomato

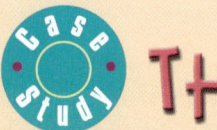

THE RED OCHRE GRILL

The Red Ochre Grill, situated in far north Queensland at Cairns, is a unique restaurant offering modern Australian cuisine.

The restaurant is decorated with the colours of the outback and Aboriginal artwork and offers a distinctive menu that utilises Australian native fruits, berries, game meat and seafood. The menu is changed regularly to reflect the seasonal nature of many of the ingredients and to maximise the flavour possibilities of the native produce. The Red Ochre Grill has been the recipient of numerous tourism and restaurant awards.

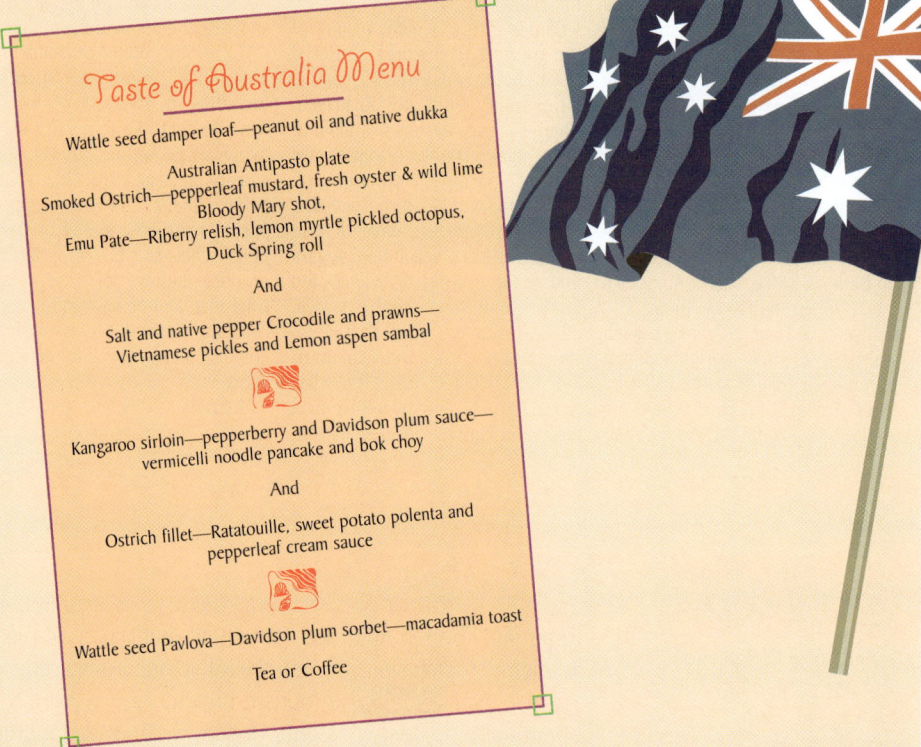

Taste of Australia Menu

Wattle seed damper loaf—peanut oil and native dukka

Australian Antipasto plate
Smoked Ostrich—pepperleaf mustard, fresh oyster & wild lime Bloody Mary shot,
Emu Pate—Riberry relish, lemon myrtle pickled octopus, Duck Spring roll

And

Salt and native pepper Crocodile and prawns—Vietnamese pickles and Lemon aspen sambal

Kangaroo sirloin—pepperberry and Davidson plum sauce—vermicelli noodle pancake and bok choy

And

Ostrich fillet—Ratatouille, sweet potato polenta and pepperleaf cream sauce

Wattle seed Pavlova—Davidson plum sorbet—macadamia toast

Tea or Coffee

QUESTIONS

Visit www.redochregrill.com.au and answer the following questions.

1 Why do you think the restaurant is named the Red Ochre Grill?
2 If you were choosing a meal from the 'Taste of Australia' menu, what would you choose and why?
3 List the names of the native Australian foods listed on the menu that you have tasted. How many in total have you tasted compared to others in your class?
4 Draw a Venn diagram to illustrate the native Australian foods tasted by you and other class members.

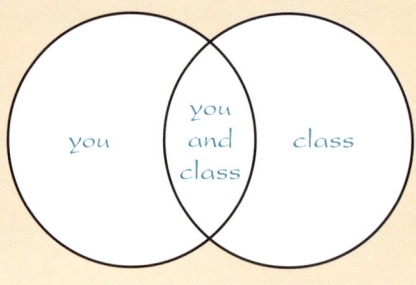

you | you and class | class

▶ Let's remember

1 How did early indigenous Australians find their food?
2 What does contemporary Australian cuisine reflect today?
3 As a result of the gold rushes, what kinds of foods were introduced to Australia?
4 Outline the impact of migration on food patterns in Australia.
5 Identify and describe three traditional Aboriginal foods.

▶ Let's investigate

1 You have been selected to enter an international essay competition. A panel of judges who have never been to Australia will judge the essay. The topic is 'Australian cuisine—the past, the present and the future'. Your essay must be between 400 and 500 words.

2 Imagine you have a friend who lives overseas and is planning to visit you. This will be your friend's first trip to Australia and he or she is very interested in finding out about Australian cuisine. Search the Internet to investigate the information available on Australian cuisine. How accurately do you think Australia and Australian cuisine are depicted on the websites that you have searched? List suitable web links to send to your friend and write an email to him or her, outlining the information that you have found.

@-Australian cuisine

www.nutritionaustralia.org./Food_Facts/Fact_Sheets/Bush_foods.pdf

1 What was Australia's first commercially produced native food?
2 Identify five native fruits.
3 What native foods can be used to flavour breads, biscuits and scones?

www.austmus.gov.au/teachers_resources/background/bush_food.htm

1 Describe the three factors on which indigenous people are dependent to obtain their traditional food.
2 Explain how indigenous men, women and children are involved in obtaining food.
3 Explain three different processing methods used with traditional Australian foods.

www.marimari.com/content/australia/food/main.html

This website contains interesting information about Australian cuisine, categorised into Australian food, bush tucker, Asian food and Australians' favourite foods.

1 Write a description of each category of food.
2 Do you agree with the website's categorisation of Australian cuisine? Explain your answer.
3 Select three de Bono hats and comment on the different types of cuisine.

WEBEXTRAS

Emotions, feelings, hunches	Caution, judging and assessing the negatives	Creativity	Optimistic, judging and assessing the positives	Information	Organising thinking
How do I feel?	What are the problems?	What new ideas can I propose?	Why is this worth doing?	What information do we have or need?	What have we achieved?

Puzzled

Go bush

Unscramble the words below to find the names of some traditional Aboriginal foods, then use the numbers to decipher the coded sentence.

NUYBA ☐☐☐☐☐
47 9 23 44

WALTET SEDE ☐☐☐☐☐☐ ☐☐☐☐
26 24 35 19 25 8 1

GAUNOQND ☐☐☐☐☐☐☐☐
12 32 30 16 38 31 50 17

LIYLL PLLYI ☐☐☐☐☐ ☐☐☐☐☐
15 11

RIYREBR ☐☐☐☐☐☐☐
33 39 6 18

RAOKJRUNG ☐☐☐☐☐☐☐☐☐
            13 36 48 37   34 10 49

LOESARL ☐☐☐☐☐☐☐
        42 3   29 45 46

DIARATMN ☐☐☐☐☐☐☐☐
      7 51   2 27 20

MOLNE MYTREL ☐☐☐☐☐   ☐☐☐☐☐☐
        22 4 43   40 52 14

WDIL LEIM ☐☐☐☐   ☐☐☐☐
      41   28   21   5

☐☐ C ☐ V ☐☐   ☐ H ☐   ☐☐☐☐☐☐
1 2 3   4   5 6   7   8   9 10 11 12 13 14

☐☐☐☐☐☐☐☐☐☐☐   ☐☐☐   F ☐☐ V ☐☐☐☐
15 16 17 18 19 20 21 22 23 24 25   26 27 28   29 30   31 32 33 3

☐ F ☐   ☐☐☐☐☐☐☐☐☐☐☐
34   35 36 37 38 39 40 41 42 43 44 45

☐☐☐☐☐☐☐☐☐   F ☐☐☐☐.
46 47 31 48 15 49 39 50 51 52   4 34 1 3

LET'S PRODUCE

Macadamia Anzac biscuits   (makes 24)

Method

1 Combine flour, oats, coconut, macadamia nuts and sugar.
2 Add bicarbonate of soda to golden syrup and water. When frothy, add melted butter.
3 Combine dry ingredients with butter mixture. Mix well.
4 Place spoonfuls of mixture onto baking tray lined with baking paper.
5 Bake at 170°C for fifteen minutes, or until biscuits are flattened and brown.

Ingredients

$\frac{3}{4}$ cup plain flour
$\frac{3}{4}$ cup cup rolled oats
$\frac{1}{2}$ cup coconut
$\frac{1}{3}$ cup macadamia nuts, chopped
$\frac{1}{4}$ cup sugar
1 teaspoon bicarbonate of soda
2 tablespoons golden syrup
2 tablespoons water
90 grams butter

e-HINT

Make sure that the bowl you use for step 2 is large enough for the bicarbonate of soda not to froth over the top.

e-HINT

Anzac biscuits will be soft when first removed from the oven and will harden once cooled.

Honey soy lamb (serves 2)

Ingredients
1 teaspoon honey
1 teaspoon soy sauce
1 teaspoon oil
1 clove garlic, crushed
2 racks lamb
1 tablespoon coriander, chopped

Method

1 Combine honey, soy sauce, oil and garlic.
2 Brush over lamb and marinate for thirty minutes.
3 Place lamb in baking tray and cook for approximately twenty-five minutes.
4 Serve with chopped coriander and orange roasted vegetables.

QUESTIONS

1 What is the difference between the terms *marinade* and *marinate*?
2 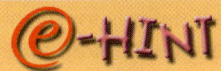 other herbs that you could substitute for coriander.

e-HINT

Before adding the honey to the marinade mix, soften slightly in the microwave. This will make it easier to brush the marinade over the lamb.

e-HINT

Covering the ends of the rack of lamb bones with foil during cooking stops them from getting burnt.

Orange roasted vegetables (serves 2)

Ingredients
$\frac{1}{2}$ sweet potato
1 potato
1 zucchini
$\frac{1}{2}$ small carrot
$\frac{1}{2}$ parsnip
2 tablespoons olive oil
1 tablespoon orange juice
sea salt and black pepper, to taste

Method

1 Peel and cut sweet potato, potato, zucchini, carrot and parsnip into large chunks.
2 Toss in bowl with olive oil and orange juice.
3 Place on baking tray lined with baking paper.
4 Sprinkle with a little sea salt and pepper.
5 Bake for forty-five minutes, or until vegetables are cooked and brown on outside.

QUESTIONS

1  your own roasted vegetables recipe. Which vegetables would you choose? Produce and evaluate this recipe ☺ ☺ ☹.
2 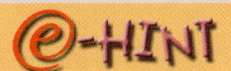 other herbs or flavourings that could be used in the recipe.

ORIENT EXPRESS: DISCOVER ASIAN CUISINE

Asia is the world's largest continent, both in land mass and population. It includes China and India, the two countries with the highest populations in the world. Australia is closest to the countries found in South-East Asia, such as Indonesia, Malaysia, Thailand and Hong Kong, and these countries are popular travel destinations for Australians. In this chapter, we will focus on the cuisines of India and Thailand and the influences that they have had on our eating patterns in Australia.

QUESTIONS

1 Using the link www.geography.about.com/library/maps/blasia.htm, you can access a free map of Asia. Download this map and label the countries of Asia.
2 How many countries in total make up Asia?
3 How many of these countries have you heard of?

e-FACT

Did you know that Asia covers more than one-third of the Earth's land mass?

WEBEXTRAS

www.lizardpoint.com/fun/geoquiz/asiaquiz.html
Test your knowledge of Asian countries by using your mouse to click on the country.

www.cia.gov/cia/ciakids/geography/asia.html
Another fun website with quizzes about regions of the world, including Asia.

www.triviaplaza.com/index.html
Test your geographical knowledge of countries at this website.

Discover Indian cuisine

India is a densely populated country, with a population of over one billion people. Being an ancient civilisation and a large country with twenty-five states, India has a very diverse culture and cuisine. India has more than fifteen official languages and more than 1500 different dialects. There are a number of main religions, although the predominant religion is Hinduism. Many Hindus are vegetarians.

Indian food can be broadly divided into vegetarian and non-vegetarian and is characterised by the use of aromatic spices. Knowing how to blend the spices is considered to be a key skill in preparing a good Indian meal. Spices are ground and blended using a mortar and pestle.

In India, the word *garam* means 'warm' or 'hot', while *masala* means 'spice'. Indian people will usually make their own garam masala, with a blend of as many as twelve spices. In other countries, a spice mix called garam masala is available.

Garam masala is used as the basis for a curry, which is probably the most common dish we associate with India. Although we associate curries with India, the word *curry* is actually an English word, most likely derived from the Indian term *kari*. It is traditional to serve curries with condiments, such as chutneys (for example, mango chutney), and also raita, a dish using yoghurt as its base. Raita helps to cool the palate

fennel

coriander seeds

mustard seeds

fenugreek

clove

turmeric

cardamom

chilli

curry leaf

when eaten with a hot curry. Unlike the chutneys we can purchase in jars at the supermarket, Indian chutneys are prepared with fresh ingredients and are an important accompaniment to an Indian meal.

Indian food is also sometimes classified as northern Indian food and southern Indian food. Wheat is a staple in the north; therefore breads such as roti or paratha are usually served with most meals. In southern regions, rice is a staple and is served as an accompaniment to curry dishes.

Indian food can be classified according to regions, some of which are Punjab, Bombay and Kashmir. Tandoori cooking, for example, is a speciality in the northern regions of Punjab and Kashmir, while Bombay cuisine includes pakoras and samosas. A tandoori oven is made from clay and brick, and the food is cooked over hot coals. Indian bread, such as naan, is slapped onto the sides of the oven to be baked.

▶ Let's remember

1   Why is Indian cuisine so diverse?
2   Explain the different ways that Indian cuisine can be categorised.
3   From where does the word *curry* originate?
4   What type of accompaniments would you serve with a curry?
5   Describe a tandoori oven and how you would cook using one.

▶ Let's investigate

1   Investigate the spices that are used to make garam masala. Find three garam masala recipes on the Internet. How do they differ? Look at a container of garam masala in the supermarket and compare the ingredients listed with those in the recipes that you found.

e-fact

Hindus believe that cows are sacred.

2   Investigate the caste system in India and food customs related to the different castes. Write your comments using each of the de Bono thinking hats.

Emotions, feelings, hunches	Caution, judging and assessing the negatives	Creativity	Optimistic, judging and assessing the positives	Information	Organising thinking
How do I feel?	What are the problems?	What new ideas can I propose?	Why is this worth doing?	What information do we have or need?	What have we achieved?

3 Using the link www.sharwoods.com/india/culture/default.htm, `investigate` the ingredients unique to each region. Choose two regions and identify a recipe from each region. (Another good link for information about regional Indian cooking is www.welcometoindia.com/home.asp. Under the heading 'Indian cuisine' you will find links to nine different regions.)

4 `Design` your own Indian curry. Choose three accompaniments for your curry. `Produce` and `evaluate` it ☺ ☺ ☹.

5 Using the links www.indianfoodsco.com/Classes/SouthIndian.htm and www.indianfoodsco.com/Classes/NorthIndian.htm, `investigate` the differences between northern Indian cuisine and southern Indian cuisine.

▶ **@-Indian cuisine**

www.cuisinecuisine.com

1 Click on 'Glossary of Indian food terms'.
   a Explain the differences between the following types of bread: naan, chapati, roti, kulcha, paratha and puris.
   b How would you describe basmati rice?
   c Find three desserts, then name and describe them.
   d What is a tandoor and how is it used?
2 Click on 'Indian kitchenware'. What is a masala dabba and what would you find inside it?
3 Click on 'Indian herbs, spices and ingredients'.
   a How would you use a mortar and pestle? Draw a diagram to illustrate what these things look like.
   b How would you store spices and how long would they normally last?
   c What is the literal meaning of the term *garam masala* and, specifically, what does it contain?

▶ **Puzzled**

Hot and spicy

Find each of the words from the box in the puzzle.

```
J G H E E M I A D A A C L S Z
O N N S I W D T T H L G A N E
G U A N O R F F A S A M O S A
H I U U A J O F Z P S L W C T
B Q Q O R K N O O L A D N I V
G I Q P A P P A D A M H K R G
J T E K I T O R G N M K C E T
N Q Z F T N N O S O A U U M B
O A T N A X M K M E R T M R N
Z X E A U O K A N R A O I U Z
B X N P O L D P Y T G K N T L
J P C P D R S X D V T M Q C B
S W V U A V U O Q P R O Q U T
T E A C Q L J V L O P T B X L
A X P E G N J G F I C W W W E
```

cardamom	pappadam
chapati	raita
cumin	rogan josh
curry	roti
dhal	saffron
garam masala	samosa
ghee	tandoori
kofta	tikka
naan	turmeric
pakora	vindaloo

LET'S PRODUCE

Ingredients

1 tablespoon peanut oil
1 teaspoon coriander, ground
1 teaspoon cumin, ground
1 tablespoon garam masala
1 teaspoon chilli powder
$\frac{1}{2}$ teaspoon garlic
salt, to taste
1 tablespoon water
6 chicken drumsticks

Ingredients

1 cup lentils
30 grams ghee
1 small onion, chopped
$\frac{1}{4}$ teaspoon chilli powder
$\frac{1}{4}$ teaspoon black pepper
$\frac{1}{4}$ teaspoon turmeric
$\frac{1}{2}$ teaspoon cumin
$\frac{1}{2}$ teaspoon coriander, ground
1 cup cauliflower, cut into florets
1 tablespoon lemon juice
275 millilitres chicken stock
1 tablespoon desiccated coconut
1 tablespoon flour
$\frac{1}{3}$ cup cashews

Indian masala chicken

(serves 4)

Method

1   Heat oil slightly. Remove from heat.
2   Blend all spices together.
3   Add spices to oil and then add water.
4   Blend spices and oil mixture together well.
5   Cut slits into chicken and baste with spice mixture. Place into refrigerator and let stand for as long as possible.
6   Preheat griller. Cook drumsticks for fifteen minutes, or until cooked, turning once.
7   Serve with jasmine rice.

Cauliflower lentils

(serves 2)

Method

1   Soak lentils for ten minutes. Drain.
2   Heat ghee in frypan. Add onion and cook until softened. Add chilli powder, pepper, turmeric, cumin and coriander. Stir until combined.
3   Add lentils and coat in spices.
4   Add cauliflower, lemon juice, chicken stock and coconut.
5   Bring to boil and simmer for twenty minutes.
6   Add blended flour. Stir into mixture until mixture has thickened.
7   Add cashew nuts.
8   Serve with jasmine rice.

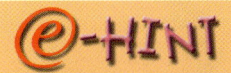

e-HINT

To blend flour, mix with a small amount of water or stock until a smooth paste forms.

Discover Thai cuisine

Thailand is situated in South-East Asia and is bordered by Laos, Cambodia, Myanmar and Malaysia.

The population of Thailand is more than 60 million, with more than 6 million people living in the capital, Bangkok. The predominant religion is Buddhism and the official language is Thai. The influence of Buddhism in Thailand has resulted in a cuisine that uses meat in small amounts. The cuisine of China has also influenced Thai cuisine, with wok cooking becoming commonplace. Whereas Chinese cooking utilises sauces such as soy and black bean thickened with cornflour, Thai cooking uses coconut milk or cream and herbs such as coriander and basil.

Being in the tropics, Thailand has a wide selection of tropical fruits available. These include fruits with which we are familiar in Australia, such as bananas, pineapples and watermelons, and other less common fruits, such as durian, mangosteen and pomelo.

banana

coconut

cantaloupe

lychee

custard apple

papaya

pineapple

jackfruit

mangosteen

rambutan

guava

durian

pomelo

watermelon

QUESTIONS

Using the following three websites, write a description for each of the fruits shown on page 108.
1 www.phuket-plaza.com/thaifruit.html
2 www.thailandontour.com/thaifruit/fruit2.shtml
3 www.welcome-to.chiangmai-chiangrai.com/fruit-tfruit.htm

Thai meals use rice or noodles as a base. Meat is usually lean and used in small amounts, with tofu being used as an alternative to meat. Thailand has many rivers and coastal areas, so it is not surprising that many Thai dishes include fish.

Unlike Indian curries, which use ghee and dried spices, Thai curries use coconut milk and fresh herbs, such as lemon grass and galangal.

lemon grass

galangal

The most common types of Thai curries are either green or red, depending on the type of chilli pepper used. In supermarkets, you can find jars of red curry paste and green curry paste; however, an authentic Thai curry will use a curry paste prepared from fresh ingredients.

Myanmar used to be known as Burma.

Thailand used to be known as Siam.

Most supermarkets today have a special section devoted to Asian food products.

Did you know that Thailand is the only country in South-East Asia that was never colonised?

Case Study

Bahn Thai

Read the restaurant review and then answer the questions that follow it.

Bahn Thai

46 St Kilda Rd, St Kilda
Tel 51 6630
Open: Wednesday–Sunday for
lunch and dinner
Parking: on street
B.Y.O.
Cards: American Express,
Bankcard, Diners Club
Seats: 50
Music: Taped
Not airconditioned
Price for two: About $15–20

Thai food is relatively new to Melbourne but its pungent combinations (based on chillies, lemon grass, coriander and a herb, generally known in this country as Vietnamese mint) deserve a wider audience.

The Bahn Thai is a small, unpretentious establishment that serves an interesting selection of regional food, with a couple of Indonesian specialities—such as satay—thrown in for good measure. Interesting offerings include kuey teow nan (rice noodles in soup), a mild curry called gang keow warn and pra neau (beef served with lemon, chilli and mint leaves). New dishes are being added to the menu as the ingredients become available here, although the owner admits there are problems in obtaining fresh coriander all year round. Don't forget to ask for a dish of nuoc cham (a combination of fish sauce and chilli) to spice up your food; the flavour is somewhat unusual but Thai food shouldn't really be eaten without this relish.

In summary: well worth a visit for unusual food.

QUESTIONS

Thai cooking has grown in popularity in Australia since this review written in 1980.

1   The review considered Thai food to be unusual. Do you agree or disagree with this? Explain your answer.
2   How do you think things have changed in Australia in relation to Thai food?
3   Have you ever been to a Thai restaurant or had takeaway from a Thai restaurant? Did you like the food? Why or why not?
4   How has Thai food influenced our eating patterns in Australia? How has it influenced what you eat at home?
5   Investigate a local Thai restaurant or search on the Internet to obtain a menu. Write a review of this restaurant (300–400 words) for your local newspaper.

Thai Terrace

CURRIES

60. Green Curry $14.90 / Prawns $17.90
A classic green curry with your choice of tender beef, chicken or king prawns, blended with coconut milk, fresh vegetables & sweet basil leaves

61. Red Curry $14.90 / Prawns $17.90
A spicy red curry with your choice of tender beef, chicken or king prawns, blended with coconut milk, fresh vegetables & sweet basil leaves

62. Yellow Curry $14.90
A delightful, mild chicken curry, cooked with onions & potatoes.

63. Mussaman $14.90
Tender pieces of beef, cooked with potatoes, peanuts & coconut milk

64. Lamb Curry $14.90
A spicy-sweet curry of tender lamb fillets, bamboo shoots & coconut milk

65. Jungle Curry $14.90
A non-coconut based curry, with your choice of beef or chicken, cooked in a flavoursome stock with fresh vegetables & herbs

Vegetarian

67. Gaeng Dang Pag $10.90
Fresh vegetables cooked with a red curry paste & coconut milk

68. Gaeng Keow Pag $10.90
Fresh vegetables cooked with a green curry paste & coconut milk

• All prices inclusive of G.S.T.
• Corkage $2 per person (Free with Set Menus)
• A 10% surcharge applies on public holidays

NOODLES & RICE

100. Pad Woong Sen $11.90
Fried glass noodles with pork fillet, tomatoes, mushrooms, onions, snow peas & spring onions.

101. Pad Thai $12.90
A popular noodle dish, with chicken, egg, green onions, ground peanuts & bean sprouts.

102. Pad See-Iw $11.90
Stir-fried noodles with your choice of either beef, pork or chicken served with fresh broccoli.

103. Chilli Noodles $11.90
Pan-fried rice noodles with chicken, shrimp, curry paste, onions, capsicums, tomatoes & mint leaves, served with fresh lettuce.

104. Chilli Pepper Fried Rice $11.90
Steamed rice with fresh red chilli, chicken, onions & mint leaves

105. Green Curry Fried Rice $11.90
Your choice of chicken or beef with fried rice, cooked with a green curry paste, fresh vegetables & sweet basil leaves.

106. Combination Fried Rice $12.90
Combination of prawn, chicken, pork, fresh vegetables & egg

Vegetarian

109. Vegetarian Fried Rice $10.90
Steamed rice cooked with fresh eggs, onions & vegetables.

110. Vegetarian Pad Thai $10.90
Glass noodles cooked with fresh eggs, bean sprouts, ground peanuts & spring onions

111. Vegetarian Chilli Noodles $10.90
Glass noodles cooked with onions, carrots, capsicum, tomatoes, basil leaves & chilli paste

115. Steamed Rice Per person $2.00
116. Coconut Rice Per person $3.00

▶ **Let's remember**

1   How has Buddhism affected Thai cuisine?
2   Explain how Chinese cuisine has influenced Thai cooking.
3   Identify three tropical Thai fruits that are not common in Australia.
4   Why is fish widely used in Thai cuisine?
5   What is the difference between an Indian curry and a Thai curry?

Let's investigate

1 Investigate tofu. What is it? How is it made? Identify three Thai dishes that use tofu. Write comments using the white, yellow and blue de Bono hats.

Emotions, feelings, hunches	Caution, judging and assessing the negatives	Creativity	Optimistic, judging and assessing the positives	Information	Organising thinking
How do I feel?	What are the problems?	What new ideas can I propose?	Why is this worth doing?	What information do we have or need?	What have we achieved?

WEBExTRaS

www.midcoast.com.au/~ttc/thailand.html
This website contains suggested curriculum activities and links to information about Thailand, Bangkok, Thai food, festivals, religion and language. You will also find some fun quizzes here.

www.tat.or.th/food/index.htm
Here you will find information about preparing or ordering and eating Thai food. You can also investigate Thai desserts, fruits and herbs.

www.butterflylearning.com/chopsticks/13thaimarket.htm
This website has some fabulous photos of food and markets in Thailand.

www.importfood.com/recipes.html
Search this website and you will find 125 Thai recipes.

2 Use these links on the *Choice* magazine website:
www.aca.com.au/articles/a101595p1.htm
www.aca.com.au/articles/a101269p1.htm
  a Investigate the difference between coconut cream and coconut milk.
  b Investigate the fat content of coconut cream or coconut milk. Evaluate the nutrient information and write a paragraph justifying your recommended brand ☺ ☺ ☹.
  c Investigate the fat content of coconut milk powder compared to coconut milk in a can.

3 Investigate lemon grass and draw a diagram of it. How is lemon grass prepared and how would you use it?

4 Investigate the different ways in which lemon grass can be purchased. How much does it cost to buy?

5 Design a low-fat Thai curry incorporating tofu, coriander and fish sauce. Give your curry a name. Produce and evaluate it ☺ ☺ ☹.

6 Investigate Thai curries by using the link www.templeofthai.com/thai_curry/thai_curry.html. How you would make a red curry paste from scratch? Design your own curry using your own red curry paste. Produce and evaluate it ☺ ☺ ☹.

7 Undertake a KWL and investigate two things you:
  a **k**now about Thai cuisine
  b **w**ant to know about Thai cuisine
  c **l**earnt about Thai cuisine

8 Draw a Venn diagram to illustrate non-Thai food that you eat, Thai food that you eat and Thai food that you do not eat.

e-Thai cuisine

www.thaicookingcenter.com

WEBExTRaS

www.tourismthailand.org
Follow the link to Thai cuisine and you will find information about Thai meals and ordering Thai food.

1 Click on 'Equipment in kitchen'.
  a What are the basic utensils required for Thai cooking?
  b Explain how Thai food is steamed using the traditional method.

2 Click on 'Rice and noodles'.
  a Explain the different types of rice.
  b What types of rice are preferred in the different Asian countries?
  c What type of noodle is used in Pad Thai dishes?
  d When would you use vermicelli?
  e Before cooking, what should you do with dried noodles?

3 Click on 'Seasoning and sauces'.
  a Identify the ingredients that you would find in chilli sauce.
  b What is palm sugar? Name a substitute for palm sugar.
  c What would you use oyster sauce for?

▶ Puzzled

Thai match

Match a word in the first column with a word in the second column to form the name of a food or ingredient associated with Thailand.

1	chilli	**a**	grass
2	pad	**b**	sugar
3	jasmine	**c**	sauce
4	coconut	**d**	paste
5	lemon	**e**	rice
6	fish	**f**	pepper
7	palm	**g**	lime
8	kaffir	**h**	Thai
9	stir	**i**	milk
10	curry	**j**	fry

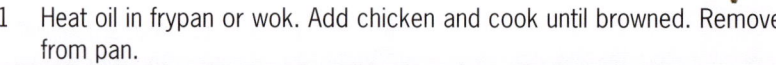

e-fact

Vermicelli is made from mung bean curd and is also known as bean thread noodles, glass noodles or cellophane noodles.

LET'S PRODUCE

Green Thai curry (serves 2)

Method

1 Heat oil in frypan or wok. Add chicken and cook until browned. Remove from pan.
2 Add onion and curry paste. Cook for two to three minutes.
3 Add coconut milk and water. Bring to boil and then simmer.
4 Add eggplant, sweet potato and browned chicken.
5 Add kaffir lime leaves, fish sauce, lime juice and brown sugar.
6 Simmer for twenty minutes. Add snow peas.
7 Simmer for a further ten minutes, or until vegetables are tender.
8 Serve with steamed jasmine rice and garnish with coriander leaves.

Variations

1 Produce a red curry by using red curry paste instead of green curry paste.
2 Select your own choice of vegetables.
3 Produce a curry with beef, pork or seafood instead of chicken.
4 Design a vegetarian green curry without meat or seafood.
5 Investigate the ingredients used to make a curry paste and design a curry paste recipe.

Ingredients

2 teaspoons peanut oil
250 grams chicken fillet
1 onion, chopped
1 tablespoon green curry paste
150 millilitres coconut milk
1 cup water
½ eggplant, diced
1 small sweet potato
3 kaffir lime leaves
1 tablespoon fish sauce
1 tablespoon lime juice
1 teaspoon brown sugar
8 snow peas
1 tablespoon fresh coriander, chopped

QUESTION

Evaluate this recipe using a Y-chart.

Tastes like
Smells like
Looks like

Ingredients

1 lime
400 grams lychees (can)
½ cup water
⅓ cup caster sugar

Lychee and lime sorbet (serves 2)

Method

1 Grate rind and squeeze juice of lime.
2 Drain lychees. Place in processor with rind and juice of lime and blend until smooth.
3 Add water and sugar and blend until smooth.
4 Pour into flat dish and chill in freezer until set.
5 Serve in scoops, garnished with mint and a lime slice.

e-fact

Another name for coriander is cilantro.

EUROPEAN VACATION: DISCOVER EUROPEAN CUISINE

Europe consists of many countries and smaller regions, from Scandinavian countries, such as Denmark, Sweden and Norway in the north, to the British Isles, including Northern Ireland, England, Ireland, Scotland and Wales, to the Eastern and Balkan countries, such as Lithuania, Poland and the Ukraine, and all of the other smaller countries in mainland Europe, including France, Italy and Greece, just to name a few. The cuisine of any country is influenced by a number of factors, including geography and culture. In Europe, where so many countries are closely situated together, the cuisine of one country often has similarities to that of its neighbours.

In this chapter, we will focus on the cuisines of Greece, France and Scandinavia.

QUESTION

Visit www.yourchildlearns.com/europe_map.htm and use the interactive map to discover all of the countries in Europe, their capitals and surrounding seas. Using your own map of Europe, label the countries, capitals and surrounding seas.

Discover Greek cuisine

Greece lies in the southeast of Europe, bordering the Mediterranean, Ionian and Aegean seas. It is a country well known for its many islands, which have become very fashionable holiday destinations. It comes as no surprise, then, that seafood is a popular part of Greek cuisine. Octopus, calamari and whole fish, either grilled or baked, are commonly found on Greek menus.

The Mediterranean climate in Greece, with its blue skies and sunny days, creates perfect conditions for olive trees. Kalamata olives, named after a town in Greece, are known throughout the world. Many herbs are also easily grown in the rocky regions of the country, such as oregano, basil, dill and fennel.

oregano

dill

basil

fennel

Greece is a mountainous country and is suited to grazing sheep and goats. Consequently, lamb is the main meat served and a well-known dish is moussaka, which contains a layer of minced lamb and a layer of eggplant topped with a cheese sauce. Dips such as taramasalata (made from fish roe) and tzatziki (the more garlic, the better!) are served with pita bread.

Greek salad is commonly served throughout the world; however, in Greece, a Greek salad is known as horiatiki salata. In Australia, we serve Greek salad on a bed of lettuce, yet in Greece it does not contain lettuce—just large chunks of cucumber, onion, tomato, green capsicum, olives and, of course, feta cheese. The dressing would include olive oil and oregano, an often-used herb in Greece. Feta cheese, made from goat's milk, is a very common ingredient in Greece. In fact, it is becoming so popular throughout the world that moves are being made to prohibit any feta cheese from being named 'feta' unless it is made in Greece.

Fish roe is another name for fish eggs.

▶ Name is food for thought

Read the newspaper article and then answer the questions that follow it.

It looks like cheddar, tastes and smells like cheddar—but don't dare call it cheddar.

After a successful legal fight to have all champagne produced outside France renamed sparkling wine, European producers have turned to other foods in a bid to stop the 'exploitation' of their brands.

Under attack are traditional staples like cheddar cheese, Spanish onions, French onion dip, Ceylon tea, Kalamata olives, Swiss chocolate, and fetta, cheddar, mozzarella and Parmesan cheeses.

The European Union wants to stop countries using 'geographical indications' to describe the food produced outside the area it is named after.

Cheddar cheese could not be called cheddar unless produced in the small British dairy town of Cheddar.

European countries, as well as India, Thailand and Sri Lanka, are lobbying to have exclusive rights over the names of their food and agricultural products.

Geographic indications protection already exists for wines and spirits.

Australian trade negotiators at World Trade Organisation talks recently succeeded in delaying any moves on geographic exclusivity until later this year.

Increased intellectual protection on basic products would cost Australian producers hundreds of millions of dollars to repackage and rebrand their products.

'I'm not sure what we will have to call the stuff we put on pizza—if we can still call it pizza, that is,' the NSW Small Business Minister, Sandra Nori, said.

Industry groups said yesterday consumers were easily able to determine what names were mostly generic descriptions and did not actually come from the regions they are named after.

But European Union farm commissioner Franz Fischler said recently: 'We will fight for preventing other countries to pirate our traditional quality names, from French Roquefort cheese to Italian Parma ham.'

On the town

Pilsener: After Pilsen, a town in the Czech republic.
Champagne: The sparkling white wine of the Champagne district of northern France.
Jasmine rice and Thai silk: Made in Thailand.
Ceylon tea: Product of Sri Lanka (formerly Ceylon).
Kalamata olives: A town in Greece.
Parmigiano and gorgonzola cheese: All from Italy.
Cheddar cheese: Named after a dairy town in England.
Parma ham: An Italian town.
Fetta cheese: Made in Greece from sheep's, goat's or cow's milk but also made in Denmark and Australia.

feta cheese

QUESTIONS

1 Why do you think European producers are trying to stop 'exploitation' of their brands?
2 Besides feta cheese, what other brands are under attack?
3 What is the possible outcome for Australian producers if other countries are successful in gaining branding rights?

In Greece, pastries are served for special occasions and celebrations. The most well-known pastry associated with Greece is called baklava, which is also a common dessert in other Balkan countries and in regions of the Middle East. Baklava is very sweet and is made with a type of filo pastry. It has lots of pastry layers, sprinkled with nuts and a honey-flavoured syrup. Sweet pastries are very popular in Greece and are served with Greek coffee, which is a strong syrupy coffee like Turkish coffee.

The Balkan countries are located in southern Europe and include Albania, Bosnia, Bulgaria, Croatia, Macedonia, Romania and Greece.

If you were to stand anywhere in Greece, you would never be more than 137 kilometres from the sea.

Throughout Greece, many tavernas, or small restaurants, can be found. These are very casual places where people congregate to talk, eat and drink. Meals served in tavernas usually consist of souvlaki or gyros. If you ordered souvlaki in Greece, you would most likely get a skewer of grilled meat, usually lamb, served on a plate. In Australia, a souvlaki would normally be the meat rolled up in pita bread with lettuce, tomato and a garlic sauce. The meat can be cooked either grilled on a skewer or on a rotating vertical spit. Increasingly in Australia, there is concern about the safety of cooking meat in this way.

 ▶ **Dob in dodgy souvlaki**

Read the newspaper article and then answer the questions that follow it.

By David Wilson

Victorians are being asked to dob in dodgy souvlaki shops after revelations 90 per cent of the takeaway food poses a health risk.

The Department of Human Services in concerned about the rise in sickness linked to eating souvlakis and it is encouraging people concerned about food poisoning or contamination to complain to their local councils.

The department is also asking consumers to report any questionable practices they see in the preparation and cooking of souvlakis.

'We would ask people who are worried about, or who have bought, contaminated material to get in touch with their local council,' said department spokesman Bram Alexander.

Meanwhile, councils have been told to have their health inspectors enforce new rules of the preparation of the popular takeaway.

The new rules for takeaway shops cooking souvlakis have been sent to local councils following a survey that found almost 90 per cent of souvlakis pose a food poisoning risk.

The Department of Human Services recorded 2683 cases of gastro-enteritis caused by campylobacter bacteria and 843 cases of salmonella poisoning from poorly cooked souvlaki meat in the first six months of the year.

Shops selling souvlakis will now have to 'second kill' meat cut from vertical cooking skewers by further cooking it on hot plates or grills before serving it.

The survey by Food Safety Victoria and local council inspectors found most lamb and chicken being cooked on the rotating skewers had an internal temperature of less than 75°C.

This creates a risk that raw meat could be mixed with cooked meat, leading to contamination when it is sliced from the cooking skewers.

Council inspectors found raw or pink meat was being cut off the spit in 23 per cent of outlets.

They also found 40 per cent of premises did not cook their meat at temperatures high enough to destroy bacteria.

A total of 65 per cent of the takeaways surveyed did not cook the meat further after it had been cut from the spit.

Food safety inspectors from councils in Melbourne's northern, western and southern suburbs surveyed 31 takeaway premises sampling raw and cooked chicken, beef and lamb from rotating vertical spits.

Four out of 12 samples of cooked meat taken from the spit drip-trays failed tests.

Eleven samples of raw meat were tested and seven failed with results finding high levels of E. coli, salmonella and bacteria.

Mr Alexander said the survey was currently being sent out to all councils food inspectors.

Souvlaki businesses would be encouraged to use probe thermometers to test the internal temperature on meat cooking on rotary spits, he said.

QUESTIONS

1 What are the food poisoning statistics caused from 'dodgy' souvlaki?
2 Identify the possible causes of the food poisoning.
3 Explain how the souvlaki meat is cooked.
4 What does it mean to 'second kill' the meat?
5 What measures could takeaway places take to ensure that their meat does not contain unsafe levels of bacteria?

▶ **Let's remember**

1 Why is seafood often part of Greek meals?
2 As a result of the climate in Greece, what kinds of ingredients are common?
3 What ingredients would you commonly find in horiatiki salata?
4 What is feta cheese usually made from?
5 Describe a typical Greek pastry.

▶ **Let's investigate**

1 Investigate how Greeks celebrate Easter and the significance of Easter eggs. Write a 500-word report.
2 Investigate how many Greek islands there are. Plan a two-week holiday to Greece, including visits to at least three islands. Explain what is unique about each island and why you have chosen each.
3 Investigate all the varieties of feta cheese by visiting your local supermarket or accessing www.colesonline.com.au. In what different ways can they be purchased? Are they made from goat's or sheep's or cow's milk? Conduct a class activity and taste at least five different kinds of feta cheese. Evaluate their appearance, flavour, texture and aroma ☺ ☺ ☹. Which type of feta cheese was the most popular in the class?

℮-Greek cuisine

www.greecefoods.com

1 Click on 'Souvlaki'. What would you get if you ordered souvlaki and gyro pita?
2 Click on 'Patsa'. Explain what patsa is.
3 Click on 'List of foods and descriptions'. Go to www.puzzlemaker.com and create your own wordsearch or crossword for other class members to try.

▶ **Puzzled**

Gobbledy Greek

Match the recipes in the first column with the ingredients listed in the second column.

WEBEXTRAS

www.thatsgreece.com
You can find a wealth of information here about Greek cuisine, recipes and festivities by just following the link to Greek food.

www.greeklandscapes.com/travel/food.html
This website provides information about Greek restaurants, tavernas and fast food in Greece.

www.greekcuisine.com
Here you can find an extensive range of Greek recipes for every course.

Recipe	Ingredient
Moussaka	Cheese
Tzatziki	Lamb and pita bread
Baklava	Vine leaves
Souvlaki	Feta cheese
Dolmades	Beef
Greek salad	Fish roe
Taramasalata	Spinach
Spanakopita	Cucumber
Saganaki	Eggplant
Keftedes	Honey

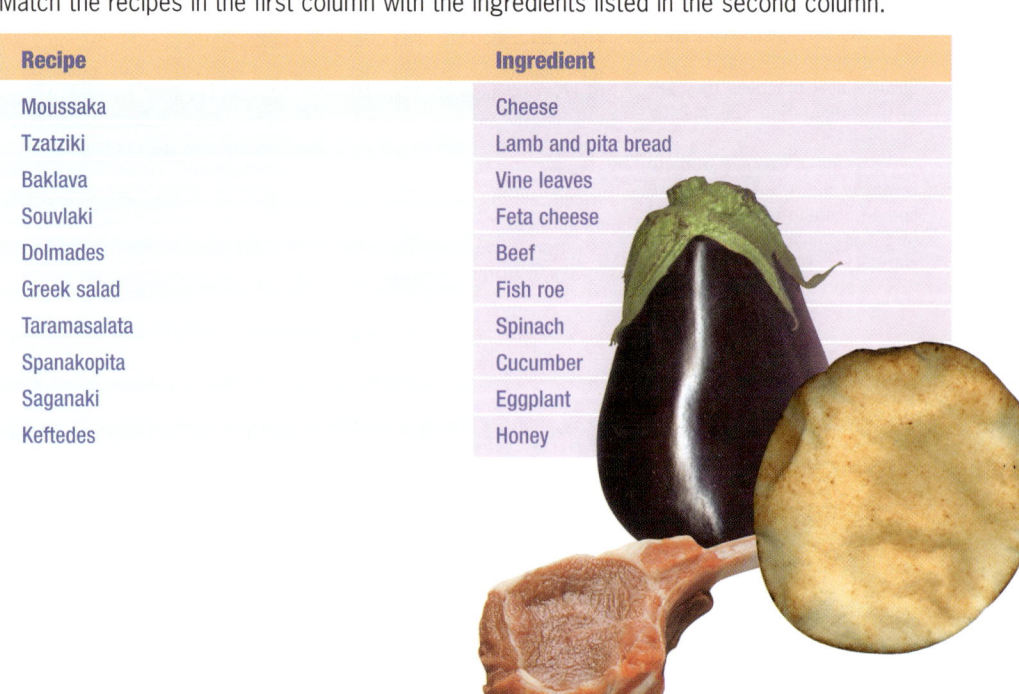

LET'S PRODUCE

Moussaka

(serves 4)

Ingredients

2 tablespoons olive oil
1 Spanish onion, chopped
2 cloves garlic, crushed
500 grams minced lamb
425 grams tomatoes, puréed
1 large eggplant, sliced
30 grams butter
2 tablespoons flour
2 cups milk
¼ teaspoon nutmeg
2 eggs, lightly beaten
60 grams feta cheese
125 grams tasty cheese
2 tablespoons parmesan cheese

Method

1. Heat one tablespoon of the oil in frypan. Add onion and garlic. Cook for one minute.
2. Add mince and cook meat until browned. Drain excess fat.
3. Add tomatoes and simmer for thirty minutes, or until liquid has evaporated.
4. Place eggplant on baking tray. Brush with remaining oil. Bake at 180°C for fifteen minutes.
5. Melt butter. Add flour. Cook for one minute.
6. Add milk and stir until thickened. Stir in nutmeg. Cook bubbling sauce for one minute.
7. Allow sauce to cool slightly. Add eggs and mix well.
8. Place eggplant slices on bottom of baking dish.
9. Sprinkle with half of the three cheeses and half of the sauce.
10. Top with mince mixture.
11. Top with remaining sauce and cheeses.
12. Bake at 180°C for thirty minutes.

Tzatziki

(serves 2)

Ingredients

½ Lebanese cucumber, chopped finely
1 cup Greek-style yoghurt
2 cloves garlic, crushed
sprinkle of salt
2 teaspoons fresh mint, chopped
1 teaspoon olive oil
mint sprigs for garnish

Method

1. Add chopped cucumber to yoghurt.
2. Add garlic, salt, mint and oil.
3. Combine all ingredients well.
4. Serve in a dish, garnished with mint.

QUESTIONS

1. With what would you serve tzatziki?
2. Evaluate the flavour of the tzatziki ☺ ☺ ☹.
3. Compare the ingredients in your tzatziki recipe with those found in commercial recipes. Explain how they differ.

e-Fact

If you sprinkle cut eggplant with salt, let stand for thirty minutes and then rinse thoroughly under cold water, you will remove any bitter flavour from the eggplant.

Discover French cuisine

A fine French meal is considered by many to be the ultimate dining experience, although it is interesting to note that the development of French cuisine is relatively new. Traditional French cuisine is also known as haute cuisine and typically includes cream-based sauces and rich pastries. The expression *haute cuisine* originated from the lavish twelve-hour feasts held during the reign of King Louis XIV. In the 1970s, the development of nouvelle cuisine brought a fresher, more casual approach to cooking as distinct from the classic, more formal cuisine of earlier days. Nouvelle cuisine relies on natural flavours and simple presentation.

In France, shopping for fresh food and produce, cooking and eating is all part of the food experience. Markets and speciality shops abound, with a wide range of patisseries, charcuteries, and boulangeries. Patisseries sell pastries and cakes, a boulangerie is also a kind of bakery and a charcuterie is like a delicatessen, which usually sells a wide range of cheeses, cold meats, pâtés, terrines and prepared salads.

Picnic-style lunches are common in France and all you need is a baguette and a visit to a charcuterie to pick up some pâté and salad, followed by a visit to a patisserie to choose from a wide range of pastry delicacies.

Baguettes are so common in France that it is not unusual to see someone eating a plain baguette on their way to or from work. They are purchased as is, not in plastic wrap or a bag, and you will often see them just being carried unwrapped in someone's hand or sticking out of a shoulder bag or backpack! Baguettes are also eaten for breakfast and a typical breakfast would consist of a baguette with jam and a café au lait.

Although dinner is usually a lighter meal than lunch, an evening meal in France for a special occasion might consist of as many as six courses, usually of small portions. The meal would begin with hors d'oeuvres, followed by soup, main course, salad, cheese and finally dessert. Set-price menus (menu prix-fix) are often available and restaurants usually offer a daily special, or plat du jour, which literally means plate of the day. Mostly, it is more expensive to order items from the menu. This type of menu is called à la carte.

Did you know that, when the Bastille was stormed in 1789, eight out of every ten French people had a staple diet of bread and cereal?

A baguette is a long, thin French bread stick with a soft inside and a crusty outside.

The expression *café au lait* is French for coffee with milk.

▶ Let's remember

1 What is the difference between haute cuisine and nouvelle cuisine?
2 Define the terms *patisserie*, *boulangerie* and *charcuterie*.
3 Describe a typical breakfast in France.
4 Which meal is the main meal of the day in France? Explain your answer.
5 Explain the different types of menu options available in France.

In France, breakfast is called *petit déjeuner* and lunch is called *déjeuner*.

▶ Let's investigate

1 Investigate and identify how many wines there are in France that are named after towns or regions.
2 Investigate the origin of crepe suzette, quiche Lorraine and Paris breast. Find a recipe for each.
3 When is Bastille Day celebrated? Investigate the historical significance of this day.

▶ *e*-French cuisine

www.ffcook.com

Did you know that France produces more than 500 different types of cheese?

1 Click on 'French recipes and menus' and follow the link to 'How is a typical French menu organised?'. What does a typical French lunch consist of?
2 Identify the basic ingredients recommended to have in a French pantry by clicking on 'French tips and tools' and then 'Basic ingredients'.
3 Using the links on the left-hand side, create your own menu consisting of entrée, main course, cheese and dessert.

▶ Puzzled

French fun

France has the largest population of any western European country.

WEBExTRaS

www.camembert-france.com
Find out all about Camembert cheese and the French village in Normandy called Camembert.

www.frenchcheese.co.uk
This website contains information about the different types of French cheeses available, including mild, medium and strong cheeses.

www.globalgourmet.com/destinations/france/
This website has information about French cuisine and descriptions of common menu items.

Match the French terms below with the descriptions found in the second column.

Term	Description
Aperitif	A thin pancake
Flambé	The French word for ham
Macedoine	A type of grape
Purée	A basic dressing of oil and vinegar
Dariole	Raw vegetables, cut into sticks or batons
Bouquet garni	A basic white sauce made with a roux and milk
Hors d'oeuvre	A water bath
Vichyssoise	The French word for lunch
Roux	A muslin bag of herbs used to flavour soups and stews
Semillon	To cut vegetables into match-like strips
Julienne	An alcoholic drink, such as champagne or sherry, served before a meal to stimulate the appetite
Béarnaise	To pour brandy over food and ignite
Jambon	An appetiser, or the first course
Crudités	A sauce made with egg, butter, vinegar, tarragon and shallots
Crepe	To put food through a processor to blend it
Béchamel	Means bread in French
Déjeuner	A mixture of flour and butter
Pain	A soup with potato and leek
Bain marie	A small dome-shaped mould used for crème caramel
Vinaigrette	A dice of vegetables

LET'S PRODUCE

Ingredients
15 grams butter
2 teaspoons oil
1 onion, chopped
3 cups beef stock
1 bay leaf
salt and black pepper, to taste
1 small baguette
45 grams extra butter
1 clove garlic, crushed
30 grams parmesan cheese
1 tablespoon fresh parsley, chopped

Ingredients
60 grams chocolate
2 eggs, separated
$\frac{1}{4}$ teaspoon rum essence
$\frac{1}{2}$ cup cream

French onion soup
(serves 2)

Method

1. Melt butter and oil. Add onion and cook gently until soft.
2. Add stock and bay leaf.
3. Season with salt and pepper. Simmer for thirty minutes. Remove bay leaf.
4. Spread sliced baguette with butter and garlic. Place on tray lined with baking paper.
5. Sprinkle bread with parmesan cheese.
6. Bake for fifteen minutes at 180°C.
7. Place bread into soup dishes and cover with soup.
8. Serve immediately, garnished with parsley.

Chocolate mousse
(serves 2)

Method

1. Melt chocolate in microwave on medium high for approximately thirty seconds.
2. Add beaten egg yolks and rum essence.
3. Whip cream until thickened.
4. Beat egg whites until firm.
5. Fold cream and rum essence into chocolate and cream mixture, then fold in the cream.
6. Pour gently into serving dishes and chill until serving time.
7. Garnish and serve with extra cream and chocolate shavings.

Discover Scandinavian cuisine

Scandinavian countries include Denmark, Sweden, Finland and Norway, although Iceland is sometimes included. These countries are also known as Nordic countries.

Parts of Scandinavia are referred to as the 'land of the midnight sun' because, during the summer months, there is still daylight at midnight! In Iceland, during the month of June, the sun never fully sets. While this sounds like it could be fun, in winter the days are very short and cold, with almost no daylight.

Scandinavian menus feature many different types of fish. This is not surprising, given the amount of land that is surrounded by sea. Salmon and herring are particularly common and in summer, crayfish, oysters and prawns are a delicacy. Cod is the main fish eaten during the winter months, because it can be dried and salted during the summer. Potatoes are a staple food, especially during the winter months, and are served boiled, baked or in dumplings.

In Scandinavia, pork is the main meat consumed, although game meat, such as venison (deer), pigeon, pheasant and partridge, is also consumed. Reindeer is especially popular for special meals or celebrations and reindeer farms can be found in the northern parts of Norway. Cheese is often served at the end of a meal and Danish cheese, such as Danish Blue and Havarti, are eaten all over the world. So too is Jarslberg, which originates in Norway. Denmark is also known for its Danish pastries.

The smorgasbord, which originated in Sweden, is a buffet meal of cold dishes. Smorgasbord-style meals have now become popular all over the world. In Norway and Denmark, the smorgasbord is known as koldbordt, which means 'cold table'. It consists of various breads, usually rye bread and crispbreads, and such foods as salmon, herring, hard-boiled eggs, pickles, spreads, cold meats and cheeses. In Denmark, open sandwiches, called smorrebrod ('buttered bread'), are served. Rye bread is normally used, topped with cured fish and cold foods similar to those served at a smorgasbord.

e-fact

Did you know that, in countries where the winter is long, cold and dark, people can be diagnosed with a condition called SAD, or seasonal affective disorder, which leaves them feeling sad and depressed? Some people just refer to it as the 'blahs'!

e-fact

In Sweden, berries belong to everyone and you can go onto someone else's land to pick them. You can even camp on their land, as long as you cannot be seen from the house!

e-fact

In Scandinavia, some people take a daily dose of cod liver oil during the winter months to ensure that they have adequate vitamin D.

Havarti cheese

Jarlsberg cheese

Danish blue cheese

Throughout Scandinavia, berries are plentiful and, in the summer months, huge trays can be found in the marketplaces for sale. Types of berries include strawberries, raspberries, blackberries, blueberries, cranberries and other varieties not available at present in Australia, called cloudberries, rowanberries and lingonberries.

▶ Let's remember

1 What countries make up Scandinavia?
2 Why are parts of Scandinavia referred to as 'the land of the midnight sun'?
3 Explain why fish and potatoes are common foods eaten in Scandinavia.
4 Describe the difference between the terms *smorgasbord* and *smorrebrod*.
5 Describe the different types of cheeses unique to Scandinavian countries.

▶ Let's investigate

1 Investigate how many words you can create from the word *Scandinavia*, using each letter only once.
2 Investigate the origins of St Lucia Day. Which country celebrates St Lucia Day? What foods are traditionally served for this celebration? What other forms of celebration occur? Present your findings as a poster.
3 In Sweden, Christmas is usually celebrated with 'five plates'. Investigate what foods and dishes are served for each plate. How does a Swedish Christmas meal differ from a Christmas meal in Finland, Norway or Iceland? This website will help you with information:
www.deliciousindia.com/InternationalRecipes/Europe/scandinavian_food.htm.
Present your information as a concept map.
4 Investigate what a cloudberry, a rowanberry and a lingonberry look like by searching the Internet. Describe each and find a recipe that uses each type of berry.
5 What is gravlax? Investigate how you would produce it. Design a recipe using gravlax. Produce and evaluate your own gravlax recipe using a Y-chart.

Tastes like

Smells like   Looks like

WEBExTRaS

www.scandinavian
cooking.com
An extensive website with
Scandinavian recipes, articles
about staple Scandinavian
foods and information about
specialities from the different
countries.
www.globalgourmet.
com/destinations/finland
This website contains information about the gastronomy
of Finland, Finnish banquets
and festive and seasonal
dishes. Find out too about
reindeer, a type of game
meat in Finland, which is
becoming a significant
export industry.

▶ 🄴-Scandinavian cuisine

www.foodiesite.com/articles/2000-09/scandanavian.jsp

1 Explain the eating ritual in Scandinavia. Include a description of food normally eaten at breakfast, lunch and dinner.
2 What are bornholmer and lukefish?
3 Scroll down the page to 'Baking'.
   a What is weinerbrod?
   b How did Danish pastries come about? Explain their origin.
   c Explain the importance of baked goods to celebrations in Scandinavia. Provide examples.

WEBExTRaS

www.foodtv.com/cuisine/
scandinaviancuisine
Here you can find infor-
mation about Scandinavian
recipes, foods and cooking
terms.

▶ Puzzled

Fish mish-mash

Unscramble the following types of fish that are synonymous with Scandinavia.

1 mnoals   7 kapolcl
2 grerihn   8 lesssmu
3 lamckeer   9 kipe
4 doc   10 campsi
5 oles   11 mreab
6 ruott   12 yfshrcai

WEBExTRaS

www.deliciousindia.com/
InternationalRecipes/
Europe/scandinavia.htm
This website will lead you
to a host of links to the
cuisine of Finland, Norway,
Sweden, Denmark and
Iceland.

LET'S PRODUCE

Grilled salmon

(serves 2)

Ingredients

300 grams salmon steak or fillet
2 teaspoons soy sauce
2 teaspoons butter
$\frac{1}{2}$ Spanish onion, chopped
2 sprigs dill

Method

1 Marinate salmon in soy sauce.
2 Melt butter and cook onion until soft.
3 Grill salmon for five minutes each side.
4 Serve topped with cooked onion.
5 Garnish with sprigs of dill.
6 Serve with braised cabbage or boiled potatoes and salad.

Almond macaroons

(makes 12)

Ingredients

1 cup ground almonds
$\frac{2}{3}$ cup caster sugar
2 egg whites
$\frac{1}{4}$ teaspoon almond essence
12 almonds, one for each macaroon

Method

1 Combine ground almonds and sugar in processor until combined.
2 Gradually add egg white and almond essence until mixture combines.
3 Divide mixture into twelve and shape into rounds.
4 Place on baking tray, lined with baking paper and flatten slightly.
5 Sprinkle lightly with additional caster sugar and place one almond in centre of each macaroon.
6 Bake at 170°C for ten to fifteen minutes, or until lightly golden brown.

QUESTIONS

1 Explain how you would separate an egg.
2 Investigate what a blanched almond is.
3 Evaluate this recipe using a Y-chart.

Tastes like

Smells like   Looks like

► Let's investigate

Investigate a European country or region of your choice, other than Greece, France or Scandinavia. Design a typical menu for your chosen country. Produce and evaluate your menu ☺ ☺ ☹.

9

aMERICaN PIE: DISCOVER THE CUISINE OF THE aMERICaS

The regions of the Americas include North America, Central America and South America. In this chapter, we will look at the cuisines of the USA, Canada and Mexico.

▶ Discover North American cuisine

When many people think of the USA, they think of takeaway restaurant chains, such as McDonald's, KFC, Burger King, Wendy's and Subway. However, like Australian cuisine, North American cuisine has early origins in the foods of its indigenous people. Some of these indigenous foods include green beans, sunflower seeds and maple syrup. Settlement in North America by people from other countries diversified the indigenous cuisine. Some of these influences are outlined in the table below.

Did you know that the French colonised Nova Scotia, one of Canada's eastern provinces, as early as 1632? In the mid-1700s, the British captured the colony and expelled many of the people known as Arcadians. As a result, many of these people of French origin settled in the south of the USA in such places as Louisiana. It is from these Arcadian people that Cajun cuisine developed. Quite simply, the word *Cajun* is derived from a mispronunciation of the word *Arcadian*.

e-Fact

During the Second World War, United States soldiers introduced hamburgers and Coca-Cola to Australia.

e-Fact

Did you know that Canada produces more than 85 per cent of the world's maple syrup?

Culture	Type of foods/dishes	Area of USA
Native American	Wild game, fish, roots, nuts and berries	Northern USA
French (Cajun)	Crawfish, gumbo, jambalaya, cayenne pepper	Louisiana, New Orleans
African	Black-eyed peas, yams, jollof rice	Southern USA—Virginia, North and South Carolina
German	Frankfurters (hot dogs), pretzels, donuts, potato salad	Minnesota, Pennsylvania
Jewish	Bagels, kofta, potato latkes,	New York
Italian	Spaghetti, pizza, pasta, ice cream	California
Mexican	Burritos, chimichangas, guacamole	Texas, New Mexico, Arizona

MaPLE SYRUP

Maple trees are so synonymous with Canada that the maple leaf is the national emblem. Maple syrup is one of the main products that we associate with Canada. There are different kinds of maple trees, mainly found in Canada's east, throughout Quebec, New Brunswick and Nova Scotia. The winter in this part of Canada can be very cold, with temperatures reaching as low as minus 30°C. The maple sugar season is at the end of winter/beginning of spring, just when the winter snow is beginning to thaw. Did you know that an average maple tree yields 40 litres of sap for just $1\frac{1}{2}$ litres of maple syrup? No wonder real maple syrup is so expensive! In Australia, we can purchase maple syrup imported from Canada. Supermarkets also sell a variety of maple-flavoured syrups, which are much less expensive than real maple syrup. Make sure you read the label if you want the real thing!

During the 'sugar' season, you can visit the maple syrup farms. Here you can see the trees being 'tapped'. To access the sap, a hole is drilled in the tree, and a pipe is inserted into the hole to allow the sap to drip into a bucket below. The buckets are then collected and the sap

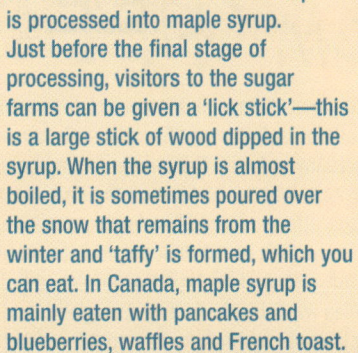

is processed into maple syrup. Just before the final stage of processing, visitors to the sugar farms can be given a 'lick stick'—this is a large stick of wood dipped in the syrup. When the syrup is almost boiled, it is sometimes poured over the snow that remains from the winter and 'taffy' is formed, which you can eat. In Canada, maple syrup is mainly eaten with pancakes and blueberries, waffles and French toast.

QUESTIONS

1 Where would you find maple trees?
2 When is the maple sugar season?
3 Why is maple syrup relatively expensive?
4 Design your own pancake recipe to serve with maple syrup.
5 Investigate recipes that use maple syrup as one of the ingredients. List three recipes.
6 What is taffy?
7 Investigate which countries maple syrup is exported to.
8 Investigate whether there are other countries producing maple syrup.

Celebrations in North America

Thanksgiving and Halloween are two celebrations that originated in North America. The national holiday of Thanksgiving was proclaimed as a day of thanksgiving and praise to God. Foods traditionally served for a Thanksgiving dinner include turkey with cranberry sauce, mashed potato, candied yams and pumpkin pie.

QUESTIONS

1 When is Halloween?
2 What foods are usually associated with Halloween?
3 What is the origin of Halloween?
4 Have you ever celebrated Halloween? If yes, how did you celebrate it?

PHILADELPHIA CREAM CHEESE

If someone asked you about the origin of Philadelphia cream cheese, you might answer that it was originally made in Philadelphia. In fact, a cheese distributor who decided that he would produce a cheese from cream and milk first made cream cheese in New York. The town of Philadelphia, Pennsylvania, was well known at the time for producing high-quality foods. Such foods were often referred to as Philadelphia quality and this is why the man who invented cream cheese named his brand Philadelphia. It was first distributed in the 1880s and it was wrapped in foil, just as it can still be purchased today. Now, it is also sold in tubs, with a range of varieties available, including spreadable and light varieties. Today, Philadelphia cream cheese is made by Kraft foods and it is sold all over the world. Kraft foods state that Philadelphia cream cheese accounts for sales of over one billion dollars worldwide. Cream cheese is very popular in the USA, where it is typically eaten with bagels. It is also used to make cheesecake, which is a popular dessert in the USA.

Adapted from: www.kraft.com/archives/brands/brands_cream.html

QUESTIONS

1 Describe the origin of Philadelphia cream cheese.
2 How was cream cheese originally packaged?
3 In the USA, how is cream cheese often used?
4 Visit www.kraft.com.au/philadelphia, click on 'Products' and identify the range of cream cheese products available in Australia.
5 Click on 'Recipes' and identify a recipe for breakfast, lunch and dinner that uses cream cheese.
6 Click on 'Frequently asked questions' and compare the fat content of the regular and light varieties of Philadelphia cream cheese.
7 Look at the label shown, which states that Philadelphia cream cheese contains 80 per cent less fat than butter or margarine. What do you think is the purpose of this statement?

▶ Let's remember

1 What takeaway restaurant chains are associated with the USA?
2 What is the origin of North American cuisine?
3 Describe the impact of settlement on North American cuisine.
4 From where does the word *Cajun* originate?
5 Identify foods that are traditionally served for a Thanksgiving dinner.

Let's investigate

1 Describe what a jack-o-lantern is. How is one made? Do you think you could make one in Australia?
2 Investigate the historical significance of Thanksgiving. When is Thanksgiving celebrated? What would a typical Thanksgiving dinner consist of?
3 How does a Christmas dinner in the USA differ from a traditional Christmas meal in Australia? Compare both of these to the kind of meal you usually eat at Christmas.
4 Investigate which fast-food chains operating in Australia originated in the USA?
5 Investigate the origin of the term *Tex-Mex*. Explain what it means.
6 Investigate your pantry or supermarket. Find five products produced in the USA. Identify the brand and product type in a table. Identify a similar product made in Australia.
7 Identify companies that have bought out Australian companies. Using each of de Bono thinking hats, make a comment about Australian-owned companies versus foreign-owned companies.

A chef called Caesar Cardini created the caesar salad in the 1920s in Tijuana, Mexico.

The waldorf salad was created at the Waldorf-Astoria hotel in New York.

Emotions, feelings, hunches	Caution, judging and assessing the negatives	Creativity	Optimistic, judging and assessing the positives	Information	Organising thinking
How do I feel?	What are the problems?	What new ideas can I propose?	Why is this worth doing?	What information do we have or need?	What have we achieved?

@-North American cuisine

www.homecooking.about.com/library/weekly/aa011998.htm

Bagels are a very popular food in the USA. Find out more about bagels by answering the following questions.

1 What are the basic ingredients in a bagel?
2 Describe the origin of the bagel.
3 Why do you think the art of bagel making was such a closely guarded secret?
4 What impact did Polish baker Harry Lender have on the bagel industry?
5 How should bagels be stored?

WEBExTRaS

www.baking911.com/bread_bagels.htm
This website provides information about the history of bagels and techniques for making them.

Puzzled

United tastes

Find each of the words from the box in the puzzle.

WEBExTRaS

www.jack-o-lantern.com
This website provides information about the history of jack-o-lanterns and techniques for making them. There is also a section showing you how to create watermelon jack-o-lanterns in summer.

www.ms.essortment.com/whathistorycor_orf.htm
Visit this website to find out more about corn, a staple food of North America.

WEBExTRaS

www.usafoods.com.au
This website will link you to the All American Grocery Store, located in the Melbourne suburb of Bentleigh, where you can order from a wide range of USA grocery products.

```
U J R E G B U P X P A Q W Y P
C L A M C H O W D E R L B P Y
S N R R O A S T T U R K E Y P
E H E N F E E B I L L I H C U
I E G K S J I S R G O D T O H
K R R W C I R T A O X T J R C
O S U E L I F T U R W Z I N T
O H B I E L H J S N S N I B E
C E M P G D C C P K O A I R K
O Y A N A Q N K D H M D L E T
E B H A B E E F J E R K Y A S
R A N C H D R E S S I N G D D
O R A E N I F F U M W R K B E
M P O P C O C A C O L A F L S
J K X J D W I T H S D V X N Y
```

bagel	fried chicken
beef jerky	hamburger
brownies	Hershey bar
caesar salad	hot dog
chilli beef	ketchup
clam chowder	muffin
Coca-Cola	Oreo cookies
cornbread	pecan pie
donut	ranch dressing
French fries	roast turkey

LET'S PRODUCE

Ingredients
1 cup butter, softened
1 cup icing sugar
1 egg
1 teaspoon almond extract
1 teaspoon vanilla
2¾ cups all-purpose flour
1 teaspoon baking powder
1 teaspoon salt
¾ cup whole blanched almonds
1 tube (19 grams) red decorator gel or ¼ cup plum jam

Ingredients
1¾ cups water
1 tablespoon dried yeast
3 tablespoons sugar
4½ cups plain flour
1½ teaspoons salt
60 grams butter, melted
1 tablespoon sugar, extra
2 teaspoons salt, extra

Witch's fingers

(makes 60)

Method

1 In bowl, beat together butter, sugar, egg, almond extract and vanilla; beat in flour, baking powder and salt. Cover and refrigerate for thirty minutes.
2 Working with one-quarter of the dough at a time and keeping remaining dough refrigerated, roll heaping teaspoonful into finger shape. Press almond firmly into one end for nail. Press in centre to create knuckle shape. Using paring knife, make slashes in several places to form knuckle.
3 Bake on lightly greased baking sheets in 160°C oven for twenty to twenty-five minutes, or until pale golden. Let cool for three minutes.
4 Lift up almond; squeeze red decorator gel onto nail bed and press almond back in place, so gel oozes out from underneath. Remove from baking sheets; let cool on racks.

Bagels

(makes 12)

Method

1 Heat ½ cup of the water. Add the yeast and sugar, allowing the yeast to activate.
2 Mix together the flour and salt in a food processor.
3 Add melted butter and pulse two to three times, until butter is distributed.
4 Gradually add the additional water and yeast mixture, until a dough forms.
5 Remove dough from food processor and knead by hand to remove any air bubbles.
6 Place dough into a greased microwave dish. Cover with plastic wrap, leaving a small area uncovered.
7 Cook on low for one minute and rest dough for five to ten minutes.
8 Repeat step 7 twice until dough is doubled in size.
9 Remove dough and divide into two.
10 Shape each mixture into six bagels, ensuring a round shape with a hole in the middle.
11 Boil a large amount of water in a large saucepan. Add additional sugar and salt.
12 When water is boiling, carefully lower one bagel into water. Boil for two to three minutes.
13 Repeat for each bagel, cooking only one at a time.
14 Place boiled bagels onto a baking tray and bake at 180°C for twenty to twenty-five minutes.
15 Toast and serve with cream cheese.

e-Fact

New Yorkers say that they can tell the difference between a genuine New York bagel and a bagel made outside of New York. They say that it is all to do with the water in the dough! They are also very particular about their pizza dough and bread because, if it is not made with New York water, it just does not taste the same!

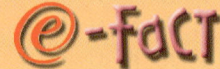

e-Fact

Did you know that it is the boiling of bagels that results in their soft chewy inside texture?

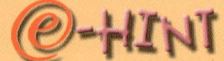

e-Hint

Make sure that the bagels are completely cooled before attempting to cut them.

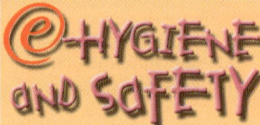

e-Hygiene and Safety

Bagels are quite hard and chewy, so it is important to use your knife carefully when cutting them in half.

Ingredients

8 chicken drumsticks
¼ cup crushed cornflakes
¾ cup flour
2 teaspoons chicken stock
½ teaspoon paprika
½ teaspoon lemon pepper
¼ teaspoon chilli powder
30 grams butter, melted
canola oil spray

Spicy fried chicken

(serves 4)

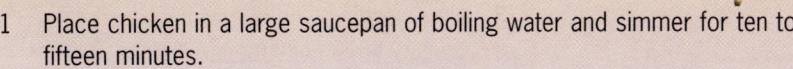

Method

1 Place chicken in a large saucepan of boiling water and simmer for ten to fifteen minutes.
2 Remove and allow chicken to cool. Remove skin.
3 Combine dry ingredients in a plastic bag and shake to combine.
4 Brush chicken with melted butter.
5 Place chicken pieces, two at a time in plastic bag and shake until mixture is coated.
6 Place chicken onto an oven tray lined with baking paper.
7 Spray lightly with canola oil.
8 Bake at 180°C for twenty to twenty-five minutes, turning once.

Did you know that there are more than 100 varieties of chilli in Mexico?

The word *tortilla* is derived from *torta*, the Spanish word for cake.

e-Fact

In the USA, there are more tortillas sold than bagels and muffins.

Did you know that the Mexicans worshipped a corn god in order to ensure a good harvest?

Discover Mexican cuisine

A number of ancient civilisations inhabited Mexico, including the Aztecs, who ruled Mexico until the early 1500s, when they were invaded by Spain. Today, Mexico is a mix of pre-Hispanic culture and Spanish culture. Although many native languages are spoken throughout the country, the predominant language is Spanish.

A number of foods are considered staples in Mexico. These include tortillas, a type of unleavened flat round bread made from wheat flour or maize (corn). Tortillas are usually cooked on a griddle and they form the basis of a number of Mexican dishes, including quesadillas, burritos, enchiladas and tacos. Mexican-style food is becoming more popular in Australia and this can be largely attributed to the meal assembly packages available from supermarkets.

▶ Let's remember

1 Identify an ancient civilisation that used to rule Mexico.
2 Which foods are considered to be staples in Mexico?
3 How would you cook a tortilla?
4 Identify three uses for tortillas.
5 Why do you think Mexican food is becoming popular in Australia?

▶ Let's investigate

1 Investigate the health benefits of corn.
2 Visit an online supermarket and investigate the number of products containing corn.
3 Investigate the different spices used in Mexican cooking. Construct a table, naming each spice and providing a description of each.
4 Investigate the contents of Mexican meal assembly packages. Identify the ingredients and compare the cost of the meal assembly packages with purchasing the ingredients separately. Evaluate which of the two ways of buying these meal ingredients is better value ☺ ☺ ☹.
5 Investigate the foods offered at Mexican takeaway chain restaurants, such as Taco Bill and Montezumas, or the Mexican restaurant closest to where you live.
6 Investigate the types of foods cultivated in Mexico. Present your information as a concept map.
7 Investigate festivals or celebrations held in Mexico. Discuss the foods eaten on these occasions and their significance to the festival or celebration.
8 Investigate the ingredients list on a taco kit, can of refried beans and a jar of salsa. Evaluate the fibre content and the flavours and additives and present your findings in a table or a concept map ☺ ☺ ☹.

▶ @ -Mexican cuisine

www.whats4eats.com/4rec_mexico.html

1 Identify the ancient civilisations of Mexico.
2 Identify the staple foods of the indigenous people of Mexico.
3 Which foods are associated with the arrival of the Spanish?
4 What is masa and how is it used?
5 Describe a typical Mexican meal.
6 Choose two regional types of cooking and compare the different types of foods or dishes that are unique to both regions.

www.recipes4us.co.uk/Cooking%20by%20Country/Mexico.htm

1 Describe where authentic Mexican food is thought to have originated.
2 What is considered to have had the greatest influence on Mexican cuisine?
3 What other cuisines were introduced with colonisation?

▶ Puzzled

Mexican mix

Match each of the following Mexican dishes with the appropriate description.

Dish	Description
Taco	A soft rolled corn tortilla filled with a spicy meat mixture, topped with melted cheese and served with salsa
Enchilada	A cocktail made with tequila and lime juice
Burrito	A spicy sauce made from a base of tomatoes and chillies
Quesedilla	A crisp folded corn tortilla served filled with a spicy meat mixture and salad ingredients
Gaucamole	A soft flour tortilla filled with such ingredients as refried beans, lettuce, sour cream and grated cheese
Chilli con carne	Corn chips covered with melted cheese and salsa, served with sour cream and guacamole
Chimichanga	A soft folded flour tortilla filled with such ingredients as refried beans, topped with cheese and grilled
Margarita	A dip made from blended avocado and Tabasco sauce
Nachos	A hot and spicy meat dish with chillies and sometimes kidney beans
Salsa	A soft folded flour tortilla that is deep-fried

Ingredients

425 grams refried beans
250 grams guacamole dip
2 tablespoons taco seasoning mix
250 grams sour cream
3 lettuce leaves, shredded
250 grams cheese, grated
2 jalapeno peppers, chopped finely
1 tomato, diced finely

Mexican bean dip   (serves 4)

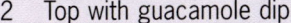 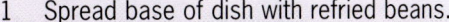

Method

1 Spread base of dish with refried beans.
2 Top with guacamole dip.
3 Place in refrigerator to chill for fifteen minutes.
4 Mix the seasoning mix and sour cream.
5 Spread over the guacamole layer.
6 Sprinkle with shredded lettuce and grated cheese.
7 Top with peppers and tomato.
8 Serve with corn chips.

QUESTIONS

1 Which ingredients in the recipe do you consider to be the healthiest? Explain why.

2 Design your own Mexican dip recipe by substituting different ingredients for the sour cream and taco seasoning mix. Produce and evaluate your recipe ☺ ☺ ☹.

3 Investigate other foods that could be served with the Mexican bean dip.

Cornbread

(serves 4)

Ingredients

125 grams butter
1 cup sugar
4 eggs, beaten
425 grams creamed corn
$\frac{1}{4}$ cup jalapeno chillies, chopped
125 grams cheddar cheese
1 cup cornflour
1 cup cornmeal (polenta)
1 tablespoon baking powder
$\frac{1}{4}$ teaspoon salt

Method

1 Mix butter and sugar together.
2 Gradually add beaten eggs.
3 Add creamed corn, peppers and cheese.
4 Blend dry ingredients together.
5 Gradually add dry ingredients into moist mixture and combine well.
6 Pour mixture into a 20 x 30-centimetre lamington pan.
7 Bake at 180°C for approximately fifty minutes.
8 Serve cornbread warm with guacamole or chilli con carne.

e-HINT

Use a skewer to test whether the cornbread is cooked. If the skewer comes out clean or with a few dry crumbs, the cornbread is cooked.

Mexican pizza

(serves 2)

Ingredients

4 tortillas
200 grams refried beans
250 grams minced beef
2 tablespoons water
$\frac{1}{2}$ packet taco seasoning mix
125 grams cheese, grated
1 Spanish onion, sliced thinly
1 tomato, chopped finely
1 red chilli pepper, chopped finely
$\frac{1}{2}$ cup sour cream
$\frac{1}{2}$ avocado
1 tablespoon black olives, chopped finely

Method

1 Heat tortillas in microwave according to instructions on packet.
2 Place the four tortillas into a round dish and spread with the refried beans.
3 Add meat and water to frying pan. Brown meat and drain any excess liquid.
4 Add seasoning mix and combine well.
5 Spread meat over refried bean mix.
6 Sprinkle with cheese.
7 Bake in oven at 180°C for approximately twenty minutes.
8 Top with onion, tomato, chilli pepper, sour cream, avocado and olives.

QUESTIONS

1 Investigate tortilla recipes by searching the Internet. Find one recipe for a wheat tortilla and one recipe for a corn tortilla. Produce both recipes and evaluate them ☺ ☺ ☹. Which one do you prefer? Why?
2 Design your own Mexican pizza recipe.
3 Investigate the ingredients in the taco seasoning mix packet. Design your own seasoning mix.

10

OUT OF AFRICA: DISCOVER AFRICAN CUISINE

Morocco

West Africa

Africa has a population of more than 500 million people, with more than 1000 languages spoken throughout the continent. The impact of settlement from other countries is evident in parts of Africa. Countries such as Ghana, which were ruled by the British, have adopted English as the official language. The official language of Senegal and the Ivory Coast is French. In Angola, the official language is Portuguese. Morocco, which we will focus on later in this chapter, was ruled by France and Spain during the 19th and 20th centuries, although it is the Arabs, who invaded Morocco in the 7th century AD, and the indigenous Berbers who have most influenced the cuisine.

Unlike Australia, where most people live in cities, the majority of African people live in rural villages. Women are mainly responsible for cooking and a traditional kitchen is often outside, where you will find large pots sitting on stones over an open fire.

e-fact

More than 75 per cent of Africa's land is sparsely inhabited, which means that the other 25 per cent is very crowded!

In North and East Africa, the main religion is Islam. In West Africa and South Africa, the predominant religion is Christianity, although some ancient religions still exist. The different religions influence the culture and food of each region; for example, Muslims must not each or drink during daylight hours throughout the holy month of Ramadan. In the following article, we learn about some of the foods eaten during Ramadan in Morocco. (For more on Moroccan cuisine, see page 138.)

▶ The distinct flavour of Ramadan in Morocco

Read the newspaper article and then answer the questions that follow it.

In the continuing examination of Ramadan traditions around the Islamic world, The Star *spoke with Raja' Alawi, the wife of the Moroccan Ambassador in Amman, about the different traditions found in her native country.*

By Lubna Khader, Star Staff Writer

As the first day of Ramadan begins, a flute player wanders the streets to announce Ramadan's arrival. This continues every night during Sahour. On the last day the wandering minstrel stops at each home asking for Zakat. Many Moroccan women put henna on their hands in celebration of Ramadan's arrival. Alawi explained how many nights during Ramadan are passed reciting prayers in praise of Prophet Mohammed.

Alawi went on to explain the traditions in Morocco. 'When children fast we prepare a special banquet for them with the main dishes of Morocco. We also decorate with incense and candles. The children wear traditional clothes. Then we recite prayers.' Alawi pointed out how, in Morocco, Iftar is divided into two separate, distinct meals. 'We break our fast with dates and a soup called 'Al Haryera', which is the main soup in every Moroccan house. It contains chickpeas soaked overnight and boiled then added to parsley, lentils, tomatoes butter, onion, flour and rice. It is served when the mixture becomes thick with boiled eggs.' After the initial small meal they drink Moroccan green tea instead of the red tea drunk in Jordan. Mrs Alawi pointed out 'The main sweet in Morocco is 'Saloo' made with flour, almonds, a pinch of Arabic gum, sesame, cinnamon and orange blossom water. Another, 'shbakeyeh,' is a pastry mixed with saffron and cinnamon then filled with almonds.' After the initial meal Alawi said a small break is taken for two to three hours where they pray the sunset and night prayer before the main meal is served. The main meal is called 'Cous Cous,' made from wheat. In Morocco there are seven different ways to cook cous cous, one with meat and raisins, another with chicken, chickpeas, carrots, and zucchini. 'In areas like Titwan and Tanjah they make it with fish. Of course all of them are spicy,' she went on the tell *The Star.*

Another dish is 'pastilla,' a pastry filled with chicken stuffing and almonds. 'It is all cut into small pieces, mixed with spices and sugar and then put into the pastry for baking.' During Lailat El Qader on the 27th day of Ramadan another ceremony takes place. 'All the young girls in Morocco wear their best traditional dresses, called 'qouftan,' as during Eid. They go down to the streets to play and take photos. After Iftar both men and women spend the night in the mosque reading the Quran,' she said. Special meals are prepared for the poor and needy. 'Some more well off families even adopt a family and send money and food to their home,' Alawi continued. During Eid the most famous sweet, called 'bagreer,' like Jordan's Qatayef, is prepared. 'All Moroccans pray in the mosque with their traditional dresses. Every Moroccan man, woman and child wears their traditional clothing on the morning of the Eid.' Alawi explained that besides the duty of a housewife, 'Moroccan women have options outside the home and can work as an Ambassador or counselor in the parliament. Illiteracy is still high, and women do face many challenges. The husband still controls the house, the final word is his, but with newly issued laws I believe Moroccan women will gain complete rights.' Alawi commented on some of the differences between Jordan and Morocco. 'We don't have the habit like here in Jordan of women and men going to cafés to drink coffee and hubbly-bubbly after Iftar. This habit is limited to men in Morocco. We don't really have the hubbly-bubbly habit as much though. We spend the nights visiting our relatives,' she concluded.

WEBExTRaS

www.lifeinafrica.com/fun/games/index.htm

This is a fun website with a drag-and-drop jigsaw puzzle. Time yourself against others in the class and see who can finish the puzzle first!

QUESTIONS

1 What happens on the first day of Ramadan?
2 How do the children celebrate Ramadan?
3 Explain what Al Haryera is.
4 Explain the types of sweets served during Ramadan.
5 Identify the different ways to cook couscous.
6 What happens on the twenty-seventh day of Ramadan?
7 Explain how Ramadan is different in Morocco compared to Jordan.
8 Investigate how Ramadan is celebrated in other parts of the world.

Discover West African cuisine

e-Fact

Did you know that an estimated twenty million Africans were shipped as slaves from West Africa to the Americas?

West Africa is made up of several countries, some of which are Ghana, Nigeria, Cameroon, Senegal and Cote d'Ivoire (the Ivory Coast).

Although parts of West Africa were settled by Europeans from Britain, France and Portugal, it is the indigenous foods and the impact of the slave trade that have provided West African cuisine with its unique character. Ghana, formerly a British colony called the Gold Coast, is well known in history as the departure point for millions of Africans who were sent to America as slaves. During the slave trade period, the ships returning from America brought back foods such as plantains, which today are still common ingredients in West African dishes. Moreover, some West African

sweet potato

yam

indigenous foods, such as yams and black-eyed peas, have become popular ingredients in the cuisine of the southern parts of the USA.

In West Africa, root vegetables such as yams, cassava and sweet potato are common foods because they are starchy and filling. They can be cooked in a variety of ways, including baking and boiling. Meals often consist of a soup or stew, cooked in the one pot. A very popular recipe in Ghana is fufu, a starchy mixture with a consistency like mashed potato. One of the main ingredients of fufu is cassava. Fufu is rolled into balls and added to soups and stews. Traditionally, it is eaten with one's fingers.

Conventional West African fufu is made by boiling the starchy cassava, then pounding it into a glutinous mass, usually in a big bowl with a long wooden pole. Sometimes fufu is made with plantains and yams. Yams belong to the banana family, although they are more starchy than sweet. Plantains can be fried; however, they are mostly served boiled and can be served as an accompaniment to any African meal.

Another well-known dish in West Africa is jollof rice, which is like a type of paella. This is also a 'one-pot' meal, with rice, rather than root vegetables, forming the starchy base. It contains chicken and is garnished with egg and lettuce.

Throughout West Africa, you will find many bustling marketplaces. Not far from Accra, the capital of Ghana, is Elmina, a coastal fishing village with over 20 000 people. Elmina is also home to Elmina Castle, one of the main slave castles, from which slaves were led onto ships bound for the Americas.

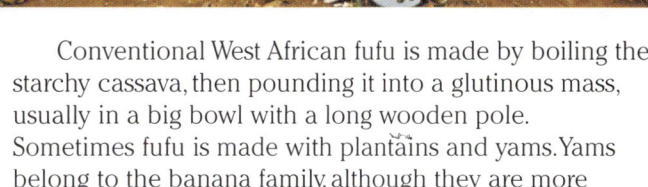

FOOD CRISIS IN AFRICA

More than 14 million people in Southern Africa and 14.3 million in Ethiopia are now facing extreme food shortages and the risk of starvation.

Worst-hit countries in Southern Africa include Zimbabwe, Malawi, Zambia, Mozambique, Lesotho, Swaziland and Angola.

The Ethiopian crisis has the potential to be a repeat of the 1984–85 humanitarian disaster without swift international action. Poor roads and remote communities mean that aid must come soon, if it is to be in time for communities in need.

QUESTIONS

When studying the food and culture of Africa, it is important to remember that many people in the sub-Sahara region face extreme food shortages and require unprecedented levels of food aid. Visit www.caa.org.au/horizons/february_2003/ethiopia.html and answer the following questions.

1   What is causing the food crisis?
2   Identify the main staple foods for the people in rural areas.
3   What are the consequences of inadequate water for the livestock?
4   How does the international coffee market impact on Ethiopia?
5   Explain how the food crisis is affecting people with HIV/AIDS.
6   The people in Afar are nomadic pastoralists. Explain what this means and describe the impact of the drought for these people.
7   Outline the results of the nutrition survey conducted in the Afar region.
8   Discuss the importance of emergency relief for the people of Africa.

28 MILLION PEOPLE
across Africa now face starvation.

Oxfam Community Aid Abroad is bringing relief to the region, but we desperately need your help.

URGENT

® **Oxfam**
Community Aid Abroad

AFRICA IN CRISIS APPEAL
Donate on 1800 088 110 or www.caa.org.au

Image courtesy of OxfamCAA

▶ Let's remember

1   Write a paragraph in your own words, describing the regions, population and languages of Africa.
2   Who is mainly responsible for cooking in Africa and what is a typical kitchen like?
3   How did the slave trade influence the cuisine of West Africa?
4   What are the main ingredients and dishes eaten throughout West Africa?
5   What is a plantain?

▶ Let's investigate

1   Investigate recipes unique to West Africa. Visit www.deliciousindia.com and follow the links to www.deliciousglobe.com/InternationalRecipes/africa/west_africa.htm.
2   Investigate the foods that were brought by African slaves to America.
3   Design, produce and evaluate your own fufu recipe ☺ ☺ ☹.
4   Investigate the countries that make up West Africa. How many are there and what are their names?
5   Investigate the Getaway website at www.travel.ninemsn.com.au/getaway, search for West Africa and read the fact sheets. Design a brochure or flyer that promotes West Africa as a tourist destination.

WEBEXTRAS

www.deliciousglobe.com/International
Recipes/africa/west_africa.htm
Here you can find recipes from all over West Africa and information about the main ingredients and dishes eaten in West Africa.

℮-West African cuisine
www.congocookbook.com

This website contains information about the cooking and culture in all regions of Africa, including West Africa. Visit the link www.congocookbook.com/c0070.html and you will find recipes for the various West African countries.

1 Choose three countries from West Africa and find a typical dish from each country.
2 Click on 'How to have an African dinner party' (www.congocookbook.com/c0073.html).
   a Explain a typical main course.
   b What sorts of food are served for appetisers, soups and desserts?
3 Click on 'Fufu' (www.congocookbook.com/c0042.html).
   a How else can you spell fufu?
   b What other African dishes are similar to fufu? What region/s of Africa are they from?
   c Outline the process for making fufu.

▶ Puzzled
Ghanaian experience

Unscramble the tiles below to reveal the message.

AND	AFRI	STA	ITIO	FUFU	IS
CA	IS A	CASS	UGHO	Y MA	TRAD
PLE	NALL	ITH	EST	UT W	THRO
DE W	AVA				

Jollof rice   (serves 4)

Method

1 Cut chicken into smaller pieces.
2 Heat oil in frypan and cook chicken until browned on both sides.
3 Add onion and chillies and cook for one to two minutes.
4 Add tomatoes, tomato paste and vegetables.
5 Add rice and cook for thirty minutes, until rice has absorbed liquid.
6 Serve, topped with lettuce, parsley and chopped egg.

Variations

1 Choose your own vegetables to add; for example, carrots or mushrooms.
2 Use brown rice instead of white rice.
3 Garnish with coriander instead of parsley.

Ingredients
8 chicken thigh fillets
2 tablespoons peanut oil
1 onion, sliced
2 red chillies, crushed
425 grams tomatoes, chopped
2 tablespoons tomato paste
75 grams green beans, chopped
½ red capsicum, chopped
200 grams long grain rice
4 lettuce leaves, shredded
1 tablespoon parsley
2 eggs, hardboiled

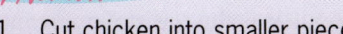

Chilled avocado soup

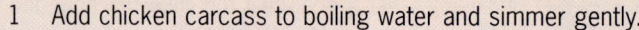

Ingredients
2 cups chicken stock, chilled
1 avocado, puréed
1 tablespoon lime juice
1 tablespoon natural yoghurt
2 shakes Tabasco sauce
black pepper, to taste

Chicken stock
1 chicken carcass
1 litre water
½ onion, sliced roughly
1 celery stalk
½ carrot, chopped
salt and black pepper, to taste

Method

1 Add chicken carcass to boiling water and simmer gently.
2 Add onion, celery and carrot.
3 Simmer for one hour. Add salt and pepper to taste.
4 Reserve two cups of chilled chicken stock for soup.
5 Gradually add stock to puréed avocado.
6 Add lime juice, yoghurt, Tabasco sauce and pepper.
7 Chill and serve garnished with chopped parsley, lime slice and a shake of Tabasco sauce.

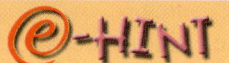

e-HINT
Be careful when preparing chillies not to rub your eyes!

e-FACT
In Morocco, women hold a 'couscous party', where they roll semolina and flour with water until the couscous grains form.

e-FACT
A couscoussière is a double saucepan, with a steamer top for the couscous and a saucepan base for cooking the meat and vegetables. As the couscous steams, it becomes flavoured by the meat and vegetables underneath.

Discover Moroccan cuisine

Morocco is situated in North East Africa, just south of Spain. The majority of Morocco's population are the Berber people, who follow Islam. Although Morocco was occupied by Spain and France, it is the Berbers and the Arabs who have most influenced the cuisine.

In Morocco, couscous is a staple food. It is made from durum wheat or semolina, which is indigenous to North Africa. It is a very versatile food, used like rice, pasta or noodles as the basis of many meals. It can also be used in salads and to thicken and add nutritional value to soups and stews.

couscoussière

In Australia, we mainly refer to couscous as a grain; however, in Morocco, couscous is also the name of a recipe that includes the couscous grain, meat and vegetables. Couscous is considered to be the signature dish of Morocco. There are now a number of instant couscous varieties available in Australian supermarkets that just require boiling water to be added. The traditional method of cooking couscous is to steam it using a couscoussière.

Moroccan cuisine is also characterised by dishes that combine meat (usually lamb) with fruit, and nuts; for example, dates, almonds or walnuts. Moroccan stews or tagines combine these ingredients and are cooked in an earthenware pot called a tagine.

tagine

▶ Let's remember

1 Which people have most influenced Moroccan cuisine?
2 Describe the difference between the grain couscous and the dish couscous.
3 What is a couscoussière?
4 What are the two meanings of the term *tagine*?
5 What combination of ingredients is used in a typical Moroccan stew?

▶ Let's investigate

1 Investigate Ramadan in Morocco by visiting these websites:
www.french.about.com/library/travel/bl-ma-ramadan2.htm
www.french.about.com/library/travel/bl-ma-islam.htm
Imagine you were explaining Ramadan to someone who had never heard of it. Write your explanation in a report of 300–400 words.

2 Design your own tagine recipe. Produce and evaluate your recipe ☺ ☺ ☹.

3 Investigate whether you can find any varieties of couscous that are not instant. Try looking at the supermarket and health food stores. Investigate the different varieties of instant couscous available at the supermarket.

4 Evaluate couscous compared to rice, noodles and pasta according to nutritional value, cooking time and price ☺ ☺ ☹. Table your results.

5 Moroccan cuisine includes the use of spices. Visit www.sallys-place.com/food.htm and investigate the most common spices used. Name three recipes and the spices used in each. Produce one of these recipes and evaluate it ☺ ☺ ☹.

6 In the city of Fez, the number seven is considered to be lucky and couscous with seven vegetables is quite common. Which seven vegetables would you choose for your lucky couscous? Design a couscous recipe that includes your seven vegetables.

WEBEXTRAS

www.foodtv.com/cuisine/moroccoindex
This website provides information about Moroccan recipes, classic dishes and commonly used Moroccan ingredients.

www.recipes4us.co.uk
This website has information about the cuisine of many countries. Click on 'Cooking by Country', scroll down to 'Morocco' and you will find information about the cuisine of Morocco and a range of recipes for different courses.

▶ @-Moroccan cuisine

www.sas.upenn.edu/African_Studies/Cookbook/Morocco.html

1 Describe the two categories of cooking in Morocco.
2 What is a dada?
3 How long might it take a hostess in Morocco to prepare a special meal?
4 Define the terms *chban*, *bstilla* and *batinjaan*.
5 What is the significance of the woman pouring water over the fingers of her guests?
6 How would you describe the dining area in Morocco?

▶ Puzzled

Moroccan mix

Form ten words related to Moroccan cuisine by matching two boxes for each word.

ves	adan	es	tag
cou	turm	ber	chic
nuts	ber	semo	wal
lina	dat	ram	scous
kpeas	ine	oli	eric

Ingredients

1 teaspoon butter
2 teaspoons cumin, ground
$\frac{1}{2}$ teaspoon coriander, ground
$\frac{1}{4}$ teaspoon cinnamon
1 clove garlic, crushed
black pepper, to taste
300 grams cod
1 onion, sliced
$\frac{1}{2}$ lemon
1 tablespoon parsley, chopped

Ingredients

$\frac{1}{4}$ cup plain flour
$\frac{1}{2}$ teaspoon baking powder
$\frac{1}{2}$ teaspoon cinnamon
$\frac{1}{2}$ teaspoon nutmeg
$\frac{1}{4}$ teaspoon cloves, ground
60 grams butter
$\frac{1}{4}$ cup caster sugar
2 large eggs, beaten
$\frac{1}{4}$ teaspoon vanilla
2 tablespoons milk
$\frac{1}{2}$ cup dates, chopped
1 tablespoon walnuts, chopped

Spicy Moroccan fish   (serves 2)

Method

1   Melt butter. Add cumin, ground coriander, cinnamon, garlic and pepper. Mix well.
2   Brush both sides of fish with butter mixture.
3   Grease a piece of aluminium foil and place half the onion on the foil.
4   Top with fish and remaining onion.
5   Loosely wrap the fish in the aluminium foil.
6   Bake in oven at 180°C for thirty minutes, or until fish is cooked.
7   Serve on a bed of couscous with chopped parsley and a lemon wedge.

Variations

Instead of cod, use another type of fish, such as bream or whiting.

Mini Moroccan date puddings   (makes 6)

Method

1   Sift together dry ingredients to ensure spices are mixed throughout.
2   Cream butter and sugar.
3   Gradually add eggs and vanilla.
4   Add flour and spice mixture. Mix well.
5   Add milk and stir until mixture is combined.
6   Add dates and walnuts to mixture.
7   Place into a greased six-muffin tray.
8   Bake at 180°C for twenty minutes, or until cooked.
9   Serve warm with whipped cream.

QUESTIONS

1   Define the term *creaming*.
2   What other types of nuts could you substitute for walnuts?
3   How would you modify this recipe to make twelve puddings?

AROUND THE WORLD: ASSESSMENT TASK 1

This assessment task addresses the outcomes TEMA0601 and TEMA0602 from the Technology Key Learning Area.

▶ Design brief

You have been appointed tour guide for a ten-day cultural and educational trip to a country of your choice or one chosen by your teacher. The itinerary must include a description of all of the towns and cities that you will visit and the tours that you will undertake. You can present your itinerary as a poster, brochure or website. You may use travel brochures as a guide and include photographs and/or diagrams. Your initial task is to find out as much as you can about the country. To do this, you will need to investigate travel websites, brochures from travel agencies and resources from your school library. You are also required to organise the itinerary for the group, which will consist of twenty students from your school.

▶ Part 1

Your itinerary must include the following:
- a site of historical significance, outlining the importance of the site
- a religious site that is representative of the predominant religion
- a site that highlights the geography of a specific region
- a market tour that highlights typical foods
- a visit to a restaurant that serves specialist dishes from the country
- a celebration or festival unique to the country

▶ Part 2

Upon your return to school, you have been asked to arrange a post-tour get-together, which you are required to cater for. Design a three-course meal (include recipes) that is typical of the country that you visited. Produce and evaluate your meal ☺ ☺ ☹.

dROUNd THE WORLd: dSSESSMENT TdSK 2

This assessment task addresses the outcomes HPIP0601 and HPIP0602 from the Health and Physical Education Key Learning Area.

▶ Part 1

globaled.ausaid.gov.au/secondary/casestud/food/1/food.html

1 Investigate and describe the terms *food security* and *food insecurity*.
2 Identify and explain food security issues for Australians.
3 How do food security issues vary for other countries in the world? Choose two examples.

▶ Part 2

Choose a developing country. Search on the Internet to find the answers to the following questions. You may find it useful to search government and tourism websites.

1 Identify the major causes of illness, injury and death in that country.
2 Choose one organisation in that country that promotes health and safety and describe its role.
3 Identify the strategies used by that organisation to promote health and safety.
4 How would you describe the nutritional status of the population for your chosen country?
5 Identify and describe a food selection model for your country. Present the information in a diagram.

3

MAKE a MEaL OF IT

START ME UP: DISCOVER BREAKFAST

Breakfast is considered by many to be the most important meal of the day because it helps to provide us with energy to get through the day. Breakfast quite literally means to 'break the fast', because the time between our evening meal and our first meal the next day is longer than any other period of time between meals. This is another reason why breakfast is such an important start to the day—to refuel the body with food after the period of 'fasting' during the night.

It is important not to skip breakfast and it needs to be quick and easy to prepare, especially if time is limited in the morning. It is becoming popular to eat breakfast and brunch outside at cafés, especially on weekends. Our outdoor lifestyle in Australia and our climate are favourable to this alfresco type of dining. Breakfast meetings during the week are also becoming more popular, especially with young professionals.

Brunch, which is a blend of breakfast and lunch, is usually eaten around 11 am. Breakfast and brunch types of foods are becoming very popular, with many cafés offering breakfast menus until 3 pm and some offering an all-day breakfast menu. In Australia, yum cha, which means to 'drink tea', is also becoming a popular alternative for breakfast. Yum cha consists of a meal of dim sum and Chinese tea. Dim sum is a range of snack foods that can be steamed, fried, baked or boiled. They are usually served on trolleys, allowing you to view and choose your own snacks.

The term *alfresco* means 'in the fresh air', or 'taking place outdoors'.

▶ **Breakfast menu**

Source: www.cafezest.com.au

Bloody Mary—spiced up tomato juice and Absolut vodka	
Seasonal fresh fruit, yoghurt, honey	$8.90
Fruit compote, yoghurt	$8.50
Cocopops	$8.90
Coconut and cinnamon porridge with condiments	$3.50
Zest muesli with yoghurt, compote and honey	$7.50
Toast—jams and spreads	$8.90
Roasted field mushrooms with thyme, toasted sourdough, taleggio, pesto	$4.50
French toast fingers—mascarpone, lemon scented spiced apple	$13.50
Buttermilk and hazelnut pancakes, berry compote, fresh strawberries	$12.50
Green eggs and ham—scrambled eggs, pesto, seared ham	$12.90
Omelette—mushroom, spinach, tomato, cheese	$12.50
Zest Eggs—poached eggs, spinach, tomato, basil béarnaise on toast	$13.50
Eggs—poached, fried, scrambled, boiled on toast	$12.50
Extras— bacon, sausage, hash browns	$6.50
tomato, avocado, mushroom, spinach, béarnaise	$3.00 ea
	$2.00 ea

e-fact

Vegemite is known all over the world as being uniquely Australian.

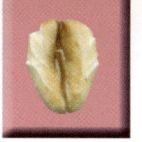

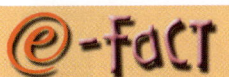

QUESTIONS

1 Use a food dictionary or the website www.foodtv.com/terms/tt-g1/0,1986,,00.html, which contains over 4000 terms, to investigate the definitions of the following terms found in the breakfast menu:
   - **a** compote
   - **b** taleggio
   - **c** mascarpone
   - **d** pesto
   - **e** béarnaise

2 What are condiments?

3 Design your own special breakfast meal that could be added to the menu.

What's for breakfast?

e-fact

Did you know that nine out of ten households have Vegemite in their pantry?

In Australia, many of us eat toast or breakfast cereal for breakfast. One of the most popular items to spread on our toast in Australia is Vegemite. Vegemite is made from yeast extract, which is a concentrated form of yeast. It is also a rich source of B-group vitamins.

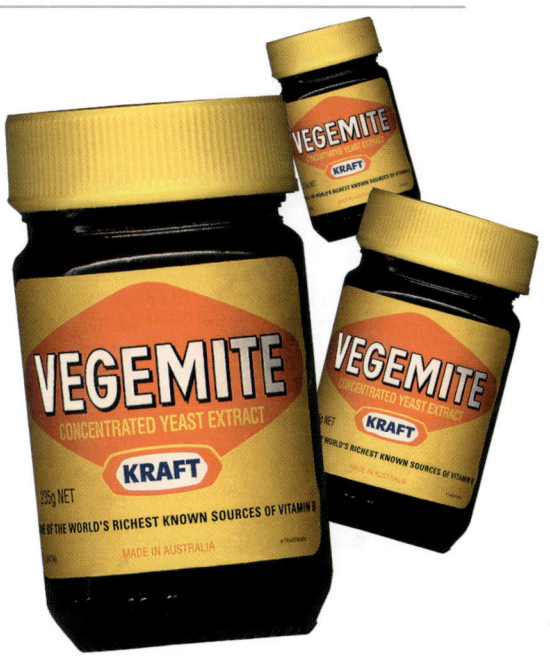

If you eat cereals for breakfast, whether it be toast or breakfast cereal from a packet, try to choose high-fibre alternatives. An average serve of rice bubbles, for example, will only provide 0.5 grams of fibre compared to a high-bran cereal, which can contain up to 9.5 grams of fibre. As we learnt in *e-Food Book 1*, fibre is important for healthy bowels and can help reduce our hunger and make us feel full. This is why having a high-fibre breakfast is important.

The following table shows a comparison of the fibre content for different types of bread.

e-fact

Marmite, which was developed in the UK, is older than Vegemite and celebrated its 100th birthday in 2002.

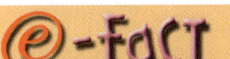

Type of bread	Fibre (grams) per two slices of bread
Sunblest	1.8
White Hyfibe	4.2
Wholemeal	3.6
Multigrain	2.7
Soy-Lin	4.4
Oat & Honey	3.8
Traditional rye	4.2

Source: www.tiptop.com.au

e-fact

Did you know that arachibutyrophobia is a fear of peanut butter sticking to the roof of you mouth?

All about coffee

Not many years ago, if you asked for a cup of coffee in Australia, you would most likely be given instant coffee. If you have a look at the supermarket shelves today, you will see many varieties of coffee beans for grinding and preground coffee for use with a dripolator, percolator or plunger.

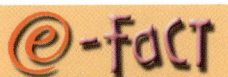

While coffee drinking is on the rise in Australia, so too is our knowledge of coffee and many people are now becoming coffee connoisseurs. Restaurants and cafés in Australia are specialising in coffee, with many of them employing a coffee-making professional, or barista.

▶ Coffee purists' short blacklash

Read the newspaper article and then answer the questions that follow it.

By Vivienne Reiner

Café owner Andrew Ryder steadfastly refuses to serve skim milk or soya milk in his coffees and says if people don't like it, they can go elsewhere.

Mr Ryder is one of the coffee purists who have had enough of the coffee phoneys asking for skinny caps, long browns and muguccinos.

'People come in and ask for all types of crap here. We say this is what we have got: just basic coffee,' said Mr Ryder, who runs Le Petit Crème in Sydney's trendy Darlinghurst.

Independent coffee consultant Gary Trye said that in the past few years, Australians had become increasingly sophisticated in their taste for coffee and more demanding, resulting in a backlash from traditionalists.

'There is an elitist group of cafés that are taking a stand, that are exceptionally proud and arrogant,' Mr Trye said. 'They argue the way they do it is the way coffee should be drunk.'

While he could sympathise with busy coffee-making professionals, or baristas, knocking out numerous drinks simultaneously to different specifications, Mr Trye said he believed baristas should ultimately give customers what they wanted. But he warned against franchises that boasted countless varieties with new-fangled names, no questions asked. A good Italian coffee, he said, was short, rich and strong.

Mr Ryder said it was not only that the fashionable new deviations from traditional coffee compromised the quality of the drink, but it was how you drank it.

'In Europe, people sit down and have a coffee at the bar, have a short black and walk out—the whole business takes about 30 seconds,' he said.

But today's Australians wanted their soy low-fat latte on the side while 'reading the newspaper and looking trendy', he said.

Across Sydney, the bustling Bar Italia, on Leichhardt's Italian strip, even displays a sign warning potentially difficult pundits against even asking for skim milk or goat's milk.

Bar Italia's owner of 10 years, Peter Cama said there were plenty of places that offered soy and skim, but 'our milk is full cream milk, period, full stop. That's the way it is'.

'You don't walk into a coffee bar in Italy and say "give me a soyaccino". They'll throw you out,' he said.

Scene from *LA Story*

'I'll have a decaf coffee.'
'I'll have a decaf espresso.'
'I'll have a double decaf cappuccino.'

'Do you have any decaffeinated coffee ice-cream?'
'I'll have a half decaf with a twist of lemon.' (Steve Martin)
'I'll have a twist of lemon.'
'I'll have a twist of lemon.'
'I'll have a twist of lemon.'
'I'll have a twist of lemon.'

Basics of all good coffees

- Machine should be running at 9-bar (atmospheric pressure)
- Use 7 g coffee for 1 standard-strength espresso, and 30 mL liquid
- Coffee should be extracted in 25–30 seconds; no more, no less
- Coffee must be below boiling or it will burn and taste bitter
- For longer coffees, add water or milk. For shorter and weaker coffees, stop extraction earlier

QuESTIONS

1. Why is there a backlash from café owners about serving skim milk or soya milk in coffee?
2. What is a barista?
3. Describe a good Italian coffee.

Quick and healthy breakfast tips

Here are some healthy breakfast tips, including some tips for when you are in a hurry in the morning.

· Prepare a Bircher muesli the night before and then all you have to do is take the bowl out of the refrigerator in the morning.
· Whip up a smoothie with whatever fruit you have on hand. If you do not have time to peel the fruit, keep some frozen fruit, such as strawberries or raspberries, in the freezer.
· Butter contains saturated fat, which is linked to cholesterol, so choose margarine instead.
· Get into the pattern of looking at labels and choose cereals with higher amounts of fibre.
· If you sleep in and are running late, take some fresh fruit with you to eat on the way to school.

Can you think of other healthy breakfast tips?

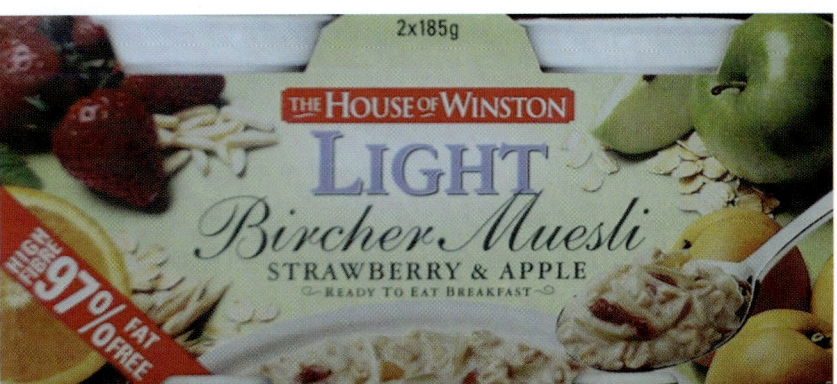

Ingredients: natural low fat yoghurt (skim milk, concentrated skim milk, live cultures) (30%), apple (17%), rolled oats (10%), water, orange juice, apple juice, strawberries (5%), sugar, thickened cream (cream, gelatin (halal), vegetable gum (407a), emulsifier (471)), raspberries, lemon juice, milk powder, coconut, almonds, vegetable gums (412, 415), flavour, cinnamon, preservative (202, 220), colour (162), food acids (300, 327, 330).

QUESTIONS

Refer to the Bircher Muesli packet.
1 The variety shown on the packet is Strawberry and Apple. What is the percentage of apple and strawberry indicated on the label?
2 Why do you think the label states 'Strawberry and Apple' rather than 'Apple and Strawberry'?
3 The packet indicates 'high in fibre'. Do you think the label should show the percentage of fibre in the nutritional information table? Explain your answer.

 ▶ **Nation goes out more for breakfast**

Read the newspaper article and then answer the questions that follow it.

Australians are eating out more often, particularly at breakfast, a study has found.

They are demanding healthier products and worry about chemical ingredients in food but are becoming less concerned about whether the food is home grown.

The survey, conducted every two years, also revealed that Australians are rapidly developing a taste for spicy foods and favour Italian cuisine.

The BIS Shrapnel analysis of food industry trends—The Australian Foodservice Market 2002–2004—now in its seventh edition, is based on more than 1500 interviews with foodservice operators in the institutional and commercial sectors and with wholesalers and distributors.

The principal author, industry consultant Sandro Mangosi, calculates the value of the foodservice industry in Australia to be more than $24 billion a year at retail prices, a figure expected to increase to $32 billion by 2011.

Australians consume 226 meals a year that are prepared away from home, including takeaways, compared with 201 meals a year a decade ago.

Most of the increase is reflected in a 38 per cent lift in breakfast meals and is attributed to cafés and a move to cheaper Asian takeaways in preference to the traditional steak or fish and chips.

The study shows multiculturalism has had, and will continue to have, a major impact on the foodservice industry, with around 75 per cent of Australians eating ethnic foods regularly.

Moreover, they are using nearly 70 per cent more spices in food preparation than a decade ago.

The study rates Italian food as the fastest growing cuisine, followed by modern Australian, and after that a variety of Asian dishes including Thai, Chinese, Vietnamese and Japanese, and Mexican food.

The survey shows a decreasing preference for Australian-made products among foodservice operators with 24 per cent of those surveyed always selecting locally produced goods compared with 29 per cent in 1999.

An increasing percentage of respondents, 37 per cent compared with 25 per cent in 1999, have no preference for local produce.

Since the 1999 survey, interest in healthy foods and beverages, particularly in additive-free and fat-free products, has increased.

QUESTIONS

1 Summarise the trends indicated in the article in relation to food patterns for Australian consumers.

2 What is the percentage increase in the number of breakfast meals eaten out?

3 How many meals per year are prepared away from home, compared to a decade ago? How can the increase be explained?

4 Explain how multiculturalism has changed our eating patterns.

5 Why do you think there has been a decrease in preference for Australian-made products?

 ▶ **Stressed-out teens need to learn how to 'chill'**

Read the newspaper article and then answer the questions that follow it.

By Huyi Jin Elizabeth Kim

No longer a child. Not yet an adult. Adolescents are in the process of developing skills they will take into adulthood—and perhaps the most important of these are healthy ways to cope with stress.

Stress is what you feel when you fail to deal with pressure, either from school, family and friends or from inside yourself, like wanting to do well in school or wanting to fit in.

Stress isn't all bad. It can help you meet deadlines and give you an edge in sports. But too much stress hurts the body and the mind.

When you're being chased by a bully or surprised by a pop quiz, your body responds by making a stress hormone called cortisol. Over time, too much stress can decrease white blood cells that help fight infections.

In a recent study published by researchers at Murdoch University in Australia, 45 children with a history of 10 or more infections in the past year were taught stress management and relaxation skills. Afterward, episodes of chronic colds were shorter and blood tests showed increased levels of infection-fighting antibodies.

Statistics confirm that stressed-out adolescents are at a higher risk of self-destructive behavior such as alcohol use, smoking and drugs, learning difficulties, depression and anxiety disorders.

Here's an example of how one adolescent in the Detroit area deals with stress:

Stacy Chen, 17, starting junior year at Pioneer High School, Ann Arbor, Mich.

• **Stressors:** 'The biggest source of stress is family,' says Stacy, who acknowledges her parents are always telling her to study harder to get into a good college.

• **The coping mechanisms:** When Stacy felt stressed out while studying for the SATs with her twin sister, Tracy, this summer, she first talked to her parents. 'They encouraged me by telling me that I will do better. I believe them, because if I study hard enough I can improve,' says Stacy.

• **What experts say:** Because the family is the most intimate social environment of an adolescent, family members are a major source of both stress and social support.

Too many familial stresses can affect a child's growth. In a study published last year by researchers at the Polish Academy of Sciences, 271 girls whose family dysfunction exposed them to prolonged

distress were more likely to have early puberty and shorter stature.

Parents are advised to make more time for talking to children about all topics, not just problems.

'Parents can be a tremendous resource for kids as they move into middle and high school with the influence of peers increasing,' says John A. Ryan, a psychologist in private practice in St. Clair Shores. 'Parents should be involved with open interest in what their kids are doing. The key is open communi-cation and listening, not pro-viding a solution. Parents tend to be solution-oriented and move too fast.'

Three ways to manage stress

THE MIND

• Maintain a positive attitude. 'I can't control what's causing the stress, but I can change how I react to things.'
• Do not demand perfection but set realistic goals.
• Talk things out.

• Take a break. Make time for things you enjoy doing, like listening to music or spending time with a pet. Research shows people with pets have healthier lives.

EXERCISE

• Regular exercise for 20 to 30 minutes three times a week is effective in reducing stress.
• Workouts can raise the amount of helpful chemicals in the brain, including endorphins, which produce a sense of well-being.

DIET

• Start the day with a healthy breakfast. Research shows eating a low-fat, high-carbo-hydrate breakfast makes students more alert, focused and in a better mood than those eating a high-fat breakfast or no breakfast at all. Skipping breakfast can lower the body's ability to cope with stress later in the day.
• Avoid having too many caffein-ated drinks. They increase the heart rate and cause feelings of anxiety.

WEBExTras

www.qsa.qld.edu.au/yrs 1_10/kla/hpe/pdf/ modules/qhm035.pdf
This module, entitled 'Breakfast is cool', has been developed by the Queensland School Curriculum Council and contains ideas for teaching about breakfast through the Health and Physical Education key learning area.

QUESTIONS

1 Write one or two paragraphs to describe what this article is about.
2 'Because the family is the most intimate social environment of an adolescent, family members are a major source of both stress and social support.' Do you agree or disagree with this statement? Include information from the article to support your answer.
3 Explain the link between stress and eating breakfast.
4 'Skipping breakfast can lower the body's ability to cope with stress later in the day.' What are your thoughts on this statement? How do you feel when you skip breakfast?
5 How do you 'chill out'? How do you react to stress? What do you do to alleviate stress?

▶ Let's remember

1 What is the literal meaning of breakfast?
2 Why is breakfast so important?
3 Alfresco dining has become more popular. Why?
4 What is the meaning of the term *yum cha*?
5 Explain the term *dim sum*.
6 Is Vegemite nutritious? Explain your answer.
7 How does the fibre content of an average serve of rice bubbles compare to an average serve of a high-bran cereal?
8 Why is it important to choose high-fibre cereal alternatives?
9 Explain why you think the breads in the table on page 145 have differing amounts of fibre.
10 Why would you choose margarine in preference to butter?

WEBExTras

www.kellogg.com.au/ DisplayPage.asp?Page ID = 319&sectionid = 1
The Australian Kellogg's website has facts about healthy eating and the importance of breakfast.

▶ Let's investigate

1 A National Nutrition Survey was conducted in 1995 by the Australian Bureau of Statistics and the Commonwealth Department of Health and Ageing. Statistics showed that 71 per cent of girls aged 12–15 regularly ate breakfast (five or more days per week) compared to 87 per cent of boys. By age 16–18, 63 per cent of girls regularly ate breakfast compared to 72 per cent of boys. (Source: Australian Bureau of Statistics, 1997.)
   a How would you explain the fact that more boys than girls eat breakfast?
   b Why do you think fewer boys and girls eat breakfast as they get older?
   c Conduct a survey in class to determine how many students regularly eat breakfast. How does the class percentage compare to the national statistics?

WEBExTras

www.nutritioncamp.com /nutrition/breakfast/ index.html
This site has breakfast information from the 'Nutrition Camp' section of the Kellogg's website.

2 Visit www.dietclub.com.au/createameal/?menu=1 to create your own McDonald's meal. The various menu items can be dragged and dropped onto a tray and you can see the kilojoule and fat content increase as each item is added. You can also click on the nutrition chart to find out the nutrient content for carbohydrate, protein and sodium. Create at least three different McDonald's breakfasts and draw up a table to show the kilojoule and nutrient content of each. Then write a paragraph on the nutritional content of a McDonald's breakfast. Include recommendations.

3 Purchase eight different bread types and conduct a sensory analysis for the breads, both fresh and toasted. Which ones are the most popular according to aroma, flavour, taste and texture? How does this compare with their fibre content? In other words, are the high-fibre breads the least or most popular?

4 Investigate the differences between a dripolator, a percolator and a plunger.

e-Breakfast

www.foodsciencebureau.com.au/health/breakfast.htm

Answer the following questions from the fact sheet 'The Facts About Breakfast'.
1 What are the reasons given for eating breakfast?
2 How can physical and mental performance be affected by missing breakfast?
3 Why do people skip breakfast?
4 What is a typical Australian breakfast?
5 Provide some breakfast tips for people who do not have much time in the morning.

www.cuisinenet.com

1 Visit www.cuisinenet.com/digest/breakfast/index.shtml. From where do we get the word *breakfast*?
2 What are the terms for breakfast in France, Germany and Portugal and what is their literal meaning?
3 Visit the link www.cuisinenet.com/digest/breakfast/cereal.shtml. Explain why the cereal industry came into being and describe what led to the creation of the first breakfast cereal.

www.twinings.com

The origin of tea can be dated back to the Chinese civilisation, almost 3000 years BC. Visit the Twinings website to learn more about the history and traditions of tea.
1 Visit the link www.twinings.com/en_int/stay_healthy/whyisteagood.html. Explain why tea is considered to be good for you.
2 Visit the link www.twinings.com/en_int/world_of_tea/australia.html. Explain how a 'billy' is unique to Australia.
3 From the homepage, click on 'Tea finder', then 'Flavour'. What four words are used to explain the flavour of tea?
4 Conduct a tea tasting and a sensory analysis in class. Use the four words from question 3 to evaluate the flavour ☺ ☺ ☹. Alternatively, you could use a Y-chart.

Puzzled

Breakfast scramble

Unscramble the following types of breakfast cereals.
1 occo sopp
2 uslime
3 sflrconake
4 lal nbar

www.coffeescience.org
An online source of information about coffee, caffeine and questions about coffee and health.

5 stju githr
6 crei ebusblb
7 itrnu-niagr
8 k pesclia
9 doller toas
10 nrab klfase

Coffee match

Match the following types of coffee with their definition.

www.gloriajeanscoffees.com.au/coffee/coffee_regions.asp
Gloria Jean's Coffees is a chain of business franchises. Their website contains information about the regions of the world where coffee is grown.

Coffee type	Definition
Café latte	Cappuccino made with soy milk
Cappuccino	A shot of espresso topped with foam
Espresso	Made with half milk, half coffee
Macchiato	A drink with equal amounts of espresso, steamed milk and foam
Café au lait	A strong method of brewing coffee by forcing high pressure water through the finely ground coffee
Soyaccino	A shot of espresso, topped with steamed milk and foam

How many cereals?

Divide into groups of three. Set a time limit of fifteen minutes and see which group can list the most number of breakfast cereals. Complete the activity for types of breads.

LET'S PRODUCE

Ingredients

2 teaspoons vinegar
2 English muffins
2 slices leg ham
4 eggs

Hollandaise sauce

60 grams butter
2 egg yolks
2 tablespoons white wine vinegar
1 teaspoon lemon juice
salt and black pepper, to taste

Eggs Benedict

(serves 2)

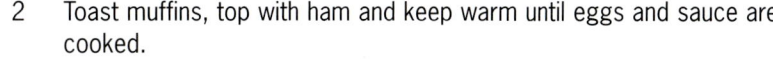

Method

1 Half fill a small saucepan with water. Add vinegar. Bring to boil.
2 Toast muffins, top with ham and keep warm until eggs and sauce are cooked.
3 Break eggs into a small cup and gently place one at a time into water.
4 Cook for three minutes, or until just soft.
5 Cut butter into smaller pieces and melt in microwave on medium high for thirty seconds, or until melted.
6 Cool slightly. Add lightly beaten egg yolks.
7 Add white wine vinegar and lemon juice.
8 Cook in microwave on medium high for thirty seconds, or until cooked, stirring occasionally.
9 If necessary, add a little water to adjust consistency of sauce.
10 Season with salt and pepper.
11 To serve, lift eggs using a slotted spoon and place on top of muffin and ham. Pour sauce over and serve immediately.

Bircher muesli

(serves 2)

Ingredients

1 cup rolled oats
$\frac{1}{2}$ cup yoghurt, any flavour
$\frac{1}{2}$ cup milk
$\frac{1}{4}$ cup sultanas
2 tablespoons slivered almonds
6 dried apricots, chopped
$\frac{1}{2}$ apple, grated

Method

1   Combine all ingredients and soak overnight in refrigerator.
2   Serve with fresh fruit of your own choice.

e-Fact

Muesli was created by Dr Bircher-Benner and in the German language the word *muesli* means 'mixture'.

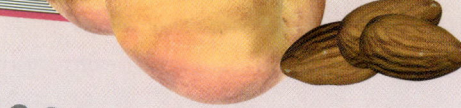

Fruit kebabs

(serves 2)

Ingredients

$\frac{1}{8}$ cantaloupe
1 banana
8 strawberries
2 kiwi fruit
$\frac{1}{8}$ pineapple
2 teaspoons lemon juice
1 cup yoghurt, any flavour

Method

1   Peel and cut all fruit into even-sized pieces.
2   Dip the banana in lemon juice to prevent browning.
3   Thread fruit onto skewers, alternating the different fruits.
4   Serve with yoghurt.

Apple cinnamon pancakes

(serves 2)

Ingredients

1 cup plain flour
$\frac{1}{2}$ teaspoon baking powder
$\frac{1}{2}$ teaspoon cinnamon
1 tablespoon sugar
1 cup buttermilk
$\frac{1}{2}$ teaspoon vanilla
2 eggs, separated
$\frac{1}{4}$ cup butter, melted
1 Granny Smith apple, peeled, cored and chopped
1 tablespoon chopped walnuts
1 tablespoon butter, extra
4 tablespoons maple syrup

Method

1   Sift together the flour, baking powder and cinnamon. Add sugar.
2   Stir in the buttermilk, vanilla and beaten egg yolks.
3   Add the butter and beat mixture until smooth.
4   Stir in the apple and walnuts.
5   Beat the egg whites until firm and gently fold into batter.
6   Melt $\frac{1}{2}$ tablespoon extra butter in non-stick frypan.
7   Add spoonfuls of mixture to pan. When bubbles appear, turn and brown other side.
8   Serve immediately with warmed maple syrup.

Ingredients

4 slices raisin bread
2 tablespoons butter
2 tablespoons brown sugar
$\frac{1}{4}$ cup walnuts, chopped
1 tablespoon golden syrup
3 eggs
$1\frac{1}{2}$ cups milk
$\frac{1}{2}$ teaspoon vanilla
$\frac{1}{4}$ teaspoon cinnamon
pinch nutmeg
200 grams yoghurt, any flavour

Breakfast bread and butter pudding

(serves 2)

Method

1 Spread raisin bread with butter and place in greased dish.
2 Mix brown sugar and walnuts together. Sprinkle on bread.
3 Drizzle golden syrup over sugar and walnut mixture.
4 In a bowl, mix eggs, milk and spices.
5 Pour over bread slices and topping.
6 Place dish into a water bath.
7 Bake in moderate oven for thirty to forty-five minutes.
8 Serve with yoghurt.

e-HINT

Place the golden syrup container into a bowl of hot water or heat in a microwave oven for twenty seconds. This will soften the syrup and make it easy to measure and pour.

QUESTIONS

1 What is the purpose of using a water bath?
2 What is the name of the process that causes the eggs to set?
3 Why is it important to cook the egg and milk mixture slowly?

12

IN THE BaG: DISCOVER LUNCH

In many countries around the world, lunch is the main meal of the day. However, in Australia, lunch has traditionally been a lighter meal, with our largest meal being dinner. Culture and climate often influence the types of lunches served in different countries around the globe. In colder climates, such as in Canada and Russia, a hot hearty meal is often served at lunchtime, whereas in Australia, especially in the warmer months, a sandwich or salad is popular.

Because we are often away from home during lunchtime, we have developed lunch meals that are portable. Lunchboxes, especially for school children, are common. Australian students eat lunch at school nearly 200 days each year.

Did you know that in Sweden school lunches are free?

A cafeteria is a restaurant where you serve yourself and collect your own food, usually on a tray.

In Australia, there are more school canteens than all other takeaway outlets combined, including McDonald's, Pizza Hut and even the small takeaway shops.

In other countries, such as the USA and the United Kingdom, school lunches are provided at cafeterias where it is possible to sit down and eat a hot meal for lunch. The 'meal of the day' is a nutritionally well-balanced meal, usually subsidised in price to make it more affordable. This encourages students to purchase a healthy meal and promotes the importance of health and well being within the school community. In Australia, most of our school canteens or tuckshops do not provide facilities for sitting down and eating a meal.

One of the problems with school canteens in Australia for many years has been the amount of junk food available for purchase. In Queensland, a tuckshop 'smart card' is being trialled, as described in the following article.

▶ Tuckshop smartcard a healthy success

Read the newspaper article and then answer the questions that follow it.

Parents now have a way to ensure their kids are not eating junk food at school with a specially-designed smart card which lets them limit the types of food that children can buy.

The smart card works just like a debit card: parents can pre-pay the monthly tuckshop bill and can top it up at anytime. When a child makes a purchase at the tuckshop, canteen staff swipe the card, debiting the purchase price from the balance.

The card also contains information supplied by parents warning of allergies to foods such as a potentially lethal allergy to peanuts or whatever restrictions they have on junk food and special dietary needs.

'To be able to put on the card that he reacts to red and green food colouring—to stop him buying that, it's just peace of mind,' said one parent.

The canteen queue is processed much faster with no cash involved. Canteen staff are enjoying a healthy rise in profits, saying because the food is healthy, parents are letting their children spend more at the tuckshop.

The smart card has been trialled successfully for five months on the Sunshine Coast, leading the Federal Government and health experts to recommend all schools implement the card, which will cost them $120 a month.

'In the long term they'll learn a lot about healthy food choices, and they'll hopefully make those choices outside the school arena,' said Sandy Towell from the Federation of Canteens.

QUESTIONS

1. Explain how the smart card works.
2. What is the cost of implementing the smart card?
3. Do you think parents should have control over limiting the types of food that children can buy? Explain your answer.
4. How can the card help children with allergies?
5. What is the reaction of canteen staff to the smart card?
6. What impact do you think the smart card might have on influencing children to purchase healthy foods in the long term?

School lunchbox ideas

Just as breakfast is important to provide you with energy to start off the day, lunch is also important because it helps you to maintain your energy during the day, especially at school when you are being physically and mentally active. Skipping lunch or buying junk food is not the best option. Taking that little bit of extra time in the morning, or even the night before, to prepare a good healthy lunch is important. If you go without lunch, you will find it harder to concentrate in the afternoon.

A healthy lunch could consist of a wholegrain sandwich (with a healthy filling, such as cheese and salad), a piece of fruit and a juice drink. In summer, freezing your drink can also help to keep the rest of your lunch chilled. In addition to your juice, make sure that you drink as much water as possible throughout the day. Water should be readily available from school taps at your school and is a much cheaper alternative than purchasing bottled water.

It is also a good idea to carry a water bottle with you so that you can drink water on your way to and from school and during class. Remember, we should all be consuming at least eight glasses of water each day. If a sandwich, fruit and juice are not enough, fill your lunchbox with additional fruit or nuts to snack on in preference to potato chips, chocolate, biscuits or cake.

Sandwich ideas

Consider the following suggestions when planning lunch. Remember that a balance of foods from those suggested in the Australian Guide to Healthy Eating is important.

Cereals, bread, pasta and noodles (preferably wholegrain)

If you get tired of eating the same thing for lunch, vary the type of bread you eat by choosing from sliced bread, rolls, bagels, lavash, pita bread, focaccia, Turkish bread, pita bread, tortillas, muffins, rye, multigrain or wholemeal breads.

Vegetables and legumes

Legumes are particularly good for us because they tend to be high in fibre and low in fat. Try a pita bread sandwich spread with hommos and filled with falafel (blended chickpeas) and salad ingredients, such as lettuce, tomato and cucumber. Consider including some vegetable snacks, such as pieces of carrot and celery.

Fruit

Any whole fresh fruit, such as apples, oranges, mandarins, pears and bananas, is an easy addition to a lunchbox. Fruit such as kiwi fruit, cantaloupe or watermelon needs to be prepared beforehand and wrapped carefully. You may like to consider adding a small can (with ring-pull top) of fruit in natural juice to a lunchbox. Dried fruit is also good to include as a snack.

Milk, yoghurt and cheese

Cheese slices are an easy sandwich filling and now come in many varieties, such as Edam, Swiss, Havarti and Gouda. Ricotta cheese and cottage cheese, especially the low-fat varieties, are also good choices.

Meat, fish, poultry, eggs, nuts and legumes

Although processed meats, such as ham, salami, pastrami and prosciutto, are relatively easy sandwich fillings to prepare, try to include canned fish, such as tuna or salmon, as these contain omega-3 fatty acids, or 'good fat'. Consider including cooked chicken legs or wings (preferably without the skin) and hard-boiled eggs as alternatives. Grated carrot, peanut butter, sultanas and peanuts are favourite sandwich fillings. Also consider a small pack of unsalted nuts for a snack.

Extras

Limit the extras, such as margarine, by choosing a low-fat cheese to spread on your bread. Also consider using spreads such as hommos, guacamole or low-fat cream cheese.

Case Study

LUNCH IDEas

QUESTIONS

1. For each of the products shown, which age group do you consider to be the target market?
2. How do you think the addition of a spoon and napkin to the Seakist Lunch Kit might influence a consumer's purchasing decision?
3. Would you consider any of these products as lunch options for you, either at school or at home? Explain your answer.
4. In relation to food safety, do you think these products would be suitable for a school lunchbox? What special food safety factors might you need to consider? Can you find any storage recommendations on any of the labels?
5. How would you store the Petit Miam yoghurt tube to ensure its safety?
6. Which of the products do you consider the most suitable, according to nutritional value, ease of packing into a school lunchbox and storage?
7. Identify the marketing strategies being used to encourage consumers to purchase these products.
8. Can you identify any slogans being used to promote these products?
9. Evaluate the different types of packaging ☺ ☺ ☹.
10. How might the age of the target market affect the type of packaging?
11. Do you consider some packaging to be more environmentally friendly than others? Explain your answer.
12. A parent has asked you to give your opinion on the suitability of these products for their child's lunchbox. Write a couple of paragraphs, summarising your advice to the parent.

School canteens

If you purchase your lunch from the school canteen, you are faced with making a choice about what you will buy. This will, of course, depend on the range of foods available. In some schools, too much of the food offered falls into the 'junk food' category. School canteens are facing increasing pressure to offer healthier choices. How healthy is your school canteen? Where possible, try to follow the lunchbox guidelines listed earlier under the Australian Guide to Healthy Eating. Remember, you can always bring some fruit and juice from home and just purchase a healthy sandwich or roll from the school canteen.

▶ Good food but there's a snag

Read the newspaper article and then answer the questions that follow it.

By STEVE DOW

Our children are ballooning, and school tuckshops may be complicit in the unprecedented obesity levels. The drive to commercial leasing and profits is compelling canteens to sell junk food alongside healthier lunches and snacks.

An estimated half of Victorian primary schools and almost all high schools have now leased their tuckshops to commercial operators, and the number is increasing.

While most schools have written into their canteen contracts that healthy food must be sold, most are forced to compromise and allow pies, chips and confectionery to also go on sale.

Parents Victoria president Lynne Reddon says schools have 'total say' over foods sold when they run their own canteen, and usually less input when they lease the canteen out. She urges schools to be forthright with canteen companies about what will go on sale.

More schools are opting out of the headache of hands-on canteen management, spurred partly by a growing reluctance of parents to volunteer their time in canteens.

Yet many of the schools that still run their own canteens also have junk food on the menu.

'The vast majority of secondary schools are built next to a shop and if kids don't get what they want in the canteen they'll go to the shop,' says the principal of Fairhills High School, in Knox, Harvey Wood. Fairhills still runs its own canteen and offers health and junk food as a compromise.

'That's the reality. We have a McDonald's and a KFC just down the road,' Mr Wood says.

Australian Medical Association president Kerryn Phelps wants parents to become more active about what is sold in canteens, given 20 per cent of boys and girls are now considered obese, up from 3 per cent in the 1960s.

Dr Phelps also wants parents to be more diligent about the food they pack in children's lunches, and says she would support censorship of the glut of junk food advertising that appears during children's television viewing hours.

But it is the call from Dr Phelps for parents to improve the quality of tuckshop fare that appears to be causing the most agitation among principals and caterers, who argue that children should be allowed to exercise choice between junk and healthy food.

Nutritionist Prue Cerin, the public officer with the Victorian Schools Canteen Association, says she tries to inform schools about healthier products.

However, since 1993 when the Kennett government stopped funding the association, Ms Cerin has run a wholesale non-perishable foods supply business that caters for 400 school canteens and sells snack foods such as chips, as well as healthy foods. Such a balance is necessary for her business to remain viable and it is what canteens demand, she says.

But Ms Cerin is critical of the trend towards leasing canteens. 'It's more profitable to downgrade the canteen,' she says. 'It's a growing trend. It often means the quality goes down. The canteen volunteers go out and the deep fryers go in.'

Mr Wood says any intervention forcing schools to stop offering junk food would be counter-productive.

'The reality is our society as a whole makes both healthy and unhealthy food available,' he says.

'We teach good nutrition in home economics classes. Most canteens would have healthy foods, and students are then in a situation where they can make a choice. If there is no junk food, the student isn't allowed to make that choice,' Mr Wood says.

Ms Reddon says that while having junk food in canteens remains an issue, such foods are required to turn a profit. Parents Victoria supports such sales as long as healthy food is also offered, she says.

School-run canteens are difficult to staff because fewer parents are now prepared to volunteer their time and, if they are available, are more interested in helping with reading and mathematics in the classroom than in serving food, Ms Reddon says.

Victorian Primary Principals Association president Lex Arthurson is, like many of his contemporaries, pragmatic about the canteen leasers and suppliers who are balancing health with junk.

'I think a packet of chips is reasonable to sell,' he says. 'Not that they're the greatest thing on earth, but if there's chips on sale at the canteen plus a range of other things that are nutritious as well, then the kids' range of interest is covered. If all that's on sale are carrots and sultanas and health bars, there's resentment of that.'

QUESTIONS

1 Why do canteens sell junk food?
2 Why are more schools opting out of operating a school canteen?

3 What suggestion does Dr Phelps make in relation to promoting healthy eating?

4 What problems have the Victorian Schools Canteen Association been facing?

5 Does your school have shops close by, where you can purchase your lunch?

6 Do you think junk food should be banned from school canteens? Explain your answer.

Salads

Lunch is a meal that many people do not spend too much time preparing. A quick healthy lunch option, especially during the summer months, may be a salad. In Australia, salads have become very popular because of our warm climate and as an accompaniment to the traditional barbecue. A salad is also a great way to increase our vegetable consumption and, with so many more salad greens available now, we have loads of options for tasty interesting salads.

Increasingly, salads are forming the basis of a meal, rather than just being an accompaniment; for example, ordering a caesar salad or a Cajun chicken salad at a restaurant for lunch or even dinner. Dressings are now becoming more varied and are also adding to the popularity of salads. We need to remember that some salads are not as healthy as others. Try to avoid having too many salads with creamy dressings, which include mayonnaise or sour cream; for example, some coleslaws, potato salads and pasta salads.

Many countries have a salad that can be associated with their cuisine. Some of these are tabouleh salad from Turkey or Lebanon, French or niçoise salad from France, caesar salad from the USA and warm potato salad from Germany.

▶ Let's remember

1 What types of lunches are popular in Australia? Why?

2 Why is lunch such an important meal of the day?

3 How do school canteens in Australia differ from those in other countries?

4 Provide an example of a healthy school lunch.

5 Identify the different types of breads available for sandwiches.

6 What kind of fruit would be suitable to include in a school lunchbox?

7 How could you limit the foods that are considered to be extras, according to the Australian Guide to Healthy Eating?

8 Why is salmon or tuna a good choice for a sandwich filling?

9 Why are salads popular in Australia?

10 Explain why salads are increasingly a meal alternative rather than an accompaniment.

▶ Let's investigate

1 Investigate what each class member had for lunch at school yesterday. How many students purchased lunch from the school canteen and how many brought lunch from home? Who prepared the lunch, if it was brought from home? Compile a list of the different range of foods consumed for lunch. On average, how many serves of fruit and vegetables are included?

2 Investigate and classify the range of lunch foods eaten by class members according to the different cultures represented. How do they vary?

3 Visit www.chdf.org.au and scroll down the links to 'School canteens'. Investigate your own school canteen and write a report on whether you think your school canteen promotes healthy eating.

4 Investigate lunch menus offered at a range of restaurants by searching the Internet. What are the most common types of lunch menu items?

5 You are going to open a new sandwich bar. Investigate the range of possible sandwich fillings. Design your own sandwich bar menu, including eight different varieties of sandwich options. Name each sandwich. What is the name of your new establishment? Produce a menu, including prices. What marketing strategies would you employ to advertise and promote your new menu?

6 Investigate the range of salad dressings and mayonnaise products that you can purchase.

7 Design your own Italian, thousand island and French dressing to make from scratch.

8 Investigate the range of pre-prepared salads that you can buy from supermarkets and delicatessens. Also, Investigate why pre-prepared salads are not sold self-serve any more.

℮-Lunch

www.tiptop.com.au

1 Click on 'What's new'. What is omega-3 DHA? What are the sources of DHA?

2 Visit the link www.tiptop.com.au/nutrition.htm. Check your body mass index and see whether it falls within the healthy range.

3 Tip Top bakeries also make Burgen bread. Use the link www.burgen.com.au.
   a Investigate the range of breads available.
   b Compare the GI ratings of the different varieties.

4 The Glycaemic Index symbol is licensed to food products that meet specific criteria. What are these criteria?

5 Visit the link www.tiptop.com.au/nutrition.htm. Scroll down to the bottom and identify the types of sandwich fillings that are suitable for freezing.

www.whatscookingamerica.net/History/SandwichHistory.htm

1 Define the term *sandwich*.
2 Write a paragraph about the history of sandwiches.
3 What is a club sandwich?
4 From where did the Dagwood sandwich originate?
5 How would you describe a submarine sandwich?

Puzzled

Know your salad

Fill in the missing words to complete the following sentences about salads.
1 A salad that includes apples, walnuts and celery is a _ _ _ _ _ _ _ salad.
2 The main ingredient in a niçoise salad is _ _ _ _.
3 A _ _ _ _ _ salad contains olives, feta cheese and tomato.
4 Another name for a green salad is a _ _ _ _ _ _ salad.
5 _ _ _ _ _ _ _ _ contains cabbage and carrot.

 ## Lunchtime

Unscramble the tiles to find out the message about eating a healthy lunch.

N A	L U N C	H C H	A U S	L T H Y	T R A L
I A N	O D S	F R O M	G U I D	H E A L	F F O
A B	A L A N	O O S E	T H E	I N G .	E T O
E A T	T H Y	C E O	T O O	B T A I	H E A

WEBEXTRAS

www.health.nsw.gov.au/public-health/health-promotion/improve/nutrition/nutindex.htm
The NSW government has a health promotion and nutrition section on its health website, which looks at lunch at school and lunchbox ideas.

www.hsc.csu.edu.au/tourism_hospitality/kitchen_ops/additional_units/sandwiches/sandwiches/THHBCC02aAMP.html
NSW has online hospitality curriculum, with information related to the Unit of Competence: Prepare sandwiches, and includes case studies, sandwich fillings, garnish sandwiches and sandwich styles.

www.sustainweb.org/g5cp/s3_dsand.htm
The Grab 5 website has curriculum activities with some interesting ideas, such as design and make sandwiches and a packed lunch.

www.abc.net.au/btn/scripts/2002/03-05/canteens.pdf
The ABC website has a story on school canteens and provides a link to a worksheet about school canteens and the effects of high sugar foods on behaviour.

Afternoon siesta

Unscramble the lunch foods, then decode the sentence below by using the numbers as clues.

AIDWCHNS □□□□□□□□ 24 9 ... 2

AFCIACOC □□□□□□□ 15 17 4

DALSA □□□□□ 5

SOPU □□□□ 14 27 8

LORL □□□□ 21 18 7 12

BAGLE □□□□□ 1 11

BICSREPRAD □□□□□□□□□□ 10 26 23 13 20 22

FITRU □□□□□ 25 16 6

IEJCU □□□□□ 19 3

□ □□□□□□Y □□□□□ □□□□□
1 2 3 4 5 6 2   7 8 9 10 2   2 11 12 13 14

Y□□ □□□□□□□□□□ □□ □□□
15 16 17 18 9 19 20 9 6 21 22 6 20 23 9 6 2 11

□□□□□□□□□
24 25 6 11 26 9 27 15 9

LET'S PRODUCE

Ingredients

30 grams butter

$\frac{1}{2}$ onion, finely chopped

1 clove garlic, crushed

1 cup Arborio rice

6 sundried tomatoes in olive oil

$3\frac{1}{2}$ cups chicken stock

3 stalks asparagus, fresh black pepper, to taste

$\frac{1}{2}$ cup parmesan cheese, grated

Tomato and asparagus risotto   (serves 2)

Method

1 Melt butter. Add onion and garlic. Cook for two minutes.
2 Add rice and tomatoes and stir for one minute.
3 Add stock gradually and simmer for fifteen minutes.
4 Cut asparagus into smaller pieces and add to rice.
5 Cook for a further fifteen minutes, or until liquid is absorbed.
6 Season with pepper. Add half of the parmesan cheese.
7 Serve and garnish with extra parmesan cheese.

Ingredients

4 chicken fillets, cut into strips

2 tablespoons olive oil

200 grams salad greens

$\frac{1}{2}$ Lebanese cucumber, sliced thinly

$\frac{1}{4}$ red capsicum

$\frac{1}{2}$ avocado, sliced thinly

2 tablespoons dressing, your choice

Cajun chicken salad   (serves 4)

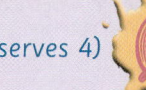

Method

1 Mix together all Cajun spice ingredients. Toss chicken in Cajun mix.
2 Place baking paper on oven tray and spray or lightly brush with olive oil.
3 Add chicken and bake at 200°C for ten minutes. Turn and cook for a further ten minutes, or until chicken is cooked.
4 Prepare salad greens and divide between four bowls. Add cucumber, capsicum and avocado. Toss with dressing.
5 Place chicken strips on top of salad.
6 Serve immediately.

Cajun mix

$\frac{1}{2}$ teaspoon garlic powder

$\frac{1}{2}$ teaspoon onion powder

$\frac{1}{2}$ teaspoon cayenne pepper

$\frac{1}{8}$ teaspoon chilli power

1 teaspoon thyme

1 teaspoon oregano

$\frac{1}{4}$ teaspoon ground black pepper

$\frac{1}{4}$ teaspoon cumin

$\frac{1}{4}$ teaspoon paprika

Ingredients
250 grams potatoes
2 slices bacon, chopped
$\frac{1}{4}$ onion, chopped finely
$\frac{1}{4}$ teaspoon sugar
1 tablespoon cider vinegar
1 tablespoon beef stock
1 egg, hardboiled, chopped
1 tablespoon parsley, chopped

Warm potato salad (serves 2)

Method

1 Peel, wash and cut potato into 2-centimetre cubes.
2 Steam for seven to ten minutes, or until tender.
3 Heat bacon gently in frypan. Add onion and cook for two to three minutes.
4 Mix sugar, vinegar and beef stock together.
5 Mix bacon, onion and potato together. Stir in dressing.
6 Gently stir in egg and parsley.

Ingredients
200 grams tuna
$\frac{1}{2}$ onion, chopped
1 stalk celery, chopped finely
$\frac{1}{8}$ green capsicum, chopped finely
1 tablespoon fresh parsley, chopped
$\frac{1}{2}$ teaspoon lemon juice
black pepper, to taste
2 large crusty rolls
2 tablespoons mayonnaise
2 small tomatoes, thinly sliced
4 slices tasty cheese

Tuna melt (serves 2)

Method

1 Mix together tuna, onion, celery, capsicum, parsley, lemon juice and pepper.
2 Cut rolls in half horizontally.
3 Spread with mayonnaise. Top with tuna mixture.
4 Place tomato slices on top of tuna mixture.
5 Top with cheese.
6 Preheat griller. Add tuna rolls and grill for five minutes, or until cheese is melted.
7 Serve immediately.

Asian noodle salad (serves 2)

Method

1 Blanch broccoli in boiling water for one to two minutes. Add snow peas and blanch for an additional minute.
2 Cook noodles in boiling water according to directions on packet. Drain.
3 Mix dressing with ginger and garlic. Add to noodles and toss.
4 Add vegetables. Toss.
5 Sprinkle with sesame seeds.

Variations

1 Make your own salad dressing.
2 Add some Vietnamese mint or coriander.
3 Replace sesame seeds with peanuts.

Ingredients
1 cup broccoli florets
$\frac{1}{2}$ cup snow peas
250 grams noodles or pasta of your choice
1/3 cup Asian-style salad dressing
1 teaspoon ginger, grated
1 teaspoon garlic, crushed
$\frac{1}{4}$ red capsicum, sliced
$\frac{1}{4}$ onion, sliced
2 teaspoons sesame seeds

QUESTIONS

1 What type of noodles or pasta would you choose for your Asian salad?
2 What ingredients would you change to make an Italian or Mexican salad?
3 What is the purpose of blanching?
4 Evaluate this recipe using a Y-chart.

Tastes like
Smells like   Looks like

THE NIGHT SHIFT: DISCOVER DINNER

In Australia, the main meal of the day for most people is dinner, which some people call tea. We probably spend more time preparing dinner than we do breakfast and lunch; however, as you will read in the article on page 176, the average time spent on preparing dinner has decreased from one hour to just twenty minutes. You will also read in chapter 14 that many people are opting for takeaway foods and home meal replacements (see page 178), not just because of busy lifestyles, but also because cooking skills are decreasing. Acquiring cooking skills is not just about knowing how to cook, but also knowing how to buy, store and prepare a range of foods. In order to be an informed consumer, it is really important to have an understanding of:

· food labelling
· what to look for when purchasing fresh foods such as meat, fish, fruit and vegetables
· how to store fresh, frozen and packaged foods
· how to prepare quick, easy, healthy foods

Food labelling

In December 2002, new food labelling laws came into effect in Australia. Some of these changes include listing ingredients by weight from biggest to smallest, listing potential allergic reactions to ingredients, storage requirements, such as store below 4°C, and including a list of food additives in the ingredients list. The new requirements provide more information for consumers; however, in order for these changes to be of benefit, consumers must be able to understand how to read labels. For more information on labelling, see chapter 20.

▶ New food rules 'to save lives'

Read the newspaper article and then answer the questions that follow it.

CONSUMERS will have a better idea of what they are putting into their body when a new food standards code comes into effect at midnight.

From tomorrow, nearly all manufactured food will have to show details of kilojoules, protein, fat, saturated fat, carbohydrates, sugar and salt content.

The requirements are part of the new Food Standards Code for Australia and New Zealand.

Foods made before December 20 can remain on supermarket shelves without the labelling changes for a maximum of two years.

Health parliamentary secretary Trish Worth said diet-related diseases accounted for 25 per cent of the total disease burden, costing between $341 million and $486 million each year.

'I urge consumers to make active use of this new nutrition information in the fight against diet-related diseases like heart disease and type-2 diabetes.'

New food labelling would also alert customers to possible allergens, as well as informing them about the main ingredient in products, she said.

'Consumers will now know how much meat is in their meat pie or strawberry in their strawberry jam.'

The government believes that up to 450 lives could be saved each year through the introduction of the mandatory labelling system.

Ms Worth said the industry would also benefit from the new code.

'Industry has been freed up to be innovative as there are no longer prescriptive, old-fashioned, recipe-based standards.'

WEBExtras

www.foodstandards.gov.au
This is the website of FSANZ, Food Standards Australia New Zealand (formerly ANZFA), whose mission is to collaborate with other bodies in order to protect the health and safety of people by maintaining a healthy food supply.

www.foodsafety.vic.gov.au
This website provides information about the Food Safety unit within the Department of Health Services, which is responsible for food regulation within Victoria.

QUESTIONS

1 What is the estimated cost of diet-related diseases?
2 Who is responsible for implementing and monitoring the new food laws?
3 What effect does the government believe the new labelling laws will have?

Shopping for food

Patterns of shopping for food have changed significantly over recent years, especially with the introduction of twenty-four-hour shopping and Internet shopping. Increasingly, people in metropolitan areas are choosing to shop online and have their purchases delivered to their door. Some people choose to just order heavy items, such as cans and packaged foods, online and only go out to shop for fresh food.

If you asked your grandparents how often they shopped for food, they would probably answer once a week. Many people now shop daily. For some, this is because they prefer to be able to buy fresh ingredients each day. For others, it is simply because they are so busy, they can only think ahead one day at a time.

Purchasing fresh food

Making sure that we eat as much fresh food as possible, especially fruit and vegetables, enhances healthy eating. In Australia, we are fortunate in that there are so many varieties of fresh foods available to us throughout the year. The impact of technology and sophisticated methods of ripening and storage of foods has assisted with this—so much so, that many of us now forget the seasonality of foods. Salad vegetables are now available all year round and summer fruits, such as strawberries, are now readily available in winter. Visit www.postharvest.com.au/Availability.htm to investigate the peak season for fruit and vegetables and compare this to the months of the year when they are available. Compile a chart for the main fruit and vegetables shown and indicate the peak season for each.

In planning meals, always try to choose foods that are in season, as they often taste better and are cheaper. Have you ever tasted a fresh tomato, picked off the tomato bush in summer? How does its taste compare to a tomato purchased in winter from the supermarket? Many fresh foods are seasonal foods—even lamb tastes better in spring! Why do you think this might be the case?

Fresh fruits and vegetables also contain more nutrients than canned varieties. Many consumers believe that frozen vegetables are less nutritional than fresh vegetables. This is not always the case. There are benefits to frozen vegetables. These include:
· availability throughout the year
· easy storage in a freezer
· less preparation and cooking time

If fresh fruits and vegetables are not stored or cooked appropriately, nutrients may be lost, in which case foods that are snap frozen may actually be more nutritious.

In addition to buying fruit and vegetables in their peak season, here are some tips to remember when purchasing fresh food:
· Look for fruit that is not bruised or too soft.
· Salad vegetables should not be brown or limp.
· Make sure that you wash fruits and vegetables before packing them away.
Can you think of any other tips?

In 1998, the United States Food and Drug Administration recognised that the nutritional value of some frozen products is equivalent to the fresh varieties.

Storage of food

Correct storage of food is essential to helping us maintain a healthy diet.
· Cover food with plastic wrap or by placing in a container with a tightly fitting lid before storing in the refrigerator.
· Store raw meat at the bottom of the refrigerator, so it does not drip onto any food below and cause possible bacterial infection.
· Make sure that cooked food cools before placing it in the refrigerator or freezer.
· Label frozen foods to ensure that you do not keep them for too long.
· Store tubers such as potatoes in a cool dark cupboard.
Can you think of any other food storage tips?

Food preparation

To prepare quick, easy and healthy meals, there are some cooking methods that are useful to know. These include stir-frying, microwaving, steaming and casseroling.

Stir-frying

Stir-fries are a great way to cook up a quick meal, because they enable you to mix meat, vegetables and sauces all together. You can add noodles to stir-fries or, alternatively, you can serve them with rice. Using a wok or a non-stick pan makes it easy to stir or toss the ingredients so that they cook quickly. Only a little bit of oil is used and vegetables retain their nutrient value because they are cooked quickly. Any water-soluble vitamins that might be lost are kept in the sauce, which is consumed. This makes stir-fries a great healthy choice and they also save on time and equipment.

Microwaving

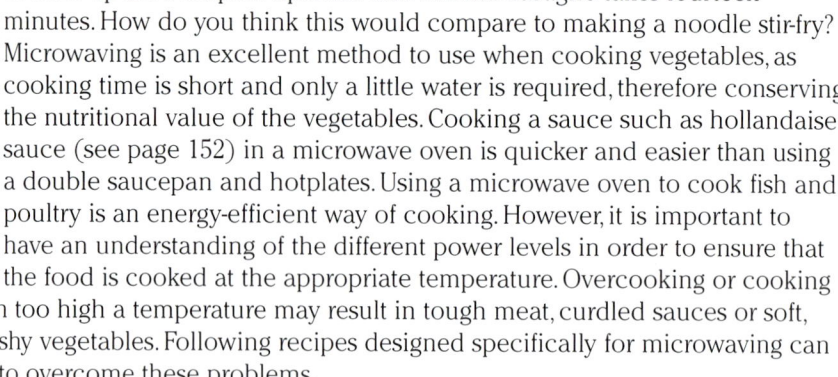

Many people use microwave ovens just to thaw food, to reheat food or to heat up home meal replacements (see page 178). Look at the Lean Cuisine packet on page 180. To heat up the Pumpkin Spinach and Ricotta Lasagne takes fourteen minutes. How do you think this would compare to making a noodle stir-fry? Microwaving is an excellent method to use when cooking vegetables, as cooking time is short and only a little water is required, therefore conserving the nutritional value of the vegetables. Cooking a sauce such as hollandaise sauce (see page 152) in a microwave oven is quicker and easier than using a double saucepan and hotplates. Using a microwave oven to cook fish and poultry is an energy-efficient way of cooking. However, it is important to have an understanding of the different power levels in order to ensure that the food is cooked at the appropriate temperature. Overcooking or cooking on too high a temperature may result in tough meat, curdled sauces or soft, mushy vegetables. Following recipes designed specifically for microwaving can help to overcome these problems.

Steaming

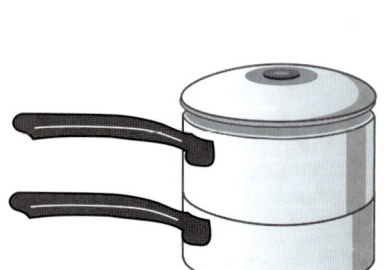

Steaming is an excellent cooking method to use for vegetables, because you can cook a number of vegetables together in the one piece of equipment. Most steamers are just like a double saucepan—that is, two saucepans—with one saucepan having holes in it and stacking on top of the other. Water goes in the bottom saucepan and allows the food in the top pan to cook via the steam coming through the holes.

Casseroling

Casseroling is an easy cooking method because it allows you to place all your ingredients in the one dish; however, the cooking time is longer than methods such as stir-frying, microwaving and steaming. If you are using your oven for something else, such as heating bread or cooking a dessert, casseroling enables you to use just the oven and be very resource-efficient!

► Seven secrets to good cooking

Conquer the kitchen with this seven-point survival plan.

By Flip Shelton

1 Roasting

The process of baking meats and vegetables in the oven (as in the great Sunday Roast). You can dry-roast your vegies by cutting them to similar size and placing them on a baking tray. Then, add a baste made of olive oil, crushed garlic, rosemary (fresh or dried) and salt and pepper. Combine in a bowl with vegies and mix well, place them on the baking tray and cook them in a hot oven. Tip: cook them until golden brown (I like some parts to go dark and crispy) or until an inserted skewer has little resistance.

2 Steaming

Not only a low-fat option but the quickest cooking method there is (apart from eating raw food). Snow peas take one to two minutes, fish 10–15 minutes, depending on size. Make sure there is enough water in the saucepan below the line of the bamboo or metal steamer so you don't boil it dry. Tip: Make sure dense vegies (potatoes and carrot) are at the bottom of the pile, 'lighter' ones at the top.

3 Microwaving

Few of us know how to utilise this tool properly. To learn more than re-heating your coffee and defrosting the pizza base, check out Janelle Bloom's book 'Microwave Cook-book'. In the meantime, remember: all microwaves are different and it is the output power that determines the speed at which food is cooked. Generally, convection microwaves cook foods in half the time of their conventional cousin. Tip: undercooking can be rectified, overcooking cannot.

4 Stir-fries

A wok is great. A fry-pan will do. Whatever you choose, stir-fry dishes are great and so easy to do. Use a vegetable oil (like peanut, which can be taken to a high heat without burning) and only use a little to assist in the flavours, in say the garlic, chilli, and food, being released. Fish sauce, while pungent, can really lift a seafood or vegie stir-fry—but use sparingly! Tip: Cut the food into bite sizes because the cooking time is short and this will ensure the food is cooked through.

5 Sauces

Provide endless options for pasta, baked spuds, rice, freekah, and cous cous. Tinned or fresh tomatoes and onions are vital ingredients in the base of a good sauce.
Try this one.

olive oil
1 onion
clove of garlic, crushed
2 small or one large zucchini
4–6 mushrooms
1 red pepper (or green)
1–2 tins of tomatoes (or fresh)
bay leaf
salt and pepper to taste

Cut vegetables into the same sized chunks. Over a moderate flame, soften the onion and garlic in a small amount of olive oil in the saucepan. Add zucchini, mushrooms and red pepper and stir to ensure they are evenly coated in oil and starting to cook. After a few minutes, add tomato, bay leaf and salt and pepper to taste. Stir. Let simmer for a minimum of 20 minutes. The longer you cook it, the thicker the sauce becomes. Remember to remove the bay leaf before serving. Tip: You can add a tin of tuna, some cooked rice, or chunks of tofu. Or eat on its own.

6 Risottos

This is an Italian way of cooking Arborio rice (a shorter, fatter, whiter grain that absorbs four times as much liquid than other grains). Once mastered, other ingredients—asparagus and Parmesan cheese, peas and corn to name just two—can be worked in. Tip: Warm 2 cups of stock in a saucepan and let simmer during the cooking process. Warm olive oil in a large, heavy-based saucepan before adding onion, garlic and bay leaf. Let onion soften before adding cup of Arborio rice. Stir using a wooden spoon so the rice is well coated. Add salt and pepper. Add cup of warm stock and stir occasionally until all the liquid is evaporated—keeping the saucepan on a medium-low heat. Repeat this process until all the liquid has been used and the rice is 'al dente'. If more liquid is needed, use either water or stock.

7 Pudding

The only way to end a meal. Tip: cut a large circle from one square puff pastry sheet and brush with melted butter. Then line the pastry with tinned fruit (peaches, pears, apricots), leaving a 1–2 cm border of pastry. Bake in an oven for 15 minutes on 180°C or until pastry is golden brown. Once cooked, sprinkle some caster sugar over the top and serve.

Time management

To enjoy food that is cooked to perfection, not only is it important to know how to cook, but also how to manage your preparation and cooking time. Learning how to prepare all of the components of a meal, so that they are all ready at the same time, not overcooked or undercooked, is a skill that takes practice and can be enhanced by using a time plan.

The following steps can assist with your time management.

1   Read the recipe right through before beginning preparation.
2   Make sure that you have a clear workspace with plenty of room.
3   Prepare a time plan and order of work. This is basically just a list of tasks written down at five-minute intervals. Sometimes you can work this out in your head, but it is often a good idea to write it down.
4   When working out what time to begin your preparation, work backwards from your serving time. For example, if you are preparing a meal in class, work backwards from the end of lesson time, making sure that you allow enough time for eating and cleaning up.
5   Collect all of the ingredients and utensils you need.
6   Clean and tidy as you go. It is much easier to work efficiently if you have a tidy, cleared working space.

Below is a time plan and order of work for preparing baked lemon chicken with sweet potato mash, yellow squash and snow peas (see recipe on page 174). This time plan is based on a time allocation of 100 minutes; that is, two fifty-minute lessons.

Time plan and order of work

10.50 am	Lesson begins.
11.00 am	Read complete recipe, collect all ingredients.
11.10 am	Prepare marinade and baste chicken.
11.15 am	Set table.
	Prepare sweet potato.
	Prepare squash and snow peas.
	Clean dishes.
11.30 am	Preheat oven.
11.35 am	Place chicken in oven.
	Boil water for sweet potato.
11.40 am	Add sweet potato to water, bring to boil and then simmer for twenty minutes.
	Bring water to boil in steamer.
11.50 am	Add squash to steamer.
11.55 am	Add snow peas to steamer.
12.00 noon	Drain sweet potato, mash and add butter and then place lid on saucepan to keep warm until serving.
12.05 pm	Serving time.
12.20 pm	Complete eating meal.
	Clean up.
12.30 pm	Finish lesson.

A canapé is an appetiser consisting of small pieces of toasted or plain bread, topped with various savoury spreads.

Entertaining at home

In Australia during the 1970s and 1980s, entertaining was very popular, with many people holding a dinner party in their home. Much of the day would be spent preparing a meal, usually three courses, and setting the table with the best dinnerware

and silver. The meal would often start with a selection of canapés and drinks, with the main meal consisting of a meat dish, usually served with a creamy sauce and a selection of accompanying vegetables. Desserts such as cheesecakes were often served and a selection of cheese would often follow the main meal. Read the following articles to see how things have changed in relation to home entertaining.

Homing in on cooking

STAYING IN has become the new going out as families try to re-create culinary and homemaking skills learned from TV experts, it emerged yesterday.

Homemakers are also likely to throw parties to unveil house conversions or renovations.

Although they are keen to be seen as accomplished chefs, time pressures cause many hosts to turn to supermarkets for pre-prepared party food.

The result, according to Datamonitor analysis who have studied the trend in Britain, is a boom in demand for gourmet ready-meals and ready-to-eat salads.

Retail analyst Neil Broome said celebrity chefs and glossy food magazines had made cooking cool.

'It has gone from being a female-dominated chore to a hugely popular hobby commanding millions of dollars from both food and the connected pro-ducts, such as cookbooks, videos and premium kitchenware.'

Consumers were now able to 'cook by numbers'.

'This allows even the most un-skilled of food lovers the opportunity to entertain and show off while they are doing it,' Broome said.

Dinner parties are becoming much more casual affairs, with guests increasingly likely to help prepare the food themselves. Some may even bring it with them, along with the obligatory bottle.

Researchers found that the wealthy increasingly preferred to entertain at home.

'Increased disposable income has not necessarily been spent at the nearest posh restaurant.' Broome said.

'People have bought bigger and better houses, spent more time and money making them look good, and want to show them off.'

Family meals a thing of the past

By Peta Hellard, Family Reporter

The home-cooked meal is becoming a thing of the past, with busy people choosing snack foods on the run instead. Research shows people are turning away from meals around the dining table with family and friends.

Supermarket aisles now are filled with packaged food that can be eaten 'on the go'—a trend that has only developed in recent years. While television cooking programs are popular and gourmet recipe books are hot sellers, researchers said many people were too snack-happy to get out the pots and pans themselves.

Instead of the traditional notion of three square meals a day, busy workers were having six or more 'eating occasions'. The research, by British firm Datamonitor, found many people were resorting to a muesli bar or yoghurt drink on the way to work and a sandwich, muffin or chocolate bar in front of the computer screen for lunch. Dinner was more likely to come out of a jar, box, packet or carton than the oven, with no-fuss time-savers replacing recipes made from scratch.

The trend for quick and easy food choices that fit in with busy lifestyles has been reflected in television programs, with characters rarely gathering around a dinner table to eat a meal. Instead, the characters in *Friends* and *Neighbours* grab quick coffees in cafés or eat while walking, working, commuting or computing. Researchers said people wanted food that did not take long to cook and could be eaten on the go.

A growing awareness of health and diet meant many were steering away from traditional snack foods such as chocolate, chips and burgers, to choose bananas, energy drinks and cereal bars. Datamonitor analyst Hugo Ehrnreich said almost all major manufacturers now offered on-the-go options in their ranges. 'With a growing range of tasks and distractions vying for traditional eating time, the daily eating occasion is coming under increasing pressure,' Mr Ehrnreich said.

For Melanie Ciantar, eating snacks is a necessity. The 23-year-old, who works as a finance officer for a fashion company, said her hectic lifestyle meant she was often eating on the go. 'I do not really have time to sit down and have big meals during the day,' she said. 'So I tend to eat lots of little meals when I find time.'

Ms Ciantar, from Avondale Heights, said that while she worked long hours and had a busy social life she always made time to eat during the day. 'I make sure I never miss out on breakfast,' she said. 'Sometimes I have to run out the door in the morning so I will take a container of cereal in the car with me and eat it while I am at the lights or when I get into work.'

'I try to eat healthily so some-times I will take packaged food like a soy milk breakfast drink which makes it really easy.' Lunch usually consists of a roll or a piece of fruit at her desk while dinner was regularly eaten in front of the television. 'Often I will have a quick bite in front of my computer screen as I usually have to work through my break, because it's so busy at work,' Ms Ciantar said.

She said her family shared an evening meal around the kitchen table once or twice a week. 'These days people are too busy and do not have time to sit down and prepare a whole meal,' she said. 'Having smaller meals is more convenient and easier to digest.'

QUESTION

Read the articles 'Homing in on cooking' and 'Family meals a thing of the past'. Write 400–500 words describing how entertaining, dinner parties and meal patterns have changed. In your discussion, include reasons for these changes and possible trends for the future.

▶ Good oil from neighbours

Read the newspaper article and then answer the questions that follow it.

By Simon Plant

Watch *Neighbours* and you could be forgiven for thinking life in Ramsay St revolves around kitchen tables.

But ask three of the show's youngest stars to discuss eating habits away from the set and you could get a different picture.

Theirs is a lifestyle that's big on takeaways and snacks and light on creative cooking.

For Krista Vendy, 27, Carla Bonner, 26, and Andrew Bibby, 19,

meal solutions often involve can openers, frying pans and hot plates.

'With the hours we do, you don't often feel like cooking a gourmet meal,' Bonner, who plays motor-cycle-riding tomboy Stephanie Sully, says.

Luckily, Carla's partner enjoys cooking.

By contrast, Vendy, who plays Teresa Bell, eats out at least four times a week.

Having traveled widely, she

wants to master some cooking skills. But as with so many members of Generation X (born between 1965 and 1978), time defeats her.

Bibby, who plays the wholesome Lance Wilkinson, lives with his parents. He enjoys home cooking when he's there to have it and hopes one day to 'get in the kitchen and really give it a go'.

'I'd love to be able to look in the fridge and think, "I know what I can do with that",' he says.

QUESTIONS

1 Why is the lifestyle of Krista, Carla and Andrew 'big on takeaways and snacks and light on creative cooking'?
2 Explain what Generation X means.
3 'I'd love to be able to look in the fridge and think, "I know what I can do with that",' Do you agree with this quote? Explain your answer.

▶ Let's remember

1 To be an informed consumer, what should you be aware of?
2 How can the new food labelling laws help consumers?
3 How have shopping patterns changed over recent years?
4 Explain the reasons why we should choose fresh fruit and vegetables.
5 Why should we buy fruit and vegetables in season?
6 List two tips to remember when purchasing fresh fruit and vegetables.
7 Why is it a good idea to label frozen meat?
8 What are the advantages of stir-fries?
9 Why is time management important?
10 In your own words, explain what a traditional dinner party used to be like.

▶ Let's investigate

1 a   Design a survey to conduct with people in the 20, 30, 40, 50 and 60+ year age groups and ask the following questions.
   i   What time do you usually eat dinner?
   ii How often do you go food shopping?

iii How often do you eat out?

iv How often do you buy takeaway food?

b Write a report and evaluate the responses ☺ ☺ ☹. Analyse possible reasons for the differences.

2 In groups of four, design a three-course meal. Compile a shopping list and prepare a time plan and order of work for the meal. Produce the meal in class and evaluate the meal and the time management of your group ☺ ☺ ☹.

3 Investigate these restaurant websites:

a www.mecca.net.au

b www.lobstercave.com.au

c www.thebengaltiger.com.au

d www.tacobill.com.au

e www.thaivillage.com.au

f www.laporchetta.com.au

For each website, investigate the:

i type of cuisine

ii ingredients common to the cuisine

iii spices and flavourings unique to the cuisine

4 Investigate how shopping patterns and food availability varies for people in metropolitan areas compared to those living in regional Victoria or another country. Your teacher may be able to connect you with students at another school. Arrange to be online at the same time and e-mail them or use a chat facility to communicate. Produce a summary of your findings for discussion in your next lesson.

▶ *@*-Dinner

www.corningware-eschool.com/about_press1.htm

Corningware, an American company that produces cookware, has an e-school with online curriculum on cooking skills. Link to the six categories of cooking methods and answer the following questions.

1 Roasting: Explain the difference between roasting and baking.

2 Baking: What are the advantages of baking as a method of cooking a meal?

3 Grilling/broiling: Write a paragraph explaining the similarities and differences between grilling and broiling.

www.formulaforlife.com.au

This website was developed by the Queensland Fruit and Vegetable Growers together with Nutrition Australia and a number of other partner organisations. Click on 'Analyse your diet' and use the dietary analysis tool to enter the foods that you have consumed for the day. Your diet can then be analysed according to the five food groups.

www.asiarecipe.com/methods.html

This website contains information about food preparation and recipes from a range of Asian countries.

1 Explain the cooking method of poaching. What types of foods are suitable to be poached?

2 Visit the link www.asiarecipe.com/cutting.html and answer the following questions.

a Describe a Chinese cook's knife and how you should hold it.

b Explain how you would perform the techniques of:

i julienne

ii dicing

iii mincing

iv roll-cutting

v parallel cutting

3   Visit the link www.asiarecipe.com/freezing.html and answer the following questions.
    a   How should you package food for freezing?
    b   What is freezer burn?
    c   For how long should meat be frozen?
    d   What foods are not suitable for freezing?
    e   Describe how frozen food should be thawed.

▶ **Puzzled**

🔴 **How's your French?**

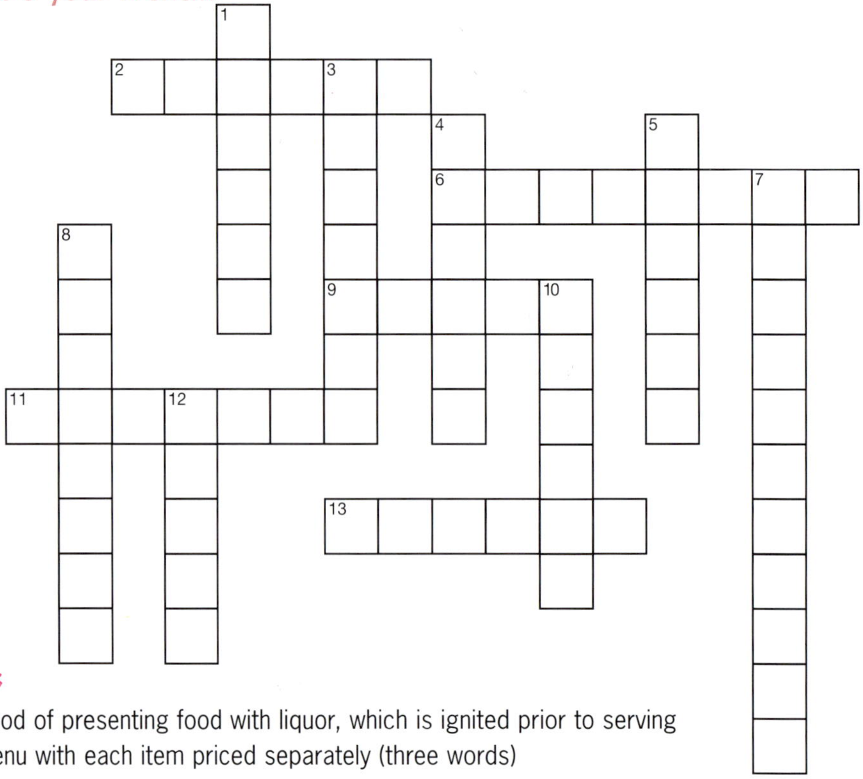

Across

2   Method of presenting food with liquor, which is ignited prior to serving
6   A menu with each item priced separately (three words)
9   A thin pancake
11 A French term referring to the style of food from a specific country
13 To remove the bones from meat or fish

Down

1   A loaf of bread slightly larger than a baguette
3   A light yeast bread that is rich in butter and eggs
4   The French word for cake
5   A type of appetiser
7   A set-price menu (two words)
8   A long thin French stick of bread
10 A dish served before the main course
12 To cook lightly in a little butter or oil

Missing words

Fill in the missing words to complete the sentences.

1   Another word for dinner in Australia is _ _ _.
2   _ _ _ _ _ _ _ _ is a method of cooking that uses two saucepans, with the top saucepan having holes in it.

3 Fresh fruits and vegetables usually contain more _ _ _ _ _ _ _ _ _ than canned or frozen varieties.

4 Meat should be stored in the _ _ _ _ _ _ of the refrigerator.

5 Time _ _ _ _ _ _ _ _ _ _ is an essential skill to learn.

 Skilled

Crack the code to complete the sentence about cooking skills.

A	B	C	D	E	F	G	H	I	J	K	L	M	N	O	P	Q	R	S	T	U	V	W	X	Y	Z
15				17						3											4				

```
_ _ _ K _ _ _      _ K _ _ _ _      A _ E  A _ _ _ _ _
1 6 6 3 22 13 2   26 3 22 11 11 26  15 7 17  15 14 6 18 8


K _ _ W _ _ _      _ _ W      _ _   _ _ _ ,   _ _ _ _ _ E ,
3 13 6 4 22 13 2   5 6 4      8 6   14 18 10   26 8 6 7 17


_ _ E _ A _ E  A _ _      _ _ _ K      _ _ _ _ _
25 7 17 25 15 7 17  15 13 20    1 6 6 3    12 6 6 20 26
```

Ingredients

1 teaspoon sesame oil
300 grams lean ground pork
1 clove garlic, crushed
1 teaspoon ginger, grated
2 teaspoons chilli sauce
2 teaspoons soy sauce
1 tablespoon hoisin sauce
¾ cup chicken stock
2 shallots, chopped
200 grams cellophane noodles
1 tablespoon coriander, chopped

Spicy pork noodles

(serves 2)

Method

1 Heat oil in frypan. Add minced pork and cook until browned. Drain excess fat.
2 Add garlic and ginger and sauté for one minute.
3 Reduce heat. Add sauces and mix well.
4 Add chicken stock, bring to boil and then cook for fifteen minutes.
5 Stir in shallots.
6 Pour boiling water over noodles, allowing noodles to soften. Drain after one minute.
7 Combine noodles and pork mixture.
8 Garnish with coriander and serve immediately.

Baked lemon chicken
(serves 2)

Ingredients

1 clove garlic, crushed

2 teaspoons extra virgin olive oil

2 teaspoons lemon juice

2 tablespoons parsley, finely chopped

2 teaspoons fresh oregano, finely chopped

2 chicken breasts

salt and black pepper, to taste

Method

1. Mix together garlic, olive oil, lemon juice, parsley and oregano.
2. Baste chicken with mixture, marinating for as long as possible.
3. Preheat oven to 180°C.
4. Place in baking dish lined with baking paper.
5. Cook for fifteen minutes. Turn and cook for a further fifteen minutes.
6. Season with salt and pepper.
7. Serve with sweet potato mash, yellow squash and snow peas.

Accompanying vegetables

1. *Sweet potato mash*: Peel 100 grams of sweet potato and cut into even-sized pieces—this means that the potato pieces will all be cooked at the same time. Place into small or medium-sized saucepan and just cover with water. Bring to boil and simmer for twenty minutes until tender—use a skewer to test if the potato is soft enough. When cooked, drain the water and add a little margarine or butter.
2. *Yellow squash*: Wash two yellow squash and cut into quarters. Place in steamer and cook for ten minutes.
3. *Snow peas*: Wash, top and tail twelve snow peas. Place in steamer and cook for three to five minutes, depending on how crunchy you like them. Be careful not to overcook them or they will go soft and lose their bright green colour.

Variation

Instead of using a steamer, cook the squash and snow peas in the microwave. Place 2 tablespoons water in microwave-safe dish, add the squash and cook for five minutes. Add snow peas and cook a further two minutes.

Microwave cabbage rolls
(serves 2)

Ingredients

4 cabbage leaves

250 grams minced lamb

$\frac{1}{2}$ egg, beaten

$\frac{1}{4}$ onion, chopped finely

$\frac{1}{8}$ green capsicum, chopped finely

1 clove garlic, crushed

$\frac{1}{2}$ teaspoon prepared mustard

$\frac{1}{2}$ teaspoon horseradish

sour cream or natural yoghurt

Sauce

150 mL tomato juice

2 tablespoons fresh basil, chopped finely

1 tablespoon fresh oregano, chopped finely

1 teaspoon fresh parsley, chopped finely

Method

1. Place cabbage leaves in microwave dish with one tablespoon water. Cover and cook for two minutes, or until cabbage is soft enough to roll.
2. Mix together all other filling ingredients. Divide filling into four.
3. Place mixture at one end of the cabbage leaf, fold in the edges and roll.
4. Place in microwave dish with seam down.
5. Combine sauce ingredients and pour over cabbage rolls.
6. Cook on high for six to eight minutes, or until meat is cooked through.
7. Serve with sour cream or yoghurt.

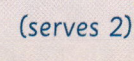

Pumpkin risotto

(serves 2)

Ingredients

1 tablespoon butter
$\frac{1}{2}$ leek, sliced thinly
1 clove garlic, crushed
200 grams butternut pumpkin, diced into 2-centimetre cubes
1 cup Arborio rice
100 grams prosciutto
$3\frac{1}{2}$ cups chicken stock
$\frac{1}{2}$ cup parmesan cheese, grated
black pepper, to taste
1 tablespoon chives, chopped

Method

1   Heat butter in frypan.
2   Add leek and garlic and cook for two minutes.
3   Add pumpkin and toss in butter mixture for two minutes.
4   Add rice and prosciutto and stir for one minute.
5   Add chicken stock and bring to boil.
6   Simmer for fifteen minutes, or until the rice is cooked and has absorbed the liquid.
7   Remove from heat and stir in half of the parmesan cheese.
8   Season with pepper.
9   Serve and garnish with chives and extra parmesan cheese.

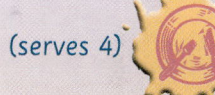

Sticky date pudding

(serves 4)

Ingredients

1 cup boiling water
1 cup dates, pitted and chopped
2 tablespoons butter
1 cup brown sugar
3 large eggs
1 cup self-raising flour

Sauce

1 cup brown sugar
1 cup cream
1 teaspoon vanilla essence
2 tablespoons butter

Method

1   Pour the water over dates in a pan and let stand.
2   Cream butter and sugar until fluffy.
3   Add eggs one at a time, beating well, and fold in the flour.
4   Add dates and flour into a lightly greased 18-centimetre cake tin.
5   Bake in a preheated oven at 180°C for thirty-five minutes.
6   Combine the sauce ingredients in a saucepan, bring to boil and simmer for five minutes.
7   Pour over pudding and serve with cream or ice cream.

IT'S A WRAP: DISCOVER FRESH VERSUS PACKAGED

Many factors have influenced our changed eating patterns in Australia. In the early years of European settlement in Australia, people largely ate foods that reflected their Anglo-Saxon heritage. It was not uncommon for families to share a traditional Sunday roast. Hearty desserts, such as apple pie or steamed puddings, were frequent. Evening meals often consisted of 'meat and three veg', with potato considered to be a staple of most meals.

In the 1950s, married women were not expected to have a job and most became responsible for being the homemaker and preparing meals for the family. There was no such thing as fast food until the 1960s, when Kentucky Fried Chicken (KFC) opened its first store. Eating out consisted of going to the neighbourhood Chinese restaurant or purchasing fish and chips wrapped up in newspaper from the local fish-and-chip shop.

Nowadays, there are many more fresh, packaged and pre-prepared foods available, as well as an enormous range of restaurants and takeaway or fast-food outlets. Juggling busy lives and working longer hours are just two factors that can influence the food choices we make. There is a range of factors, such as social, cultural and religious, economic, nutritional knowledge and media influences, as we read about in chapter 2 of *e-Food Book 1*, that can influence our food decisions. In making food choices between fresh foods versus packaged foods, it is often a matter of balancing resources, such as time, energy and money. For example, if you were going to have a meal of spaghetti bolognaise, would you choose to make it from scratch or prepare it using a bottled sauce? Would you go out to a pasta place or order in takeaway from a nearby Italian restaurant? Think about the factors that would influence your choices.

▶ Time not on cooks' side

Read the newspaper article and then answer the questions that follow it.

FOR THE TIME-CHALLENGED Bridget Jones generation, it's a decision that takes only seconds.

Do they devote an hour to making the main meal of the day, or do they grab a ready-made dinner that saves on the washing up?

Researchers have found that women are taking the latter option as their busy lives put the squeeze on time in the kitchen.

Research for Marks and Spencer, based on interviews with 11 000 male and female shoppers, revealed that young working women are devoting less than 20 minutes to making the main meal of the day, in contrast to the average of an hour spent 20 years ago.

Market researchers Taylor Nelson Sofres said: 'Meal preparation times have decreased because of an increase in consumption of ready meals, more women working longer hours and the increase in disposable income.'

'A third of meals are chosen because of convenience and on the basis of how easy it is to clear up after eating them.'

QUESTIONS

1 How does the amount of time spent on meal preparation twenty years ago compare to now?
2 What factors are influencing the amount of time spent on meal preparation?
3 Can you think of other factors that might influence the amount of time spent on food preparation?

▶ Pre-prepared meals

Read the newspaper article and then answer the questions that follow it.

Is cooking becoming a lost art?

- Only a quarter of the population are cooking an evening meal 7 nights a week and 85% of those are over 55 years of age.
- Around two thirds of people who cook an evening meal spend less than 30 minutes preparing it, with 18% spending less than 15 minutes.

- In 1999, 45% of those cooking the evening meal used pre-prepared ingredients. In 2001, this is up to 50%.

Cooked anything from scratch lately?

- Only 50% of those cooking the evening meal state that they prepare a meal from scratch.

- Older people are more likely to be cooking from scratch.
- Reflective of this change in behaviour, sales of core baking ingredients like butter, flour and sugar over time have been in decline, and there have been significant increases in sales of pre-prepared meals.

QUESTIONS

1 Why do you think older people are more likely to cook from scratch?
2 What reasons could you provide for the decrease in sales of core baking ingredients, such as butter, flour and sugar?
3 How many different kinds of pre-prepared ingredients can you think of?

▶ Recipe for nutrition disaster

Read the newspaper article and then answer the questions that follow it.

By Joel Dullroy

A generation of young people lacks basic cooking skills—which has long-term health ramifications for our nation.

Few home leavers could shop properly for groceries or prepare a nourishing meal, Aloysa Hourigan of Nutrition Australia said.

And Katherine Warth of the Dietician Association of Australia said that even tossing a salad might become a lost art amid the welter of pre-packaged fruit and vegetables—with a loss of fresh-

food nutrition. 'It's not hard to imagine that young people could grow up never learning how to chop up fruit and vegetables,' Ms Warth said.

The loss of cooking skills was contributing to the deteriorating health of the nation, Ms Warth said. Once, teenagers learnt how to cook from their parents—but with adults spending less time in the kitchen, knowledge was not passing on to the next generation. 'The family's evening meal can be a very rushed affair. Kids don't get

a chance to observe or learn how to do it properly,' she said.

Nutrition Australia is lobbying for a basic cooking skills program to go into the primary school curriculum.

In the Food For Life Program, which has had trials in several schools, secondary school home economics teachers teach year 7 classes how to prepare a meal and learn for themselves along the way. 'You can prepare a meal in less time than it takes to order a pizza.'

QUESTIONS

1 'A generation of young people lacks basic cooking skills.' Do you agree or disagree with this statement? Explain your answer.
2 How do you think teenagers today learn to cook?
3 Think about your own family members and then have a class discussion. Who does the cooking? Do they prepare meals from scratch or do they use pre-prepared ingredients? How did they learn to cook?
4 How would you define cooking skills? Do you think cooking skills include shopping skills, such as reading food labels and knowing what to look for when purchasing fresh ingredients like meat, fish, fruit and vegetables?
5 'You can prepare a meal in less time than it takes to order a pizza.' Do you agree or disagree with this statement? Explain your answer.
6 Write down a list of what you consider to be essential cooking skills. Compare your list to others in your class and compile a class list of 'what we need to know'. Perhaps your teacher can incorporate some of your suggestions into your classes.

Focus on home meal replacements

Convenience food is the term used to describe food that is partially or fully pre-prepared, therefore requiring less preparation and cooking time. There are many foods today that fall into this category. Some of these include:

- heat-and-serve foods, such as frozen pastry products
- cereal products, such as breads, breakfast cereals, biscuits, pasta, noodles and rice
- canned products, such as fruits, vegetables and fish
- dairy products, such as ice cream and yoghurt
- bottled products, such as pasta sauce, curry paste and chutney
- dehydrated products in packets, such as soup, risotto and couscous

Convenience foods also include home meal replacements (HMRs)—a relatively new term referring to fully prepared meals that can be purchased chilled, frozen or heated. These types of meals are sold at retail outlets, including supermarkets and specialty delicatessens, and at restaurants.

With so many convenience foods and HMRs available, it is important to be an informed consumer in order to know how to make healthy choices. Just because a food is convenient—that is, quick and easy to prepare—does not mean that it is unhealthy or falls into the category of junk food. It is also important to remember that not all takeaway food is bad for us either.

With so many more products to choose from today, we can use food selection models, such as the Australian Guide to Healthy Eating, to assist us with the sorts of choices that we should be making for healthy eating patterns. Our decision-making can also be made easier by:

· having an understanding of food labelling
· knowing what to look for when purchasing fresh foods such as meat, fish, fruit and vegetables
· knowing how to store fresh, frozen and packaged foods
· knowing how to prepare quick, easy, healthy foods

Case Study

HOME MEAL REPLACEMENTS

Lean Cuisine® 97% Fat Free*

PUMPKIN SPINACH & RICOTTA LASAGNE

A vegetable lasagne combining layers of spinach & ricotta, al dente pasta and creamy pumpkin sauce, garnished with a cheese & herb topping.

GOOD SOURCE OF FOLATE

FROZEN
NET 400g
SERVING SUGGESTION

INGREDIENTS: WATER, COOKED PASTA (WATER, WHEAT SEMOLINA), VEGETABLES (21%) (SPINACH, PUMPKIN), RICOTTA CHEESE (WHEY, MILK, SKIM MILK POWDER, FOOD ACID (260), SALT, PRESERVATIVE (202)), SKIM MILK POWDER, SOUR CREAM, THICKENER (1422), PARMESAN CHEESE (CONTAIN CULTURES, ANTICAKING AGENT (460), ENZYMES), CHEESE POWDER, SALT, BROWN SUGAR, ONION POWDER, WHEAT SEMOLINA, SPICES, COLOUR (160b), HERBS, YEAST EXTRACT.
MADE IN AUSTRALIA BY EST. NO. 85 FOR:
NESTLÉ AUSTRALIA LTD, 6/123 EPPING ROAD, NORTH RYDE NSW 2113, AUSTRALIA.
NESTLÉ NEW ZEALAND LIMITED, 1 BROADWAY, NEWMARKET, AUCKLAND, NEW ZEALAND.
NESTLÉ SINGAPORE (PTE.) LTD, 200 CANTONMENT ROAD, #03-01 SOUTHPOINT, SINGAPORE, 089763.
NESTLÉ HONG KONG LTD, 28/F PCCW TOWER, TAIKOO PLACE, 979 KING'S ROAD, QUARRY BAY, HONG KONG.

QUESTIONS

Refer to the Lean Cuisine packet and visit www.leancuisine.com.au.

1 Who do you think is the target market for Lean Cuisine meals? Explain your answer.
2 How many people would this meal serve?
3 Visit www.woolworths.com.au, do a search for 'Lean Cuisine' and find out the price of Lean Cuisine meals.
4 Lean Cuisine is '97 per cent Fat Free', yet the total fat content per serving is 8.8 grams. Write an explanation as to whether or not you think this is a low-fat meal.
5 Would you choose a Lean Cuisine meal? Explain your answer.

▶ Home meal replacements—where to now?

Read the newspaper article and then answer the questions that follow it.

By Debbie Kerslake, Marketing Director, ACNielsen Retail Measurement and Customised Research Services

In the late 1990s Home Meal Replacement or Meal Solutions were identified as one of the key opportunities for supermarkets. Both retailers and food manufacturers wanted to replicate in Australia the success that 'HMR' were having overseas. There was speculation about future kitchens being built without stoves (this is already the case in New York), and whole industry conferences were devoted to the subject.

It is fair to say that Australian supermarkets came a long way in the 1990s in terms of offering the consumer products which took some of the work out of meal preparation. Ready chopped and peeled vegetables, fruit and salad appeared in the produce aisles, and 'meal assembly' offerings such as fresh pasta and pasta sauces consistently proved to be amongst the fastest growing supermarket categories.

However, the value-added 'ready to heat' chilled meals has never fulfilled early expectations in Australia, and remains relatively underdeveloped compared with Europe and the US.

At the recent Australian Food Congress held in Melbourne in November, I asked a panel of retailing experts their opinions on why this was the case. Was it because retailers had not put enough effort behind them, or because there was less demand? Was it down to geographical issues based on the size of Australia and the intricacies of the cold chain, or to the fact that private label is relatively small in Australia (many HMR products overseas are retailer brands).

The consensus of the panel was 'all of the above'.

I asked this question based on findings from the recently published ACNielsen/Australian Retailers Association 'The Way We Shop'. One section of the report focuses on people's eating habits, comparing the number of meals eaten in the home versus out of the home. A number of findings from the report support the fact that Australians are still looking for convenient meal solution offerings:

- Only 54% of Main Grocery Buyers (MGB) agree with the statement 'I like to cook'. That leaves 46% of people feeling ambivalent towards cooking or worse.
- Despite this, six out of seven main evening meals are eaten at home with five of those prepared 'from scratch'. NB this survey was conducted in winter, and there may be seasonal variations.
- Over half of the MGB's expressed an interest in 'freshly prepared meals which you can heat up and serve'.
- Younger people cook from scratch less than older people.

The question that the research does not answer, is why young main grocery buyers cook less from scratch? Is it simply a life stage issue, and they will cook more as they get older? Or, as some believe, are today's youth simply not learning to cook? If the latter, grocery retailers need to scrutinise their ready to serve and meal assembly offerings to meet the future demand of a generation who may be less likely and able to prepare meals from raw ingredients.

One thing that may depress demand for home meal replacements in Australia is the abundance of affordable and high quality take away offerings.

However there is no doubt that people are getting busier. Moreover, cooking is seen as a chore by many and the cooking skills of younger people are possibly inferior to those of older generations. All this leads to the conclusion the convenient meals, both ready to serve or in a meal assembly format, is one area where there is still opportunity for both food manufacturers and retailers.

QUESTIONS

1. Why were HMRs considered to be a good marketing opportunity for the Australian market?
2. Describe what the term *meal assembly* means.
3. Provide some examples of products that have taken the 'work out of meal preparation'.
4. Why have ready-to-eat chilled meals not fulfilled early expectations?
5. Why do you think younger people cook less from scratch than older people?
6. What might reduce the demand for HMRs in Australia?
7. In New York, some kitchens are being built without stoves. What do you think about this? Could you imagine having a kitchen without a stove?

Promoting fresh fruit and vegetables

The 1995 National Nutrition Survey found that one in three children did not consume fruit or vegetables. As a result of the National Nutrition Survey, the Commonwealth Department of Health and Aging has identified four priority areas as part of the National Public Health Nutrition Strategy. One of these priorities is to increase the consumption of fruit and vegetables for all Australians. Why do you think Australians are eating less fruit and vegetables?

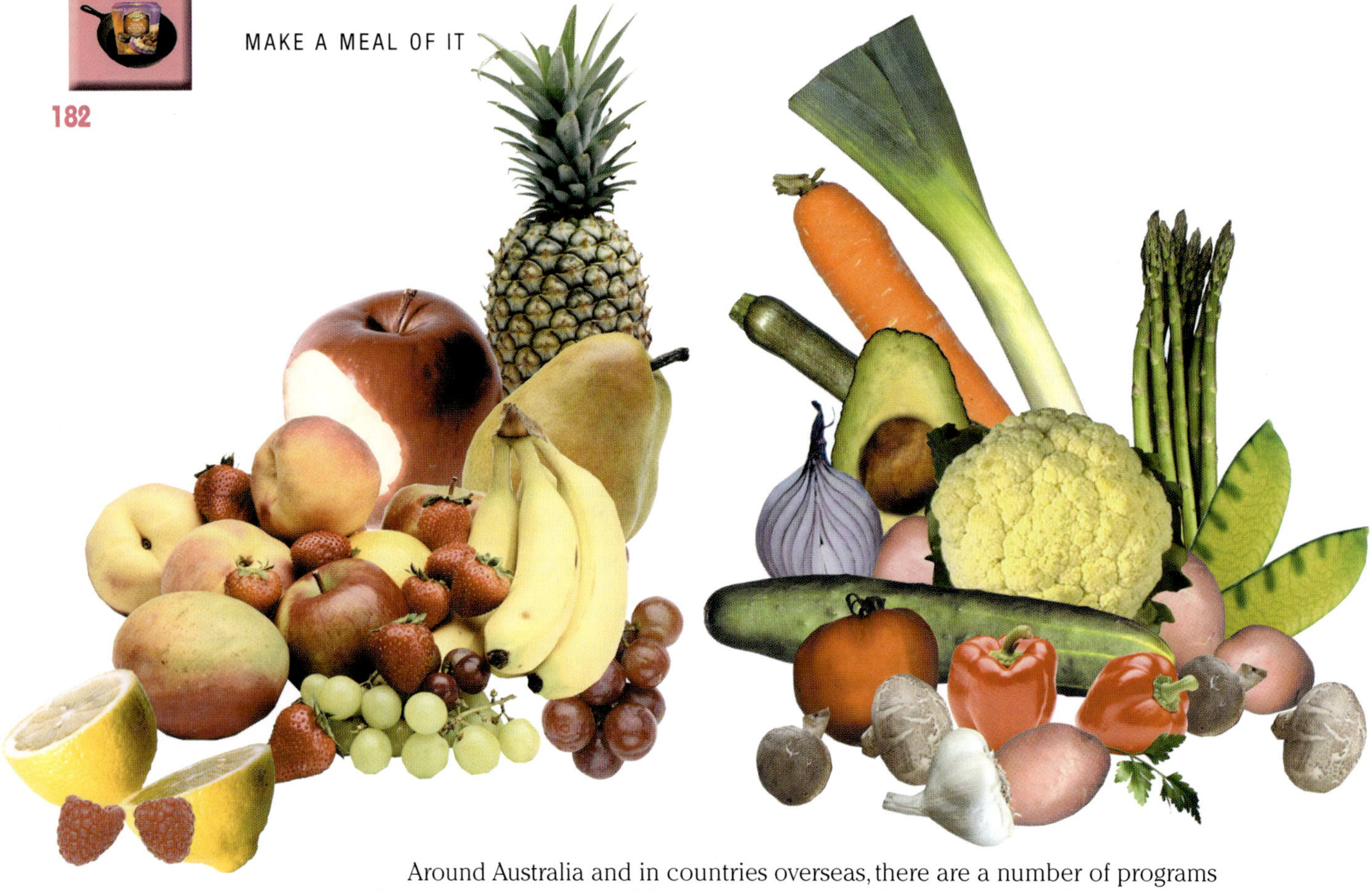

Around Australia and in countries overseas, there are a number of programs aimed at encouraging children to increase their fruit and vegetable intake. In Western Australia, the Department of Health has been running a '2 Fruit and 5 Veg' campaign for over ten years. Coles Supermarkets and the Dietitians Association of Australia have been working together on the Coles 7-a-day program, which encourages Australians to eat at least seven serves of fruits and vegetables each day.

The Australian Guide for Healthy Eating sample serves for fruit and vegetables are shown below.

Go for 2 & 5
FRUIT   VEG

Coles seven a day
7
5 veg + 2 fruit

Fruit

1 medium piece, e.g. apple, banana, orange, pear
2 small pieces, e.g. apricot, kiwi fruit, plum
1 cup diced pieces or canned fruit
$\frac{1}{2}$ cup fruit juice
dried fruit, e.g. 4 dried apricot halves
$1\frac{1}{2}$ tablespoons sultanas

Vegetables

75 grams ($\frac{1}{2}$ cup) cooked vegetables
75 grams ($\frac{1}{2}$ cup) cooked dried beans, peas or lentils
1 cup salad vegetables
1 potato

There are many ways that we can increase our fruit and vegetable consumption. Some of these ways include:
·   adding fruit to breakfast cereal
·   cooking stir-fries or soups with a variety of vegetables
·   serving additional salads or vegetables with meat dishes
·   choosing fruit or vegetables, such as carrot or celery sticks, for snacks
Can you think of other suggestions?

▶ Tuck in at Tucker Road

Read the newspaper article and then answer the questions that follow it.

By Ian Royall, Educational Reporter

A health plan that lets children eat in class should be spread state-wide, Victoria's former chief health officer said yesterday.

Professor John Catford, dean of health and behavioural science at Deakin University, said the program at Tucker Rd Primary in Bentleigh would improve the long-term health prospects of students.

The school is developing a vegetable garden, revamping the tuckshop menu and building a running track.

Produce grown in the vegetable patch would be delivered to the canteen and the classrooms.

Children will be allowed for the first time to eat during class, if it is fruit or vegetables.

Professor Catford said while not all schools would fit the Tucker Rd model, some aspects may be useful.

'With very little resources and a lot of commitment, schools can very quickly turn things around,' he said.

The school council has offered to share its ideas with other schools.

The moves follow an address by Professor Catford to parents at the school in May when he warned childhood obesity was reaching epidemic proportions and was a health time bomb.

Principal Stan Oakley said the program was not just about his school.

'This is about the health of all young Australians whose lives and lifestyles are at risk unless we do something about it,' he said.

QUESTIONS

The article highlights the value that some schools are placing on healthy eating patterns and the importance of consuming fruits and vegetables.

1   Do you think that your school would allow eating in class, so long as it were fruit or vegetables?
2   What do you think about the idea of creating a vegetable or herb garden so that the produce can be utilised in your practical food classes or by the school canteen?

▶ Let's remember

1   Where did early Australian eating patterns originate?
2   Describe a typical meal in Australia in the early years of European settlement.
3   In the 1950s, what did eating out consist of?
4   What are some of the factors to consider when choosing between fresh and packaged foods?
5   How would you describe the term *convenience food*?
6   Identify some examples of convenience foods.
7   What does HMR stand for?
8   Where can HMRs be purchased?
9   Why should we be informed consumers?
10 What skills do we need to make better food choices?

▶ Let's investigate

1   Investigate the pre-prepared products that you have at home in your pantry. Design some different recipes using whatever canned or packaged products you can find.
2   Visit www.colesonline.com.au or www.woolworths.com.au and search under meals or prepared foods. List as many different types of convenience foods and HMRs as you can. Categorise them into home meal replacements, dinner starters, canned foods, dried foods, dinner sauces and any other categories that you can think of.
3   Investigate five ways to incorporate fruit and vegetables into your diet at breakfast, lunch and dinner.

WeBExTRas

www.dietclub.com.au/
foods/?
The Diet Club website
contains a food database
that enables you to search
from a wide range of
foods, including brand
products, to find out
nutrient values.

WeBExTRas

www.dolmio.com.au
The Dolmio website has
information about its range
of pasta sauces and recipes
that use their products.

www.masterfoods.com.au
The MasterFoods website
has information about
convenience products,
including canned products,
sauces, recipe bases and
stocks. Visit the link
www.masterfoods.com.au/
cookbook/meals.asp, which
contains a collection of
recipes that can be prepared
in thirty minutes or less.

www.health.qld.gov.au/t
pch/Diet/convenience.pdf
The Queensland government
has produced this
information sheet about
healthy eating. It provides
information about foods to
avoid and includes
suggestions of convenience
foods to stock in the pantry,
refrigerator and freezer.

4 Have each class member write down the ingredients from their evening meal the night before. Evaluate their meals by working out the percentages of fresh ingredients versus pre-prepared or convenience ingredients ☺ ☺ ☹. Collate the results for the class. Work out the average number of fruit and vegetables consumed by class members for the meal. Are you surprised by the results?

5 Design a menu (three meals) for one day that includes two serves of fruit and five vegetables. Include foods that you would consume.

6 Investigate the range of washed, cut and prepared fruits and vegetables that can be purchased from supermarkets. Compare the unit cost of purchasing pre-prepared fruits and vegetables compared to purchasing them whole or unprepared.

▶ @-Fresh versus packaged

www.heinz.com.au

Click on 'Food in a minute', then the map of Australia and then 'Menu planner', where you can find menu suggestions for the week. Investigate the recipes section and design your own weekly menu. Prepare a time plan and order of work for one of the meals and produce this meal in class. Evaluate your meal according to its appearance, flavour, texture and aroma ☺ ☺ ☹.

www.goldencircle.com.au

Click on 'Fun factory' and then 'Let's go shopping'. Select the level of difficulty and test your mathematical skills.

www.sanitarium.com.au/article/article.do?art-id=21

Go to the convenience foods shopping list and look at the foods suggested to stock the cupboard. How many of these foods do you have in the pantry at home?

www.cannedfood.org

Visit the link www.cannedfood.org/nutrition.html#Head-4.

1 What reason is given for preservatives not being required in canned food?

2 Click on peaches, pineapples and tomatoes and look at the nutrient comparison for fresh versus canned. For all three, which nutrient is lower in the canned form compared to the fresh form? How could you explain this difference?

3 'There are no practical differences between the value of fresh and canned foods'. Write a couple of paragraphs to explain what you think this statement from the website means?

▶ Puzzled

Convenience foods

Crack the code to complete the sentence about convenience foods.

A	B	C	D	E	F	G	H	I	J	K	L	M	N	O	P	Q	R	S	T	U	V	W	X	Y	Z
				5							17						4	23							

```
_   _   _   E      _   E   L      R   E   L   _   _   E   _   E   _   _   S      _   R   E
11  13  26  5      26  5   7   17     4  5  22  17   7  24   5  26   5  19  2  23     7   4   5

_   _   L   L   _      _   R   E   _   R   E   _      _   E   _   L   S      _   _   _   _   _
9  16  17  17  3     22   4   5  22   7   4   5  15    26   5   7  17  23     18  11   8  24  11
```

```
___  _E  __R___SE  ____LLE_ ,
24 7 19  10 5  22 16 4 24 11 7 23 5 15  24 11 8 17 17 5 15

_R_E__  _R  _E__E_
9 4 13 6 5 19  13 4  11 5 7 2 5 15
```

Know your fruit 'n' veg

Find each of the words from the box in the puzzle.

```
E B O P E R S I M M O N B A N
X G Z T E L H A B U E O R E O
Z X A M A C A E V K X S O P L
R O I B A T E C O A Q M C W E
D L H N B T O H U U U A C O M
D H I T R A C P A M G G O N R
U P R O I I C S T X Q D L S E
S F O A T W H T K E O U I V T
E T L R S Y L C B D E X A S A
N F A S E P G D Q Q H W W T W
D H O B R A B U H R O G S V W
I E G N A R O E P A R S N I P
V N N F I G P Q R G F A Z V X
E A A A S M W W F R I Q F O B
I R M V U U Q D K H Y C D K R
```

artichoke	orange
beetroot	parsnip
broccoli	persimmon
cabbage	raspberry
cumquat	rhubarb
endive	snowpea
fig	spinach
guava	squash
lime	sweet potato
mango	watermelon

LET'S PRODUCE

Ingredients
1 tablespoon olive oil
1 clove garlic, crushed
¼ onion
200 grams mince
1 can (425 grams) tomatoes, crushed
1 small red chilli, finely chopped
1 stalk celery, finely chopped
1 tablespoon tomato paste
1 tablespoon fresh oregano, finely chopped
black pepper, to taste
200 grams pasta
parmesan cheese, freshly grated

Chilli bolognaise   (serves 2)

Method

1   Heat olive oil in pan for approximately one minute. Add garlic and onion and cook for a further two minutes.
2   Add mince, stir and cook until meat is browned. Drain excess fat.
3   Add tomatoes, chilli, celery, tomato paste and oregano. Simmer for twenty minutes.
4   Three-quarter fill medium saucepan with water. Bring to the boil. Add a splash of olive oil to prevent the pasta from sticking together. Add pasta and cook for twelve minutes, or until al dente.
5   Drain pasta and place in serving bowls. Top with sauce and parmesan cheese.

QUESTIONS

1   What does the term *al dente* mean?
2   Could you substitute fresh tomatoes for canned tomatoes, and how might you need to modify the recipe?
3   Describe two ways in which you could crush garlic.

Bean burritos

(serves 2)

Ingredients
200 grams mince
$\frac{1}{4}$ onion, finely chopped
$\frac{1}{4}$ green capsicum, chopped
$\frac{1}{2}$ can tomatoes
$\frac{1}{2}$ can (420 grams) kidney beans
1 clove garlic, minced
1 teaspoon chilli powder
2 teaspoons cayenne powder
2 teaspoons paprika
4 burritos
100 grams cheese, grated

Method

1. Add a little water to the pan. Add the mince, onion and green capsicum. Cook until meat is browned. Drain excess fat.
2. Add remaining ingredients. Cook for thirty minutes.
3. Heat burritos according to instructions.
4. Divide filling into four and place in middle of tortilla. Roll and wrap.
5. Sprinkle with cheese. Place in microwave and heat until cheese is melted.
6. Serve immediately.

QUESTIONS

1. Find out the definition of a burrito.
2. From where do chillies originate? (Hint: Read the label on the chilli powder bottle.)

Salmon frittata

(serves 2)

Ingredients
15 grams butter
2 shallots, finely chopped
100 grams salmon
1 can (100 grams) corn kernels
1 tomato, chopped
$\frac{1}{4}$ green capsicum, finely chopped
1 tablespoon parsley, finely chopped
black pepper, to taste
2 eggs, beaten
50 grams cheese, grated

Method

1. Melt butter in small omelette pan. Add shallots and cook for one to two minutes.
2. Mix salmon, corn, tomato and capsicum together. Add to pan. Stir in parsley and pepper.
3. Pour beaten eggs over ingredients. Top with cheese.
4. Cook gently for ten to fifteen minutes, or until eggs are cooked.
5. Place pan under griller for about five minutes, until top is browned.

Variations

1. Replace salmon with tuna or other canned fish.
2. If you don't have canned corn, use frozen corn kernels.
3. **Design** your own frittata with your choice of ingredients.

Spicy vegetable couscous

(serves 4)

Ingredients
1 tablespoon olive oil
1 onion, chopped finely
$\frac{1}{2}$ teaspoon cumin
$\frac{1}{2}$ teaspoon paprika
$\frac{1}{2}$ teaspoon cinnamon
1 tablespoon coriander
$\frac{3}{4}$ cup vegetable stock
1 clove garlic, crushed
1 can tomatoes, chopped
$\frac{1}{2}$ small eggplant, diced
$\frac{1}{2}$ carrot, diced
100 grams mushrooms, sliced
$\frac{1}{4}$ red capsicum, chopped
$\frac{1}{2}$ can chickpeas
150 grams couscous
1 tablespoon parsley, chopped

Method

1. Heat oil, add onion and cook for one to two minutes.
2. Add cumin, paprika, cinnamon and half of the coriander.
3. Add stock, vegetables and chickpeas.
4. Bring to boil and then simmer for twenty to thirty minutes.
5. Cook couscous according to directions on packet.
6. Serve couscous and top with vegetable mixture.
7. Top with parsley and remainder of coriander.

Thai pumpkin salad

(serves 2)

Ingredients
4 Roma tomatoes

250 grams pumpkin, cut into 3-centimetre cubes

2 teaspoons olive oil

$\frac{1}{4}$ teaspoon nutmeg

100 grams rocket

75 grams snow pea sprouts

$\frac{1}{4}$ red capsicum, roasted and peeled

2 tablespoons pepitas (pumpkin seeds)

Dressing
4 tablespoons olive oil

2 tablespoons balsamic vinegar

1 teaspoon sugar

1 teaspoon soy sauce

$\frac{1}{2}$ lime, juiced

$\frac{1}{2}$ lemon, juiced

2 tablespoons Vietnamese mint, chopped

2 teaspoons coriander, chopped

2 teaspoons basil, chopped

Method
1 Cut tomatoes in quarters and brush with oil.
2 Brush pumpkin with oil and sprinkle with nutmeg.
3 Roast pumpkin in oven for thirty minutes.
4 Add tomatoes to pumpkin and roast for a further thirty minutes.
5 Mix all dressing ingredients together.
6 Place rocket and snow pea sprouts into bowl.
7 Add dressing to pumpkin and tomatoes and toss gently.
8 Place on salad vegetables and top with red capsicum and pepitas.

CHAPTER 15

SNACK ATTACK: DISCOVER SNACKS AND JUNK FOOD

Junk food is considered to be food that is energy-dense and low in nutrient value. We consider junk food to be high in fat, sugar and salt, often providing 'empty' kilojoules. This means that, although junk food provides us with energy or kilojoules, it is often of little nutritional value to us. Many takeaway foods fall into the junk food category and we sometimes mistakenly think of fast food as being junk food. Not all fast food is bad for us. For example, a piece of fruit, a tub of yoghurt or a handful of unsalted nuts are good choices when hungry and in a hurry.

We can categorise junk food as the 'extras' that do not fall within the Australian Guide to Healthy Eating (see page 156). These 'extras' include biscuits, ice cream, doughnuts, cakes, soft drinks, chips, cream, mayonnaise, alcoholic drinks and pastry products, such as pies, sausage rolls and pasties.

Energy-dense foods are high in kilojoules, while nutrient-dense foods are low in kilojoules.

QUESTION

For each of the five groups shown in the Australian Guide to Healthy Eating on page 156, identify three healthy snacks.

The main problem with junk food is that we are eating too much of it, our serving sizes are increasing and we are engaging less in physical activity. By eating too much junk food, we risk health problems, such as obesity, diabetes and heart disease. These health problems are discussed in more detail in chapter 3. The problems associated with junk food are a major problem for high-income or industrialised countries, such as Australia, the United Kingdom and the USA. We often refer to the problems associated with junk food as diseases of affluence. Increasingly, these diseases of affluence are becoming an issue in low-income or developing countries, as multinational fast-food companies spread their market into the developing world.

If you were in the USA and you wanted to order takeaway, you would order food 'to go'.

When we think of takeaway food outlets, we often think of fast-food chains, such as McDonald's, KFC and Red Rooster. However, takeaway outlets also include the local fish-and-chip shop, pizza shop or any type of restaurant that will allow you to take the food away, such as Chinese, Thai or Indian.

In the USA, the most popular meal to order at a sit-down restaurant is fried chicken.

Unhealthy appetites—value comes at a cost

Read the newspaper article and then answer the questions that follow it.

AUSTRALIANS are risking their health in the pursuit of value for money—buying fast food 'value deals', bonus-pack groceries and accepting meal 'up sizes'.

Experts warn our desire for a bargain is increasing consumption and making us fatter, thereby increasing risk of heart problems, diabetes and obesity.

Research shows value for money is the priority among shoppers. A 2001 survey of 1000 parents, by consumer analyst group Good Business Sense, found 35 per cent were influenced by value for money when buying snack foods.

A quarter were influenced by health factors.

Half were influenced by in-store promotions and 44 per cent were attracted to special offers, like two-for-one or bonus pack sizes.

Experts say increasing competition in the confectionery, fast food and soft drink markets was prompting offers of extra portions free, or for a slightly higher price.

Analyst Anne Roze said firms were 'realising customers are looking for value for money and getting into the habit of eating larger portions'.

The 2002 AC Nielsen Grocery Report found 'overwhelming evidence of strong growth of large pack sizes', despite smaller average households and increasing shopping frequency. Bulk juice, like three-litre bottles, doubled its market share in five years, according to the report.

NSW vice-president of the Australian Medical Association, Dr John Gullotta, said that consumers were being tricked into eating more.

'They're trying to trick people to (buy) a bigger amount with that perception of it being cheaper,' he said.

'It's detrimental to our health because of the higher fat and sugar content.'

QUESTIONS

1 What are the disadvantages of 'value deals' and 'up-sizes'?
2 What percentage of people are influenced by 'value for money' when purchasing snack foods?
3 What factors influence consumers when buying snack foods?
4 What is said to be prompting offers of free extra portions?
5 'Consumers are being tricked into eating more.' Do you agree or disagree with this statement? Explain your answer.

Children's junk food slammed

NINE OUT OF TEN products aimed at children are 'junk food', says a new report from the UK Food Commission. It looks at the high levels of fat, sugars and sodium in foods targeted at children and sold in cartoon wrappings featuring toys, giveaways, puzzles, and games.

The study looks at 358 products and finds that 77% have high levels of fat, sugar and salt. Only four products, which declared their nutritional content, are low in fats, sugar and salt. These include frozen vegetables from Iceland with cartoon packaging. More than a third of the products were insufficiently labelled for any judgement to be made.

Companies and products criticised included:
• Nestlé: for a 50-mL sachet of milk called Maxi Mooze, which was 56% sugar
• Yeo Valley: for producing a children's yoghurt, which was 25% sugar when its general sale yoghurt was made up of 12% sugar
• Beans, bangers and mash: 43% product, the rest was water, starch and rusks

American diet of junk food causing increased health concerns

One-third of the average American's diet is made up of 'junk' foods, according to a recent study in the American Journal of Clinical Nutrition. In addition to being high in calories and fat, these junk foods take the place of healthier foods, so Americans are depending on just two-thirds of their diet to get 100 per cent of the recommended dietary intake of vitamins and nutrients, according to researchers.

The study used data from the third National Health and Nutrition Examination Survey, which examined eating patterns of among over 15 000 American adults. The investigator analyzed consumption of energy-dense, nutrient-poor foods, which were defined as foods that do not belong in any of the five major food groups: dairy, fruit, grains, meat and beans and vegetables. These foods include: butter and margarine; sweeteners; desserts; salty snacks; and coffee and tea.

Results show that the average American gets 27 per cent of their total daily energy from junk foods and an additional 4 per cent from alcoholic beverages. About one-third of Americans consume an average of 45 per cent of energy from these foods. Such patterns of eating may have long-term health consequences. While it is common knowledge that junk foods are unhealthy, there is convincing evidence that too much junk food can actually replace the healthy food a person needs and may lead to life-threatening consequences, say researchers.

Experts want ban on junk food advertising

Health experts have called for a ban on the advertising of junk food to slow the disturbing trend of adult and child obesity.

They also want to raise taxes on all junk food, saying the money should be used in a campaign to warn that obesity is linked to cancer.

A nutrition conference in Sydney was told of a new link between obesity and cancer which comes from a World Health Organisation study of half a million people.

Researchers found that eating too much food increases our insulin levels which can lead to type two diabetes and now appears to cause damage to cells in the kidney, breast, colon and prostate.

'We can unfortunately expect the rates of some cancers will increase due to this epidemic of obesity,' said Elio Riboli, from the World Health Organisation.

With the number of overweight children doubling and child obesity levels trebling over the past 10 years, nutritionists are calling on doctors to support a ban on junk food advertising.

'It's a disgrace that we advertise junk food to kids, then damn them for getting fat as a result of eating them,' said dietician Rosemary Stanton.

With 16 Australians dying from cancer each day, governments are being urged to increase GST on junk food to fund awareness campaigns.

The theme of the conference is 'eat and run' and nutritionists are tyring to emphasise a key finding that too many of us are only getting half the equation right when it comes to the obesity problem. As a nation, we're conscious of our diet but we're not exercising enough.

'Weight gain is a result of more energy in than energy out and we've all got to lift our energy output … and avoid the further epidemic of obesity,' said Professor Graham Colditz from Harvard University.

Facts on cancer in Australia

One in three men and one in four women in Australia will be directly affected by cancer before the age of 75. Cancer accounts for 29 per cent of male deaths and 25 per cent of female deaths in Australia each year.

Diet and physical activity play a major role in the prevention of cancer. In Australia, more than 6000 deaths from cancer each year have been attributed to inadequate intake of vegetables and fruit, insufficient exercise or being overweight.

1 Enjoy a balanced diet rich in vegetables and fruit.
 —Of all dietary factors, vegetables and fruit have the greatest effects on reducing cancer risk. In particular, diets high in vegetables and fruits reduce the risk of digestive tract, bowel and lung cancer.
 —More than 10 per cent of premature cancer deaths and cancer disabilities in Australia are attributed to inadequate diet.
 —The latest National Nutrition Survey shows Australians need to double their intake of fruit and vegetables.
 —Australian adults should aim to eat at least two serves of fruit and five serves of vegetables each day.
2 Eat a variety of wholegrain cereals, breads and pastas.
3 Maintain a healthy weight and be physically active.
4 Drink alcohol in moderation, if at all.
5 Select foods low in salt and fat.

QUESTION

Read the three articles 'Children's junk food slammed', 'American diet of junk food causing increased health concerns' and 'Experts want ban on junk food advertising', which provide perspectives on junk food in the United Kingdom, the USA and Australia. You have been asked to deliver a presentation titled 'The problem with junk food is …' Your presentation must include information about the problems associated with junk food in addition to offering possible solutions for dealing with these problems. Deliver your oral presentation of five to ten minutes to the class.

Aussie fat epidemic

Read the newspaper article and then answer the questions that follow it.

By Robyn Riley

OVERWEIGHT AUSSIES have been put on notice to shape up, cut out the fat in their diets and start moving.

We are a nation of overweight and obese people and health experts have warned it is time to treat the problem seriously or face the deadly consequences.

David Crawford, a nutrition research fellow at Deakin University in Geelong, said that for too long Australians have viewed obesity as a trivial issue, 'when it really is a serious health problem,' he said.

Mr Crawford said Australia was facing an obesity epidemic that would cause a massive increase in diabetes, heart disease, stroke and certain cancers.

Obesity defines people who score higher than 30 on the inter- nationally-recognised body mass index (BMI) scale. This formula measures your height in metres squared with your body weight in kilograms.

It is a simple test. Using a calcu- lator, start with your weight in kilograms (for example 60 kg) and then divide it by your height in metres (1.7 m), then divide this by your height again (1.7 m). This will give you a score (20.76 for this example). A healthy range is 20–25, as above 25 is considered overweight and 30 and above is obese.

Mr Crawford, who was involved in producing the National Health and Medical Research Council's *Acting on Australia's Weight*, a study of the country's obesity problems, said Australia should be leading the world in the fight against fat.

Instead:
- Obesity has been increasing in Australia for the last decade.
- Five million Australians are now obese.
- Almost half the male population is overweight.
- Some 60 per cent of Aboriginal and Torres Strait Islanders are overweight.
- Our children are not immune, the NHMRC survey found 5.3 per cent of Australian children aged 12 to 15 were overweight.
- Men rapidly increase their weight between 25 and 40; women during the menopausal years (45 to 55).
- An international study predicts that within 25 years, 40 per cent of Australians will be obese.

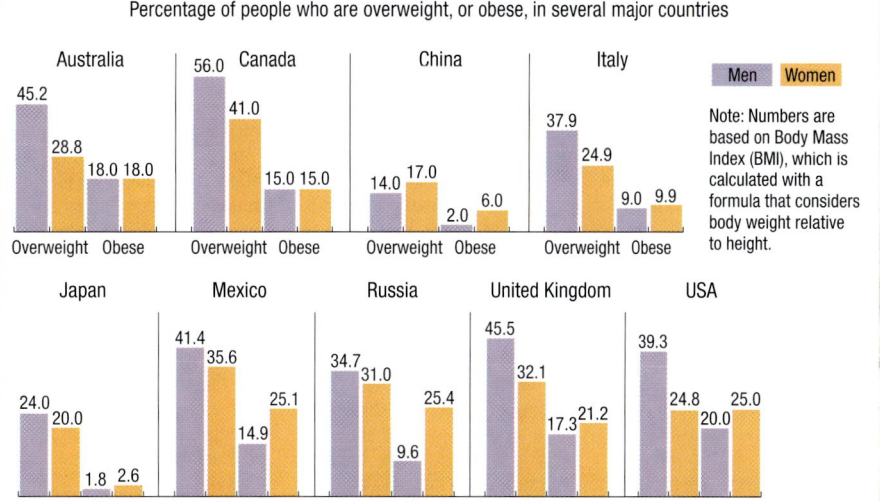

Percentage of people who are overweight, or obese, in several major countries

Note: Numbers are based on Body Mass Index (BMI), which is calculated with a formula that considers body weight relative to height.

Supporting Mr Crawford's concern is a recent report by the International Obesity Task Force (IOTF), a group representing 30 countries including Australia, which found Australian men were among the most obese in the world, second only to the US.

And Australian women did not fare much better in the study. They came in fifth behind Russia, Mexico, the US and the United Kingdom.

The cause of obesity, according to *Acting on Australia's Weight*, were a mix of inherited characteristics, lifestyle and social factors. And the cost to Australia is about $850 million.

'Basically, Australians are enjoying too much of a good life; eating too much and doing too little,' Mr Crawford said.

Professor Joe Proietto is the head of the Royal Melbourne Hospital's Metabolic Disorder Clinic, one of only two specialist obesity units in Victoria (the other is at Monash Medical Centre). Prof. Proietto is also a former president of the Australian Society for the Study of Obesity.

He agrees obesity is rising rapidly in Australia. 'Not only because people are eating more, but because people are moving less,' he said.

'With all these modern gadgets today, people are sitting down more, not moving or exercising and it is causing major health problems.'

And men are more at risk. Prof. Proietto said although the percentage of obese Australian men and women was the same, it was a much more serious health problem for men because of the way their bodies stored fat.

'Men always store fat around the abdomen and abdominal fat is related to heart attack, diabetes, high cholesterol and strokes,' he said.

'Women tend to store fat predominantly on the thighs and hips, which is not as dangerous.'

Prof. Proietto said obese people needed only to achieve a 10 per cent weight reduction to significantly lower health risks.

He said gross obesity was caused by a generic disorder.

'People who get really big do so because of medical reasons and scientists have now identified five genes which can lead to severe obesity,' Prof. Proietto said.

In September, Professor Greg Collier, also from Deakin University, was part of a team which discovered a human gene which might lead to the first gene-based drug to treat obesity.

Prof. Collier found that the gene, which he called Beacon, cranked up the appetite.

The Beacon gene produces a protein that stimulates the appetite. Another gene, known as NPy, does the same, but the body also produces a hormone, leptin, which can switch off the appetite.

Prof. Proietto said some obese people had a mutation in their genes which stopped leptin doing its job.

Leptin was discovered in 1994 and identified as the hormone which signalled a message to the brain to stop overeating.

It is made in fat cells and as we accumulate fat in our bodies, these cells release more leptin to control our appetite.

Prof. Proietto said those deficient in leptin had no control over their appetite.

'And that is why large people who lose weight on a diet start to feel very hungry all the time,' Prof. Proietto said.

'Most lose the battle because their drive to eat is just too strong and eating is a very basic human instinct, much stronger than reproduction.'

QUESTIONS

1. According to the article, what is the definition of obesity?
2. Explain how you would calculate your Body Mass Index (BMI).
3. How many Australians are now obese?
4. At what age do men and women increase their weight rapidly?
5. What is the predicted rate for obesity in the future?
6. How do the obesity statistics for Australia compare to those in other countries?
7. Identify some possible causes of obesity.
8. Why is obesity a more serious concern for men as opposed to women?
9. What causes gross obesity?
10. Explain what the Beacon gene is.

▶ Meet Macca's Number 1 fan

Read the newspaper article and then answer the questions that follow it.

CORALEE NIELSEN-NEEDHAM is a walking, talking advertisement for McDonald's.

The 77-year-old great-grandmother has eaten McDonald's for breakfast, lunch and dinner, seven days a week, for the past eight years.

She even sold her house to move closer to her favourite fast-food restaurant.

'It's the only place I can eat where the food doesn't disagree with me,' said Mrs Nielsen-Needham, a spritely pensioner who walks everywhere to keep fit.

'I've eaten at other places and ended up in hospital on a drip,' she said.

Mrs Nielsen-Needham sold her home in Stirling, in Perth's northern suburbs, three years ago to move closer to her favourite McDonald's in nearby Tuart Hill.

'I would never have sold my house if this one hadn't been so close,' she said.

Her daily pilgrimage to McDonald's runs like clockwork: at 6 a.m. she has an egg and cheese McMuffin and coffee and does the crossword, at 11 a.m. she returns for a hot apple pie, and she's back at 5 p.m. for a McOz burger— 'because it has lots of salad'.

When the *Sunday Herald Sun* called in at her home at lunchtime, a neighbour said we could find her at the local McDonald's. She practically lived there, he said.

And there she was, drinking coffee over a hot apple pie with a group of regulars and so much at home that, at one stage, she disappeared behind the serving counter, returning minutes later with the store manager.

To critics of fast food, Coralee says her own slight frame is proof that the food doesn't make you fat.

'People get fat because they eat too much and they are not active,' she said.

Her own exercise regime is a case in point.

The nimble former single mother and business manager walks about 5 km every day and thinks nothing of a 12 km hike.

'I don't ever want to be a burden to my family and I love it. It is the main part of my life,' she said.

Needless to say, they are all fond of McDonald's too.

'My great grand-niece calls me "Auntie Donald",' she said.

A VIP guest on McHappy days, Coralee insists she gets none of her food for free.

'I come here so often because I like it and because this is where all my friends are.'

QUESTIONS

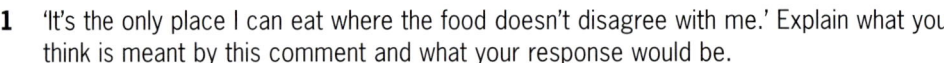

Did you know that McHappy Meals account for 40 per cent of McDonald's profits?

1 'It's the only place I can eat where the food doesn't disagree with me.' Explain what you think is meant by this comment and what your response would be.

2 Visit www.dietclub.com.au/createameal/?menu=1.
   a 'Drop and drag' Coralee's food items onto the tray.
   b Click on 'Nutrition Chart All Menu Items' to determine the nutrient value of Coralee's daily diet.
   c Chart her diet in a spreadsheet and compare the results with the Recommended Daily Intake (RDI) for a person of her age. You can find the RDIs at www.medicalonline.com.au/medical/nutrition/rdi.htm.

3 What recommendations would you make to Coralee in relation to her diet?

▶ New McMenu

Read the newspaper article and then answer the questions that follow it.

By Chloe Adams

YOUNG health-conscious Australians have forced fast-food giant McDonald's to review its traditional burger and fries menu.

On Friday McDonald's will introduce its New Tastes Menu, its largest menu change in 30 years.

And the marketing catchcry 'Things that make you go mmmmmm', takes a cue from C&C Music Factory's early 1990 hit song, not to mention Homer Simpson.

About 30 products will appear on the menu on a rotational basis.

McDonald's 1.2 million daily customers can expect to see healthy alternatives, such as salads and fruit parfaits, by early next year.

'The research we did showed customers are looking for healthy alternatives,' a McDonald's spokeswoman said today.

'The mid-20 and 30 something's are more health-conscious than ever before.'

The spokeswoman said white meat was on the desired list.

The first instalment on Friday will feature a cheese and tomato toasted sandwich, pikelet drippers with hotcake syrup and cinnamon sugar, a honey mustard crispy chicken burger and a Cadbury Crunchy McFlurry.

Other menu ideas are fish and chips, pies and the flavours of Italy and Thailand.

The spokeswoman said the healthy changes were not based on keeping up with competitors

who were increasingly turning to low-fat menu options.

They were based on extensive customer research, she said.

'Qualitative and sensory research was conducted earlier this year which resulted in planning and product development,' Liz Dangar of Dangar Research said.

'It was clear from this research that those questioned believed that McDonald's plans for New Tastes were keeping up with the changing times.'

QUESTIONS

1 Why is McDonald's introducing a new menu?
2 Identify the marketing strategies being used to introduce this new promotion.
3 Which target market is becoming more health conscious?
4 Do the new changes appeal to you? Explain your answer.
5 Write two paragraphs on whether or not you consider the McDonald's New Tastes Menu to be healthy or nutrient-dense.

Shopper strike:

Italy's pizza resistance

Italy is famous for strike action by everyone from transport workers to doctors, from teachers and even prostitutes.

Now the first pizza strike has been called for tomorrow by consumer group ADUC which says prices are too high.

It estimates that the ingredients for a classic pizza margherita—tomato, mozzarella and basil—costs about 90 cents, but restaurants charge about $9.

Using the same mark-up, the group says, a fish dish in a good restaurant would cost a ridiculous $268.

In protest, the group wants all Italians not to buy pizzas all day tomorrow.

Focus on fat, salt and sugar

Fat

As we read in *e-Food Book 1*, we often refer to fat as being good fat or bad fat. Good fats are those that can reduce the amount of cholesterol in our blood and consequently the risk of heart disease. Saturated fats can raise our blood cholesterol and contribute to heart disease. Polyunsaturated and monounsaturated fats are considered to be good, while saturated fats are considered to be bad.

Another type of fat that we are beginning to hear more about are trans-fats, or trans-fatty acids. You will notice that food labels will now list trans-fatty acids in the nutrient information, along with saturated, monounsaturated and polyunsaturated fats. Trans-fatty acids are actually unsaturated fats that have been hydrogenated so that they have a chemical composition similar to saturated fats. We mainly find trans-fatty acids in margarine and some commercial cooking oils.

One of the problems with junk food is that it contains bad fat. This means that it is often high in saturated and/or trans-fatty acids. To avoid bad fat, we should reduce the amount of junk food eaten, as it often contains or is cooked in oil that is high in saturated fat, such as palm oil, or is cooked in oil that contains trans-fatty acids. We should also avoid products that contain hydrogenated fat, including some types of margarine, and avoid saturated fats found in animal products.

The Kettle Chip Company produces a range of potato chips, including the original salted variety shown.

250g NET

Original Salted

THE AUTHENTIC CHIP

NO CHOLESTEROL

BEST BEFORE

16 APR 03 A 3 11:44

WE ONLY USE THE BEST AUSTRALIAN
GROWN POTATOES - WASHED,
SLICED, THAT'S IT!

WE HAVE THE BEST FLAVOURS...
BECAUSE WE ONLY USE NATURAL
INGREDIENTS – NO ARTIFICIAL
COLOURS, FLAVOURS,
PRESERVATIVES, AND NO MSG!

Why do
Kettle Chips
taste so good?

WE HAVE A LOUD
CRUNCH BECAUSE
OUR CHIPS ARE SLOWLY
COOKED THE AUTHENTIC WAY.
WE USE SUNFLOWER OIL - MAKING THEM
CHOLESTEROL FREE AND 75% LESS IN
SATURATED FAT THAN CHIPS COOKED
IN PALMOLEIN.

THIS PACK IS SOLD BY
WEIGHT NOT VOLUME.
IT IS PACKAGED WITH
AIR TO CUSHION AGAINST
BREAKAGES. SETTLING
MAY OCCUR DURING
TRANSIT. STORE IN
A COOL DRY PLACE.

FOR MORE
INFORMATION ABOUT
KETTLE CHIPS
CALL US ON 1800 806 128
OR FIND US AT
www.kettle.com.au

PRODUCT OF AUSTRALIA
INGREDIENTS:
POTATOES, SUNFLOWER OIL,
SEA SALT.

9 313611 250117

THE KETTLE CHIP COMPANY,
11 GEORGE STREET, HOMEBUSH, NSW, 2140
©2001 ®REGISTERED TRADEMARK ™TRADEMARK.

034779-01

NUTRITION INFORMATION

SERVES PER PACKAGE 2.5
SERVING SIZE 100g

	PER 100g*
ENERGY	2280kJ
PROTEIN	6.3g
GLUTEN	NIL
FAT, TOTAL	32.3g
SATURATED	2.8g
TRANS	0.0g
POLYUNSATURATED	3.6g
MONOUNSATURATED	25.9g
CHOLESTEROL	NIL
CARBOHYDRATE, TOTAL	55.3g
SUGARS	1.0g
DIETARY FIBRE	4.6g
SODIUM	250mg

*Average Quantities-Subject to Seasonal Variation

QUESTIONS

1   Using your knowledge about cholesterol and saturated fat, why do you think the package highlights 'No cholesterol'?

2   Analyse the types of fat and total fat content. How does this packet of chips compare to others? Find two other chip packets and draw comparisons between those and the Kettle chips.

3   Do the Kettle chips contain good or bad fat? Explain your answer.

4   Compare the ingredients listed on the Kettle chips packet to those listed on the two other chip packets and write a paragraph describing the similarities and differences.

5   What is palmolein?

Salt

Junk food that is high in fat is also often high in salt. A diet with too much salt can lead to problems such as dehydration, high blood pressure (hypertension) or stroke. We should avoid adding salt to our food and eating snack foods that have high amounts of salt. Junk food that is high in salt includes takeaway pizza, potato chips and hot dogs (processed meat and white bread).

Salt is made up of sodium and chloride. The recommended dietary intake (RDI) for sodium is 920 to 2300 milligrams per day. The table below shows the high sodium content of common takeaway foods. If you consumed one large pizza supreme, you would be consuming 6000 milligrams of sodium!

Food item	Average serving size (grams)	Sodium content (milligrams)	Grams of sodium per 100 grams of food
Meat pie	175	798	46
Sausage roll	130	819	63
Pastie	170	1080	64
Hot dog	160	1160	73
Pizza supreme (one slice)	130	750	58
Corn chips	200	1150	600

Source: www.dietclub.com.au

Sugar

Just like fat and salt, sugar adds flavour to food, which people find appealing; however, eating sugary or sweet foods in excess is unhealthy. Many snacks, such as sweets, chocolate, lollies and ice creams, are high in sugar. Soft drinks also have high amounts of sugar and it is preferable to drink water or milk (which contains a natural sugar called lactose and other nutrients such as calcium and protein) instead.

Consuming junk food or snacks high in sugar contributes to 'empty kilojoules' in the diet, filling us up with foods that are low in nutrient value and energy-dense. This makes us feel full and allows less room for the nutrient-dense foods, which we require in order to maintain healthy eating patterns. Also, one of the main health problems associated with consuming foods that contain too much sugar is dental caries. Although dental health has been improved by introducing fluoride into the water supply and toothpastes, we still need to be mindful of reducing our intake of sugary snack foods outside of meal times.

Rather than snacking on sugary junk foods, it is best to consume sugar as part of a meal, as many foods contain sugar; for example, fruits, milk and bread. If snacking between meals, choose a piece of fruit instead of chocolate or lollies. Remember, sugary junk food should only be consumed occasionally as a treat and should not be given as a reward to children.

Focus on healthy snacks

It is almost impossible to expect people to remove all junk food from their diet; however, it is important to remember that consumption of junk food should be kept to a minimum and considered only to be suitable on occasion. It is far better to focus on the consumption of healthy snacks and to try to promote healthy eating patterns based on good nutritional principles. The Dietary Guidelines for Australians aim to assist us by providing general principles or guidelines for us to follow. In particular, we are encouraged to limit our intake of fat (especially saturated fat), salt and sugar.

While these guidelines are very useful, they are very general and rely on additional knowledge and skills to actually know how to do as the guidelines say. This is why it is important for all of us to gain an understanding of the properties of food, cooking and decision making in relation to the purchase and preparation of food.

▶ Dietary Guidelines for Australian Adults

Enjoy a wide variety of nutritious foods
- Eat plenty of vegetables, legumes and fruits
- Eat plenty of cereals (including breads, rice, pasta and noodles), preferably wholegrain
- Include lean meat, fish, poultry and/or alternatives
- Include milks, yoghurts, cheeses and/or alternatives. Reduced-fat varieties should be chosen, where possible
- Drink plenty of water

and take care to:
- Limit saturated fat and moderate total fat intake
- Choose foods low in salt
- Limit your alcohol intake if you choose to drink
- Consume only moderate amounts of sugars and foods containing added sugars

Prevent weight gain: be physically active and eat according to your energy needs

Care for your food: prepare and store it safely

Encourage and support breastfeeding

▶ Dietary Guidelines for Children and Adolescents in Australia

Encourage and support breastfeeding

Children and adolescents need sufficient nutritious foods to grow and develop normally
- Growth should be checked regularly for young children
- Physical activity is important for all children and adolescents

Enjoy a wide variety of nutritious foods

Children and adolescents should be encouraged to:
- Eat plenty of vegetables, legumes and fruits
- Eat plenty of cereals (including breads, rice, pasta and noodles), preferably wholegrain
- Include lean meat, fish, poultry and/or alternatives
- Include milks, yoghurts, cheeses and/or alternatives
  - Reduced-fat milks are not suitable for young children under 2 years, because of their high energy needs, but reduced-fat varieties should be encouraged for older children and adolescents
- Choose water as a drink
  - Alcohol is not recommended for children

and care should be taken to:
- Limit saturated fat and moderate total fat intake
  - Low-fat diets are not suitable for infants
- Choose foods low in salt
- Consume only moderate amounts of sugars and foods containing added sugars

Care for your child's food: prepare and store it safely

▶ **Let's remember**

1 Define the term *junk food*.
2 Define the term *takeaway food*.
3 Identify the foods that are categorised as extras according to the Australian Guide for Healthy Eating.
4 'All fast food is bad for us.' Do you agree or disagree with this statement? Explain your answer.
5 What problems do we risk by consuming too much junk food?
6 What are the disadvantages of consuming empty-kilojoule foods?
7 What are trans-fatty acids?
8 Define the term *hydrogenation* and explain why hydrogenated products should be avoided.
9 What kinds of junk food are high in salt?
10 What are the main problems associated with consuming too much sugar?

▶ **Let's investigate**

1 Investigate the sodium content of a range of potato chips by visiting www.dietclub.com.au. Use the search facility to do your investigating and then design a table to collate your results. Evaluate the different varieties and draw comparisons ☺ ☺ ☹.
2 Have each class member bring in an empty margarine tub. Compare and evaluate the types and amounts of saturated, unsaturated and trans-fatty acids present ☺ ☺ ☹. Are there any margarines that are hydrogenated or partly hydrogenated? Which margarines do you rate as the healthiest?
3 Do a search for 'dental caries' on the Internet. Produce a list of rules for good dental hygiene.
4 Design a poster or collage that is divided into two sections. On one side, paste junk food pictures to be avoided and on the other side, paste pictures of healthy alternatives.
5 Create a jingle or poem about eating less fat, salt and sugar.

▶ *ℯ*-**Snacks and junk food**

www.betterhealth.vic.gov.au

The Better Health Channel is a website established by the Victorian Government aimed at providing the community with information about a range of health issues. Search the articles section under 'J' and read the article on junk food.

1 On average, what percentage of the household budget do Australians spend on takeaway and convenience foods?
2 Fat is energy-dense. What does this mean?
3 Outline some of the suggested healthier choices for takeaway foods.
4 Junk food should only be eaten in moderation. What is the general rule of thumb to apply?
5 'Junk food can be enjoyed occasionally as part of a healthy diet.' Do you agree or disagree with this quote from the website? Explain your answer.

www.dav.org.au

Visit the Diabetes Australia—Victoria website. Click on 'What is diabetes?'

1 Describe Type 2 diabetes.

WEBExTRaS

www.youngmedia.org.
au/mediachildren/
03_03_ads_food.htm
This website provides
information about food
advertising for children and
statistics about the number
of advertisements
promoting food high in fat,
salt and sugar during
children's viewing times.

www.foodsciencebureau
.com.au/nutrit/salt.htm
This website has an information fact sheet about salt.

2 Who is most at risk of being diagnosed with Type 2 diabetes?

3 Click on 'Healthy Eating'. Describe what kind of healthy eating plan is recommended for managing diabetes.

www.heartfoundation.com.au

Go to the National Heart Foundation website and click on 'Cardiovascular Disease—Australia's Major Health Problem'.

1 How many Australians die every ten minutes from cardiovascular disease?

2 Define the term *cardiovascular disease*.

3 How can cardiovascular disease be prevented?

4 Scroll down to 'A comprehensive national physical activity program'. How many deaths in 1996 were attributable to physical inactivity?

5 Scroll down to 'A comprehensive national nutrition program'. Explain how diet has been linked to cardiovascular disease and outline the dietary recommendations suggested.

▶ **Puzzled**

◉ **Hi-lo**

Crack the code to complete the sentence about the nutritional value of junk food.

A	B	C	D	E	F	G	H	I	J	K	L	M	N	O	P	Q	R	S	T	U	V	W	X	Y	Z
				20									7					1		10					

_ _ _ _   _ O O _   _ _   E _ E _ _ _   _ E _ _ E
15 4 13 17   23 7 7 25   26 14   20 13 20 2 9 22   25 20 13 14 20

_ _ _   _ O _   _ _   _ _ T _ _ E _ T   V _ _ _ E
12 13 25   24 7 6   26 13   13 4 1 2 26 20 13 1   10 12 24 4 20

◉ **Junk food criss-cross**

Across

3 An example of a healthy snack

5 A mineral found in salt

6 Soft drinks contain empty _____

9 Too many lollies may cause this (two words)

10 More than 10 per cent over recommended weight

Down

1 A snack that is high in saturated fat and salt

2 Type of oil used in many takeaway food outlets

4 Junk food is generally high in fat and low in _____

7 More than 20 per cent over recommended weight

8 Junk food is energy- _____

Which takeaway?

Name the takeaway outlets that are identified by the slogans.

1 Things that make you go mmmmmm …
2 Nobody does chicken like …
3 The best ice cream treat experience
4 Thank goodness … make great pizzas
5 You deserve a muffin break
6 The greatest tasting donuts in the world!
7 The burgers are better at …
8 The best pizzas under one roof

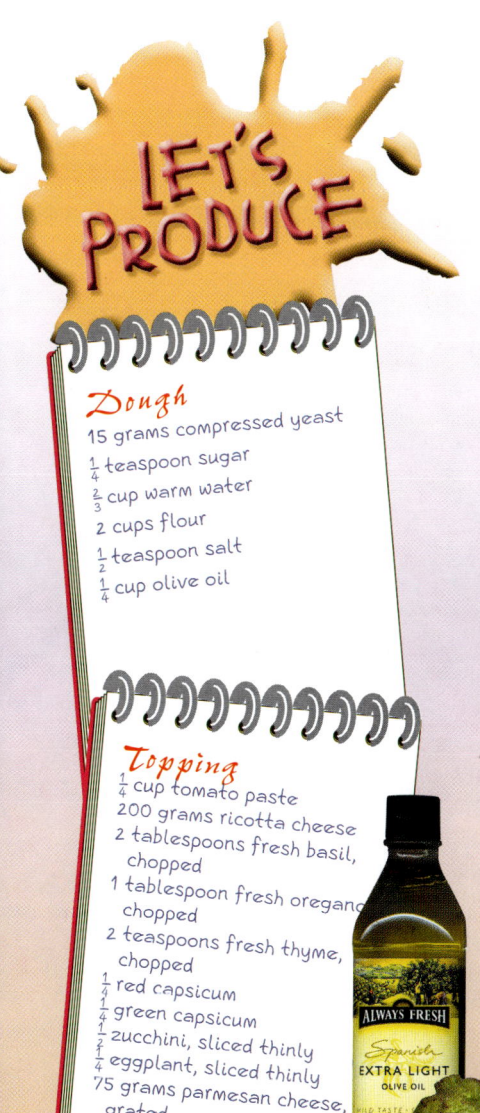

LET'S PRODUCE

Dough

15 grams compressed yeast
$\frac{1}{4}$ teaspoon sugar
$\frac{2}{3}$ cup warm water
2 cups flour
$\frac{1}{2}$ teaspoon salt
$\frac{1}{4}$ cup olive oil

Topping

$\frac{1}{4}$ cup tomato paste
200 grams ricotta cheese
2 tablespoons fresh basil, chopped
1 tablespoon fresh oregano, chopped
2 teaspoons fresh thyme, chopped
$\frac{1}{4}$ red capsicum
$\frac{1}{4}$ green capsicum
$\frac{1}{2}$ zucchini, sliced thinly
$\frac{1}{4}$ eggplant, sliced thinly
75 grams parmesan cheese, grated
2 tablespoons pine nuts

Vegetarian ricotta pizza   (serves 2)

Method

1 Mix together yeast, sugar and warm water. Allow five to ten minutes for yeast to activate.
2 Sift flour and salt. Add yeast mixture and oil to form dough.
3 Knead on lightly floured board for five minutes.
4 Place dough in a lightly greased bowl, cover with plastic wrap and allow to rise for thirty minutes.
5 Prepare topping ingredients.
6 Remove dough from bowl, 'knock back' and then knead for a further two to three minutes. Shape dough to fit pizza pan.
7 Blend together ricotta cheese and herbs.
8 Spread dough with tomato paste and ricotta cheese mixture.
9 Sprinkle with toppings.
10 Top with parmesan cheese and pine nuts.
11 Bake in preheated oven for twenty to thirty minutes.
12 Serve with garden salad.

QUESTIONS

1 Describe how to knead. Draw a diagram to illustrate the process.
2 Investigate what happens when yeast is combined with sugar and warm water.
3 What ingredients do you think you would find in a garden salad?

Souvlaki

(serves 2)

Method

1. Mix oil, lemon juice and herbs together.
2. Cut meat into cubes.
3. Baste meat with oil mixture.
4. Thread meat onto skewers.
5. Marinate for as long as possible.
6. Preheat griller.
7. Cook meat for three minutes on each side.
8. Serve on pita bread with shredded lettuce and tzatziki dip.

Ingredients

1 tablespoon olive oil
2 teaspoons lemon juice
1 tablespoon fresh oregano, chopped
1 teaspoon fresh thyme, chopped
300 grams lamb
2 rounds pita bread
4 lettuce leaves, finely shredded
2 tablespoons tzatziki dip

QUESTIONS

1. From which country does souvlaki originate?
2. Investigate the ingredients in tzatziki.
3. Evaluate the souvlaki according to appearance, flavour, texture and aroma ☺ ☺ ☹.
4. Design your own souvlaki using different ingredients.
5. Investigate a range of recipe books and produce your own tzatziki dip.

Fish burgers

(serves 2)

Method

1. Break bread into smaller pieces and place in food processor to make breadcrumbs.
2. Add fish, egg, chilli sauce, parsley and pepper.
3. Shape fish mixture into round shapes and coat in flour.
4. Cut tomato into slices and shred lettuce.
5. Heat oil in frypan. Add fish and cook for two to three minutes each side.
6. Serve on toasted hamburger bun with tomato, lettuce and tartare sauce.

Ingredients

1 slice bread
300 grams fish fillets, chopped roughly
1 egg, lightly beaten
2 teaspoons sweet chilli sauce
2 teaspoons parsley
black pepper, to taste
2 tablespoons flour
1–2 tablespoons oil
½ tomato
4 lettuce leaves
1 hamburger bun
1 tablespoon tartare sauce

Variations

1. Use your own selection of herbs and sauces to flavour the fish burgers.
2. After coating the fish in flour, dip in a mixture of egg and milk and then coat in breadcrumbs.
3. Add your own selection of extras to the burger, such as cheese or beetroot.

Baked chicken nuggets

(serves 2)

Ingredients

300 grams chicken breast
$\frac{2}{3}$ cup plain yoghurt
1 cup cornflake crumbs
butter for greasing

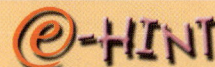

Method

1. Cut chicken into small strips or nugget-sized pieces.
2. Baste with yoghurt.
3. Coat with cornflake crumbs.
4. Line baking tray with baking paper and brush a little butter onto the paper.
5. Cook in oven at 180°C for approximately twenty minutes, or until chicken is cooked and browned on both sides.

e-HINT

Place crumbed chicken into refrigerator for fifteen to twenty minutes before cooking to 'set' the crumbs.

Banana and macadamia muffins

(serves 2)

Ingredients

$1\frac{1}{2}$ cups self-raising flour
1 tablespoon brown sugar
2 teaspoons cinnamon
$\frac{1}{2}$ cup macadamia nuts, chopped
2 eggs
2 over-ripe bananas, mashed
$\frac{3}{4}$ cup milk

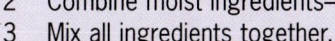

Method

1. Combine dry ingredients—flour, sugar, cinnamon and nuts.
2. Combine moist ingredients—eggs, bananas and milk.
3. Mix all ingredients together.
4. Spoon into greased muffin tray.
5. Bake at 200°C for approximately twenty-five minutes.

MakE a MEal of It: ossEssmEnt Task 1

This assessment task addresses the outcomes TEMA0601 and TEMA0602 from the Technology Key Learning Area.

▶ Part 1   Design brief—meal planning

Your task is to plan a two-course menu for yourself and a friend. The meal may be breakfast, lunch or dinner and is to celebrate a special occasion of your own choice. Your assignment must include the following:

- a menu, which includes two new products—you can find these new products by searching www.woolworths.com.au or www.colesonline.com.au
- a description of these two new products and an explanation as to why they are appropriate to the menu
- recipes for both courses, including title, ingredients and method
- a balance of healthy foods in accordance with the Australian Guide to Healthy Eating
- a time plan and order of work
- a shopping list detailing the specific quantities of each ingredient required
- a description and diagram explaining how you would decorate the table for your chosen theme

▶ Part 2

Prepare your meal in class and  it according to appearance, flavour, texture and aroma ☺ ☺ ☹. In your evaluation, also include a paragraph about the compatibility of your chosen menu and theme.

MaKE a MEaL of IT: assEssmENT Task 2

This assessment task addresses the outcomes HPIP0601 and HPIP0602 from the Health and Physical Education Key Learning Area.

▶ Part 1

Answer the questions below for the food selection models listed.

- Australian Guide to Healthy Eating (www.health.gov.au/pubhlth/strateg/food/guide)
- Dietary Guidelines for Australians (www.health.gov.au/nhmrc/advice/diet.htm)
- Healthy Eating Pyramid (www.nutritionaustralia.org)

1 Describe the role of each food selection model in promoting the health of Australians.
2 Analyse each food selection model by identifying its positive and negative points.
3 Explain how each food selection model caters for the nutritional needs of different age groups.
4 Which food selection model would you prefer to follow? Explain your answer.

 **Part 2**

Use the following websites to answer the questions below.

- Go for 2 & 5 (www.gofor2and5.com.au)
- 7-a-day (www.7aday.coles.com.au)
- Adelaide markets (www.adelaidemarkets.com.au/kef/links.htm)
- Sydney markets (www.sydneymarkets.com.au/fandv/homeindex.html)

1 Explain why there are programs aimed specifically at increasing fruit and vegetable consumption.

2 Which groups of people are being targeted for each of the programs identified?

3 How many serves of fruit and vegetables do you consume on an average day of the week and weekend?

4 Identify five ways that you could include fruits and vegetables in your diet at breakfast, lunch and dinner.

4

TECHNO FOOD

16

MAKES SENSE: DISCOVER SENSORY EVALUATION

As consumers of food, we use our senses to form an opinion of food products; we assess food according to its appearance, flavour, texture and aroma.

Appearance

The way a food looks in terms of colour, shape and texture will impact on whether we decide to consume it.

We have expectations about the colour of particular foods. For example, a pie should have pastry that is golden brown, a lemon should be yellow and milk should be white.

We expect the texture of the outside of an apple to be smooth and not wrinkly; its inside texture should be crisp and crunchy. The texture of marshmallow should be soft.

We expect that the shape of an orange will be round, while the shape of a boiled egg will be elliptical.

Colour, in particular, will help us to form an opinion about the quality of the food. Green mould on bread indicates that it is not suitable to eat. Green tomatoes indicate that they are not ripe. Black bananas indicate that they are overripe.

e-Fact

Did you know that when Heinz launched its green tomato sauce in 2000, the highest increase in sales in its history was recorded?

▶ Glowing chook—food from the X-files?

Read the newspaper article and then answer the questions that follow it.

CHICKEN glowing in the dark?! This case could have come from an *X-files* episode, but in fact is real. Not one but two CHOICE subscribers have contacted us in the past few months to tell us about their experiences with 'glowing chicken'.

In both cases the raw chicken leftovers had been left out of the fridge for the family cat. Both subscribers noticed that in the dark the chicken was a bright fluorescent colour—it was

glowing! One said he 'thought it was the moonlight shining on the sink'.

Still, the explanation behind this isn't nearly as sinister as you might expect. We contacted the health department to see if it could shed some light on this strange phenomenon and, lo and behold, it's a fairly common occurrence. Apparently a spoilage bacterium called *Pseudomonas fluorescens* is the culprit. This is a water-borne bacterium that could

be present in meat that's been stored at too high a temperature, and could continue to grow slowly under refrigerated conditions.

Even though it may be present, it's not considered a food-poisoning bacterium, so you won't become ill if you ingest it. It's quite common in meat, but chicken would have to be subject to temperature 'abuse' at some point, like being left out for pets. And let's face it, how many people would normally have the

opportunity to observe chicken glowing in the dark!

So there you have it.

If you've got any strange or interesting food experiences or questions you'd like to ask, go to the food forum.

We can't answer all questions individually; but we'll add the most-often asked or the most interesting questions to our upcoming Food files. So stay tuned for more exciting instalments!

QUESTIONS

1 What would you think if you saw chicken that glowed in the dark?
2 Identify and describe the bacterium that causes raw chicken to become bright fluorescent in colour.
3 What causes the bacterium to be present in chicken?
4 Why is this bacterium not considered to be a food-poisoning bacterium?

Flavour

Flavour is the impact of the combination of taste and the more discerning sense of smell. The sense of smell is said to be about 10 000 times more sensitive than the sense of taste. You usually smell more flavours than you taste!

There are about 10 000 taste buds located on your tongue; children have more taste buds than adults. The four basic taste sensations are bitter, sour, salty and sweet.

If you poke out your tongue, you will notice a V-shaped line of lumps called papillae. The much smaller papillae are found at the front of your tongue, while the larger ones are found at the back.

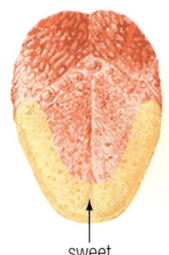 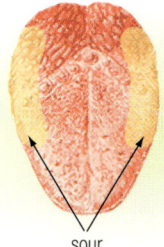 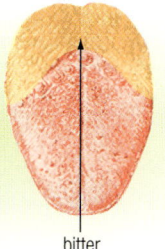 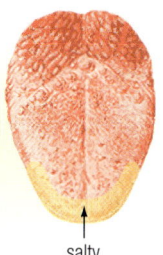

sweet   sour   bitter   salty

Saliva is necessary to dissolve tastes in food and arouse the taste buds so that we enjoy our food. The salivary glands are located underneath the tongue.

Particular foods exhibit a particular taste, or combinations of tastes. Think about the sweetness of sugar or the bitterness of coffee.

Texture

Texture refers to the way food feels in your mouth; it may be referred to as 'mouth feel'. You can also experience texture by touching food with your hands, such as when you select fruits like avocado and peaches.

Aroma

The way food smells impacts on our senses. The olfactory receptors are located in the nose and convey the smell via the nasal passages to the brain.

Most people adore the smell of freshly baked bread from a baker or the smell of chocolate from a chocolate shop. They do not like the smell of curdled milk or mouldy bread.

► Electronic nose—sniffing out commercial applications

Read the newspaper article and then answer the questions that follow it.

FRUITY, cowy, foxy and austere are words used by specialists to describe the smell of food. This vivid language indicates the complexity and sensitivity of the olfactory system.

The electronic nose is an analytical tool that uses special sensors to mimic the human nose. It generates a character-istic fingerprint of an odour, which is compared with data from different samplers, batches and blends.

Brian Young from Food Science Australia commented, 'Over the past four years, our researchers have used electronic nose tech-nology to assist the food industry. We have investigated commercial applications, including monitoring odours released from production plants, batch-to-batch viability and assessing food quality.'

Electronic nose and quality testing of food

Consistent flavour and aroma are important in our appreciation of food. Deviations in these qualities may force a producer to adjust the manufacturing process or with-draw a product from sale. Food Science Australia researchers are using electronic nose technology to assess food quality and variability. For example, this system has discriminated between the types of coffee, cheese and olive oil and has also detected off-colours and food taints.

The distinctive aroma of Brazilian coffee or the attributes of a Greek olive oil can be visualised by plotting its fingerprint on an aroma map. The positioning of its fingerprint on an aroma map illustrates similarities and differences between a selection of imported and local olive oil products.

The electronic nose is also being used to monitor changes and detect foreign aromas in foods. For example, studies have shown that storage and seasonal variation affect the aroma of cheese. The electronic nose has also helped to identify the source of a flavour taint in confectionery. It was found that a residual compound in the packaging had permeated through the wrapping and altered the flavour of the sweets.

The public is becoming increasingly aware of environmental and health issues associated with production plant emissions, and as a consequence of increasing development into rural areas.

Researchers from Food Science Australia have used a new type of artificial nose that combines sensor technology and gas chromatography. Its value is its portability, which allows sampling and analysis of odours *in situ*, enabling the monitoring of odours from facilities, such as meat-rendering plants, chicken farms and piggeries, without having to take air samples back to the laboratory for analysis.

Benefits

Traditional methods employed for measurement of odours such as gas chromatography/mass spectroscopy (GC/MS) and human sensory panels using olfactometry are expensive and labour-intensive. In addition, sensory analysis may be affected by an individual's sensitivity to aromas.

The electronic nose provides an objective, cost-effective, labour-saving method of analysing odours. This technology gives comparative information, making it suitable for quick quality control testing.

For further information contact: Brian Young, Food Science Australia, Werribee, (03) 9731 3492.

QUESTIONS

1. What is the electronic nose?
2. How has the electronic nose assisted the food industry?
3. Why is consistent flavour and aroma important in the food industry?
4. How are the distinctive characteristics of particular foods determined by sensor technology?
5. What are the other uses for the electronic nose?
6. What are the advantages of using sensor technology with gas chromatography?
7. Identify traditional methods usually used for the measurement of odours, and outline the disadvantages with using these methods.
8. What are the advantages with using the electronic nose?

▶ Send in the sensors

Read the newspaper article and then answer the questions that follow it.

By BIANCA NOGRADY, CSIRO Communicator

AS YOU TAKE a bite, the chocolate flavour rolls around your mouth like a smooth, sweet thundercloud, coating your tongue with a satin blanket that almost playfully clings to the roof of your mouth. Then, you encounter the flavour equivalent to a sharp pebble in a soft shoe—a sour, bitter taste that sends you scurrying for something to wash it all away.

This scenario is something that food manufacturers spend hundreds of thousands of dollars trying to avoid. The unwanted aftertaste, the unpleasant gluggy texture and the 'not-quite-right' taste are things that can condemn a food product to the dusty bargain bin or, at worst, force a product recall or product failure.

At Food Science Australia—a joint venture of CSIRO and the Australian Food Industry Science Centre (AFISC)—the methods for tailoring and testing food products for the consumers' palates are well developed. Finely tuned and calibrated instruments—both mechanical and human—are used to analyse every possible nuance of flavour and texture with the aim of shaping a food product that is in every way appealing to the consumer.

Take, for example, a piece of chocolate. Few other food products arouse such passions and loyalty in consumers, as chocolate manufacturers can often find out the hard way. To a novice, a change as seemingly insignificant as the source of the cocoa liquor may have a barely perceptible effect on the flavour of the chocolate. However, for loyal consumers who have been eating this brand of chocolate for years and are as familiar with its flavour as they are with their own body scent, the new strangeness can be enough to send them in search of another favourite.

Enter the sensory evaluators, otherwise known as tasters or trained panellists. Their task is to seek out, identify and quantify these flavour nuances, whether desirable or detestable. Like airport sniffer dogs, the panellists' taste buds and nasal odour receptors are trained to detect even the most minute trace of a flavour or odour that might indicate a change in quality or evidence of spoilage.

While a wave of technological advance in this field has produced such marvels as the electronic nose and electronic tongue, scientists are yet to come

up with a machine that can rival the sensitivity of the human palate and nose. Food Science Australia employs trained panels of tasters around Australia. Ms Vivian Boghossian manages Sensory Research at Food Science Australia and has worked in the area for ten years.

'These trained panels of tasters act like instruments. They are screened and selected for their sensory acuity and sensitivity, then they are trained and "calibrated" to detect specific odours, flavours and textures in food, such as bitterness in chocolate or a nutty flavour in cheese,' she says.

The tasters are given a sample of the food in question, which could be a piece of chocolate, slice of cheese or, if they're unlucky, a few drops of fish oil. They sniff, chew and suck the sample thoroughly, then enter their findings into their computer. Despite being isolated in booths with only their samples and a computer screen for company, a panel of tasters is selected for their ability to get on with each other.

'Taste panel members are carefully selected for their abilities to work as part of a team and to be forthcoming with their findings. For example, if nine out of ten team members don't detect a flavour but one does, we need to make sure that person will speak up about their finding,' says Ms Rachel Marsh, who is involved with recruiting and training taste panellists.

According to two of these 'highly trained human instruments', putting their palates on the line is actually a lot more fun than it sounds.

'It doesn't feel like I'm coming to work, it's more like a social gathering,' says Mrs Lysette Sanchez, who has been a taster for two years. 'My friends' kids all think I have the coolest job.'

Mrs Dianna Mudie, also a taster for two years, agrees. 'We all find tasting interesting and challenging, although sometimes we get samples of things like fish oil, where we all go "Oh, yuk"'.

Assessing the good and bad flavours of food is considerably more complex than the 'yummy' or 'yuk' reaction that would satisfy most of us. At a basic level, there are four 'tastes': bitter, sweet, sour and salty. A fifth basic taste has recently been identified called umami, which is used to describe the savoury, 'beefy' taste common in Asian cuisine.

However, to a professional taster, the sweet flavour of a chocolate bar can then be broken down further into 30 or so sub-flavour factors, such as vanilla, caramel and hazelnut.

Cheese can be even more complex. The distinctive whiff of your favourite cheddar can be described by a range of sub-flavours, including sweet, fruity, nutty, buttery and milky.

And the testing doesn't just cover flavours, it also explores the 'interactive' elements of the food; its fat content, texture, colour, melting properties, thickness of melt—how thick the chocolate feels when it melts in your mouth—and aftertaste.

Assessing aftertaste requires tasters to actually swallow the food, rather than spit it out as a wine taster would do. And while the perils of too much alcohol after a long day's tasting can't be underestimated, the ingestion of food—especially full-fat—products raises some interesting conundrums.

'I started putting weight on as soon as I joined the panel,' says Dianne. 'Now I walk here and walk home, which hopefully takes care of it.' Keeping tasters happy and healthy is vital, as good tasters certainly aren't easy to come by.

Establishing a trained sensory panel is expensive and involves putting candidates through rigorous testing to ensure they have the ability to detect all the basic tastes, a variety of flavours, odours and textures. They are also screened for their ability to work as part of a team, and they cannot be smokers, have any food allergies and must be in possession of a full set of their own teeth!

Not all sensory evaluation relies solely on humans. Technology still plays a part, and this is where inventions such as the electronic nose come in. This electronic instrument has sensors that differentiate between trace amounts of different types of volatiles that may be released from food samples.

'An electronic nose can be useful for routine quality control. It can tell if one sample is different from another, but it can't tell us in what way they are different,' says Ms Boghossian.

As a dedicated chocolate-eater, I for one am grateful that these expert gourmets are putting their palates on the line for my epicurean delight, protecting me from unwanted surprises in my daily bread. Sensors, we who are about to dine salute you!

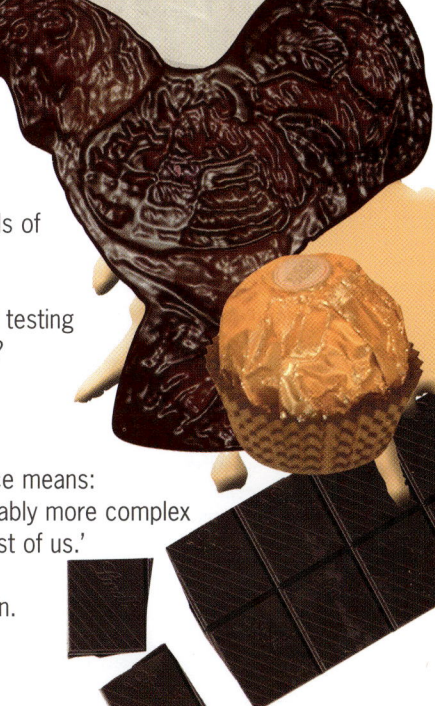

 e-fact

e-fact

QUESTIONS

1 What do food manufacturers spend hundreds of thousands of dollars trying to avoid?
2 What is Food Science Australia?
3 Why are Food Science Australia methods for shaping and testing food products for the consumers' palates well developed?
4 Explain the importance of the role of sensory evaluators.
5 Identify important key criteria for selection as a sensory evaluator.
6 In terms of a sensory evaluator, explain what this sentence means: 'Assessing the good and bad flavours of food is considerably more complex than the "yummy" or "yuk" reaction that would satisfy most of us.'
7 Explain the term *interactive elements of food*.
8 Will technology replace human sensory evaluators? Explain.

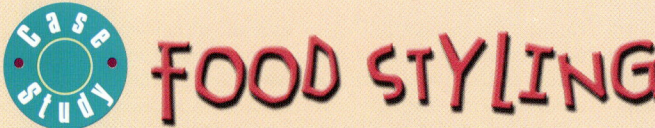

FOOD STYLING

IF YOU'VE EVER flicked through the pages of a glossy food magazine you've seen what a food stylist can do. But how do they get that fabulous, luscious look that says 'Eat me'?

To the uninitiated, the lengths to which food stylists go to make food look perfect may be surprising. As one person commented when we started on this story, 'Surely if you want a photo of a chook, you just photograph a chook.'

The problem with food photography is that food tends to dry out, shrink, discolour and sag—food styling is about counteracting these forces. As the photos on the following pages show, there's a definite art to getting a picture of food that looks good enough to eat, rather than looking destined for the bin. Here's what goes on to get that one apparently simple pic.

Real or fake?

We talked to food stylists and found two schools of thought. Some try to use real food no matter what. Others use whatever techniques get the shot to look right—fake or not. And most are somewhere in between.

In Australia the real-food camp seems to hold sway, with most photos aiming for a natural look using the real thing (albeit with a make-up job). On the other hand, in the US, while they're moving towards a more casual approach to food shots, the art of faking the parts of a shot that don't fall foul of consumer protection laws seems to have been perfected.

Of course, there are different types of food photography. A shot for packaging or an ad has to show the real food being advertised, though that doesn't mean it can't be tweaked, titivated and made-up. And an advertising picture is aiming for perfection. A photo for a glossy recipe mag is more likely to want

a casual 'real' look than perfection. As one stylist put it, 'Editorial is about drawing people into the experience of the food, while advertising is about capturing the perfect vision of the food.'

Much food styling could be summarised as lateral thinking and patience, patience, patience —just keep setting up the food over and over or keep it constantly refreshed until the photographer gets the perfect shot. In fact, the photography itself is an art—it's not unusual to spend most of a day getting the lighting perfect for a single shot.

Of course, these days fixing a shot that isn't quite right can be as simple as a photo touch-up by computer—for example, one picture has the perfect cheesecake, while another has the perfect dollop of cream. Combine the two and the result is just what the client wanted.

Tricks of the trade

So what are some of the techniques stylists might use to counteract the tendency for food to discolour, sag and drip? Try these for size.

- Meat tends to dry out and shrink when you cook it, so chances are the meat in the photo is only partially cooked to keep it plump and juicy. Then it may be browned up with a coat of gravy browning or soy sauce and a hot air gun or blowtorch called upon to crisp up the edges. A final coat of oil gives a hot, fresh-looking shine. The perfect chook, right, gives an idea of the effect. You can do something similar with sausages to avoid explosions and burnt bits: simmer them first, dry them, then apply the paint, torch and oil.
- A hamburger straight out of the wrap doesn't usually look too inspiring (as most people would have experienced).

That's why creating a burger photo is a long and involved process. First find the perfect bun—you might have to trawl through hundreds, and even then it might need a few more sesame seeds glued on in strategic places. The meat patty is given a make-up job as described above, and perfect tomato slices and lettuce frills are chosen —hard to believe, but one stylist told us it might take her four lettuces to find the perfect leaf. Then you've got to construct the thing— layers are separated with cardboard or plastic to stop sogging and squashing, and pins hold it all in place and make sure the lettuce sits just so (see above).

- You know what happens to breakfast cereal when it sits in milk—soggy cereal's not a good look. How to fix it? PVA glue does a much better job than milk. The flakes stay put and stay crisp.
- If you're shooting a slice of cake, the air and lights make it dry out—but a shot of hairspray gets it back looking fresh and yummy.
- Ever noticed chocolate sauce doesn't stay put on top of ice cream for long? Get it to stay by cutting out a sauce-splodge-shaped piece of paper towel and putting it on the ice cream—then the sauce sticks to the towel.
- And on the subject of ice cream—it melts, and fast. Some stylists still work with real ice cream—in editorial shots a bit of melt is OK: it makes the reader feel they want to lick it right off the page. But in product shots, it's got to look perfect and that's not easy—one tutorial on getting the perfect scoop of real ice cream is almost five A4 pages long and advises having as many as twenty 2-litre tubs of ice cream on hand for each shot, not to mention more than

20 kilograms of dry ice and an electric saw.

If you're not advertising the ice cream, you might decide to go fake—coloured mashed potato can make a reasonable substitute. Or instead there are various recipes using corn syrup, margarine, icing sugar and colouring to achieve just the right consistency—depending whether you want super-premium ice cream or a lower-fat look.

- Maple syrup soaks into pancakes and goes a nasty dark colour—but not when you've sprayed the pancakes with fabric protector. Pin your carefully 'scattered' blueberries in place so they don't get swept away with the syrup flow.
- Plastic ice cubes (usually acrylic) don't melt and spoil a drink shot. And to get that frosted look on the glass, spray it with a dulling spray and then give it a spritz with water spray.
- Anyone who's served up a slice of pie knows how it can disintegrate before you get it to the plate. Make it more stable by baking a pie full of instant mashed potato, then cut a slice, scoop out a little potato and put the filling on the side—the chunks neatly pinned in place.
- If you want a perfect drip of sauce glistening on the side of your dessert, use a small piece of soft wax shaped like a drop and put it in place, then coat the drop with sauce for a perfect mid-drip shot.
- If you don't want tomato sauce to run everywhere, mixing it with some tomato paste thickens it enough so it stays perfectly in place. Put it exactly where you want it with a syringe.
- A simple white sauce with the right mix of colouring can double for sauces that are much more delicate beasts, like hollandaise.

- A thin painted-on coat of glycerine makes seafood look juicy. And tossing some liquid glucose through noodles makes them keep a hot, fresh look.
- Stir-fries and things like pasta sauce are often not cooked according to the recipe—each vegie is selected and individually cooked, then put together with the sauce. Often the careful arrangement designed to look random is the result of painstaking work.

The wacky

We came across some truly bizarre techniques and suggestions while researching this article. The stylists we spoke to were by degrees horrified or amused by them—but they generally weren't surprised that someone, somewhere (usually in the US) may have given it a go:

- Maple syrup is much more popular in the US than here, and there are all sorts of tricks to getting it looking right, the most bizarre of which we heard being to use motor oil instead (as long as it's the pancakes being advertised, not the syrup).
- If your Swiss cheese isn't looking photogenic enough, enhance its holes—use little round cutters or even straws for small holes.
- Spray deodorant can give a nice frosting to grapes.
- The perfectly shaped chicken leg can be achieved by

injecting mashed potato under the skin and coating.

Food magic: behind the scenes

We started with identical chooks, muffins from the same batch and the same ingredients, and it was a hard day's work for four professionals to get their shots looking perfect—especially compared with how they looked without titivation. No wonder yours doesn't look the same.

The perfect chook

The styling challenge: Regular roast chook dries up, shrinks and browns unevenly. And while it may smell great at the dining table, it looks pretty unappealing in a photo.

How to style it: First decide on the chook's best angle—in this shoot, the stylists consulted the photographer and his assistant and the raw chook's credentials were discussed at some length. Then the skin at the foot and neck ends is trimmed and sewn in place. It's carefully trussed, firmly stuffed with paper and oven-cooked for about twenty minutes to 'set' the flesh. The skin is 'cooked' to brown crispiness using a coat of soy sauce and paprika and a heat gun. A coat of oil makes it look hot and juicy. In our shot a skin graft has even been used to get a pasty area near the wing looking perfect.

The result: Plump, juicy, perfect roast chicken.

Muffin magic

The styling challenge: Cake and muffins can look flat, dry and uninteresting.

How to style it: The muffin is carefully broken apart and placed on the plate. Tweezers are used to tease out the crumbs to give pleasing shadows and a moist, crumbly look. The fruit in the muffin is excavated so you can see it more clearly. Fresh blueberries—only ever handled with tweezers or gloves to avoid fingerprints—are blue-tacked in place. The blueberry leaves are the most difficult part of the shot. It takes twenty-five minutes to get them arranged to the stylist's and photographer's satisfaction. A shake of icing sugar and an artistically placed fork finish the shot.

The result: Still life with muffin—true art.

More food magic

A BEAUTIFUL BURGER
The styling challenge: The meat is heavy and squashes everything beneath it. The salad slides sideways and the sauce and beetroot ooze out.

How to style it: The meat is only lightly cooked and the edges browned with a blowtorch. The bun, like the other ingredients, is selected for perfection (in this

case the top and base come from two different buns). After lettuce frills are carefully pinned in place, a cardboard platform supported by pieces of toothpick is constructed to hold the weight of the meat off the lettuce and bun. The other ingredients are artistically arranged and may also need to be pinned in place. Make-up remover pads do a good job of soaking up beetroot juices. The final touch is an artistic injection of tomato sauce thickened with tomato paste.

The result: A tall, symmetrical, balanced hamburger creation.

A SPECTACULAR STIR-FRY
The styling challenge: Stir-fries and pasta sink flat onto the plate and rarely do the ingredients land in a balanced way. The noodles look dull and cold and some ingredients may end up overcooked.

How to style it: First the carefully selected ingredients are cooked individually so they're perfect. A mound of instant mashed potato is used as a base to get some height and stability. Noodles are coated with liquid glucose to make them look hot and shiny. The ingredients are arranged to give a casual appearance that belies the amount of time spent with tweezers to get perfectly looped noodles and balanced colour.

The result: An appetising and colourful stir-fry that looks fresh and hot.

QUESTIONS

1 What are the two schools of thought in regard to food styling? In your response, identify which style is more common in Australia and which is more common in America.
2 Why are there different types of food photography?
3 Why can food stying be summarised as 'lateral thinking and patience, patience, patience…'?
4 How can computer technology assist with food styling?
5 Using the following foods as examples, describe some of the tricks of the trade to counteract the tendency for food to discolour, wilt or drip:

a	meat	f	ice cream	j	sauce for a dessert
b	hamburger	g	maple syrup on	k	tomato sauce
c	breakfast cereal		pancakes	l	white sauce
d	cake	h	ice cubes	m	seafood
e	chocolate sauce	i	pie	n	stir-fries and pasta sauce

6   List some of the more bizarre techniques used by some food stylists, using maple syrup, Swiss cheese, grapes and chicken legs as examples.
7   Using one of the following examples, describe how the *Choice* team ensured that the finished food photo would look great: cooked chicken, muffin, hamburger or stir-fry. Ensure that you outline the challenging aspects of the food and how it was styled, providing an overview of the end result.
8   Select a food from the recipes at the end of this chapter and, using a camera (for example, digital), take a photo of the end product. Investigate what you could do to make the photo more appealing.

▶ Let's remember

1   Identify the four criteria usually used to assess food products.
2   How does appearance influence our selection of foods?
3   Describe the expected appearance of the following foods:
   a red delicious apple   **c** chocolate bar   **e** pea
   b shaved ham   **d** wholegrain bread roll   **f** raspberry-flavoured jelly
4   What is flavour?
5   How many taste buds does an adult usually have?
6   Draw a diagram of a tongue and identify the four basic taste sensations.
7   How are taste buds aroused?
8   When tasting food, what is the role of saliva?
9   What are the olfactory receptors and where are they located?
10 List five foods that you love the smell of.

▶ Let's investigate

1   As a class, brainstorm a range of terms that could be used to describe the appearance, flavour, texture and aroma of food. Some examples are listed below to assist you. Summarise the information in a classroom display, such as a collage of words, a table or a concept map.

Appearance	Flavour	Texture	Aroma
Colourful	Bitter	Grainy	Fruity
Golden	Spicy	Hard	Sweet
Undercooked	Burnt	Crunchy	Spicy
Well risen	Creamy	Doughy	Yeasty
Dull	Tangy	Soft	Mild
Curdled	Sweet	Lumpy	Strong

2   Identify the taste of the following foods:
   a lime   **f** potato crisps
   b golden syrup   **g** vinegar
   c coffee   **h** beer
   d chocolate   **i** table salt
   e butter   **j** grapefruit

3   Bring in an assortment of foods and describe the appearance, flavour, texture and aroma of each. Put your findings in a table like the one below.

Food	Appearance	Flavour	Texture	Aroma

▶ Focus on fussy eaters

Read the newspaper article and then answer the questions that follow it.

By BRAD CROUCH

FOOD FIGHTS with fussy bubs may be more than just a mess—it may be a sign of future speech problems. Researchers at Flinders Medical Centre (FMC) say the same muscles used for eating are used for speaking, so feeding skills can have an effect on speech development. FMC has started a feeding assessment service with three paediatric speech pathologists checking children who are not feeding 'properly' for their age. Speech pathologist Mr Phill Hunt estimated up to 80 per cent of youngsters referred with speech problems have had previous feeding difficulties.

Many such children have 'oral hypersensitivity', so they do not like the sensation of some types of food textures in their mouths. This can lead to difficulty pronouncing some sounds. 'We use the same group of muscles and nervous system to speak and to eat, so if a child isn't developing their eating skills properly there's a high likelihood of ending up with speech problems down the track,' Mr Hunt said. 'All kids are fussy with food, but it is when it starts to affect their weight and energy levels that it becomes a problem.'

As a rule of thumb, a child should be fairly well understood by most people by age two to three, and by three to four be able to form most sounds. Mr Hunt cautioned parents against making food a big issue, noting children often eat when hungry, rather than at set mealtimes.

The feeding assessment service works with allied professionals at FMC such as lactation consultants, occupational therapists, physiotherapists and dietitians. Babies who suffer colic or reflux also can be fussy eaters due to associating negative experiences with eating. However this is not related to muscles used for eating, so they are not likely to develop speech problems.

Two-year-old Brad Pankhurst's speech and feeding both have improved dramatically since he joined the FMC program. His mother, Kylie Walton, said the youngster has been a little slow in speech development and meal-times were a battle. 'When he was younger he used to gag on his food to a point he just was not interested in eating,' she said. 'He seemed to be scared of swallowing food because he gagged. He wouldn't put food in his mouth and was under-weight—the milk was the thing that kept him going.'

The FMC program encouraged Brad to chew his food while working on his speech. 'They said it was all linked together, they wanted to get him to eat to get his muscles moving,' Kylie said. 'His speech now is so much better and really came on very quickly once he started the program. The Flinders people have been great, they got him to chew and he has improved ever since.'

QUESTIONS

1   Why do researchers say that feeding skills can have an effect on speech development?
2   What percentage of children referred to the Flinders Medical Centre with speech problems have experienced previous feeding difficulties?
3   Define the term *oral hypersensitivity*.
4   Describe how a child with oral hypersensitivity may develop difficulties pronouncing sounds.
5   All kids tend to be fussy with foods. However, when should parents become concerned with their child's eating habits?

▶ *e*-Sensory evaluation

www.sydneymarkets.com.au/homeindex.html

Browse through the selection of fruits and vegetables, then select ten for analysis. Try to select fruits or vegetables with which you are unfamiliar.

1   Complete the table below by:
   • predicting the appearance, flavour, texture and aroma of each fruit or vegetable
   • visiting a supermarket and purchasing the selected fruits and vegetables, and recording the actual appearance, flavour, texture and aroma of each
2   Compare your predictions with the actual results. Were you able to accurately predict the appearance, flavour, texture and aroma of each fruit or vegetable?

Name of fruit/ vegetable	Appearance		Flavour		Texture		Aroma	
	Prediction	Actual	Prediction	Actual	Prediction	Actual	Prediction	Actual

Puzzled

Word pile

Can you place these words in their correct places below: red capsicum, ice cream, nectarine, honey and raw sugar? The boxed letters will identify one of their sensory characteristics.

```
___ __□____
   __□ _____
___ __□__
   __□_
   __□_____
```
Answer: _____

Can you make your own word pile using another descriptive term? Ask a classmate to solve it.

Sensory scramble

Unscramble the following words to identify sensory evaluation terms.

1 ymraec   3 ccnuryh   5 teribt   7 brutn
2 toomsh   4 uros   6 yipcs

LET'S PRODUCE

Ingredients

2 cups flour, sifted
1 tablespoon baking powder
1 cup caster sugar
125 grams butter, melted
2 eggs, lightly beaten
$\frac{1}{4}$ cup natural yoghurt
125 millilitres lemon juice
2 teaspoons lemon rind, grated

Lemon muffins

(makes 12)

Method

1 Preheat oven to 180°C.
2 Grease muffin pan.
3 Sift flour and baking powder and stir in caster sugar and make a well.
4 Combine melted butter, eggs, yoghurt, lemon juice and lemon rind, and stir into the dry ingredients with a metal spoon until just combined.
5 Spoon into muffin pans and bake for twenty minutes, or until cooked. Remove from oven and stand for five minutes before turning onto a cake cooler.
6 Serve warm.

Variations

- Blueberry muffins: Replace lemon juice, lemon rind and yoghurt with $\frac{3}{4}$ cup of buttermilk and 300 grams of blueberries (frozen or fresh). Replace caster sugar with $\frac{3}{4}$ cup of brown sugar. Sift 2 teaspoons of cinnamon with the dry ingredients.
- Banana and nut muffins: Replace lemon juice and rind and yoghurt with $\frac{3}{4}$ cup of milk, three mashed bananas and 100 grams of nuts, such as walnuts, hazelnuts, pecans or almonds. Replace caster sugar with $\frac{3}{4}$ cup of brown sugar.
- Apple muffins: Replace lemon juice and rind and yoghurt with $\frac{3}{4}$ cup of milk, 2 teaspoons of cinnamon and two Granny Smith apples (peeled and chopped) and $\frac{3}{4}$ cup of sultanas. Replace caster sugar with $\frac{3}{4}$ cup of brown sugar.

QUESTIONS

1 Identify the appearance, flavour, texture and aroma of the muffins.
2 Investigate other ingredients that could be used in the muffins. Design, produce and evaluate your own muffin ☺ ☺ ☹. Provide your new muffin recipe with a name.

Poached chocolate pears   (serves 2)

Method

1 Remove the core from the base of the peeled pears, leaving the stems intact.
2 Place water, cocoa, star anise and honey in a saucepan over a medium heat and combine with a whisk until sugar dissolves.
3 Bring mixture to the boil and reduce heat to medium low. Place the pears in the saucepan; they should be lying down. Cook uncovered for about ten minutes, or until tender, turning occasionally.
4 Transfer the pears to a shallow dish and cover with foil to keep warm.
5 Bring the liquid in the saucepan to the boil by increasing the heat. Boil uncovered for twenty minutes, or until reduced to a thick syrup.
6 Stand each pear in a serving bowl and spoon thick syrup over the top.
7 Serve with cream.

QUESTION

Describe the appearance, flavour, texture and aroma of the pear.

Beef kebabs with salsa   (serves 2)

Method

1 Soak four bamboo skewers in water.
2 Boil potatoes until just tender. Drain and cool. Cut lengthways into 1-centimetre-thick slices. Combine butter, garlic and pepper and add potatoes. Toss to combine.
3 Combine beef with oil and cumin and thread onto skewers.
4 Grill kebabs until cooked. Transfer to a plate and cover with foil to keep warm.
5 Grill potato slices until golden.
6 Combine salsa ingredients in a bowl.
7 Divide potato slices onto serving plates, place kebabs on top and place salsa over the kebabs.

QUESTION

Describe the appearance, flavour, texture and aroma of the meal.

Ingredients
2 pears, peeled
2 cups water
1½ tablespoons cocoa
1 star anise
2 teaspoons honey
cream

Ingredients
250 grams new potatoes, washed
1½ teaspoons butter
1 clove garlic
3 shakes black pepper
400 grams round beefsteak, cut into 2-centimetre cubes
2 teaspoons olive oil
½ teaspoon cumin

Salsa
1 tomato, finely chopped
½ Spanish onion, finely chopped
½ Lebanese cucumber, finely chopped
1 green chilli, finely chopped
2 teaspoons red wine vinegar

Spicy dhal (serves 2)

Ingredients
½ cup dried red lentils
2 teaspoons oil
½ teaspoon yellow mustard seeds
1 teaspoon cumin
½ brown onion, thinly sliced
2-centimetre piece ginger, grated
1 clove garlic, crushed
1¼ cups vegetable stock or water
3 shakes black pepper
1 green chilli, thinly sliced
naan, warmed

Method
1   Rinse lentils in cold water.
2   Heat oil in saucepan, add mustard seeds and cumin and cook until aromatic and mustard seeds begin to pop. Add onion, ginger and garlic and increase heat to medium hot. Stir constantly for three minutes.
3   Add lentils and stir through for one minute. Add stock and cook covered for an additional twenty minutes, stirring occasionally. Remove lid and cook for another ten to fifteen minutes or until thick. Add black pepper and top with chilli.
4   Serve with naan.

Variation
Replace mustard seeds and cumin with half a teaspoon of garam masala. Replace chilli with one tablespoon of fresh chopped coriander.

Spiced lamb cutlets with potatoes (serves 2)

Ingredients
200 grams Sebago potatoes, peeled
2½ teaspoons coriander, ground
1½ teaspoons cumin, ground
1 teaspoon paprika
½ teaspoon ginger, ground
1 clove garlic, crushed
pinch cardamom, ground
pinch cayenne pepper
1 tablespoon olive oil
6 lamb cutlets
1 tablespoon fresh lemon juice
50 grams spinach leaves

Method
1   Preheat oven to 160°C.
2   Boil potatoes until almost tender. Drain and set aside to cool. Cut into 1-centimetre-thick rounds.
3   Combine coriander, cumin, paprika, ginger, garlic, cardamom and cayenne pepper and sprinkle over both sides of the cutlets. Rub the spices into the cutlets with your fingers.
4   Heat oil in a frypan and cook potato slices for five minutes, or until golden and tender. Transfer to a plate and keep warm.
5   Add cutlets to the frypan and drizzle with lemon juice. Cook on each side according to your preference.
6   Place potatoes on serving plates with the lamb. Serve with spinach leaves.

Variation
Replace potatoes with 400 grams of sweet potatoes. Use 3 teaspoons of garam masala, ½ teaspoon of turmeric and a pinch of ground chillies instead of coriander, cumin, paprika, ginger, garlic, cardamom and cayenne pepper.

QUESTION
Describe the appearance, flavour, texture and aroma of your meal.

HOT PROPERTIES: DISCOVER PROPERTIES OF FOOD

When selecting, storing and preparing food, it is important that you are aware of its properties. Each food has its own physical and chemical (nutritional) properties, so it can carry out various functions in food preparation.

Denaturation and Coagulation

Protein is found in such foods as meat and eggs. Protein is made up of amino acids joined together. It is the sequence of amino acids that determines the characteristics and properties of each protein food.

    The shape of some of the proteins can be altered by applying heat, as this causes the amino acid chains to uncoil. This chemical process is known as denaturation. Protein is said to be denatured because the change cannot be reversed.

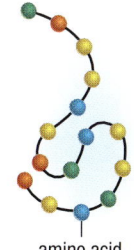

Chains of amino acids = protein

Each different protein food has a unique amino acid composition and arrangement

amino acid

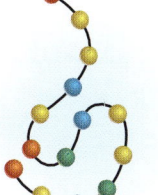

Before denaturation

After denaturation

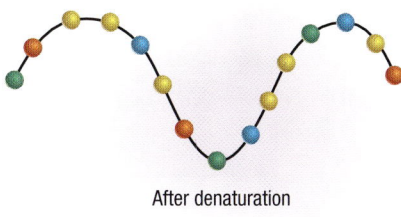

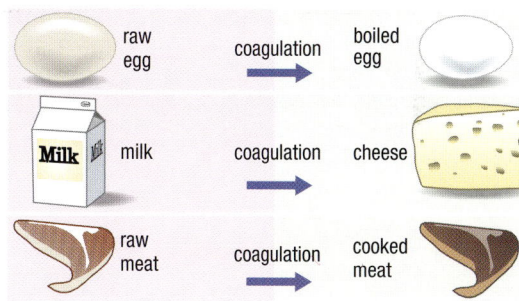

raw egg → coagulation → boiled egg

milk → coagulation → cheese

raw meat → coagulation → cooked meat

    Applying heat for a longer period of time will cause the protein to coagulate, as the protein structure creates a network and entraps the liquid, forming a gel. For example, when an egg is cooked, both the liquid yolk and white will become firm and change colour.

    Cooking protein foods too long will result in the protein becoming overcoagulated. The product becomes dry and tough because the protein shrinks and forces the moisture out. This is evident when meat or poultry is overcooked.

    Proteins can also be denatured by beating (see 'Aeration' on pages 130–1).

e-fact

The starchy substance in a recipe could be flour, cornflour or rice and is often referred to as the thickening agent.

Gelatinisation

When starch is dissolved in a liquid and then heated, it will swell and produce a thick paste. This process is known as gelatinisation.

    Recipes for cakes, sauces and gravies rely on the gelatinisation of starch for their consistency. The starch is blended with a separating agent to keep the starch grains apart, ensuring that they will not bunch together.

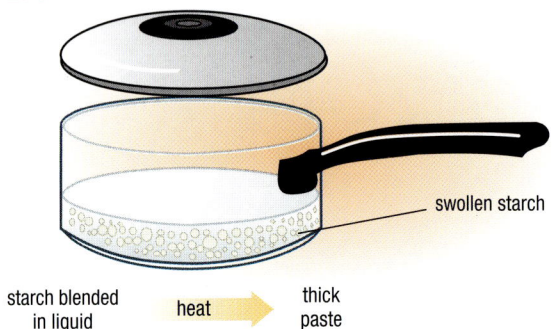

swollen starch

starch blended   heat   thick
in liquid   paste

The blended starch is then mixed into the liquid to be thickened, and this mixture is heated. To stop the starch grains bunching together, the liquid must be stirred during the heating process.

The liquid softens the cell walls of the starch grains, resulting in the cell walls bursting. The starch inside the cell walls then absorbs the liquid, causing the starch to become bigger. The liquid then forms a gel.

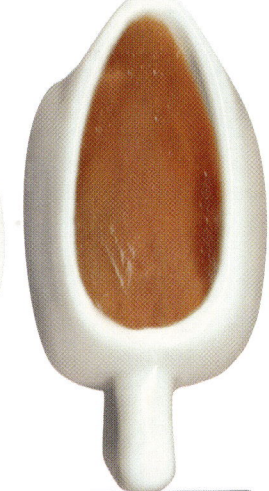

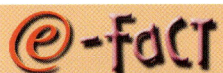
Instant mashed potato and instant pudding mixes contain modified starches that gelatinise without heating. These modified starches have been developed so that they gelatinise at specified temperature ranges or in acidic conditions.

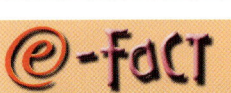
Emulsions

Water and oil do not mix unless an emulsifying agent is added, such as lecithin found in egg yolks. Emulsions form the basis of products like mayonnaise and salad dressings. Lecithin holds the water and oil together to form an emulsion.

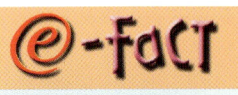

Mayonnaise

oil droplet

egg yolk

vinegar

The egg yolk around the oil droplet acts as an emulsifying agent

Mayonnaise

egg yolk

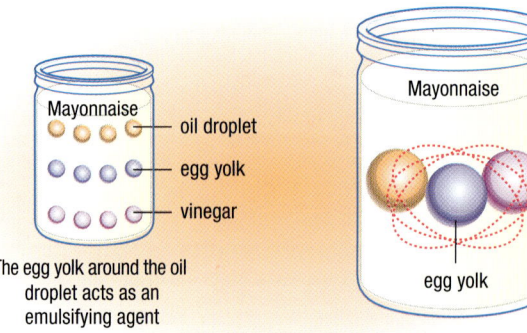

HELLMANN'S MAYONNAISE

1903	1912	1924	1932	1986	1992	1996	1998
German immigrant Richard Hellmann arrives in the United States. Two years later, in New York, Hellmann opens a delicatessen featuring salads containing his wife's mayonnaise. Hellmann's Mayonnaise becomes very popular, so he decides to sell it in 'wooden boats' that were used for measuring butter.	Two versions of the mayonnaise recipe were initially sold; to distinguish between the two, a blue ribbon was tied around one of the 'wooden boats'. In 1912, due to demand for the 'blue ribbon' variety, Hellmann creates a 'Blue Ribbon' label which he places on larger glass jars. Best Foods, Inc. introduces a self-named variety of mayonnaise in California.	Hellmann's Mayonnaise is exported to Canada.	As Hellmann's extends on the East Coast, Best Foods Mayonnaise benefits from enormous success on the West Coast. Best Foods, Inc. acquires Richard Hellmann, Inc. Today, Hellmann's Mayonnaise is sold east of the Rockies and Best Foods Mayonnaise is sold in the West.	Hellmann's Light Mayonnaise is introduced. The product contains half the fat and half the kilojoules of the original Hellmann's Mayonnaise. It is selected as 'the best tasting light' mayonnaise in a countrywide consumer taste test when introduced.	Hellmann's introduces a Dijonnaise Creamy mustard blend—a blend of mustard, spices and white wine. It is low in fat, cholesterol and sodium.	Hellmann's introduces an ultra-low-fat mayonnaise-type dressing. It contains less than 1 gram of fat per serving and no cholesterol.	An online version of the Hellmann's Diner is opened on 1 July.

QUESTIONS

1   Using the information above, create your own timeline on poster paper to illustrate the history of Hellmann's Mayonnaise. Use pictures, diagrams and phrases to depict key events on your timeline.

2   Investigate other brands of mayonnaise, identifying the country from which each mayonnaise originates.

3   Investigate what is aioli. Which country does it come from?

e-FACT

In 1756, the French chef of the Duke de Richelieu created a victory feast after the Duke defeated the British at Port Mahon. Part of the victory feast was to include a sauce made of eggs and cream. When the chef became aware that there was no cream in the kitchen, he improvised by adding olive oil instead of the cream, and so a new culinary masterpiece was born! The chef called it 'Mahonnaise' after the Duke's victory at Port Mahon.

Browning Reactions

The following three processes outline browning reactions in food:

·   dextrinisation
·   caramelisation
·   enzymatic browning

Dextrinisation

Another name for complex carbohydrate is starch. When starch is cooked by dry heat methods, dextrinisation occurs. The starch is changed to dextrin, which is brown and sweeter in flavour; for example, when bread is toasted.

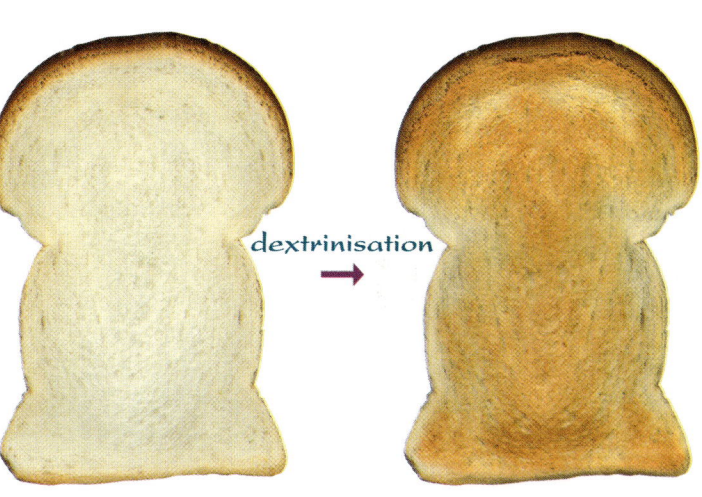

dextrinisation

Dry heat cooking methods include grilling and baking.

Dextrins are starch chains, made up of glucose molecules.

Caramelisation

When heated to a high temperature, sugar will melt and become a brown liquid. This chemical process is known as caramelisation. It occurs when making toffee, caramel sauce and fruit cakes. Caramelisation does not require oxygen. Browning in vegetables with high sugar content, such as carrots and sweet potatoes, is likely to be caused by caramelisation.

Enzymatic browning

Blanching is when food is immersed in boiling water for a short period of time and then plunged into cold water to prevent the cooking process.

Enzymatic browning occurs in particular raw fruits and vegetables that are peeled and exposed to air. Enzymatic browning has no effect on the flavour or texture of the food, but it does detract from the visual appeal of the food. Unlike dextrinisation and caramelisation, this type of browning is not desirable. Oxygen activates enzymes in fruits and vegetables such as bananas, apples and potatoes, causing a chemical reaction and resulting in surface browning. An acid such as lemon juice can act to inhibit the chemical reaction. Other ways to prevent enzymatic browning include covering the food with water or, as in the case of fruit, a sugar syrup. Blanching the food can also destroy the enzymes.

O_2 + enzyme enzyme =

oxygen + enzymes = enzymatic browning

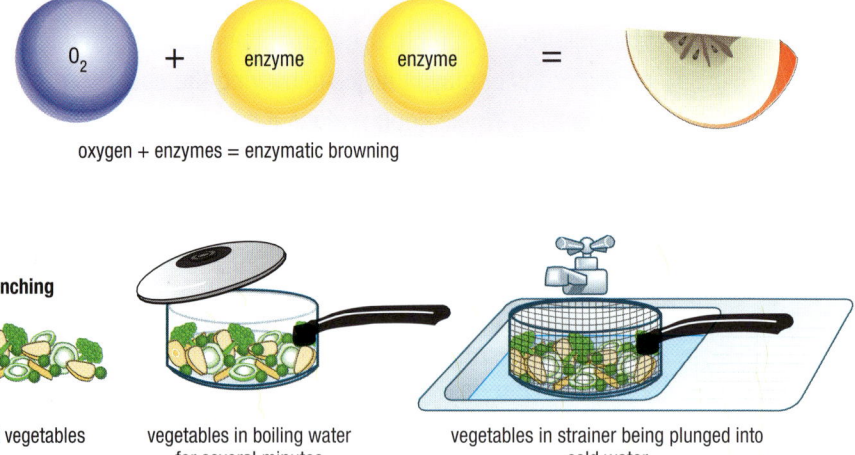

Blanching

cut vegetables   vegetables in boiling water for several minutes   vegetables in strainer being plunged into cold water

Aeration

Aeration is the process of incorporating air into food products. It can be done:
· mechanically
· chemically
· biologically

Mechanical aeration

Mechanical aeration includes the following processes:

Process	Description	Example of process	Examples of application in food preparation
Whisking and beating	Agitating protein will cause it to become denatured—the protein structure unwinds, and air is entrapped in the network. Entrapping air in the protein network creates a foam, as when egg whites are beaten for soufflé or meringues.	bonds holding chains of protein together / agitation results in protein unfolding / new weak bonds start to form / new bonds entrap pockets of air	
Sifting	When flour and similar ingredients are sifted, the particles are separated and air is incorporated. Sifting ingredients several times can increase the amount of air entrapped. Sifting is usually not the only method of aeration—other processes will usually also be used to aerate the product. Sifting can also be used to mix ingredients together and remove any impurities in dry ingredients.	flour / air being incorporated	
Rubbing in	Rubbing fat into flour aerates the product, as it encourages the flour particles to separate and incorporate air. The process of lifting the mixture while rubbing in also aerates the mixture. Fats are incorporated into pastries to tenderise the product. Fat is referred to as shortening in this case, as it surrounds the gluten strands and prevents them from reacting with the liquid. This means that the gluten will not be tough.	using fingertips to rub butter into flour / flour / chunks of butter	
Creaming	Fats are able to entrap air within their structure as well. When butter is beaten with sugar, this process is known as creaming. The sugar crystals split the fat molecules and dissolve, enabling air to be incorporated into the mixture, which becomes lighter in colour and texture, increases in volume and resembles 'whipped cream'. This technique is used when making butter cake.	sugar / chunks of butter	
Addition of liquids	When heated, liquids will convert to steam. The steam will expand and rise, assisting the food product to increase in volume. Usually, this method is combined with another method of raising, such as beating or the use of yeast. Choux pastry, however, relies solely on this method.	water in mixture / heat / water converts to steam / increase in volume and mixture rises	
Rolling and folding	When making pastry, the action of rolling and folding incorporates air.	a / b / c	

Chemical leavening

Chemical leavening involves adding agents to food products. Usually an acid is added to an alkali and heated in the presence of water to produce a gas called carbon dioxide.

Some examples of combinations are listed below.

Alkali	Acid
Bicarbonate of soda	Cream of tartar
Bicarbonate of soda	Sour milk
Bicarbonate of soda	Golden syrup

Biological leavening

Yeast is a single-celled micro-organism that is used to leaven food products.

yeast + sugar + warm water + warmth = growth of yeast

Focus on yeast

All yeasts that ferment bread, beer, wine and cider correspond to the simple, single-celled organism *Saccharomyces cerevisiae*, a type of fungus. Many varieties of *Saccharomyces cerevisiae* exist and they are essentially suitable for the various types of fermentation. Baker's yeast is manufactured especially for bread making.

The yeast in bread will grow and ferment carbohydrates, manufacturing ethyl alcohol and carbon dioxide gas in the process. The alcohol will evaporate during the cooking process. The carbon dioxide gas is trapped within the elastic dough and expands when heated, causing the dough to rise, providing a light, appetising bread.

When yeast is in the presence of oxygen and sugar, it produces carbon dioxide, water and energy. This is the process of respiration. The oxidation of glucose is complete in these conditions:

Glucose + Oxygen → Carbon dioxide + Water + Energy

When there is no oxygen present, yeast can use sugars to produce the energy it requires to maintain its life. Pasteur defined this process as the fermentation process. Sugars are converted into carbon dioxide and alcohol:

Glucose $\rightarrow$ Carbon dioxide + Alcohol + Energy

Yeast is an astonishingly versatile and adaptive organism. If its oxygen supply is closed off, yeast is able to still reproduce anaerobically; deprive yeast of moisture and it will become inactive, but still be alive. Without yeast and fermentation there would be no bread. Flavour and texture are not the only benefits of yeast. Yeast is also an excellent source of the B group vitamins and the action of fermentation makes grains more digestible.

Fresh yeast is also known as compressed yeast. It is pressed firmly together. It has a distinctive fruity smell and looks like putty. It crumbles quite easily. It needs to be stored in the refrigerator to keep it inactive. Its shelf-life is about five days. It is typically used by bakeries.

Dried yeast that comes in granular form is inactive until moisture is added. It has a longer shelf-life than fresh yeast. It is also more concentrated than fresh yeast, so less is needed in food preparation.

Liquid creamed yeast is used in plant bakeries.

▶ Let's remember

1 Explain the process of denaturation.
2 When does coagulation occur?
3 How does overcoagulation occur and what happens to the end product?
4 How does gelatinisation occur?
5 Why does starch contain a separating agent?
6 What is an emulsion?
7 Identify three processes that cause browning in food and describe each process in detail. Which of the browning processes are desirable and which are not desirable?
8 Identify the three ways to aerate food, and discuss three processes in detail.
9 Why is caster sugar used in the creaming method?
10 Outline the differences between fresh and dried yeast.

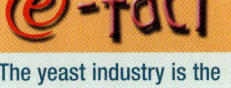

▶ Let's investigate

1 Complete the table by finding a recipe that incorporates each of the following processes.

Process	Recipe
Denaturation	
Coagulation	
Gelatinisation	
Emulsion	
Dextrinisation	
Caramelisation	
Whisking and beating	
Sifting	
Rubbing in	
Creaming	
Addition of liquids	
Rolling and folding	
Chemical leavening	
Biological leavening	

2 Investigate the differences between mayonnaise and salad dressing.

3 Investigate the coagulation of eggs when boiled for varying lengths of time. Copy and complete the table.

Length of time (minutes)	Description
1	
3	
7	
10	

4 Investigate the denaturation of egg whites by whisking them with an electric beater for varying lengths of time. Copy and complete the table.

Length of time (minutes)	Description
1	
3	
5	
10	

5 Design a menu for your family that incorporates all of the following processes: dextrinisation, creaming, denaturation, coagulation, chemical leavening. Produce and evaluate your menu ☺ ☺ ☹.

6 Investigate ways to prevent enzymatic browning in fruits and vegetables. Design and produce a pamphlet to inform others. A computer package could be used to present your work. Get a classmate to evaluate your pamphlet ☺ ☺ ☹.

7 How many processes can be found in one recipe? Investigate a range of recipes and find one that has the most number of processes. Make sure that you identify all of the processes.

8 Design a recipe that has the most number of processes that you can include.
Produce and evaluate your recipe ☺ ☺ ☹. Which processes did you include? Investigate the number and types of processes that your classmates included.

℮·Food properties

www.gelatin.com

1 Where does gelatin come from and what is it used for in food preparation?

2 Identify five products that use gelatin in the food industry.

3 What happens when gelatin is heated and cooled in milk? Describe the texture of the end product.

4 Outline the advantages of using gelatin in dairy products.

5 Describe the use of gelatin in the following dairy products by copying and completing the table.

Dairy product	Function of gelatin	Other comments
Yoghurt		
Sour cream		
Soft cheese products		
Acidic milk desserts		
Flavoured milk-based desserts		
Frozen desserts		
Thickened cream		
Low-fat butters/spreads		

6 Gelatin is also used in a variety of meat products. Identify the function of gelatin in the following meat products:

a cooked ham   **c** canned meat products   **e** aspics
b sausage   **d** paté   **f** decorative jellies, coatings and glazes

7   Describe the role of gelatin in the following confectionery:
   a   gelled confectionery   e   cream pastes
   b   aerated confectionery   f   lozenges
   c   sugar-pulled confectionery   g   compressed tablets
   d   toffees and caramels   h   liquorice

8   Complete a PMI of the following applications of gelatin in farinaceous foods—identify one 'Plus', one 'Minus' and one 'Interesting point' for each application.

	Plus	Minus	Interesting point
Biscuit marshmallow			
Icing and frostings			
Bakery glazes			

9   Gelatin is considered to be a truly remarkable protein that has many diverse and varied uses in the food industry. Identify seven other uses for gelatin.

10 Complete the following statements about the physical and chemical properties of gelatin.
   a   Gelatin is fairly _____ in water.
   b   Gelatin _____ readily in warm water.
   c   The granules of gelatin will _____ when added to cold water.
   d   Gelatin can absorb about _____ its weight in water.
   e   The dissolved gelatin particles dissolve in temperatures of about 40°C and form a _____.
   f   When this solution is cooled, a _____ is formed.
   g   The rate of _____ is affected by temperature, concentration, and particle size.
   h   Gelatin is _____ in alcohol.
   i   The rigidity of gelatin gels increases with _____.
   j   The strength of gelatin gels depends upon various factors, including _____, _____ and _____.

▶ Puzzled

Process scramble

Unscramble the following words to find the names of six processes.
1   niotlcaaoug   3   leimsationarac   5   gniotleaiitnsa
2   nndeioattaur   4   mreacngi   6   xtrediinnitaso

Fill in the gaps

Complete the following sentences by using the words from the box.

gelatinisation	compressed	denatured	increase	foam
separated	caramelisation	incorporates	overcoagulate	mechanical

1   Overcooking protein foods will cause the protein to _____.
2   Beating protein will cause it to become _____.
3   Sifting dry ingredients a number of times can _____ the amount of air entrapped.
4   The process of heating sugar until it melts and turns brown is known as _____.
5   When making a meringue, air is entrapped in the protein network to make a _____.
6   The process of _____ is when starch is dissolved in a liquid and then heated.
7   When making pastry, the action of rolling and folding _____ air.
8   Rubbing in is a type of _____ aeration.

9 When flour is sifted, the particles are _____ and air is incorporated.

10 Another name for fresh yeast is _____ yeast.

 Recipe process match

Match each recipe with its main process.

Recipe	Process
Focaccia	Creaming
White sauce	Rubbing in
Chocolate éclairs	Emulsion
Shortbread	Caramelisation
Butter cake	Gelatinisation
Mayonnaise	Addition of liquid
Toffee	Biological aeration

Fruit salad with praline   (serves 2)

Method

1 Combine sugar and water in a saucepan and heat until sugar is dissolved.
2 Increase heat and bring to the boil, without stirring, until the mixture turns pale caramel in colour.
3 Pour mixture over almonds on a greased oven tray. Set aside to harden and form praline.
4 Break praline into pieces and process in a food processor until finely chopped.
5 Dip tops of cones in honey and then into praline.
6 Spoon fruit into cones and serve immediately.

Ingredients
4 tablespoons caster sugar
¼ cup water
½ cup roasted flaked almonds
2 ice-cream or waffle cones
2 tablespoons honey, warmed
¾ cup chopped fruits, such as bananas, strawberries, peaches, grapes, apricots

e-HINT

Praline can be stored in an airtight container for up to two weeks.

e-HYGIENE AND SAFETY

Be careful when pouring hot syrup into your greased pan. Sugar will increase the boiling point of the mixture.

QUESTIONS

1 What process caused the heated sugar mixture to turn brown?
2 **Investigate** what other recipes use this process.
3 **Investigate** what other nuts and fruits you could use.
4 **Design** your own recipe. **Produce** and **evaluate** this recipe ☺ ☺ ☹.

Berry puffs   (serves 2)

Method

1 Preheat oven to 220°C.
2 Whisk egg and egg white together.
3 Combine the water and butter in a saucepan until the mixture comes to the boil.

Ingredients
1 egg
1 egg white
½ cup water
1 tablespoon butter
½ cup plain flour, sifted
250 grams berries, such as strawberries, raspberries
2 teaspoons icing sugar
¼ teaspoon orange rind, finely grated
1 teaspoon fresh orange juice
ice cream

4   Remove from heat and add flour. Mix quickly with a wooden spoon.
5   Stir over a medium heat until mixture forms a ball—about one minute. Remove from heat and let sit for five minutes.
6   Gradually add the whisked egg, beating well. Mixture should appear smooth and glossy.
7   Place tablespoonfuls of mixture onto baking tray lined with non-stick baking paper.
8   Sprinkle with water and place in oven. Reduce temperature to 200°C, until puffed and slightly browned—approximately twenty-five to thirty minutes.
9   Make a slit in each puff and return to the oven for five minutes. Turn off the oven and leave the puffs inside until cool.
10 Cut puffs in half and remove any doughy pastry.
11 Purée half the berries, together with the icing sugar, orange rind and juice. Toss in the remainder of the berries.
12 Fill puff with a tablespoon of ice cream and place in bowl, topping with berry mixture.

e-HINT

Whipped cream could be used instead of ice cream.

QUESTIONS

1   Identify two processes that are used to aerate the choux pastry.
2   What was the purpose of slitting the puffs during the cooking process?
3   Why were the puffs left in the oven until they cooled?
4   Investigate what other fruits could be used in this recipe. Design your own purée. Produce and evaluate this recipe ☺ ☺ ☹.

Meringue and raspberry pudding (serves 2)

Method

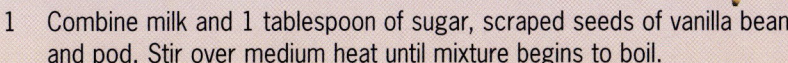

1   Combine milk and 1 tablespoon of sugar, scraped seeds of vanilla bean and pod. Stir over medium heat until mixture begins to boil.
2   Remove from heat and cool for ten minutes. Remove vanilla pod and stir in brioche crumbs.
3   Whisk egg yolks and stir into mixture.
4   Place mixture into two small ramekins and bake at 180°C, until nearly set in the centre—about fifteen minutes.
5   Remove from oven and spread with jam.
6   Beat egg whites until soft peaks form and steadily whisk in remainder of sugar.
7   Top each pudding with beaten egg-white mixture and return to oven for another fifteen minutes, or until meringue is light golden brown in colour.

Ingredients

200 millilitres milk
$\frac{1}{3}$ cup caster sugar
$\frac{1}{2}$ vanilla bean, split lengthwise
40 grams fresh brioche crumbs
1 egg, separated
1 egg yolk
$\frac{1}{4}$ cup raspberry jam

QUESTIONS

1   Explain how the mixture thickens. Diagrams may be useful.
2   Explain what happens to the egg whites when beaten.
3   Investigate what other jams could be used. Design, produce and evaluate your recipe ☺ ☺ ☹.

Ingredients

¾ cup plain flour
1 teaspoon dried yeast
¼ teaspoon sugar
¼ teaspoon salt
⅓ cup warm water
1 teaspoon olive oil

Topping

¼ cup pizza sauce
1 tomato, thinly sliced
4 slices proscuitto
1 clove garlic, crushed
125 grams mozzarella, grated
⅓ cup fresh basil, chopped
black pepper, to taste
2 teaspoons olive oil

Italian pizza   (serves 2)

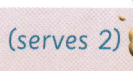

Method

1 Preheat oven to 230°C.
2 Combine flour, yeast, sugar and salt. Add water and oil and mix to a soft and sticky dough.
3 Knead dough for about two minutes on a lightly floured board until the dough is smooth.
4 Brush bowl with oil and place dough in it. Cover with plastic wrap and set aside to prove.
5 Roll out dough until 2 centimetres thick and place onto greased tray.
6 Prick dough with fork and spread with pizza sauce.
7 Bake for twelve minutes and remove from oven and top with tomato, proscuitto, garlic and mozzarella.
8 Bake for a further five minutes and remove from oven.
9 Sprinkle with basil and pepper and drizzle with oil.

QUESTIONS

1 What type of leavening is yeast?
2 What is yeast?
3 Identify the three requirements for yeast to grow.
4 How does yeast cause leavening?
5 Investigate what other recipes require yeast as a leavening agent. Include both sweet and savoury recipes. Represent your findings as a collage of recipes.
6 Design your own pizza topping. Produce and evaluate your pizza ☺ ☺ ☹.

Cheesy corn pasta   (serves 2)

Ingredients

250 grams small spiral pasta
2 teaspoons olive oil
½ onion, sliced thinly
1 clove garlic, crushed
½ cup corn kernels
2 teaspoons cornflour
½ cup cream
1 cup vegetable stock
½ cup tasty grated cheese
black pepper, to taste

Method

1 Cook pasta and drain.
2 Meanwhile, heat oil in frypan and cook onion and garlic for five minutes. Add corn.
3 Blend cornflour with 1 tablespoon of cream. Stir in remaining cream and stock.
4 Add cornflour to frypan and stir over medium heat until sauce boils and thickens. Reduce heat and simmer for five minutes uncovered.
5 Stir through cheese and pasta and season with pepper.

QUESTIONS

1 Identify and explain the process that caused the pasta sauce to thicken.
2 At what temperature did the thickening occur?
3 What was the starchy substance in the recipe?
4 Why was the starchy substance premixed with a liquid prior to heating?
5 What liquid was used to initially combine with the starchy substance?
6 Why was the pasta sauce stirred when being heated?
7 Investigate other recipes that use this process for thickening. Make a collage of recipes, clearly identifying the starchy substances and liquids used in each recipe.

BRANDED!: DISCOVER FOOD PRODUCTS

Line Extensions

A line extension occurs when a company produces a group of products that are similar in nature and function. Line extensions involve adapting existing products while maintaining their central characteristics. This results in a greater choice of products for the consumer.

A line extension may occur when:

· the product is reformulated to reduce its fat, sugar or salt content, increase its fibre, vitamins and minerals or alter its colouring, flavouring or texturising ingredients

· presentation of the product is modified; the size and shape of the product may be altered or the packaging and labelling may be changed

· the product is redeveloped to create a more convenient or attractive product

Milk is an excellent example of line extension, as there are many different varieties of milk on the market today: low fat, no fat, added calcium, added iron and so on. Milk also comes in a range of packaging, such as cartons and bottles.

Another example of line extension is the Tim Tam biscuit. How many varieties have you consumed?

e-fact

One batch of Tim Tams makes more than one million biscuits. The ingredients include 7.5 tonnes of milk chocolate, 6 tonnes of Tim Tam cream, 2 tonnes of flour and 1.5 tonnes of sugar.

Other examples of line extension include Heinz baked beans, dry biscuits such as Vita Weat and breakfast cereals such as Weet-Bix.

'Me-toos'

'Me-toos' are copies of products developed by competing companies. This allows for an increase in the range of products and provides the consumer with greater choice and improvements in quality.

Examples of 'me-too' products include:
- canned tuna
- rice crackers

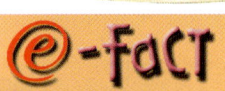

Functional Foods

Foods that assist with protection against disease or foods that enhance one's health are described as functional foods. These are foods that offer health benefits beyond basic nutrition. Such components of food may occur naturally, such as the soluble fibre found in oat bran. On the other hand, functional foods also include processed foods that have been modified during processing, such as calcium-enriched milk. The interest in functional foods lies in their possibility to decrease the frequency of dietary related diseases, principally those typically occurring in later life.

The following components of food are causing great interest among scientists and nutritionists in regard to their health-promoting benefits.

Lycopene 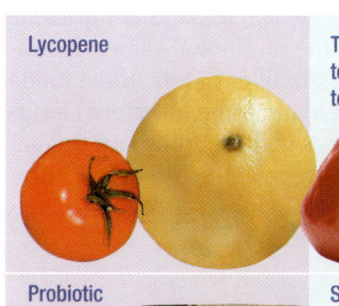	This antioxidant is a carotenoid, and is found in foods such as tomatoes, ruby red grapefruit and red capsicum. Lycopene is thought to reduce the risk of prostate cancer. Processed foods such as tomato paste are considered to have higher amounts of lycopene than their unprocessed form—fresh tomatoes
Probiotic lactobacilli and bifidobacteria 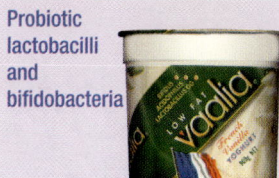	Some studies have identified the likely effects of components of food intended to improve the quality of microflora in the bowel, and to promote the growth of 'good bacteria' connected with a healthy gut. Yoghurt that is enhanced with the probiotics is considered to be a functional food.
Oligosaccharides	In Japan, a number of new natural carbohydrates, known as oligosaccharides and developed as potential sugar substitutes, are also believed to enhance intestinal microflora.
Garlic 	A few studies have indicated that garlic may have cancer-preventive effects. However, further research is needed to confirm whether garlic has these properties.
Soy protein 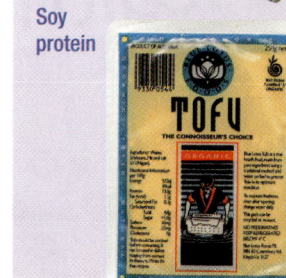	Various studies have indicated that the consumption of soy protein has resulted in the reduction of low-density lipoproteins (LDL) or 'bad' cholesterol levels in the blood, without reducing the levels of high-density lipoproteins (HDL) or 'good' cholesterol. Soy protein may have a role in reducing the risk of heart disease.

e-Fact

Caroteniods are pigments that produce carotene. They are a group of substances that are converted to vitamin A.

Other areas in which functional foods may have health potential are:
·   foods that offer cardiovascular protection
·   foods with advantages for the digestive system
·   foods that are intended to guard against certain cancers
·   foods with carbohydrate or fat alternatives
·   foods with favourable fat ratios for the elderly, people with diabetes, those at risk of heart disease and those with inflammatory disease
·   foods to enhance resistance against allergenicity
·   foods that are intended for athletes and recreation
·   foods for enhancing mood or cognition

Currently, in Australia, it is illegal to use health claims on food labels, although nutrition information is allowed. The exception to this is folate (see case study on page 167). The exclusion of health claims centres around concerns that any acknowledgment of functional foods in Australia would have to depend entirely on the demonstration that they are completely risk-free, effective and capable of delivering the health benefits promised.

If functional foods are consumed as part of a balanced diet, in addition to regular exercise, they could play an essential part in enhancing one's health and well being.

Individuals should benefit from a wide variety of foods, paying particular attention to those foods with specific functional properties for additional health promotion and so incorporating many potentially beneficial food components. With over thirty years of research related to enhancing the nutritional value of foods, the scientific community is greatly hopeful about the possibilities of functional foods.

However, it has been argued that some functional foods are promoting a 'techno fix' and aiming to create foods as good as fruits and vegetables. If this is the case, why not just consume the fruits and vegetables? There is no doubt that nutrition drives the marketing push for many functional foods.

Case study
UNCLE TOBYS HEalTHWISE BREakFast CEREals

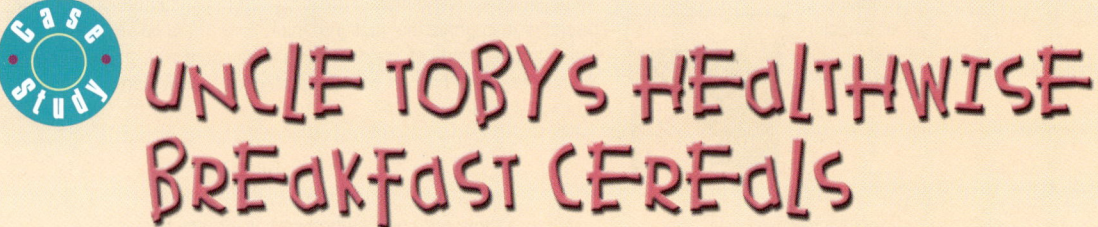

Uncle Tobys has developed a range of functional breakfast cereals, such as:

- Healthwise for improved heart health
- Healthwise for improved bowel and digestive health
- Healthwise for women 40+

These breakfast cereals are targeting diseases in the community that can be improved by modifying one's diet. Heart disease and bowel cancer account for a significant number of deaths in Australia. The Healthwise range of breakfast cereals was developed after a great deal of scientific and consumer research, in which it was found that many consumers were concerned about their health and endeavoured to make wise food decisions.

Uncle Tobys Healthwise breakfast cereals contain the following ingredients:

- soluble fibre, to slow digestion in the small intestine, which results in improved satiety and absorption of nutrients
- insoluble fibre, which ensures regularity and removes toxins from the body
- resistant starch, which resists digestion in the small intestine and so has positive effects in the large intestine by encouraging the growth of 'good' bacteria and discouraging the growth of 'bad' bacteria and increasing the bulk of stools

One of the main ingredients found in Healthwise for improved heart health is Oat Gold, also known as beta-glucan, which is a natural oat nutrient concentrate shown to lower cholesterol. High cholesterol is a risk factor for people with heart disease. Healthwise for improved bowel and digestive health contains Hi-Maize, which is a concentrated form of resistant starch. Resistant starch protects against the risk of bowel cancer, as it plays an important role in bowel and digestive health.

QUESTIONS

1 Why did Uncle Tobys create functional breakfast cereals?
2 Outline the three different types of fibre found in the Healthwise range and the different functions of each type of fibre.
3 What is Oat Gold and what is its function?
4 What is Hi-Maize and what is its function?

Lowan repositions itself in cereal market

Read the newspaper article and then answer the questions that follow it.

By Anna Hoate

Consolidated Foods Australia, (CFA), is a company that is reinventing itself, claiming a position with its Lowan Whole Foods brand as the 'nutrition educator' in the breakfast cereal category. Breakfast cereal is the fourth largest category in the dry grocery market, worth $760 million. Lowan Whole Foods general manager, Daryl Bird, puts the Lowan Whole Foods' share at 4 per cent of branded cereals, as well as having a significant share of the generic cereal business.

Building market share in a category dominated by sophisticated marketers like Kellogg, with a total corporate share of 44.8 per cent, Uncle Tobys on 20.7 per cent, and Sanitarium on 17.2 per cent, is being achieved with a plan to deliver consumers the promise of 'nutrition made simple' (ACNielsen MAT July volume).

CFA has a new managing director, Theng Dar Teng, with the departure of one of its founders, Evan Cross, six months ago. Mr Bird said Consolidated Foods Australia chose to concentrate on the healthier end of the breakfast cereal market in mid 1997. This decision was reinforced after a *Choice* magazine article was scathing in its analysis of the healthy benefits of most breakfast cereals. Mr Bird believes this was the beginning of a consumer shift away from pre-sweetened cereals.

The four cereal brands Lowan inherited, over 100 retail products in nine different categories, have been relaunched under the Lowan Whole Foods brand. Mr Bird said, 'The size of the project changing 100 products in the space of 12 months, together with the $3 million decision to drop ten Willow Valley products, was a high risk for us because of our relative sales performance and mix. We had traditionally relied on all our products, not just a few.'

The Lowan rebranding exercise, including research and advertising, has been an over $5 million investment by CFA over the past two years. A long transitional period of change was designed to let consumers know what was happening with their products.

A promotional ribbon ran on the old cereal packs, letting consumers know what the new pack would look like. The promotional ribbon also ran on the new packs, with a picture of the old pack so that consumers would recognise their favourite brand. Mr Bird said, 'The trade particularly liked that, because it was a managed process of change'.

Backing up the claim to be the 'nutritional educator', Lowan Whole Foods invested in three full-time nutritionists who make up the consumer services department. 'If a consumer rings our 1800 number, a qualified nutritionist will answer,' Mr Bird said. When the 1800 number was first advertised on the Lowan Whole Foods television ads in July 1998, consumer services took an average of 50 calls a day. This has grown to about 140 contacts a day, a very high response rate when benchmarked against other companies, according to Mr. Bird. 'The 1800 nutrition line is invaluable in building consumer brand loyalty,' Mr Bird said. Strict branding and marketing guidelines for the development of the Lowan Whole Foods brands include the 'what you see is what you get' image of cereals, with simple product names such as Multiflakes, Soy Flakes and FlakeMedley.

A simple, consistent pack design with a maximum of six communications on the pack, aims to make it easy for consumers to choose from the over 200 products in the cereal aisle.

Purchase intent time, if the item is not on the shopping list, is two or three seconds, so if you are an up and coming brand, you have to cut through.

All the Lowan Whole Foods cereals promote their health benefits and functionality. In a world first pilot program, Lowan Whole Foods is part of a trial conducted by the Australia New Zealand Food Authority, ANZFA.

The program allows the participating manufacturers to claim the health giving benefits of folate in the diet for women of child bearing years.

Slim, an animated stick figure, developed to continue the theme of simplicity, is the Lowan Whole Foods spokesperson in its television commercials.

Twelve months into the relaunch of breakfast cereals, Mr Birds said, 'We are the spark, not the flame, to the category. That's what we told retailers. We are providing a real alternative, a real choice. It has been a great success for us and for our trade partners, and we think we have read consumers correctly thus far.'

While the major focus for the company is on breakfast cereals, the Lowan Whole Foods brand has been leveraged in to the bread mix market. As an unknown bread mix producer, Mr Bird says retailers were persuaded to put the new range of three packs on shelf because of the innovative pack design.

Mr Bird said, 'We will enter into any market that can deliver the whole food promise.'

QUESTIONS

1 According to the article, how is Consolidated Foods Australia reinventing itself?
2 Graph the market share that the following companies have in the breakfast cereal market:
   a Kellogg   **b** Uncle Tobys   **c** Sanitarium   **d** Lowan Whole Foods
3 Why did Consolidated Foods Australia decide to concentrate on the healthier end of the breakfast cereal market?
4 What does the term *rebranding* mean?
5 What did the Lowan Whole Foods' rebranding exercise involve? Why?
6 How did the company let consumers know that they were rebranding their products?
7 How has Lowan Whole Foods supported its claim as the 'nutrition educator'?
8 Why was a simple, consistent pack design developed?

9 Outline the world-first pilot program in which Lowan Whole Foods is involved.

10 Who is Slim?

▶ Brains nut out answer

Read the newspaper article and then answer the questions that follow it.

Physicists are a step closer to solving one of the most troubling dilemmas of science—why Brazil nuts always rise to the top in a box of muesli.

Since the 1930s, they have racked their brains over the Brazil-nut Effect, puzzling why the big bits in a mix of different sizes head for the surface when the container is shaken.

A team from the University of Chicago replicated the problem in a lab, filling a ball with variable amounts of foam and lead shot, which was then placed in a transparent cylinder and surrounded by glass beads and poppy seeds. The cylinder was then shaken vertically to see how quickly the ball rose to the top. They found that the ball's speed was not just to do with its size, but with the density of the surrounding particles and the pressure of the air in the gaps between those particles.

Their complex equation, published in the British science magazine *Nature*, may have applications for industries where particles, such as grains or minerals, are separated.

QUESTIONS

1 What issue regarding muesli has perplexed scientists?

2 Explain the Brazil-nut Effect.

3 How have scientists in Chicago tried to work out the problem?

4 What were their findings?

▶ Japanese woman finds finger tip in rice ball

Read the newspaper article and then answer the questions that follow it.

A Japanese woman in her twenties made a grim discovery when she bit into a rice ball snack bought at a local convenience store and found a human fingertip.

The woman bought the Korean-style flavoured 'onigari' snack on Friday in Sendai, 300 km north of Tokyo, at a Lawson convenience store, the second largest convenience store chain in Japan with 7734 outlets nationwide.

But when she took a bite, she experienced a strange texture which she immediately spat out, a local government official said.

She took the meaty centimetre-long substance to a local hospital where a doctor confirmed it was a human finger.

Nihon Fresh Delica, which supplied the rice ball, confirmed it had come from a 46-year-old female part-timer who had lost her finger in a factory press the night before.

'We deeply apologise for causing the trouble,' local factory chief Noboru Mikawa told Jiji news agency, who revealed that despite knowing of the lost finger, the factory only disposed of some tens of 560 products produced at the time of the accident.

'Our foresight was very lax,' Mikawa said.

Lawson spokesman Takashi Fujii said the chain was taking the incident 'very seriously'.

It had halted all supply from the manufacturer with an eye to cutting completely its daily 45 000 rice ball order.

'While we did not make the product, we feel responsibility as the retailer,' said Fujii.

'To ensure this never happens again, we will thoroughly re-examine our business relationships.'

QUESTION

Undertake a PMI of the article—list three 'Pluses', three 'Minuses' and three 'Interesting points' related to the article.

▶ Let's remember

1 Define the term *line extension* and outline why companies create line extensions.

2 Provide an example of line extensions for:

    a dry biscuits   **b** yoghurt   **c** bread

3 Define the term *me-too* and provide an example of a 'me-too'.

4 Define the term *functional food*.

5 What are the benefits of functional foods?

6 Outline the health benefits associated with the following foods or components of food:

   a lycopene   **c** probiotic yoghurt   **e** oligosaccharides

   b garlic   **d** soy protein

7 What are caroteniods?

8 List other areas where functional foods may have health benefits.

9 What is your opinion of functional foods? Do we need functional foods? Explain your answer.

10 In Australia, are statements regarding health benefits allowed to be placed on food labels? Explain your answer.

► Let's investigate

1 Read the case study below and identify the functional foods. Complete a table like the one shown, listing the health benefits associated with each functional food.

Functional food	Health benefits

Lewis empties some wholegrain cereal, containing both insoluble and soluble fibre, into his bowl and then pours some low-fat, calcium-enriched milk on top. He tops his cereal with vanilla yoghurt that contains probiotic bacteria. After eating his cereal, Lewis then gets a slice of soy and linseed bread from the freezer and puts it in the toaster. Lewis then pours himself a glass of orange juice with added iron and waits for his bread to toast. He spreads his toast with a low-fat spread containing plant sterols, and tops it with grilled tomato.

2 Bring in a range of supermarket catalogues and magazines. Create a collage of one of the following food products:

   a 'me-toos'   **b** line extensions   **c** functional foods

3 Investigate a range of recipes and find examples of line extensions.

4 Design a new version of your favourite recipe so that it becomes a functional food. Indicate reasons for the inclusion or exclusion of particular foods.

@-Food products

1 Visit an online supermarket, such as Coles Online at www.colesonline.com.au or Safeway at www.woolworths.com.au.

   a Identify five original products and their line extensions.

   b Identify five 'me-too' products. Include the names of the various manufacturers that make the 'me-too' products.

   c Identify five functional foods. Can you identify the health benefits associated with each product?

   d Can you identify any original products that do not have any line extensions or 'me-too' products?

2 Visit *Choice* magazine at www.choice.com.au/articles/a102413p1.htm (click on 'New Probiotic Foods') for the latest information on probiotics.

   a What is so special about Inner Balance cheese?

   b What is the principle of probiotic bacteria?

   c Identify factors that may influence the effect of probiotic bacteria.

d What factors determine if probiotic bacteria can have any effect on the gut?

e How much probiotic bacteria needs to be present per gram to have an effect?

3 Visit *Choice* magazine at www.choice.com.au/articles/a100237p1.htm (click on 'Yoghurt for Inner Balance'). Complete the following sentences.

a Our gut contains _____ of bacteria, many of which are _____.

b Bacteria aid _____, stimulate the _____ and inhibit the growth of _____.

c Healthy people tend to have a good balance of _____, but factors such as a _____ diet, _____, _____ and ageing can put your digestive system out of balance.

d Probiotic bacteria are found in many yoghurts and make up over _____ of the yoghurt marker.

e Probiotic bacteria are _____ that are said to have a _____ and bring one's digestive system back into balance.

f Probiotic bacteria are said to prevent and control _____, decrease the effects of _____, relieve _____, lower _____, prevent and control thrush and prevent _____ as well as _____ the immune system.

g Most of these claims have a _____ scientific foundation as the evidence is _____; this means that the evidence comes from studies conducted _____.

▶ **Puzzled**

Finding functions

Match the examples below with their functions listed in the table.

a low-fat cheese
b calcium-enriched milk
c Hi-Maize (resistant starch) bread
d margarine with added plant sterols
e no-fat yoghurt
f yoghurt with probiotic bacteria
g iron-enriched milk
h soy and linseed muffins
i breakfast cereal with added wheat bran
j skim milk

Function foods	Examples
1 Fat-reduced foods	
2 Foods with added vitamins and minerals	
3 Foods with added ingredients	

What a word!

How many words can you create from the word *oligosaccharides*? You can only use each letter once.

Find a food product

Find each of the words from the box in the puzzle.

```
L  C  B  M  U  B  H  D  T  M  C  Z  G  F  D
I  E  I  K  E  F  V  Y  V  I  T  B  O  E  U
N  Z  R  T  M  T  L  M  L  Y  N  O  H  N  W
E  P  Q  P  O  H  O  R  T  O  D  C  E  E  M
E  O  Q  I  Q  I  A  O  I  P  I  S  V  J  A
X  H  A  W  G  G  B  T  R  R  P  M  V  R  Q
T  F  U  N  C  T  I  O  N  A  L  F  O  O  D
E  T  S  D  X  R  D  E  R  Y  N  L  H  Y  N
N  A  M  F  T  U  M  A  C  P  V  E  S  G  H
S  F  Q  U  C  U  C  O  N  S  U  M  E  R  S
I  W  N  T  I  B  P  P  W  C  G  L  K  N  A
O  O  F  C  D  E  T  A  L  E  R  T  E  I  D
N  L  L  X  N  E  C  N  E  I  C  S  S  L  V
L  A  A  E  B  U  K  W  T  H  E  A  L  T  H
C  M  K  W  W  U  Q  B  U  W  J  H  G  I  Q
```

calcium enriched	line extension
consumer	low-fat
diet related	lycopene
food product	me-too
functional food	nutrition
garlic	probiotic
health	science

Which product?

Identify the following foods as a line extension, a 'me-too' or a functional food.

1 oat-bran-enriched muffins, to decrease blood cholesterol
2 tomato sauce, garlic-flavoured tomato sauce and basil-flavoured tomato sauce
3 yoghurt containing live cultures of bifidus and acidophilus, to assist with digestion
4 margarine with added sterols, to reduce LDL-cholesterol
5 Fantastic rice crackers, Sakata rice crackers, Lanes rice crackers
6 French dressing, salt-free French dressing, oil-free French dressing
7 Leggo's flavoured tomato paste, Dolmio flavoured tomato paste, Edgell flavoured tomato paste
8 canned spaghetti, salt-free canned spaghetti, canned spaghetti with added cheese
9 calcium-enriched milk, to increase bone-density mass
10 breakfast cereal with added psyllium, to decrease blood cholesterol

LET'S PRODUCE

Basic biscuits

(makes 24)

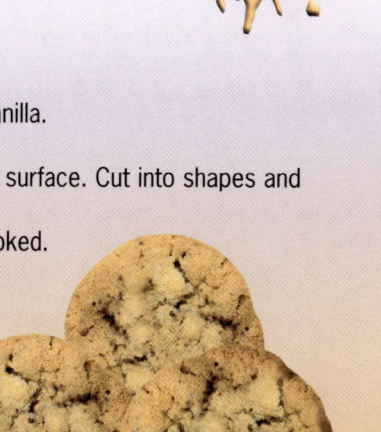

Method

1 Preheat oven to 160°C.
2 Sift flours.
3 Cream butter and sugar. Mix in egg and vanilla.
4 Add flour and mix into a firm dough.
5 Roll to $\frac{1}{2}$-centimetre thickness on a floured surface. Cut into shapes and glaze with milk.
6 Bake for ten to fifteen minutes, or until cooked.

Ingredients
$\frac{1}{2}$ cup flour, sifted
$\frac{1}{2}$ cup self-raising flour, sifted
60 grams butter
$\frac{1}{4}$ cup caster sugar
$\frac{1}{2}$ egg
$\frac{1}{4}$ teaspoon vanilla
1 tablespoon milk

Ingredients
1 tablespoon butter
½ onion, diced
½ cup Arborio rice
2 cups stock
30 grams parmesan cheese, grated

QUESTIONS

1 **Investigate** what ingredients you could add to the recipe to turn it into a line extension.
2 **Design** your line extension.
3 **Produce** and **evaluate** your line extension ☺ ☺ ☹.
4 Identify a new name for your line extension.

Basic risotto   (serves 2)

Method

1 Melt butter in frypan and sauté onion for two minutes.
2 Stir in rice and cook for two minutes.
3 Stir in flavouring ingredients.
4 Add half of stock and stir until it is absorbed.
5 Add remainder of stock and stir until it is absorbed.
6 Garnish with cheese and serve.

QUESTIONS

1 **Investigate** what ingredients you could add to the recipe to turn it into a line extension.
2 **Design** your line extension.
3 **Produce** and **evaluate** your line extension ☺ ☺ ☹.
4 Identify a new name for your line extension.

Ingredients
1 tablespoon olive oil
1 onion, diced
1 clove garlic, crushed
4 tomatoes, skins removed and diced
1 tablespoon basil
black pepper, to taste

Basic pasta sauce   (serves 2)

Method

1 Heat oil and gently fry onion and garlic.
2 Add tomatoes, basil and pepper and simmer gently for fifteen minutes.

Basic couscous   (serves 2)

Method

1 Pour water over couscous and stir.
2 Cover and stand for five minutes.
3 Add butter and mix in with a fork.

Ingredients
2 cups water, boiling
1 cup couscous
1 teaspoon butter

QUESTIONS

1 **Investigate** what ingredients you could add to this recipe to make it into a functional food.
2 Identify the foods or food components that have a health benefit.
3 **Design** your couscous.
4 **Produce** and **evaluate** your couscous ☺ ☺ ☹.
5 Identify a new name for your couscous recipe.

Sushi rolls

(makes 6 rolls)

Ingredients

3 cups short-grain rice, such as koshihari
3½ cups water
1 teaspoon sugar
½ cup mirin (rice wine)
6 sheets nori (seaweed sheets)
½ cup egg mayonnaise
150 grams flavoured tuna
½ carrot, peeled and cut into matchsticks
½ Lebanese cucumber, halved, deseeded and sliced into strips
½ avocado, sliced
320 millilitres Asian sauce for dipping, such as sweet soy

Method

1 Wash rice and place in saucepan with water. Bring to the boil and simmer, covered for twelve minutes.
2 Combine sugar and rice wine and add to rice. Remove from heat and let stand for ten minutes.
3 Place one sheet of nori on the bamboo mat and spread about one-sixth of the rice on top of the nori, ensuring that one edge of the nori has a 2-centimetre strip free of rice.
4 Place the mayonnaise down the centre and place the tuna on top. Next arrange the carrot, cucumber and avocado on the tuna.
5 Roll up the sushi, so that the filling is firmly enclosed. Cut into 2-centimetre slices.
6 Repeat with remaining ingredients and serve with soy sauce.

e-HINT

Most supermarkets have a Japanese section where you can purchase your ingredients.

QUESTIONS

1 Investigate the range of flavoured tuna on the market. Select a variety and design your own sushi rolls. Select vegetables that would complement your tuna variety. Produce and evaluate your sushi rolls ☺ ☺ ☹.
2 Is the flavoured tuna a 'me-too' or a line extension? Explain your answer.
3 Design your own variety of flavoured tuna. Investigate what ingredients you could use. Produce and evaluate your flavoured tuna ☺ ☺ ☹.

Wedges with salsa

(serves 2)

Ingredients

400 grams Sebago potatoes
2 tablespoons olive oil
pinch salt
black pepper, to taste
tomato salsa

Method

1 Preheat oven to 220°C.
2 Line baking tray with non-stick baking paper.
3 Peel potatoes and cut into 1.5-centimetre thick wedges.
4 Mix oil, salt and pepper together and pour over potato wedges.
5 Rub oil mixture into potatoes with hands to ensure each is well coated.
6 Place potatoes in single layer on baking tray and drizzle with leftover oil.
7 Bake for ten minutes and turn potatoes over.
8 Reduce temperature to 200°C and cook for another ten minutes.
9 Turn potatoes over and continue cooking for an additional twenty to twenty-five minutes, turning every ten minutes, until crisp and tender.
10 Serve with tomato salsa.

e-HINT

Other suitable potatoes for making wedges include russet burbank, King Edward and bintje.

QUESTION

Investigate the range of potato wedges on the market. Design your own flavouring to create a line extension. Produce and evaluate your recipe ☺ ☺ ☹.

CHAPTER 19

all wrapped up: DISCOVER packaging

Packaging

In today's society, packaging plays a vital role in the production, preservation, distribution and marketing of manufactured foods.

Packaging should contain the food product. Defective packaging, or under packaging, can result in spillages and therefore major losses and serious damage.

e-fact

Various packaging systems engage in independently sterilising both the food and the packaging and then carrying out the filling and sealing operations in a hygienic environment. This permits preservative-free foods, retains a food's flavour, nutrition and colour, and includes long-life qualities without necessitating refrigeration.

Prehistoric	*Early civilisation*	*Pre-1800*	*1800s–1850s*
• Leaves are used for wrapping and storing small amounts of food. • Skins and hides are used for moving and storing larger quantities of food. • Leather flasks, carved wooden vessels and gourds (dried shells of melons and pumpkins) are used.	• Pottery is first made in Japan (10 000 BC). • The first recorded pottery is produced in Europe, in Mesopotamia (3500 BC). • Hollow glass vessels are made (1500 BC). • The Romans create the first blown glass vessels (100 BC).	• Sacks, chests and barrels are utilised when transporting and storing large amounts of food. • Grocers and shopkeepers measure out portions of food and wrap them in paper. • Hand-printed labels are used on glass bottles and stoneware.	• Individual cartons and boxes are used. • Hand-printed labels are used on bottles and cartons. • Box construction and metal packaging are developed. • Moulded glass is developed. • The first airtight glass container is created (1809). • There is wide use of airtight metal cans (1840s).

The definitive assessment of packaging is whether or not it achieves its essential responsibilities —to contain, preserve, protect and provide information

In 1795, Napoleon offered a 12 000 franc prize for a means of preserving food for his armies. Nicolas Appert, a French confectioner, experimented with preserving food by sterilisation and won the prize in 1810.

Packaging should preserve and protect the contents. This is because the consumer wants a food product that is acceptable to consume and has not been damaged because it was not packaged correctly. The product should be protected:

- during transport and distribution
- from climatic effects, such as heat and cold, moisture, vapour, drying atmospheres
- from dangerous substances and contaminants
- from infestation

Packaging should act as a communication tool and provide information about the food product, such as price, ingredients and nutritional values, cooking instructions and recommended use-by date. Trends in marketing are placing greater emphasis on the appearance, sales appeal and quality of the packaging. Packaging can increase sales by identifying product differentiation and presentation, greater brand awareness and convenience. The ongoing evolving consumers' demands will require greater quality graphics and promotional links between graphics and advertising to support brand identities, plus the ability to reflect current consumer trends and images.

Packaging is also a significant part of our contemporary lifestyle.

- In the move to convenience and prepackaged foods, packaging allows for single or small serves, to cater for families of varying sizes and lifestyles. Individually wrapped butter provides the consumer with a specific amount of the product, reducing wastage. Containers can also be resealed if all the contents are not consumed.
- Packaging allows for quick preparation of foods. Examples include microwavable soups and pasta dishes, and the simple use of the product by way of spouts, squeeze bottles and aerosols.
- Packaging results in fewer visits to the supermarket.
- Packaging provides evidence if the food has been tampered with, such as secure packaging for jars of jam.

The usage of different types of packaging is often changing as new materials become accessible and innovative processing techniques are developed. Today, packaging is produced more quickly and efficiently than ever before.

Packaging timeline

Packaging has progressed from a fairly limited range of heavy, inflexible containers made of wood, glass and steel to an extensive collection of rigid, semi-rigid and

Industrial Revolution

- A paper bag making machine is invented (1852).
- Glass bottles with screw stoppers are manufactured (1870s).
- There is growth of branded materials, due to mass production, folding cartons and colour printing (1880s).
- Metal tubes are developed for toothpaste, but later used to package food products, such as condensed milk (1892).
- Bottling of Coca-Cola occurs (1894).

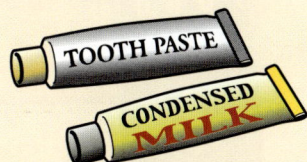

Age of Invention

- Waxed paper cartons are used for cream (1910s).
- Tins are used to keep potato crisps fresh (1920s).
- Cellophane is used to wrap sweets and other food products (1920s).
- Birdseye makes the first frozen foods that are sealed in cartons and wax-paper wrappers (1923).
- Polythene is invented in Britain (1933).
- The beer can is patented (1934).
- Milk bottles have aluminium foil caps (1934).
- Aerosols become popular (1940s).
- Printing directly on metal and glass packaging occurs (1940s).
- Plastic is used as a packaging material (1940s).

Age of Technology

- The aseptic milk carton is invented by Tetra Pak (1950s).
- Polythene bags are widely used (1950s).
- Tamper-evident closure is developed (1960s).
- Various new plastics for packaging are developed, such as the PET bottle for carbonated drinks (1970s).
- Bar coding is introduced (1970s).
- Plastic tubes replace metal tubes for food items such as condensed milk and tomato paste (1980s).
- Convenience food packaging becomes popular, especially microwave oven designs (1980s).
- Plastics to be used for cooking foods in a hot oven are developed (1990s).
- Technology is able to alter the composition of inert gases in packaging to preserve foods longer (1990s).

flexible packaging choices, progressively constructed from particular lightweight materials.

Compared to earlier forms of packaging, today's packaging usually:
- is lighter in weight
- uses less material
- is easier to open, dispense from, reseal, store and dispose of

Types of Packaging Materials

The chief packaging materials used in Australia are:
- plastic
- paper and board
- metal
- glass

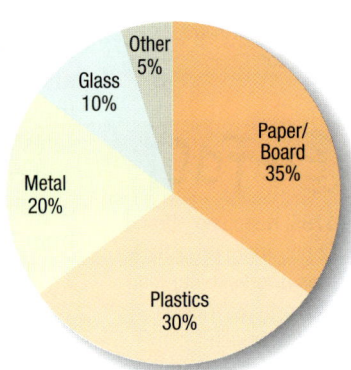

Plastic

Plastics for packaging are made in chemical factories. The six major plastics are shown below.

Raw materials used to make plastics are called polymers; they come in granular or powder form. Heat and pressure are used to convert the polymers into bottles, tubs, films, crates and so on.

Plastic bottles used to look opaque and were easily identifiable as plastic when compared to transparent glass bottles. However, in recent times, the ability to stretch plastics in a special way has enabled plastic to become clearer and tougher. This type of plastic is known as polyethylene terephthalate (PET). PET bottles include soft-drink bottles. PET film is manufactured by stretching the plastics in a different way. Stretched PET film is used in oven roasting bags.

Major plastics used in packaging
LDPE: low-density polyethylene
HDPE: high-density polyethylene
PP: polypropylene
PVC: polyvinylchloride
PSE: polystyrene
PET: polyester (polyethylene terephthalate)

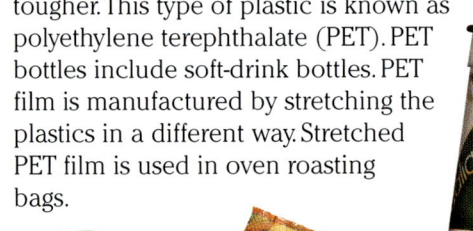

Paper and board

Paper is primarily used for paper bags and labels. It is also used in lamination—layers of paper, foil or plastics bound together. Board is used in cartons. Corrugated board is another product that is made from layers of paper. It is used where strong protection is required, such as in food packaging. The wavy layer in corrugated cardboard boxes can absorb acceptable impact, making it very useful for transport by road, air or sea. A lot of recycled paper is used to make paper and board for packaging.

Paper and board packaging is functional because:
· the materials are light and easy to handle, store and fold
· if combined with foil or plastic to produce laminated packaging, distinctive features are possible, such as a seal that stops evaporation and safeguards the product
· colour printing to a high quality is possible

e-fact

Paper and board are manufactured from wood pulp, which comes from fibres found in trees, and waste paper. Most paper is made from softwood trees that are grown and managed in forests purposely planted for this reason.

e-fact

Australia was the first country in the world to change completely to retained tab can ends for beer and soft-drink cans.

Metal

Steel and aluminium are the main metals used to make packaging for food products such as cans, aerosols, foil containers and metal closures.

There are a variety of ways to manufacture cans. Most food cans are made of three pieces of steel. Drink cans are usually made from two pieces of metal, either aluminium or steel.

There are many advantages to using cans, as outlined below.
· Canned food lasts for a long time if the cans are kept in a cool, dry cupboard.
· Some canned foods are very convenient because the food has been pre-cooked and can be consumed directly from the can or reheated without additional preparation.
· The cooking and canning process preserves the contents until the can is opened. Therefore no preservatives are necessary.
· There is little or no waste.
· Canned food can be purchased in convenient sizes; for example, canned soft drinks are easily opened, lightweight and easy to chill.

The canning process

The food is prepared for canning.

⬇

The cans are washed by strong jet blowers and rinsed in purified water.

⬇

Food is placed into the cans as they move along a conveyor belt; a liquid is also added. This liquid could be brine for vegetables and tuna or syrup or juice for fruits.

⬇

A machine seals the cans. Each can is inspected to ensure that it has the correct content level. Cans that do not have the correct content level are rejected automatically.

⬇

If appropriate, the food is cooked and sterilised in a giant pressure cooker and then cans cooled.

⬇

Usually the cans are packed in groups of twenty-four and covered by a layer of outer packaging. A machine places each group of cans on a cardboard tray and the whole pack is shrink-wrapped in film and heat-sealed. Some cans may be packed in cases made from corrugated board.

⬇

The trays are placed onto pallets and transported to a warehouse. Trucks collect the packaged cans and take them to shops and supermarkets.

Glass

Glass is one of the oldest forms of packaging and it has many advantages.

· The contents are clearly visible.
· Glass containers can be easily opened and resealed.
· The flavour of the food is not affected.
· Liquids and gases cannot leak into or out of glass packaging because it is impermeable.
· Glass containers are environmentally sound, as they can be washed and reused or recycled.
· Materials used to make glass—sand, limestone, soda ash—are inexpensive and in abundant quantity.

Disadvantages of using glass containers are that they can be easily broken and are heavier than other types of packaging.

Environmental Considerations with Packaging

There has been much debate about the waste problems and the environmental concerns associated with packaging. Environmental considerations are extremely important in packaging design. However, it is important to find the right balance between sometimes conflicting requirements. Packaging should be designed to reduce the amount of materials required while, at the same time, ensuring that it carries out its functional performance and satisfies consumer demands. Manufacturers make decisions about how the packaging is constructed and which materials are used based on many considerations, including:

· protecting the goods—the cost of damaged food products or the danger from spoilt foods needs to be carefully considered against using extra resources to make a stronger pack
· protecting the health of the consumer
· protecting the environment
· protecting company profits through reducing costs
· providing what the consumer needs, such as smaller quantities for individuals who live alone and easy-opening packaging for the elderly
· providing information about the food product

Significant resource conservation has occurred across the industry in the last twenty years through lightweighting.

• The weight of the 375-millilitre glass beer stubby has decreased by 35 per cent since 1980. The weight of 375-millilitre aluminium beer and soft-drink cans has decreased by 29 per cent since their introduction in 1969.
• Since its introduction in 1980, the HDPE milk bottle has been reduced in weight by 30 per cent.
• The PET soft-drink bottle weight has been reduced by 38 per cent since it was first introduced in the late 1970s.
• The weight of a standard 440-gram can has been reduced by 18 per cent since 1980.
• Since 1970, a weight saving of 30 per cent has been made to corrugated shipping boxes used for general grocery products.
• Folding cartons, as used for products such as breakfast cereals, have had their weight reduced by 15 per cent since 1970.
• The weight of gable-top milk and juice cartons has decreased by 23 per cent since 1975.
• 'Long-life' aseptic cartons have been reduced in weight by 15 per cent since they were introduced in 1979.
• The weight of 200-millilitre polystyrene yoghurt tubs has been reduced by 20 per cent since 1986.

Adapted from: www.packcoun.com.au

The National Packaging Covenant in Australia is endeavouring to manage packaging waste. This covenant was signed by the Australian and New Zealand Environment and Conservation Council ministers, local government and a range of industries in the packaging supply chain in 1999. It is a self-regulatory agreement between industries and government and is based on the shared responsibility for the ultimate disposal of waste packaging. The covenant is in effect for five years. It is not prescriptive—it does not tell companies how to create their packaging or what kind of packaging to use; nor does it require businesses to take back materials recovered from curbside recycling collection programs.

The goals of the National Packaging Covenant in Australia are to reduce the environmental impacts of consumer packaging waste throughout the complete lifecycle of the packaging product, close up the recycling loop, improve economically viable and sustainable recycling collection systems and ensure that the voluntary process is maintained.

Case study: Breakfast Cereal Packaging

The aims of breakfast cereal packaging are to contain and protect the contents as well as provide a barrier against moisture.

Cereals are edible grains. A mixture of cereals, nuts and fruits found in a packet of Just Right would appeal to the health-conscious adult.

Investigation of requirements of breakfast cereal packaging

Cereals have very specific requirements, so the packaging has to:
- protect the cereal and prevent it from being crushed
- keep the cereal dry and uncontaminated
- comply with food packaging regulations
- market the product
- supply essential information about the product
- be able to be easily displayed on supermarket shelves
- be stackable and not collapse when other packages are stacked on top of it
- fit into the supermarket's shelf space
- withstand being opened and closed numerous times

A designer will create the graphics for the package, ensuring that it is eye-catching, appeals to the target audience and includes essential labelling information. Market research will gauge consumer reaction and this feedback will influence the selected design.

Design brief
- An outer board package is required to provide strength and protection.
- An inner plastic material is necessary to prevent moisture penetration and contamination.

The external packaging must be sturdy enough not to crumple during transportation or when handled in supermarkets. Because it is not in direct contact with the food, recycled paper-based material can be used.

Breakfast cereal cartons often appear bigger than required because the cereal takes up extra space when packed, then settles as the package is transported.

The inner packaging is constructed from high-density polyethylene because it:
- prevents dust and other contaminants from entering
- provides an acceptable moisture barrier, as most cereals are hygroscopic

Hygroscopic means absorbing moisture.

- allows odours to escape
- has the correct stiffness for forming a bag shape on the machine
- is not easily split or punctured
- is economical to use
- can be heat-sealed and is easily opened by the customer

The inner packaging is put through shelf-life trials to make sure that the breakfast cereal is still suitable after the time specified by the best-before date. A panel of 'tasters' test the product after varying lengths of storage time. Samples may be kept in increased temperatures and humidity to replicate conditions in export countries or to accelerate testing as the product may have a twelve-month shelf-life.

Australia and New Zealand developed modified atmosphere packaging in the 1930s, exporting fresh bulk meat to the United Kingdom in an atmosphere rich in carbon dioxide.

QUESTIONS

1. List the steps in the design process.
2. Using the design process, outline the steps that a manufacturer of a breakfast cereal must work through when creating a new packaging for a breakfast cereal.

Case study — DIET PEPSI

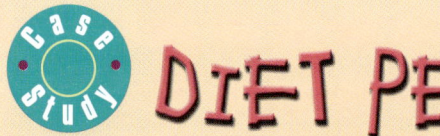

The taste of Diet Pepsi has frequently been described as 'light, crisp and refreshing'. The packaging of this product was redesigned to reflect the recollections of the consumer.

The redesigned labels and multipacks with the Diet Pepsi logo on a light blue background now feature on store shelves. A 'bubbly' background suggests a crisp, fresh taste, while the blue colour is associated with the packaging of regular Pepsi. The new three-dimensional red, white and blue globe icon creates a powerful identity for Diet Pepsi, yet ties it in with the Pepsi family of products, and so provides Diet Pepsi with marketing support. Pepsi consumers consistently say that what they prefer about the beverage is its light, crisp and refreshing taste. Diet Pepsi's light blue graphics are designed to reinforce those attributes and create a closer link to the Pepsi trademark.

QUESTIONS

1. What message is the new packaging for Diet Pepsi endeavouring to convey?
2. How does the packaging communicate this message?
3. How is marketing support provided from the Pepsi trademark?

Case study — REUSING, REUSING

In former times, tea used to be bought in an attractive tea caddy and biscuits in a decorative tin. The consumer would reuse the container once the original contents were consumed. The consumer would purchase the item in a basic pack and empty it into the fancy container. There was no real need for the basic packaging to be very durable, as it would be disposed of soon after purchase. This concept is still used by many producers today, such as Cottee's, who sell their product in concentrated form for dilution at home. The manufacturer is able to increase the ratio of product to packaging further.

Reusable crates are associated with the bakery industry, where bread products are often supplied without individual packaging. A number of supermarket chains are also investigating the use of returnable crates for other products. South Australia is currently the only state to offer monetary incentives for the return of glass and plastic beverage bottles. However, there is a push for other states to offer this incentive to assist with the recycling process.

QUESTIONS

1   Provide an example of how packaging was traditionally reused.
2   Why did the packaging of the basic pack not have to be very durable?
3   How are cordial manufacturers reusing packaging today?
4   List the advantages of reusing packaging.
5   Identify other foods that could have their original packaging reused.
6   How do bakeries reuse packaging?
7   List other foods that could be presented in reusable packaging like bread products.
8   Should other states follow South Australia's lead and offer money for the return of glass and plastic bottles? Explain your response.

Let's remember

1   Identify the three main roles of packaging and discuss each in detail.
2   Why is packaging considered to be important in today's society?
3   How does packaging today compare with packaging of the past?
4   Identify the types of materials commonly used in packaging in Australia.
5   What is PET? What foods use PET for packaging?
6   Why is paper and board packaging considered to be functional? Provide some examples of foods that use paper or board packaging.
7   Outline the advantages of using metal as a form of packaging.
8   Identify the advantages and disadvantages of using glass as a form of packaging.
9   Identify the environmental advantages of manufacturers 'lightweighting' their packaging.
10 What is the role of the National Packaging Covenant in Australia?

Let's investigate

1   Investigate one of the following forms of packaging: aseptic packaging, modified atmosphere packaging, active packaging. Provide information about the packaging technique, advantages and disadvantages of the technique and foods that use this form of packaging.
2   Investigate the various forms of packaging that could be used for sweet biscuits. Also investigate what information should be included on the package. Design and produce a package for sweet biscuits. Place your biscuits in your package and evaluate how effective the package is ☺ ☺ ☹.
3   Investigate the range of packaging that is used for the following food products. Include some of your own examples of foods as well. Supermarket websites, such as www.colesonline.com.au and www.woolworths.com.au, may be useful.

Food product	Packaging examples
Preserved peaches	
Coffee	
Beetroot	
Butter	
Flavoured milk	
Tomato paste	
Yoghurt	

Discuss the advantages and disadvantages of each form of packaging and evaluate which form of packaging you consider to be the most suitable for each food product ☺ ☻ ☹.

4   Investigate ways in which companies such as McDonald's have changed their packaging to be more environmentally friendly. Investigate ways in which packaging could become more environmentally friendly. Create a poster to outline your findings.

5   NuWave is a unique plastic product created by VisyPak. Visit the Visy website at www.visy.com.au and write a 250-word report outlining the development, benefits and uses of this form of packaging.

6   Investigate ways in which food packaging also serves a useful function, such as noodle boxes whereby the consumer can eat straight from the package. Identify a list of functional packaging and display your findings by redrawing your examples on poster paper.

7   Investigate ways in which manufacturers could produce packaging that would suit the needs of the elderly. Factors to consider would be the physiological process of ageing, such as decrease in strength, eyesight and energy requirements, as well as perhaps the likelihood of more people living alone. Design your packages for a range of foods suitable for the elderly and identify key features. Write up a report outlining issues that you have addressed with your packaging designs.

8   Select five different food products. Investigate the various types of materials that are used to package each product. Make an assessment about the package. Is there too much? Is there too little? Could another material be used? Evaluate the effectiveness of the packaging of each food product and discuss any environmental concerns that you may have ☺ ☻ ☹. Identify suitable alternatives if necessary.

▶ e-Packaging

www.visy.com.au

Click on 'Visypak'. Select three of the following types of packaging and research how they are used in food packaging.

*   PET bottles and jars
*   two-piece aluminium beverage cans
*   tinplate food cans
*   gable-top paperboard cartons
*   aseptic paperboard cartons
*   dual-ovenable trays and shelf-stable barrier containers
*   aseptic filling systems
*   confectionery or dry-food foils and laminations
*   plastic tubes, cubes, bottles, drums and pails
*   general-line cans
*   steel drums and pails and flexible intermediate bulk containers (FIBCs)

▶ **Puzzled**

Packaging puzzle

Across

1 Type of metal used in packaging
3 Name of first plastic
4 HDPE, PET and PVC are abbreviations for this type of packaging
5 The name given to the raw materials used to make plastic
6 In the 1920s, this food product was kept fresh in tins (two words)
8 Who offered a prize for a method of preserving food in 1795?
12 Type of material that is primarily used in packaging in Australia today
15 The aseptic milk carton was invented by this company (two words)
16 The name of the company that first made frozen foods in cartons in 1923

Down

2 The main aims of packaging are to contain, preserve, protect and provide _____
3 The bottling of this product first occurred in 1894 (two words)
7 Type of wrapping used for food products in the 1920s
9 Today's packaging is considered to be _____ in weight than packaging of the past
10 One disadvantage of glass packaging is that it can be easily _____

11 This type of bag was commonly used in the 1950s as a form of packaging

13 Abbreviation for polyethylene terephthalate

14 This material accounts for about 10 per cent of packaging today

Packaging purposes

Unscramble the tiles below to complete a sentence about the aims of packaging.

O F	A G I N	F O R M	T A I N	N .	O V I D
C O N	E I N	S E R V	A T I O	P A C K	G A R
O T E C	D P R	T H E	E P R	A I M S	T A N
E T O	P R E				

Plastic match

Match the following words with their abbreviations.

Name	Abbreviation
Polyvinylchloride	PP
Polyethylene terephthalate	PSE
Polystyrene	PVC
Low-density polyethylene	PET
High-density polyethylene	LDPE
Polypropylene	HDPE

LET'S PRODUCE

Ingredients
1 tablespoon olive oil
1 leek, sliced
1 clove garlic, crushed
1 teaspoon dried oregano
1 teaspoon dried basil
3 chat potatoes, quartered
1 carrot, cut into 4-centimetre long batons
1 stick celery, diagonally sliced
200 grams whole peeled tomatoes, chopped
2 cups vegetable stock
1 zucchini, thickly sliced
black pepper, to taste
parmesan cheese
crusty bread

Simple vegetable soup   (serves 2)

Method

1 Heat oil in saucepan and cook leek, garlic, oregano and basil for five minutes.
2 Add potatoes and cook for ten minutes, stirring occasionally.
3 Add carrot, celery, tomatoes and stock and bring to boil.
4 Add zucchini and simmer for ten minutes, or until vegetables are tender.
5 Season with pepper and serve with shaved parmesan cheese and crusty bread.

QUESTIONS

1 Investigate which target groups would consume this soup. Make alterations and design your own soup to ensure that it would cater for a niche market that you select.

2 Investigate what type of packaging would be most suitable for your soup. Visiting a supermarket or website such as www.colesonline.com.au or www.woolworths.com.au may help you to gain ideas about the various ways in which soup is packaged.

3 Design your own packaging to market your soup.

4 Investigate the current labelling laws in Australia and design a label for your soup.

5 Produce your packaging and label for your soup and evaluate how successful you were in catering for your target group by asking people in this group if they would buy your soup ☺ ☺ ☹.

Ingredients
2 tablespoons dried bread-crumbs

$\frac{1}{3}$ cup short-grain rice

$\frac{3}{4}$ cup canned cream-style sweet corn

$\frac{1}{2}$ cup canned tomatoes, chopped

2 eggs, slightly beaten

50 grams grated tasty cheese

1 tablespoon fresh basil

2 shakes black pepper

1 tomato, sliced into 6 thin pieces

chutney

Savoury rice cakes

(makes 6)

Method

1 Preheat oven to 180°C.

2 Grease six large individual muffin pans and dust with breadcrumbs.

3 Cook rice, drain and set aside to cool.

4 Mix corn, canned tomatoes, eggs, cheese and basil. Add cold rice and season with pepper.

5 Place mixture evenly into six individual muffin pans and place a slice of tomato on top.

6 Bake for thirty-five to forty minutes, or until skewer comes out clean.

7 Serve with chutney.

QUESTIONS

1 Identify and list the various forms of packaging of the ingredients. Evaluate the effectiveness and the environmental soundness of each package ☺ ☺ ☹. A table like the one below may be useful.

Food product	Type of packaging	Effectiveness of packaging	Environmental soundness of packaging

2 Investigate what factors should be considered when designing a package for the savoury rice cakes.

3 Design and produce your packaging.

4 Evaluate the effectiveness of your packaging, listing the criteria that you used in descending order of priority ☺ ☺ ☹.

5 Investigate which groups of people would buy this product.

6 Investigate what line extensions could be created if this product were successful.

7 Design, produce and evaluate one of your line extensions ☺ ☺ ☹.

Golden syrup and chocolate dumplings

(serves 2)

Ingredients

1 cup water
1½ tablespoons golden syrup
⅓ cup sugar
30 grams butter
2 tablespoons marmalade
30 grams extra butter, chopped
½ cup self-raising flour, sifted
3 tablespoons milk
60 grams chocolate, chopped into squares
ice cream

Method

1 Place water, golden syrup, sugar, butter and marmalade into a saucepan and stir to combine. Bring to boil and reduce heat to simmer.
2 Rub extra butter into flour, make a well and add milk to form a dough.
3 Turn dough onto floured surface and shape into 10-centimetre log. Divide into six even-sized pieces.
4 Place a cube of chocolate into each piece of dough, ensuring that the dough totally covers the chocolate.
5 Place dough into simmering sauce, cover and cook for twenty minutes.
6 Serve dumplings with ice cream.

QUESTION

Investigate and evaluate the packaging of each ingredient ☺ ☻ ☹. Present your information as a poster.

Mini meat loaves

(serves 2)

Ingredients

250 grams pork mince
½ apple, peeled and finely grated
¼ onion, finely chopped
½ tablespoon fresh parsley, chopped
1 clove garlic, crushed
½ egg, lightly beaten
½ cup stale breadcrumbs
2 tablespoons barbecue sauce
50 grams lettuce
½ tomato
½ Lebanese cucumber

Method

1 Preheat oven to 180°C.
2 Lightly grease two one-cup capacity muffin trays.
3 Combine mince, apple, onion, egg, breadcrumbs, garlic and parsley and press into muffin tins.
4 In the meantime, prepare the barbecue sauce.
5 Heat butter in small saucepan and fry onion and garlic until light brown.
6 Add flour and cook until mixture is light brown. Remove from heat.
7 Combine stock, vinegar, brown sugar and mustard together and gradually add to onion mixture, stirring constantly.
8 Return to heat and bring to boil, stirring constantly.
9 Add Worcestershire sauce and reduce heat, simmering for one minute.
10 Cook meat loaves for twenty minutes, turn out and place onto a greased oven tray and top with barbecue sauce.
11 Increase oven temperature to 200°C and cook meat loaves for an additional twenty minutes, or until cooked through and browned.
12 Serve with salad vegetables.

Barbecue sauce

1 tablespoon butter
½ onion, finely diced
1 clove garlic, crushed
1 tablespoon flour
½ cup stock
2 teaspoons vinegar
½ teaspoon brown sugar
½ teaspoon wholegrain mustard
½ teaspoon Worcestershire sauce

QUESTION

Investigate the packaging of each ingredient and evaluate how environmentally sound each package is ☺ ☻ ☹. Can the packaging be reused, recycled or reduced? Present your findings and recommendations in a written report.

LaBELLED!: DISCOVER LaBELLING

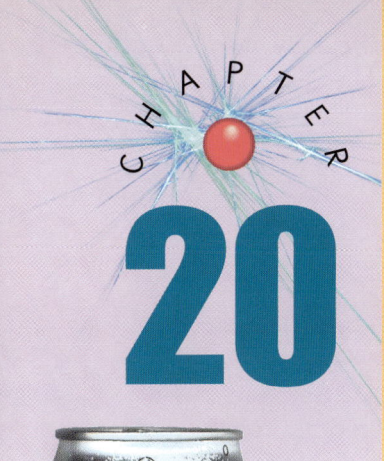

The labelling of food packages must provide information that allows the consumer to make informed choices. The Food Standards Codes stipulate that a food label must include the following information:

- the name of the food product
- the name and address of the manufacturer, packer, importer or vendor
- the country of origin
- identification of where the food was produced and a 'batch' number, so that the food can be traced to its packaging plant
- the date of packing or a use-by date
- a list of ingredients
- a nutritional breakdown of the key nutrients
- percentages of the key nutrients listed
- information to notify consumers if the food product contains ingredients likely to have unpleasant effects, such as the laxative effect of sorbitol

1 Use-by or best-before date and lot number
These are for safety reasons. The lot number makes the identification and notification of contaminated food products much more efficient.

2 Name/description of the product
It is illegal to deceive consumers about products; for example, a product called raspberry jam must include raspberries.

3 Characterising ingredients
Characterising ingredients (in this case, raspberry) must be listed as a percentage of the product.

4 Supplier's address
This is required in the rare case of recall.

5 Use or storage directions
This informs consumers how to safely store the product.

6 Country of origin
This provides information to the consumer about where the product was made.

7 Food additives
Food additives must be identified by their internationally recognised food number.

8 Ingredients
The ingredients, including water, are listed in order of ingoing weight

9 Nutrition information
Information concerning nutrients, such as fat, protein, energy, carbohydrates (total and sugars) and sodium, is required.

Note: The food label must be prominent, legible and in English. It also must be quite distinctive from the background and warning statements must be printed in a font that is at least 3 millimetres high.

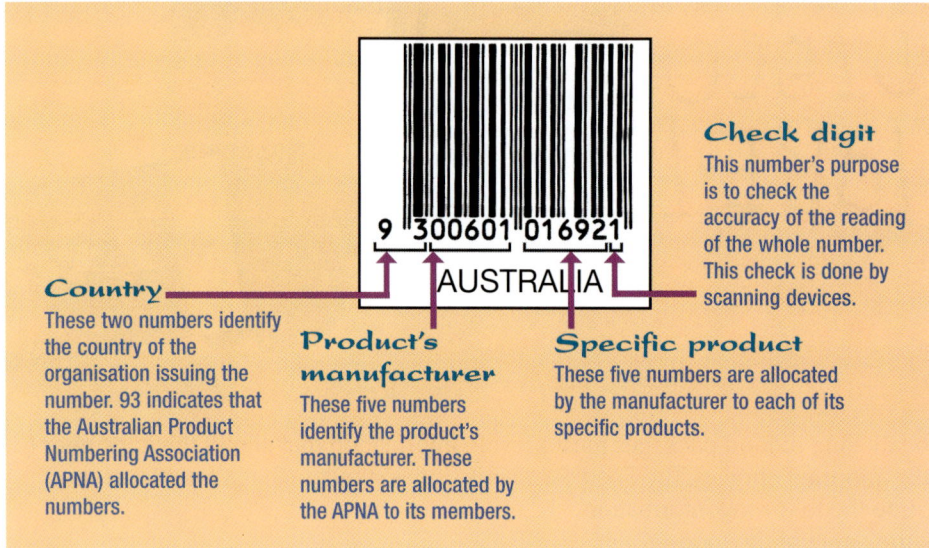

Country
These two numbers identify the country of the organisation issuing the number. 93 indicates that the Australian Product Numbering Association (APNA) allocated the numbers.

Product's manufacturer
These five numbers identify the product's manufacturer. These numbers are allocated by the APNA to its members.

Specific product
These five numbers are allocated by the manufacturer to each of its specific products.

Check digit
This number's purpose is to check the accuracy of the reading of the whole number. This check is done by scanning devices.

AUSTRALIA

9 300601 016921

The new labelling laws are quite informative. The chicken soup pictured here contains only 0.5% chicken. Would you call it chicken soup?

Focus on Food Additives

The role of food additives in food production is often not understood and therefore perhaps wrongly disapproved of. Food additives allow us to benefit from a diversity of safe, nutritious and flavoursome foods year-round, and enable us to have access to a range of foods in our home without having to shop daily.

A food additive is a substance that is added to a food for a precise technological intention and is not a food itself. Food additives are not necessarily complex chemical compounds, but may include substances such as salt, baking powder and vanilla. Additives are identified in the ingredients list on the label of packaged foods.

Additives are approved for various functions in foods, such as to:
· improve the nutritional value of particular foods
· enhance the taste, texture, consistency or colour of particular foods and therefore make them more appealing
· preserve foods so that they remain wholesome and appealing while being transported to their place of sale; preservatives also extend the storage life of foods
Here are some examples of how additives are used in food processing:
· Stabilisers and thickeners provide a smooth, consistent texture in food products.
· Vitamins and minerals may be added to particular foods, such as breakfast cereals, flour, dairy products, margarine and fruit juice, to compensate for nutrients likely to be deficient in a person's diet or lost during the processing. Such vitamins and minerals include folate, thiamin, vitamin C, riboflavin, niacin, calcium and iron.

- Preservatives delay food spoilage triggered by bacteria, mould, fungi, yeast or contact with air. Antioxidants are preservatives that delay fats and oils in baked goods from turning rancid and so retain flavour and goodness. Antioxidants also impede fruits such as apples from becoming brown when cut and exposed to air.
- Additives also supply leavening or control acidity or alkalinity. Leavening agents release acids. When heated, these acids react with baking powder and help baked goods such as cakes and biscuits to rise during baking.
- Additives are also used to improve flavour or impart desired colour. Various natural and synthetic flavours increase the taste of foods. Colours are used to enhance the appearance of particular foods to satisfy the expectations of consumers. Soft drinks, cordials, soups, confectionery, baked goods and jams are some foods that have additives added to them to improve flavour and impart the desired colour.

Government authorities and various international organisations carefully control all food additives to make certain that they are safe for their proposed use and that foods containing the additives are precisely labelled. In Australia, Food Standards Australia New Zealand (FSANZ) is the government food regulatory body. FSANZ must approve additives prior to them being legally added to foods. All additives are subject to constant safety reviews as scientific knowledge and techniques of testing continue to be developed.

The Australian Food Standards Code demands that food additives be identified, either by name or number, on food product labels. The numbering system for food additives is known as the International Numbering System (INS).

Functions of food additives

Additive	Function
Antioxidants	Foods containing fats and oils are prevented from becoming rancid
Colours	Replace colours that are lost during processing
Flavour enhancers	Boost the flavours in foods
Food acids	Maintain the level of acid in food where there are variations in the food's acidity
Humectants	Mainly used in baked goods to control moisture levels and keep foods moist
Preservatives	Enhance shelf-life by controlling the growth of mould, yeast and bacteria
Thickeners	Change the texture and consistency of food, including thickening and stabilising emulsions

SOME ADDITIVES IN DETAIL

Case study

Propionates

Certain baked goods may have propionates, which are used in strictly controlled amounts to preserve foods such as bread, biscuits, cakes, pastries and other flour products.

Propionates help keep baked goods fresh and reduce the growth of mould and other micro-organisms. They afford consumers the convenience of having soft, freshly baked goods in the home without having to buy them daily.

Various food companies also manufacture a range of propionate-free foodstuffs, so that the minority of the Australian population who may be sensitive to propionates are able to consume alternative products.

Colour additives

A colour additive is any dye, pigment or substance that conveys colour when added to food. Colour additives are not only used in foods, but also in drugs and cosmetics. They are used in foods for various reasons, including compensating for colour loss due to storage or processing of foods and to adjust variations in natural food colour.

Aspartame

Aspartame is considered a food additive. Aspartame is a concentrated sweetener that is about 200 times sweeter than sugar. It was approved for use in Australia in 1982 and is used extensively in various foods and beverages to add sweetness without kilojoules.

Aspartame's components break apart when heated, resulting in a loss of sweetness. Therefore, aspartame is not recommended for use in recipes that are to be heated or baked. If a food containing aspartame were accidentally heated, it would still be safe, but would merely not give the preferred sweetness.

e-fact

Propionates occur naturally in particular foods, such as cheese, and are naturally present in the body. Did you know that propionate is produced every day in our intestines when dietary fibre is fermented? Propionate is consequently absorbed into our bloodstream.

QUESTIONS

1 Identify the types of foods that may contain propionates.
2 Why are propionates used in such foods?
3 What is the advantage to the consumer of buying foods that contain propionates?
4 What is a colour additive?
5 Why are colour additives used in foods?
6 What is aspartame?
7 Why is aspartame not recommended for use in recipes that are to be baked or heated?
8 What would happen to food containing aspartame if it were heated?
9 Investigate a range of 'diet' foods and identify which contain aspartame. Compile a list of other artificial sweeteners that are used in such foods.
10 Collect five food labels and identify the food additives. Investigate one such food additive (other than propionates, colour additives and aspartame) in detail and present your information in a 400-word report.

▶ Would you like meat with that pie?

Read the newspaper article and then answer the questions that follow it.

By Sarah Stock

FANCY some minced gristle, connective tissue, offal and a blob of fat about the size of a golf ball for lunch?

If you eat a meat pie, that could be what you consume, according to an analysis of the frozen variety.

The Australian Consumers Association study, published today in its journal *Choice*, tested 18 brands of frozen meat pies that mostly sell in supermarkets in four- and six-packs.

It found three meat pie brands—Patties, Tastee and The Great Southern Pie Company – failed to meet the quality requirement of 25 per cent meat content, despite the definition of meat including buffalo, camel, deer and goat in any form, from fat and gristle to trimmings and meat scraps removed from bones.

The Australia New Zealand Food Authority and the Victorian and NSW governments plan to examine the results and possibly tighten enforcement of food standards.

NSW Health Minister Craig Knowles said he would ask the Health Department to investigate the pies involved in the study after the 'alarming' findings.

Tastee Pty Ltd and Patties Pies Pty Ltd yesterday rejected the analysis, saying it conflicted with external audits of their pies, which they regularly conducted to ensure quality.

The pies contained a whopping 15 g to 35 g of pure fat, and 20 to 40 per cent of the upper recommended daily limit of sodium for adults.

If pie-lovers wanted beef or steak meat, they should buy fresh pies from a bakery. Shakespeares Pies, for instance, used only fresh ingredients and its traditional meat pie contained prime lean beef in much greater amounts than the 25 per cent required.

QUESTIONS

1 What ingredients are found in some meat pies, according to the Australian Consumers Association?
2 What percentage of meat content is required in meat pies?
3 What is Australia New Zealand Food Authority's definition of the term *meat*?
4 Does Australia New Zealand Food Authority's definition of meat differ from your definition? In what ways is it similar or different?
5 Outline the amount of fat found in the pies tested. Why is this finding a concern?

Let's remember

1 What information must be included on the labels of food products?
2 Outline the recent changes to food labelling in Australia.
3 Identify information that should not to be included on food labels in Australia.
4 What does a nutritional panel provide information about?
5 Identify the information that a barcode provides.
6 Define a food additive and outline the functions of food additives in food preparation.
7 Who determines what food additives are safe to include in food products?
8 How do consumers know whether additives have been added to food products?
9 What are propionates and why may they be added to food products?
10 Why would food products have food additives included?
11 Outline the advantages and disadvantages of using aspartame as a food additive.

Let's investigate

1 Investigate the Heart Foundation's 'Pick the Tick' logo. What selection criteria are used to enable a food label to display this logo? If a food product contains this logo, does it mean that it is 'healthier' than a competitor's food product that does not contain this logo? Explain your response.
2 Investigate and design your own label for a flavoured milk drink. Produce the label.
3 Investigate the differences between a nutritional message and a health claim. Are nutritional messages and health claims allowed on food labels? Explain your response.
4 Select a well-known food product, such as milk, frozen pizza, soft drink or chocolate bars, and design a new label for it. Try to keep elements of the original label, so that consumers can still identify with the product. Produce your label and ask your classmates to evaluate the new label ☺ ☺ ☹.
5 Investigate the Glycemic Index now appearing on Australian food labels.
6 Construct a questionnaire to investigate if people are able to read and understand information on a food label. For example, questions could be asked about order of ingredients on the ingredient list, serving sizes and nutritional claims. Graph your results using a computer graphing package and analyse the information that you have collected. What conclusions can you draw?
7 Investigate recent changes to food labelling. Outline the changes. Ask a range of people if they are aware of the changes. Do they approve of the changes? Do the changes have an effect on their food selection? Are there any other changes that they would like to see in regard to food labelling?
8 How often do you read food labels? What information do you read? Do you understand how to read food labels? Compare your responses to those of others. Graph your findings. What type of information is most often collected from food labels? What conclusions can you draw?
9 Many food additives may appear to be unfamiliar to you, but their compounds are actually quite common. Find out the common names for the following additives:
   a ascorbic acid
   b alpha-tocopherol
10 Investigate the responsibility of Food Standards Australia New Zealand in regard to labelling.

1   Why is it important to know how to read food labels?
2   Identify what food labelling requirements specify must appear on all packaged food products.

Click on the 'Food Label Articles' hyperlink at the bottom of the page to take you to three articles related to food labels.

What will we see on the new food labels?

1   Outline what information is mandated on food nutrition panels.
2   a   Describe some of the differences between new and old food labels, and provide a reason why you think each change would be useful to the consumer.
    b   Which information would be most important for you to know?
3   Predict changes that you think will occur to food labels by 2020.
4   Why are some products exempt from displaying the mandatory panel?

Reading nutrition information panels

The nutrients on a food label are displayed in a standard format, providing amount per serve and per 100 grams (or 100 millilitres of liquid) of the food. List the advantages and disadvantages of displaying nutrients in this way.

Making sense of food labels

1   One of the major changes to food labels is that the percentage of each key ingredient in a product will be listed. What do think this means to you as a consumer?
2   Why would the percentage of whole wheat be listed in the nutrition panel on a package of whole wheat breakfast cereal?
3   Using the food labels on the following products, investigate the accuracy of the name of each product. Make a judgement about the reliability of each food label in helping the consumer to make informed food choices. Discuss ways in which the consumer may be misled. If appropriate, rename each food so that the consumer can make a more educated selection by using the new name.
    a   Berri Tropical Fruit Salad
    b   SPC Peaches in Mango and Natural Juice
    c   Continental Cup A Soup Asian Seafood Laksa
    d   Continental Cup A Soup Gourmet Chicken and Sweet Corn Soup
    e   IXL 100% Raspberry spreadable fruit
    f   Cottee's Apple Blackcurrant Crush Cordial
    g   San Remo La Pasta Carbonara Fettuccini Pasta in Creamy Bacon and Onion Sauce
    h   Uncle Tobys Real Fruit Strawberry Bars

www.woolworths.com.au/recipes/foodadditives.asp
www.foodstandards.com.au (click on the 'Food Additives Shoppers' Guide' on the left-hand side)

Using either of the above websites investigate one of the following food additives:

1	emulsifiers	4	thickeners or vegetable gums	6	colourings
2	preservatives			7	humectants
3	flavour enhancers	5	anti-caking agents	8	food acids

Puzzled

INS match

Match the following preservatives with their International Numbering System category.

Preservatives	International Numbering System category
Nitrates/nitrites	249–252
Sorbates	310–321
Sulphites	210–213
Antioxidants	280–283
Benzoates	220–228
Propionates	200–203

WEBEXTRAS

www.glycaemicindex.com
This website provides information about the Glycaemic Index including a link to a list of carbohydrate foods and their GI.

www.glycemicindex.com
This is a link to the University of Sydney's Glycemic Index website.

Add the additives

Unscramble the tiles below to complete a sentence about food additives.

R E U	C O L O	R T A I	T E X	O D S	H E T
F C E E S	A N F O	U R O	S E D		F O O D
A S T E	C E T	T O E	T U R E	O R	S I S T
C O N	A D D	N H A N	E N C Y	I T I V	

LET'S PRODUCE

Ingredients

½ sheet puff pastry
1 teaspoon peanut oil
1 spring onion
80 grams button mushrooms
125 grams chicken thigh
    fillet, cubed
1 tablespoon satay sauce
1 tablespoon roasted
    peanuts, chopped
¼ cup coconut cream
2 teaspoons fresh coriander,
    chopped
lightly beaten egg for
    glazing

Satay chicken pie

(serves 1)

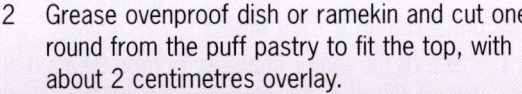

Method

1 Preheat oven to 200°C.
2 Grease ovenproof dish or ramekin and cut one round from the puff pastry to fit the top, with about 2 centimetres overlay.
3 Heat oil in frypan and cook spring onion and mushrooms for two minutes.
4 Add chicken and cook until brown.
5 Add satay sauce and peanuts, then coconut cream and coriander.
6 Bring to boil and reduce heat and simmer for ten minutes, or until sauce thickens slightly.
7 Spoon chicken mixture into ovenproof dish and cover with pastry round.
8 Glaze with egg and cut a steam hole in the centre of the pastry.
9 Bake for twenty minutes, or until pastry is golden brown.

Ensure that the chicken mixture does not completely fill the ovenproof dish. There should be a gap between the chicken mixture and the pastry.

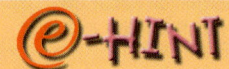

Beat together several eggs for glazing that can be shared among the class.

QUESTIONS

1 Investigate the various ways in which satay sauce is packaged, by visiting a supermarket or a website such as www.colesonline.com.au or www.woolworths.com.au.
2 Investigate the information that is provided on the label of a satay sauce container. Does it comply with the Australian labelling laws? Are there any additives? Visit www.woolworths.com.au/foodadditives or www.foodstandards.gov.au to find out the names of these additives.
3 Investigate the difference between coconut cream and milk. Should you use 'light' coconut cream or milk? The website of *Choice* magazine (www.choice.com.au) may provide some useful information.

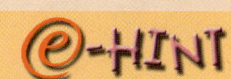

Apricot puffs

(makes 12)

Ingredients

2 sheets puff pastry
2 teaspoons honey
20 grams butter
125 grams apricot halves
2 teaspoons brown sugar

Method

1 Preheat oven to 210°C.
2 Line baking tray with non-stick baking paper.
3 Cut twelve 8-centimetre rounds of pastry and place on baking trays.
4 Melt honey and butter in a small saucepan and brush mixture over pastry rounds.
5 Thoroughly drain apricots and dry with a paper towel.
6 Slice each apricot half into four pieces and arrange into centre pastry rounds, leaving a 1-centimetre border.
7 Sprinkle with brown sugar and bake for twelve to fifteen minutes, or until puffed and golden.

e-HINT

Microwave honey and butter for about one minute, or until butter just melts. Stir to combine the mixture.

QUESTIONS

1 **Investigate** the various ways in which puff pastry is packaged, by visiting a supermarket or a website such as www.colesonline.com.au or www.woolworths.com.au.

2 **Investigate** and **evaluate** the various marketing strategies used to sell the puff pastry that you used in the recipe ☺ ☺ ☹.
Investigate the information that is provided on the label. Check that the information that is meant to be provided on a food label is evident. Use a checklist to ensure that all information is included on the puff pastry packaging. Include any other additional information that is evident.

3 **Investigate** the label of the canned apricots that you used in the recipe. Are the apricots canned in natural juice, fruit juice or syrup? **Investigate** the differences between these liquids.

Duo-choc muffins

(makes 12)

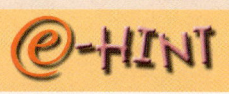

Ingredients

200 grams dark cooking chocolate, roughly chopped
120 grams low-salt butter
$\frac{2}{3}$ cup low-fat milk
300 grams cream cheese, softened
2 teaspoons vanilla essence
4 eggs
2 tablespoons baking powder
3 cups plain flour, sifted
2 cups brown sugar
4 tablespoons cocoa powder

Method

1 Preheat oven to 180°C.
2 Grease muffin pans.
3 Combine chocolate, butter and $\frac{1}{3}$ cup of milk in a saucepan and stir over a low heat until melted. Remove and set aside.
4 Beat cream cheese and vanilla essence until smooth, and gradually add remaining $\frac{1}{3}$ cup of milk.
5 Lightly whisk two eggs and add to cream cheese mixture.
6 In one bowl, sift 1 tablespoon baking powder and $1\frac{1}{2}$ cups flour, and add 1 cup brown sugar.
7 Add the cream cheese mixture, and mix using a metal spoon until just combined.
8 Sift the remaining $1\frac{1}{2}$ cups flour and 1 tablespoon baking powder with cocoa in another bowl and add the remaining 1 cup brown sugar.

e-HINT

The chocolate, butter and milk can be combined in the microwave. Place in the microwave for one to two minutes and stir after each minute.

9   Lightly beat two remaining eggs and add to chocolate mixture.
10 Place spoonfuls of chocolate mixture into one side of each muffin pan.
11 Repeat process with the cream cheese mixture.
12 Bake for twenty-five minutes, or until golden.

QUESTIONS

1   Investigate the labelling laws for milk. What are the requirements
    for milk to be labelled in each of the following ways?
    a full cream   **b** low fat   **c** no fat
2   Investigate the various ways in which milk is packaged. Evaluate
    the advantages and disadvantages of each type of packaging
    ☺ ☺ ☹. Discuss how each type of packaging could be reused or
    recycled.
3   Investigate the labelling laws for butter. What are the requirements
    for butter to be labelled 'low salt'?
4   Investigate and identify the various ways in which butter is
    packaged.
5   Investigate the labelling laws for cream cheese. What are the
    requirements for cream cheese to be labelled 'low fat'?
6   Investigate and identify the various ways in which cream cheese is
    packaged.
7   Investigate the difference between cooking chocolate and
    confectionery chocolate.

Chicken meatballs and pasta   (serves 2)

Method

1   Combine chicken mince, parsley, basil and one clove of garlic and shape
    into walnut sized balls.
2   Heat oil in frypan and cook for five to seven minutes, or until golden.
    Transfer to a plate.
3   Add onion and the remaining clove of garlic and fry for five minutes. Add
    pasta sauce and bring to boil. Reduce heat and add chicken balls and
    pepper. Simmer for ten minutes, or until sauce thickens.
4   In the meantime, cook pasta until al dente.
5   Serve pasta topped with meatballs and tomato sauce.

Ingredients

250 grams chicken mince
2 tablespoons fresh parsley, chopped
1 teaspoon fresh basil, chopped
2 cloves garlic, crushed
2 teaspoons olive oil
½ onion, finely chopped
400 millilitre jar tomato-based pasta sauce
3 shakes black pepper
200 grams pasta, such as spaghetti or fettuccini

QUESTIONS

1   Investigate the different varieties of tomato-based pasta sauces
    that are available.
2   Investigate and identify the various types of pasta available in the
    supermarket that could be used in this recipe.

Risotto cakes (serves 2)

Ingredients
1 tablespoon olive oil
1 onion, finely chopped
1 clove garlic
1 cup Arborio rice
210 grams cream chicken soup
   ($\frac{1}{2}$ can)
$\frac{3}{4}$ cup water
$\frac{1}{4}$ zucchini, grated
1 tablespoon sweet corn kernels
2 button mushrooms, finely
   chopped
$\frac{1}{2}$ cup parmesan cheese
2 tablespoons fresh parsley,
   chopped
$\frac{1}{2}$ cup dry breadcrumbs
1 tablespoon olive oil (extra)
sweet chilli sauce

Method
1   Heat oil in saucepan and sauté onion and garlic.
2   Add rice and stir to coat with oil.
3   Add soup, water, zucchini, sweet corn kernels and mushrooms.
4   Cover and simmer for ten minutes, or until rice is tender.
5   Stir in cheese and parsley.
6   Cool and shape into four patties and coat with breadcrumbs.
7   Heat extra oil in frypan and fry for five minutes, until golden.
8   Serve with chilli sauce.

QUESTION
1   Investigate the label of the can of soup and graph the nutrients.
2   Design your own label.

Dukkah (serves 2)

Ingredients
$\frac{1}{3}$ cup hazelnuts
$\frac{1}{4}$ cup sesame seeds
1 tablespoon coriander seeds
1 tablespoon cumin seeds
1 teaspoon black pepper,
   freshly ground
$\frac{1}{2}$ teaspoon sea salt
extra olive oil
crusty bread

Method
1   Preheat oven to 180°C.
2   Toast hazelnuts in oven for three to four minutes and remove skins.
3   Process hazelnuts until coarsely chopped.
4   Heat frypan over medium heat and cook sesame seeds, stirring constantly for one minute, until golden brown.
5   Place sesame seeds and hazelnuts in bowl.
6   Add coriander and cumin seeds to frypan and cook for one minute, or until seeds begin to pop, stirring constantly.
7   Crush seeds finely in mortar and pestle or grinder.
8   Combine seeds with sesame seeds and hazelnuts and add pepper and salt.
9   Serve dukkah with olive oil and crusty bread.

QUESTION
Investigate the labels on a variety of spice jars, and categorise the types of information provided.

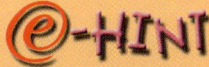
e-HINT
Hazelnuts can be toasted by placing in an oven bag and twisting the opening to seal. Microwave on high for three to four minutes, shaking the bag gently every minute.

e-HINT
Coriander and cumin seeds can be purchased from most Asian grocery stores.

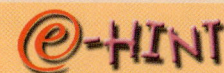
e-HINT
Dukkah can be stored at room temperature in an airtight container.

e-FaCT
Dukkah is an Egyptian blend of spices.

TECHNO FOOD: aSSESSMENT Task 1

This assessment task addresses the outcomes TEMA0601, TEMA0602, HPIP0601 and HPIP0602 from the Technology and Health and Physical Education Key Learning Areas. Library research can be used as the basis for the assessment task and the following websites may be useful:

- www.foodstandards.gov.au
- www.safefood.net.au
- www.foodsafety.vic.gov.au
- www.science.org.au/nova/030/030box02.htm
- www.howstuffworks.com/food-preservation.htm
- www.sydneymarkets.com.au/fandv/homeindex.html

▶ Tasks

1   Investigate the various ways in which the following foods can be prepared and stored to guarantee that they are not spoilt or contaminated prior to consumption.
   a   apples
   b   milk
   c   chicken
   d   bread

2   a   Using the Internet or newspapers, locate an article that relates to food standards not being met; for example, foreign objects found in food or food poisoning.
   b   Why do you think it is important to have food standards in Australia?
   c   Investigate how food safety and hygiene is controlled in Australia.
   d   Design a pamphlet entitled 'Tips for safe shopping', outlining reasons why it is important to consider food safety when shopping. Include a discussion about the health consequences of consuming unsafe foods.

3   Investigate which fruits and vegetables are in season.
   a   Investigate and select an appropriate recipe to preserve a fruit or vegetable.
   b   Design a work plan to preserve the fruit or vegetable. Ensure that you have enough time to complete all tasks.
   c   Preserve your fruit or vegetable, following safety and hygiene guidelines.
   d   Evaluate your end product ☺ ☺ ☹. What criteria did you use for evaluation?

TECHNO FOOD: aSSESSMENT Task 2

This assessment task addresses the outcomes HPIP0601, TEMA0601 and TEMA0602 from the Health and Physical Education and Technology Key Learning Areas. Library research can be used as the basis for the assessment task and the following websites may be useful:

- www.woolworths.com.au/dietinfo/index.asp
- www.foodwatch.com.au
- www.foodsciencebureau.com.au

▶ Tasks

The associations between dietary related diseases and diet are still the subject of scientific investigation. However, it appears that our selection of food might decrease our risk of developing such diseases. Some organisations have made recommendations about which foods to consume more frequently and which to consume less frequently.

Your responsibility is to create a functional food that you can promote as being linked to a decrease in a specific dietary related disease. The food that you create must be a snack food that could be made in less than twenty minutes and would appeal to adolescents.

1 Investigate a range of dietary related diseases and determine which stages of the life span each disease affects. Include information about which nutrients or particular foods are associated with particular dietary related diseases.

2 Discuss whether particular diseases are more common in adolescents. Why are some diseases not evident until adulthood?

3 Investigate a range of ingredients that are said to be functional foods because they offer health benefits beyond basic nutrition. Complete a table similar to the one shown below.

Ingredient	Functional properties

4 Identify the criteria listed in this section that must be addressed in the development of a snack food.

5 Develop a series of at least three detailed designs in which at least three of the ingredients listed in the table in question 3 are included in a recipe. Detail how the criteria identified in question 4 are addressed.

6 Identify your preferred option and justify why this design was selected.

7 Design a work plan in order to create this functional food. The table below may assist with this.

Task	Time	Equipment	Safety/hygiene considerations

8 Produce your functional food.

9 Ask five classmates to evaluate your design ☺ ☺ ☹. What criteria did they use to judge the success of your functional food?

10 Based on the information provided by your classmates, was your functional food design a success? Provide reasons to support your answer. Include suggestions for future improvements, if necessary.

11 Discuss how your functional food would be packaged. Create packaging that would be appealing to adolescents. Provide reasons for the packaging design and materials that you have selected.

12 Design a label for your functional food.

GLOSSARY

adrenalin a hormone that stimulates the conversion of glycogen in the liver to glucose to restore sugar levels in the blood

alfresco in the fresh air or taking place outside

baguette a long thin French bread stick with a soft inside and a crusty outside

barista a professional coffee maker

blanching when food is immersed in boiling water for a short period of time and then plunged into cold water to prevent the cooking process

canapé an appetiser consisting of small pieces of toasted or plain bread topped with savoury spreads

cilantro another name for coriander

connoisseur an expert in the matters of taste

convenience foods term used to describe food that is partially of fully pre-prepared

couscoussière a double saucepan for cooking couscous

dextrins chains of starch that are made up of glucose molecules

dry-heat cooking methods includes methods such as grilling and baking

energy-dense foods foods high in kilojoules

fatigue lacking energy

fermentation process by which yeast is able to obtain energy through the breakdown of glucose and other simple sugar molecules without requiring oxygen

functional food food that offers health benefits beyond basic nutrition

glucagon a hormone produced in the pancreas that causes glucose to move from the liver to the blood

Glycemic Index an approach to rating carbohydrates in food, with the rating being between 0 and 100 and based on the carbohydrates' effects on blood glucose in the body

home meal replacements fully prepared meals that can be purchased chilled, frozen or heated

hydrogenation a process whereby hydrogen atoms are added to polyunsaturated fatty acids in oil, thus allowing oils to become solid

irradiation the process of exposing food to radiation to prevent spoilage

junk food food that is energy-dense and low in nutrient value

line extension when an existing food product is adapted while maintaining its central characteristics

me-toos copies of food products developed by competing companies

nutrient-dense foods foods that are low in kilojoules

obesity being 20 per cent or more over recommended weight

phytates compounds found in the outer layers of cereal grains; they can trap minerals such as iron, calcium and zinc and make them unavailable to the body

rancid when fats become oxidised and develop an 'off' flavour and odour

trans-fatty acids unsaturated fats that have been hydrogenated so that they have a chemical composition similar to saturated fats

triglyceride type of fat that consists of one glycerol + three fatty acids

INDEX

RECIPE INDEX

CSF Grid

Each chapter contains a range of activities, with each type of activity being indicated by a different symbol. This activity-based approach enables students to demonstrate specific learning outcomes from the Technology and Health and Physical Education Key Learning Areas as indicated in this grid.

Key

- ☺ Let's remember
- ⚲ Let's investigate
- ? Puzzled
- 📁 Case studies
- @ e-Food section
- ▣ Newspaper articles
- 🍴 Let's produce

Outcome	Chapter 1 Food Stuff: Discover Nutrients	Chapter 2 Science Fiction: Discover Food Myths	Chapter 3 Bad Taste: Discover Dietary Related Diseases	Chapter 4 What's Hot?: Discover Nutritional Issues	Chapter 5 Food For Thought: Discover Impact of Technology
TEMA0601	☺ ⚲ @ 🍴	☺ 📁 ▣	☺ ⚲ ? @ ▣	☺ ⚲ 📁 @ ▣ 🍴	☺ ⚲ 📁 ? ▣
TEMA0602	☺ ⚲ @ 🍴	☺	▣	⚲ 🍴	
TEMA0603	☺ ⚲ @ 🍴	☺ 📁 @	⚲ @ ▣	☺ ⚲ 📁 @ ▣	☺ ⚲ 📁 @ ▣
TEMA0604	☺ ⚲ @ 🍴	☺ 📁 @	☺ ⚲ @ ▣ 🍴	☺ ⚲ 📁 ▣	⚲ 📁
HPIP0601	☺ ⚲ ? @ @ 🍴	☺ ⚲ ? 📁 @	☺ ⚲ ? @ ▣ 🍴	☺ ⚲ ? 📁 ▣ 🍴	☺ ⚲ ? ▣ @
HPIP0602	☺ ⚲ ? @	☺ ⚲ ▣	☺ ⚲ ? @ ▣	☺ ⚲ 📁 @ ▣	☺ ⚲ ? @ ▣
HPIP0603	☺ ⚲ @	▣	☺ ⚲ @ ▣	☺ ⚲ @ ▣	⚲ @ ▣
HPIP0604	☺ ⚲ @		☺ ⚲ @	☺ ⚲ @ ▣	☺ ⚲ ? @
HPSR0601	☺ ? ⚲ @ 🍴	📁	☺ ⚲ @	☺ ⚲ ? @ ▣ 🍴	☺ ⚲ ? ▣
HPSR0604	@	📁	☺ ⚲ @	☺ ▣	☺ ⚲ @ 📁

271

Outcome	Chapter 6: Advance Australia Fare: Discover Australian Cuisine	Chapter 7: Orient Express: Discover Asian Cuisine	Chapter 8: European Vacation: Discover European Cuisine	Chapter 9: American Pie: Discover the Cuisine of the Americas	Chapter 10: Out of Africa: Discover African Cuisine
TEMA0601					
TEMA0602					
TEMA0603					
TEMA0604					
HPIP0601					
HPIP0602					
HPIP0603					
HPIP0604					
HPSR0601					
HPSR0604					

Outcome	Chapter 11 Start Me Up: Discover Breakfast	Chapter 12 In the Bag: Discover Lunch	Chapter 13 The Night Shift: Discover Dinner	Chapter 14 It's a Wrap: Discover Fresh Versus Packaged	Chapter 15 Snack Attack: Discover Snacks and Junk Food
TEMA0601					
TEMA0602					
TEMA0603					
TEMA0604					
HPIP0601					
HPIP0602					
HPIP0603					
HPIP0604					
HPSR0601					
HPSR0604					

Outcome	Chapter 16 Makes Sense: Discover Sensory Evaluation	Chapter 17 Hot Properties: Discover Properties of Food	Chapter 18 Branded!: Discover Food Products	Chapter 19 All Wrapped Up: Discover Packaging	Chapter 20 Labelled!: Discover Labelling
TEMA0601					
TEMA0602					
TEMA0603					
TEMA0604					
HPIP0601					
HPIP0602					
HPIP0603					
HPIP0604					
HPSR0601					
HPSR0604					

274